Database Publishing with FileMaker Pro on the Web

D0206412

MARIA LANGER

Database Publishing with FileMaker Pro On the Web
Maria Langer

Peachpit Press
1249 Eighth Street
Berkeley, CA 94710
510/524-2178
800/283-9444
510/524-2221 (FAX)

Find us on the World Wide Web at:
http://www.peachpit.com

Peachpit Press is a division of Addison Wesley Longman
Copyright © 1998 by Maria Langer

Editor: Corbin Collins
Copyeditor: Terry Wilson
Technical editor: Andrew Knasinski
Cover design: Gee + Chung Design
Cover illustration: © Joseph Kelter / www.badcat.com
Interior design: Mimi Heft
Production: Maria Langer, Mimi Heft

Colophon
This book was created with QuarkXPress on a Power Macintosh 8500/180. The fonts used were ITC Officina Sans and Sans Serif, NIMIX Quirks, OCRA and B, and Versailles. Direct-to-plate imagesetting and printing were done at Edwards Brothers in Ann Arbor, MI, onto 50# Arbor Smooth paper.

Notice of Rights
All rights reserved. No part of this book may be reproduced or transmitted in any form by any means, electronic, mechanical, photocopying, recording, or otherwise, without the prior written permission of the publisher. For information on getting permission for reprints and excerpts, contact Gary-Paul Prince at Peachpit Press.

Notice of Liability
The information in this book is distributed on an "As Is" basis, without warranty. While every precaution has been taken in the preparation of the book, neither the author nor Peachpit Press, shall have any liability to any person or entity with respect to any loss or damage caused or alleged to be caused directly or indirectly by the instructions contained in this book or by the computer software and hardware products described in it.

ISBN 0-201-69665-7

9 8 7 6 5 4 3 2 1

To Julia and Frank Soricelli,

my favorite aunt and uncle

Acknowledgments

This book would not be possible without the help and guidance of the following people...

First, a big thanks to the folks at Peachpit Press: Corbin Collins, Mimi Heft, Paula Baker and the Peachpit Marketeers, and Nancy Aldrich-Ruenzel. Also, thanks to the editors who didn't stick around to see the completion of this book: Jeremy Judson and the man who started it all, Nolan Hester.

Next, thanks to my editors: Terry Wilson, who never ceases to amaze me with the glaring problems that I miss but she finds, and Andy Knaskinski, FileMaker Pro Web publishing guru. Another big thanks goes to Andy for working up the Web publishing solutions in Chapters 8, 9, and 12.

More thanks go out to the folks who make and support the products discussed throughout this book: Bill Shissler and Geri Hyde at FileMaker, Inc. (formerly Claris Corporation), Eric Zelenka at StarNine, Bill Doerrfeld at Blue World Communications, Eric Bickford at Web Broadcasting, and Chris Moffett at Everyware Development.

Finally, thanks to Stu Gitlow, Dianna Tangen, and Tom Heffernan for their miscellaneous support. And to Mike, of course, for the usual reasons.

Table of Contents

Introduction 1

Overview 1

Static vs. Dynamic Publishing 2

Database Publishing with FileMaker Pro 4

What You Need 6

About this Book 8

Organization & Contents 8

Companion Web Site 10

Elements 10

What this Book Assumes 10

About Me 11

Part I FileMaker Pro's Built-In Web Publishing Features **13**

Chapter 1 ◉ Instant Web Publishing **15**

Overview 15

How it Works 15

Benefits 16

Drawbacks 16

Step-by-Step Setup 17

Enabling & Configuring the Web Companion Plug-In 17

Preparing a Database for Instant Web Publishing 19

Enabling & Configuring Web Companion Sharing 20

Accessing Published Data 24

Opening a Database File 24

Browsing Records 25

Modifying the Database 32
Returning to the Home Page 34
Getting Help 34

Chapter 2 ◉ Custom Web Publishing 35

Overview 35
How it Works 36
Benefits 37
Drawbacks 37
A Closer Look at Format Files 38
Types of Format Files 38
The Role of HTML in a Format File 39
Static vs. Dynamic Forms 39
A Closer Look at CDML 40
Types of CDML Tags 40
CDML Tag Syntax 40
Links vs. Form Actions 42
Tools for Creating Format Files 44
The CDML Reference 44
The CDML Tool 45
Claris Home Page 3 49
Step-by-Step Setup 57
Enabling & Configuring the Web Companion Plug-In 57
Preparing a Database for Custom Web Publishing 60
Creating & Saving Format Files 61
Enabling Web Companion Sharing 63
Accessing & Testing Your Custom Web Publishing Solution 64
Opening the Database Home Page 64
Testing Your Solution 64
Troubleshooting Problems 65

Chapter 3 ◉ Web Companion Configuration & Security 67

Web Companion Configuration Options 67
Web Companion User Interface Options 68
Remote Administration 70
Log Activity 70
Security 71
TCP/IP Port Number 71
Security 72
Overview 72
Securing a Database with Access Privileges 73

Securing a Databse with the Web Security Database 76
Accessing a Secured Database File 83
Dealing with Security "Loopholes" 84
Remotely Administering the Web Security Database 85

Chapter 4 ◉ Static Web Publishing **89**

Export to HTML Table 90
Overview 90
Exporting Data as an HTML Table 90
Using Exported Data as a Web Page 92
Generating HTML with Calculation Fields 93
Overview 93
Before You Start 94
Creating the Calculation Field 94
Exporting the Records 98
Checking (and Troubleshooting) Your Work 99
Using Exported Data as a Web Page 99

Part II Third-Party Solutions 101

Chapter 5 ◉ Lasso **103**

Overview 105
Lasso Products 105
How it Works 106
Benefits & Drawbacks 107
A Closer Look at Format Files 107
Types of Format Files 108
The Role of HTML in a Format File 109
Directing Actions to Lasso 109
Pre-Lasso & Post-Lasso Modes 111
A Closer Look at LDML Tags 112
Types of LDML Tags 112
LDML Syntax 115
URL-Embedded Actions vs. Form Actions 116
Using FM Link 119
Opening FM Link 120
Using a Template 120
Building a Format File from Scratch 122
Using FM Link with WYSIWYG Web Authoring Tools 130

Step-by-Step Setup 131
Installing & Registering Lasso *131*
Preparing a Database for Publishing with Lasso *133*
Creating & Saving Format Files *134*
Lasso Security 135
Setting Up Security *135*
Accessing a Secured Database File *141*
Dealing with Security "Loopholes" *141*
Remotely Administering the Lasso Security Database *142*
Accessing & Testing Your Lasso Web Publishing Solution 143

Chapter 6 ◉ Tango for FileMaker 147

Overview 148
Tango for FileMaker Products *148*
How it Works *149*
Benefits & Drawbacks *149*
A Closer Look at Query Documents 150
Types of Query Documents *150*
Query Document Contents *151*
A Closer Look at Tango Meta Tags 152
Using Tango Editor to Create Query Documents 153
Starting Tango Editor *153*
Setting Tango Editor Options *154*
Creating a Query Builder File *158*
Saving the File *159*
Using the Database Palette *160*
Specifying Search Options *160*
Specifying Record List Options *165*
Specifying Record Detail Options *168*
Specifying New Record Options *171*
Generating a Query Document *173*
Working with the Query Document Editor *174*
Step-by-Step Setup 176
Installing Tango *176*
Opening the Data Source *178*
Creating & Saving Query Documents *178*
Adding a Link to a Query Document on another Web Page *178*
Accessing & Testing Your Solution 179
Testing Your Solution *179*
Using Debug Mode *179*
Troubleshooting Problems *180*

Chapter 7 ◉ WEB•FM 181

Overview .182
WEB•FM & Related Products .182
How it Works .183
Benefits & Drawbacks .183
WEB•FM & HTML .183
The Role of HTML .183
Directing Actions to WEB•FM .184
A Closer Look at WEB•FM Codes .185
Basic Commands .186
INPUT Variables .186
Reserved Field Names .186
Substitution Tokens .187
WEB•FM Code Syntax .187
URL-Embedded Actions vs. Form Actions .188
Using TAG•FM to Create HTML Documents .190
Opening a Database File with TAG•FM .190
Setting Preferences .191
About the TAG•FM Window .191
Adding WEB•FM Codes to an HTML Document .192
Other Ways to Use TAG•FM .193
Step-by-Step Setup .194
Installing WEB•FM .194
Preparing the FileMaker Pro Database File .197
Creating & Saving HTML Documents .205
WEB•FM Security .207
Naming Files with the .fm Suffix .207
Securing the Admin Database .207
Securing Your Database Files .208
Accessing & Testing Your WEB•FM Web Publishing Solution . . .211

Part III Real-Life Database Publishing Examples 213

Chapter 8 ◉ Basic Data Publishing 215

About the Database .215
Database Fields .216
Database Layouts .216
Database Records .216

Exporting to an HTML Table .217
Preparing the Database for Export .217
Exporting the Records .217
Checking (and Troubleshooting) Your Work .217
Improving the Appearance of the Exported Table .218
Publishing the Page .218
Exporting Calculation Fields .218
Creating the Calculation Fields .219
Exporting the Records .222
Checking (and Troubleshooting) Your Work .222
Publishing the Page .222
Instant Web Publishing .222
Moving the File to the Web Folder .222
Creating a New Layout .223
Setting Up Views .223
Checking the Instant Web Publishing Solution .224
Custom Web Publishing .225
Creating a Project Folder in the Web Folder .226
Creating the Format Files .226
Checking the Custom Web Publishing Solution .230

Chapter 9 ◉ Including Graphics in Published Data 231

About the Database .232
Database Fields .232
Database Layouts .233
Database Records .233
About the Images .233
Exporting Calculation Fields .235
Creating the Fields .235
Exporting the Records .240
Checking (and Troubleshooting) Your Work .241
Publishing the Page .241
Instant Web Publishing .241
Moving the File to the Web Folder .241
Creating New Layouts .241
Setting Up Views .243
Checking the Instant Web Publishing Solution .244
Custom Web Publishing .245
Creating a Project Folder in the Web Folder .246
Creating the Format Files .246
Checking the Custom Web Publishing Solution .251

Chapter 10 ◉ Making Published Data Interactive 255

About the Database 256
Database Fields *256*
Value Lists *257*
Database Layouts *257*
Database Records *258*
Instant Web Publishing 258
Moving the File to the Web Folder *258*
Creating New Layouts *258*
Setting Up Views *259*
Setting Access Privileges *260*
Checking the Instant Web Publishing Solution *262*
Custom Web Publishing 263
Planning the Solution *264*
Creating a Project Folder in the Web Folder *265*
Creating Additional Fields *265*
Creating the Format Files *267*
Checking the Custom Web Publishing Solution *299*

Chapter 11 ◉ Performing Calculations 301

About the Database 302
Database Fields *302*
Database Layouts *303*
Database Records *303*
Custom Web Publishing Solution 304
Creating a Project Folder *304*
Creating the Format Files *304*
Checking the Solution *314*

Chapter 12 ◉ Handling Transactions 315

About the Databases 316
Products.fp3 ....*316*
OrderItems.fp3 ....*318*
Customers.fp3 ....*320*
Orders.fp3 ....*322*
Custom Web Publishing Solution 325
Planning the Solution *326*
About Token Passing *328*
Creating Project Folders *329*
Creating the Format Files *329*

Creating the Include File *371*
Checking the Solution *373*

Appendixes 375

Appendix A ◉ Online Resources **377**

Appendix B ◉ Claris Dynamic Markup Language Tags **381**

Action Tags 381
Variable Tags 385
Replacement Tags 394

Index **413**

Introduction

Need to find the OfficeMax closest to Wickenburg, AZ? Check http://www.bigbook.com/.

Want a list of all books about FileMaker Pro currently in print? Try http://www.amazon.com/.

Need to buy some freeze-dried food for that camping trip in the canyon next week? Shop at http://www.campmor.com/.

All of these Web sites have one thing in common: they display database information on the World Wide Web. Like many other organizations, the companies that maintain these sites—BigBook, Amazon.com, and Campmor—utilize the Web as a cost-effective way to distribute information that is recorded and maintained in database files.

Overview

Webmasters and content providers are always looking for effective ways to publish timely, useful information on their Web sites. What many of them are finding is that database files may offer the best solution in many Web publishing situations.

There are several benefits to maintaining Web-published information in database files:

- Huge quantities of database information can be maintained and published with relatively little effort.
- Database information can be served up on request, thus ensuring that the most recent information is made available.
- Database information can be searched or sorted based on the needs of Web site visitors.
- Database information can be updated or added by Web site visitors.
- Database files linked to the Web can handle complex tasks such as cost estimating and order processing.

This book shows you examples of these benefits—as well as many others—in action. For now, let me provide a little background information that'll help you understand how you can publish database files created and maintained with FileMaker Pro.

HyperText Markup Language

If you want to be a Web publisher, you must have at least a basic understanding of HTML, which stands for *HyperText Markup Language*. HTML is the language of the World Wide Web; it determines the appearance and functionality of Web pages.

While it's true that you can use a Web publishing tool like Claris Home Page, Adobe PageMill, or Microsoft FrontPage to create HTML documents without knowing a single HTML tag, some of the database publishing solutions discussed in this book require that you know how to insert tags into HTML documents. If you've never even seen an HTML document, you might go into cardiac arrest when you get to those chapters—HTML can look pretty scary to the uninitiated.

If you don't know HTML, start learning it. It isn't tough and you can't be a real Webmaster without knowing it. Peachpit Press's *HTML for the World Wide Web: Visual QuickStart Guide* by Elizabeth Castro is an excellent book to get you started.

Static vs. Dynamic Publishing

Database information published on the Web is either *static* or *dynamic*. This is an important distinction, one that you must understand before you continue.

Static Publishing

In static publishing, you create a standard HTML file based on the contents of a database file. That HTML file is then published on the Web server. There is no interaction between the Web site visitor or the Web server and the database file itself. If the database file changes and a new HTML file is not created, the existing HTML file will not reflect the contents of the database file.

Dynamic Publishing

In dynamic publishing, database information is retrieved and displayed in the Web browser window when a request for it is made to the Web server.

For example, say you visit BigBook looking for Office Max stores in Arizona. You enter your search criteria in a form, submit your request, and the server tells the database what you're looking for. The database then sends the information to the server, which sends it to your Web browser. Somewhere along the way, an HTML document is created so the information is neatly formatted as a Web page. Since the HTML document is generated when needed, it contains the most up-to-date information, straight from the database—even if the database was updated two minutes before you made your request.

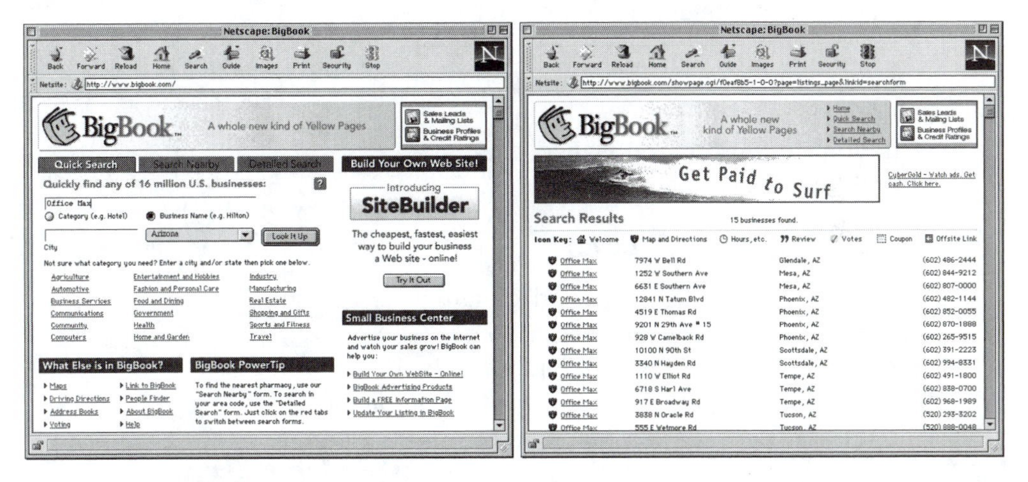

Which is Better?

This may seem like a dumb question, but it isn't. Let me explain.

On the surface, it appears that dynamic publishing is better than static publishing because the information is always up-to-date and does not require manual updating when the database is changed. While this is true, dynamic publishing has two main drawbacks:

- Dynamic publishing requires that the Web server interact with a database file. This can only be done with CGI software and/or special HTML tags that enable communication between the CGI and database applications. This means you must have additional software and expertise.

- Dynamic publishing usually requires that the database file be open and accessible to the Web server. This means you must have control, either directly or indirectly, of the Web server.

Does that mean that static publishing is better? Of course not. It just means that it's easier. And in many instances, it's all you need.

Here's an example. One day I decided to publish a database of all companies that made Macintosh products. I started collecting company names, locations, phone numbers, and Internet addresses. I put them in a FileMaker Pro database. Then, using calculation fields and scripts, I exported the information to HTML documents that I could copy to my Web site. Since I didn't have access to the server and couldn't run a CGI (I had an evil ISP which forbid running CGIs), this was the only way to publish the information. Because the information didn't need to be searched or sorted and it was rarely updated, the solution was fine. (If you're really interested, you can find the published database at http://www.gilesrd.com/mcd/.)

> **CGIs**
>
> CGI stands for *Common Gateway Interface*. A CGI is a program that, when called by the Web server, performs a task. In the case of database publishing, a CGI may submit search criteria to a database, collect the information returned as a result of the search, create an HTML document containing the information, and send the HTML document back to the server.
>
> Lasso, Tango for FileMaker, and WEB•FM are three examples of CGIs that work with FileMaker Pro on Macintosh Web servers. You can also write your own CGIs from scratch with a little C/C++ or AppleScript programming, but that's far beyond the scope of this book.

Which Does this Book Cover?

This book covers both static and dynamic publishing. I do, however, use a lot more ink and paper discussing dynamic publishing because of its additional power and complexity.

Database Publishing with FileMaker Pro

There are a number of methods you can use to publish FileMaker Pro databases on the Web. The method you choose depends on the answers to three questions:

- What version of FileMaker Pro are you using? As I explain in a moment, version 4 offers Web publishing features that are not available in version 3.
- On which computer platform does your Web server run? Macintosh users have more options than Windows 95/NT users. (If you're a UNIX user, you bought the wrong book.)
- Do you want to take advantage of third-party solutions and, if so, which one(s) do you want to use? Macintosh users can choose from a variety of third-party CGIs.

In this section, I tell you more about your options.

FileMaker Pro Web Companion

FileMaker Pro version 4 introduces FileMaker Pro Web Companion. This plug-in, which comes with FileMaker Pro 4, enables you to dynamically publish FileMaker Pro database files on the Web. You don't even need Web server software!

FileMaker Pro Web Companion is like a highly specialized Web server and a CGI rolled into one. It handles all of the interaction between a Web browser and FileMaker Pro. It enables you to publish databases using two different methods:

- INSTANT WEB PUBLISHING lets you publish a FileMaker Pro database by simply opening it and selecting a few configuration options. Web pages are automatically created on the fly based on the contents of the database and the options selected by Web page visitors. I tell you about Instant Web Publishing in Chapter 1.
- CUSTOM WEB PUBLISHING lets you publish a FileMaker Pro database with highly customized Web pages. Although this method is much more powerful and flexible than Instant Web Publishing, it requires that you create custom Web pages that contain HTML and CDML (*Claris Dynamic Markup Language*) tags. I tell you about Custom Web Publishing in Chapter 2.

Although you don't need a Web server to take advantage of FileMaker Pro Web Companion, that doesn't mean you can't have one. After all, FileMaker Pro Web Companion can only serve up FileMaker Pro database files—not the regular HTML documents that you may have on your Web server. And in case you're wondering, there's nothing to stop you from using the third-party solutions discussed next with FileMaker Pro version 4, even if you're also using FileMaker Pro Web Companion.

Third-Party Solutions

Mac OS users have additional options that are not available to Windows 95/NT users. (Sorry folks, but let's face it: you get some stuff that the Mac folks never see.) These three popular solutions work with FileMaker Pro versions 3 and 4 on Macintosh systems:

- LASSO is a family of three products developed by Blue World Communications, Inc. The *Lasso CGI* and the *Lasso plug-in* work with a Web server to dynamically publish FileMaker Pro database files. You can use one or the other; you don't need to use both. The *Lasso Server* is a highly specialized Web server designed specifcally to serve Lasso format files. I tell you more about Lasso in Chapter 5.
- TANGO FOR FILEMAKER consists of a pair of programs developed by EveryWare Development Corp. The *Tango Editor* lets you create query documents that the *Tango CGI* uses to interact with FileMaker Pro database files

and the Web server. Together, they enable you to dynamically publish FileMaker Pro database files. I tell you more about Tango for FileMaker in Chapter 6.

- **WEB•FM** is a Web server plug-in developed by Web Broadcasting Corporation. It interacts with the Web server and FileMaker Pro databases to dynamically publish FileMaker Pro database files. Web Broadcasting also develops *PICT•FM,* which enables you to publish images on the Web and *TAG•FM,* which enables you to create Web pages that include WEB•FM commands. I tell you more about all of these products in Chapter 7.

Static Web Publishing Options

If you're interested in static Web publishing, there are two options to consider:

- **Export to HTML Table** is a new feature of FileMaker Pro version 4. It enables you to quickly create an HTML document that displays FileMaker Pro data in table format. I tell you more about this feature in Chapter 4.
- **Calculation Fields** within FileMaker Pro 3 or 4 database files can create HTML by concatenating text. You can then export the fields containing the HTML to create HTML documents. This isn't fun, but it works. I tell you more about this technique in Chapter 4.

What You Need

Here's a shopping list you can use to gather the things you'll need to publish your FileMaker Pro database files on the Web.

Hardware

By hardware, I mean your computer system. Your requirements depend on your publishing plans:

- For dynamic publishing of FileMaker Pro database files on the Web, you need a computer with a live connection to the Internet (more about that later). The computer must be able to run all of the software you'll use to implement your database publishing solution (more about that next). Specifically, it must have the correct processor, sufficient RAM, and enough hard disk space to provide storage for all application and data files. Check your software documentation for details on system requirements.
- For static publishing of FileMaker Pro database files on the Web, all you need is a computer capable of running FileMaker Pro. Check the software documentation that came with your copy of FileMaker Pro for details on system requirements.

Software

By software, I mean the programs that you need to run to publish database files. Again, your requirements depend on your publishing plans:

- If you plan to take advantage of FileMaker Pro version 4's new Web publishing features and don't plan on publishing anything other than FileMaker Pro database files, then all you need is FileMaker Pro version 4.
- If you already have FileMaker Pro version 3 running on a Macintosh and you're not interested in upgrading to version 4 right now, you also need one of the third-party solutions discussed above (Lasso, Tango for FileMaker, or WEB•FM) and Web server software such as WebSTAR. Check the documentation that comes with the third party solution of your choice to see which Web server packages are compatible. If you haven't chosen a third party solution yet, check the Web sites for these three programs for more information; you'll find their URLs in Appendix A. Or, better yet, browse through Chapters 5, 6, and 7 of this book to learn how each package works. Then decide which one is right for you.
- If you don't plan on doing any dynamic Web publishing, all you need is FileMaker Pro. With version 4, you can take advantage of the Export to HTML Table option to have FileMaker Pro create HTML documents for you. With FileMaker Pro version 3, you'll have to work a little harder for the same results.

You may also need a Web page creation tool like Claris Home Page, Adobe PageMill, or Microsoft FrontPage. This will help you create the Web pages you'll need for Custom Web Publishing with FileMaker Pro version 4 and other database publishing solutions discussed in this book. If you don't have any of these packages yet, I recommend Claris Home Page version 3 or later since it includes features specifically for use with FileMaker Pro.

Finally, you'll need a Web browser like Netscape Navigator or Microsoft Internet Explorer. You'll use one or both of these to test your database publishing skills. The way your database appears when you view it with these programs is the way it will appear when viewed by the rest of the world.

Internet Connection

Your Internet connection also depends on your database publishing plans:

- For dynamic Web publishing on the World Wide Web, you must have a full-time Internet connection using TCP/IP. For best results, you should have a T1 or better connection, but a full-time dial-up or ISDN connection will also work.

- For dynamic Web publishing on an intranet, you must have a full-time connection to the intranet via TCP/IP.
- For static Web publishing, you only need access to the Internet (or intranet) when it's time to upload HTML documents created from your database to the Web server.

About this Book

This book will tell you what you need to know to publish FileMaker Pro database information on the World Wide Web. Rather than focusing on a single method or computer platform, however, it provides information for a variety of FileMaker Pro Web publishing solutions:

- FileMaker Pro version 4 for Macintosh and Windows 95/NT:
  - FileMaker Pro Web Companion's Instant Web Publishing
  - FileMaker Pro Web Companion's Custom Web Publishing
  - Export to HTML Table Feature
- FileMaker Pro version 3 or 4 for Macintosh and Windows 95/NT:
  - Calculation Fields for Generating HTML
- FileMaker Pro version 3 or 4 for Macintosh:
  - Lasso for Macintosh
  - Tango for FileMaker Pro
  - WEB•FM for Macintosh

This approach enables you, the Web publisher, to select a database publishing method based on the hardware and software that you already have. At the same time, however, you can see how other software tools can be used to publish FileMaker Pro databases. FileMaker Pro version 3 users will find this approach especially useful—they can learn what publishing methods are available to them now, as well as what methods they can take advantage of when they upgrade to FileMaker Pro version 4.

Organization & Contents

This book has three parts, each containing at least three chapters. The first two parts provide basic information and step-by-step instructions for each Web publishing method. This makes it easy for you to find and learn about the method that interests you most. The last part provides real-life database publishing examples and their solutions, using each appropriate method.

Here's a brief outline so you know what to expect.

Part I: FileMaker Pro's Built-In Web Publishing Features

This part of the book provides overviews and step-by-step instructions for using the Web publishing features available in FileMaker Pro. Its four chapters are:

- Chapter 1: Instant Web Publishing
- Chapter 2: Custom Web Publishing
- Chapter 3: Web Companion Configuration & Security
- Chapter 4: Static Web Publishing

Part II: Third-Party Solutions

This part of the book provides an overview and step-by-step instructions for using the most popular third-party CGIs for publishing FileMaker Pro version 3 or 4 databases on the Web. Its three chapters are:

- Chapter 5: Lasso
- Chapter 6: Tango for FileMaker
- Chapter 7: WEB•FM

Part III: Real-Life Database Publishing Examples

This part of the book provides examples of FileMaker Pro databases. It includes instructions for publishing them on the Web using FileMaker Pro using the Static, Instant, and Custom Web Publishing techniques (as appropriate) discussed in detail earlier in the book. It starts out with simple publishing problems and works its way up to more complex problems. Its five chapters are:

- Chapter 8: Basic Data Publishing
- Chapter 9: Including Graphics in Published Data
- Chapter 10: Making Published Data Interactive
- Chapter 11: Performing Calculations
- Chapter 12: Handling Transactions

Appendixes

Like all of my books, this one also includes appendixes where I provide reference information:

- Appendix A: Online Resources
- Appendix B: Claris Dynamic Markup Language Tags

Companion Web Site

To get the most out of this book, it's a good idea to try the real-life examples for yourself. Rather than put the database and solution files on a CD, thus forcing Peachpit to charge you an extra $10 for the book, I've set aside some space on my Web server for a companion Web site. That's where you'll find the files you need to try the book's examples, as well as updated information, corrections (if necessary), and other useful tidbits.

You can visit the site at http://www.gilesrd.com/fmproweb/. While you're there, be sure to enter your comments in the guestbook or use the feedback link to let us know what you think about the book and the site.

Elements

Like almost every other computer book on the planet, this one uses icons and special text formatting to flag certain types of information.

I'm sure you've seen lots of tip icons. But my tip icons indicate real tips that'll save you time, effort, or money.

Note icons indicate interesting information that isn't exactly vital to completing a task or using a software product.

When you see a warning icon, read the text beside it! Failure to do so could result in the self-destruction of your Web server. Well, maybe not, but ignoring a warning can cause trouble.

Sidebars

A sidebar isn't an icon. It's a box like this one with its own little story to tell. I use them to provide background information that you may or may not already know. Sometimes I use them to tell stories or jokes.

What this Book Assumes

In writing this book, I've made a few assumptions:

- **You know how to use your computer.** That means you can click, drag, select and edit text, and use menus. You also know how to use dialog boxes to open and save documents. (If you can't do all of these things, put this book down. You're not ready to publish anything on the Web.)
- **You know how to use FileMaker Pro.** You don't have to be an expert, but you should know all about creating database files, defining fields, working with layouts, and setting preferences. I could recommend a good book about FileMaker Pro, but since I wrote it for another publisher, I'll keep quiet and let you find it for yourself.

- **If necessary, you know how to use your Web server software.** That means you can set it up and successfully publish Web pages. Well, if you're not the Webmaster, you don't have to know all that. But you should know how to be nice to the Webmaster so he or she will be glad to help you when you need help.
- **You know how to use your Web browser.** That means you can use it to open and browse HTML documents on a remote server or your own computer.

Anyone who's seen all the *Odd Couple* reruns knows that "to assume is to make an ass of you and me." I know it, too. But without these assumptions, I'd have to start from scratch. This book would take a year to write, be 2,000 pages long, and cost about $100. I don't think any of us wanted that.

About Me

I've been writing computer books since 1992 and, if you look hard enough, you could probably find at least ten of my books on the computer bookshelves of your favorite bookstore. My background is in Macintosh training and consulting, although I "do Windows" when asked nicely by people I like. I was an auditor and financial analyst in a prior life, but that's all a fading memory now (thank heaven).

I'm no stranger to FileMaker Pro or Web publishing. I've written books about FileMaker and Web publishing tools like Claris Home Page and Adobe PageMill. I've also created a number of Web sites, including the one for Giles Road Press (http://www.gilesrd.com/), publisher of the ever-popular but sporadically published newsletter, *Macintosh Tips & Tricks*.

My training experience helps me to identify and organize the information that I need to cover, present it in a way that's easy to understand, and anticipate questions so I can answer them before they're asked. (It's kind of difficult to ask a book a question, isn't it?) I've also learned that humor is an important part of any learning experience. If I don't keep you entertained, you'll put the book down and you won't learn a thing. I'm no stand-up comic and I don't believe in dummies jokes, but I'll do my best to hold your attention.

Oh, one more thing about me. I'm *not* a geek. I love computers and the Internet because of the power they give us, but I turn off my computer when I'm done working. There's more to life than what we can see on a CRT.

If you're ever in Wickenburg, look me up. I'll show you my motorcycles and, if you're up to it, take you for a ride that you'll never forget.

I

FileMaker Pro's Built-In Web Publishing Features

FileMaker Pro version 4 for Macintosh and Windows has a number of built-in Web publishing features utilizing the new Web Companion plug-in. This part of the book explores these new features, as well as some static Web publishing techniques. Its four chapters are:

Chapter 1: Instant Web Publishing

Chapter 2: Custom Web Publishing

Chapter 3: Web Companion Configuration & Security

Chapter 4: Static Web Publishing

CHAPTER 1

Instant Web Publishing

The easiest way to publish a FileMaker Pro database on the Web is with Instant Web Publishing, one of the brand new features of FileMaker Pro version 4. In this chapter, I tell you all about Instant Web Publishing: what it is, why you might or might not want to use it, how you set it up, and how you and your Web site visitors can access the data you publish with it.

Overview

As the name suggests, Instant Web Publishing requires very little preparation. Better yet, you can take advantage of it without knowing a single HTML tag. Sounds like a dream come true, doesn't it? For many people, it is. But as you'll see later in this section, it may not be the perfect solution for you.

How It Works

Instant Web Publishing utilizes FileMaker Pro Web Companion's Web serving capabilities to create Web pages on the fly. You set up the Web Companion plug-in and configure the database files that you want to publish. Then you use your Web browser to point to the IP address of the computer on which FileMaker Pro and the databases are running.

Web Companion automatically generates a Home page that lists all open databases. When you click a link, Web Companion generates a page that displays the file's data in a standard Table View. Clicking other buttons on the page let you change the view, search for and sort records, and modify the database. All without manually creating a single Web page!

Benefits

There are a number of benefits to using Instant Web Publishing, some obvious, others not so obvious:

- **Quick and Easy.** No doubt about it, Instant Web Publishing is the quickest and easiest way to publish a database on the Web. Once you know the steps required to publish a database, you can put a file on the Web in minutes.
- **No HTML Required.** You can use Instant Web Publishing to publish a database on the Web without knowing any HTML.
- **Consistent Pages.** Instant Web Publishing prepares all pages with a consistent interface. This makes it very easy for the people who access your database files to find, edit, and otherwise work with published data.

Drawbacks

Instant Web Publishing has some drawbacks, too. Consider these when deciding whether this technique is right for you:

- **Limited Customization of Page Appearance.** Although you can select the fields that appear in a database published with Instant Web Publishing, you can't customize the elements or layout of Web pages.
- **Limited Customization of Access.** Instant Web Publishing lets you specify the fields that appear as well as security privileges that govern access. It does not, however, offer a full range of access features that are only available through the use of Custom Web Publishing or another FileMaker Pro Web publishing solution.
- **Inability to Run Scripts.** If your database includes scripts to automatically find, sort, or otherwise manipulate data, these scripts cannot be made available to users with Instant Web Publishing.

Step-by-Step Setup

Ready to try your hand at Instant Web Publishing? If so, fire up your copy of FileMaker Pro 4 and open a database that you'd like to publish. Then follow along with the steps in this section to put your database online.

Throughout this chapter, I work with the file named Book Catalog.fp3, which is an illustrated catalog of books by one of my favorite authors. If you'd like to work with the same database file, look for it at http://www.gilesrd.com/fmproweb/.

Enabling & Configuring the Web Companion Plug-In

The first step in publishing a database using FileMaker Pro version 4's new Web publishing features is to enable and configure the Web Companion plug-in, which is part of FileMaker Pro. You do this with the Application Preferences and Web Companion Configuration dialog boxes.

You only need to follow these steps once, no matter how many databases you publish.

Enabling the Web Companion Plug-In

Start by choosing Application from the Preferences submenu under the Edit menu.

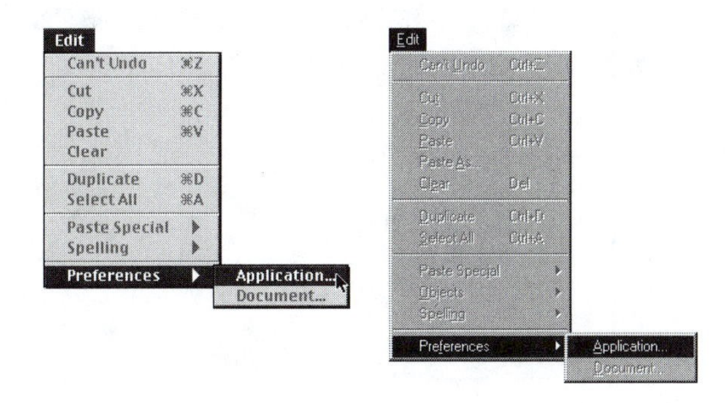

The Application Preferences dialog box appears. Choose Plug-Ins from the pop-up menu (Macintosh) or click the Plug-Ins tab (Windows). The dialog box changes to display a list of all plug-ins. The Web Companion plug-in should appear in the list—in fact, it may be the only item in the list. To enable it, simply turn on the check box beside it.

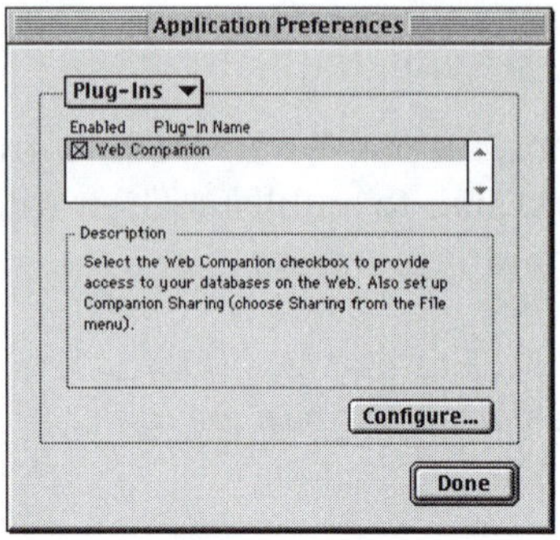

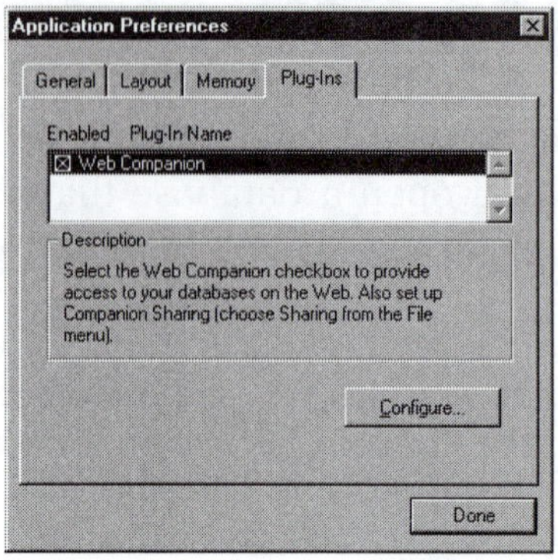

TIP

If the Web Companion plug-in does not appear in the Application Preferences dialog box, it was probably not installed with FileMaker Pro. Quit or exit FileMaker Pro and use the FileMaker Pro installer to reinstall FileMaker Pro. When installing, choose the Easy (Macintosh) or Typical (Windows) Install option or, if you choose the Custom Install option, be sure to turn on the check box for Web Support. Restart your computer and try again. The Web Companion plug-in should be properly installed.

Enabling Instant Web Publishing

Select the Web Companion plug-in in the Application Preferences dialog box and click the Configure button. The Web Companion Configuration dialog box appears.

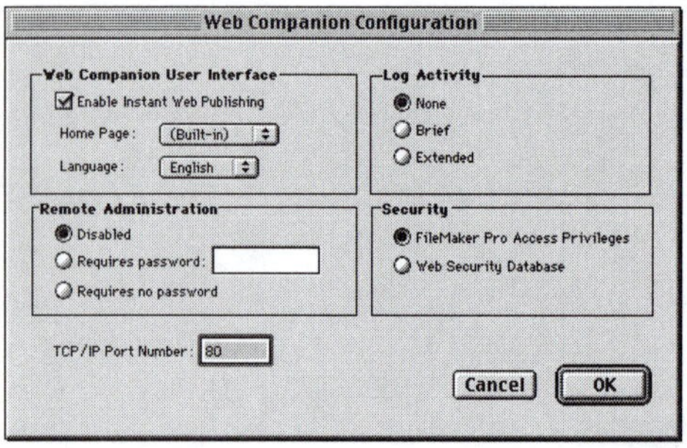

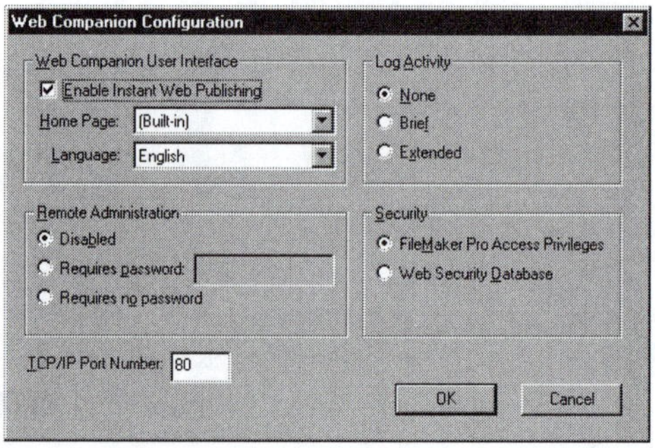

Make sure the Enable Instant Web Publishing check box is turned on. (It's turned on by default.)

Selecting the Built-In Home Page

Make sure (Built-in) is chosen from the Home Page menu. (It's selected by default.) This insures that the databases you open for publication automatically appear on the Home page that Web Companion displays to visitors. I tell you more about choosing a Home page in Chapter 3.

Setting Other Web Companion Configuration Options

The other options in the Web Companion Configuration dialog box apply to both Instant Web Publishing and Custom Web Publishing. I discuss them in Chapter 3, where I discuss a number of options that apply to FileMaker Pro version 4's new Web publishing features.

Saving Your Settings

Once you've enabled the Web Companion Plug-In and Instant Web Publishing, click OK to dismiss the Web Companion Configuration dialog box and click Done to dismiss the Application Preferences dialog box. Your settings are saved to the FileMaker and Web Companion preferences files.

Preparing a Database for Instant Web Publishing

Next, you need to prepare the database that you want to publish. This can be as easy as opening the database or it may require that you create new layouts with the fields that you want to appear in table and form views. It's also a good time to think about security and what privileges you want users to have.

Opening a Database

If you haven't already opened the database that you want to publish, choose Open from FileMaker's File menu. Use the dialog box that appears to locate and Open the database file.

WARNING

The database must be open for its contents to be published on the Web. If you close a database, it will no longer be available to users who access it via the Web.

Creating Layouts

You have two options for choosing the database fields that you want to appear on the Web:

- To display all fields in Table and Form Views and on the Search form, no additional layouts are required.
- To display specific fields, your database must include a layout containing the fields that you want to display, in the order in which you want to display them. The layout itself does not appear on a Web page; just the fields included in that layout and any special date, time, or number formats associated with the layout's fields. If you want to display a different collection of fields in Table View, Form View, and the Search form, your database must include a separate layout for each.

Look at your database file and decide which fields you want to display. To display them all in both Table and Form Views and on the Search form, do nothing. To display only certain fields, check your database to see if it already has a layout that contains only the fields that you want to display. If it does, do nothing. If it doesn't, switch to layout mode and create a layout that includes only the fields that you want to display, in the order in which you want to display them. Do this as necessary for Table View, Form View, and the Search form.

TIP *If you've been using the database for a while, it may already have all of the layouts you need to publish it on the Web using Instant Web Publishing. In that case, you don't have to do a thing.*

Setting Security Options

FileMaker Pro's built-in Web publishing features offer two ways to maintain security over your database:

- FILEMAKER PRO ACCESS PRIVILEGES, when set, can also control access when the database is published on the Web.
- THE WEB SECURITY DATABASE is a separate database file that offers additional security for databases that are published on the Web.

I tell you more about both of these options in Chapter 3. If you decide to secure your database, be sure to set up security *before* making your database available to the public.

Enabling & Configuring Web Companion Sharing

The final step to publishing a database with Instant Web Publishing is enabling and configuring Web Companion Sharing. This is done individually for each FileMaker Pro database file that you want to publish on the web.

Enabling Web Companion Sharing

Start by choosing Sharing from the File menu.

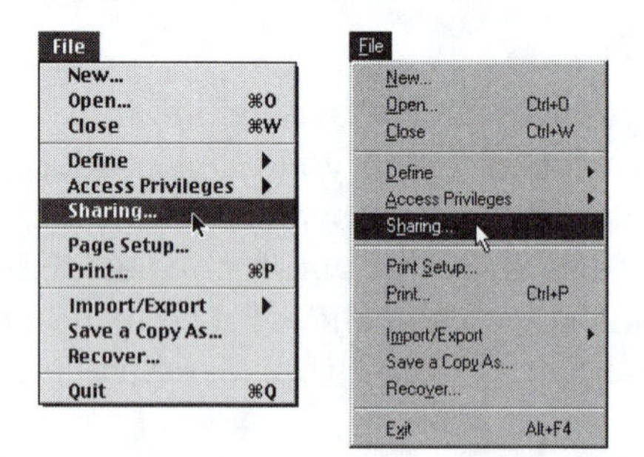

The File Sharing dialog box appears. In the Companion Sharing section of the dialog box, turn on the Web Companion check box.

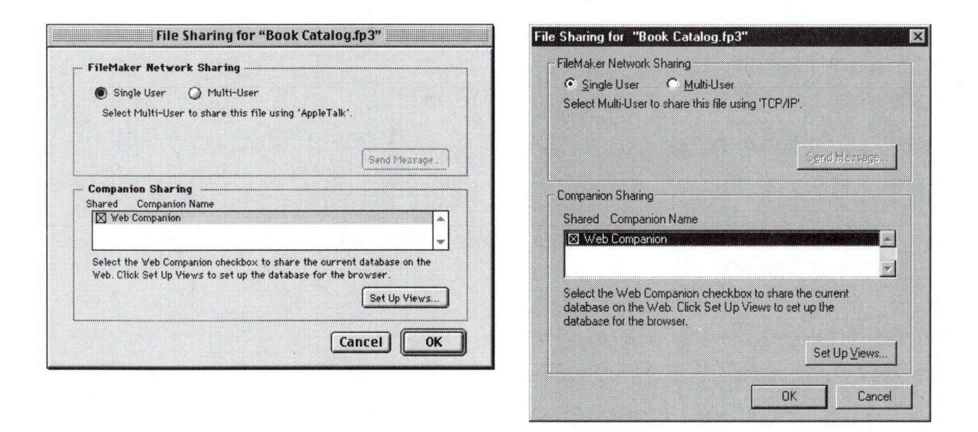

Specifying Fields for Table and Form Views and the Search Form

Make sure Web Companion is selected in the File Sharing dialog box. Then click the Set Up Views button. The Web Companion View Setup dialog box appears.

To set the fields that will appear in Table View, choose Table View from the menu (Macintosh) or click the Table View tab (Windows) in the Web Companion View Setup dialog box. Then choose an option from the Layout menu. You'll have at least two options:

- **ALL FIELDS (NO LAYOUT)** will display all fields in the order that they appear in the Field Name list. In case you're wondering, field order is determined by the order in which fields were created and, unfortunately, cannot be changed.
- ***LAYOUT NAME*** will display all fields in the specific layout in the order they appear in the layout. When you choose a specific layout, a list of its fields

appears in the Field Name list. The Layout menu includes an option for each layout in your database.

TIP

To display a related field, you must choose a layout that includes the related field. If you choose All Fields (no layout), related fields do not appear.

To set the fields that will appear in Form View, choose Form View from the menu (Macintosh) or click the Form View tab (Windows) in the Web Companion View Setup dialog box. Choose an option from the Layout menu.

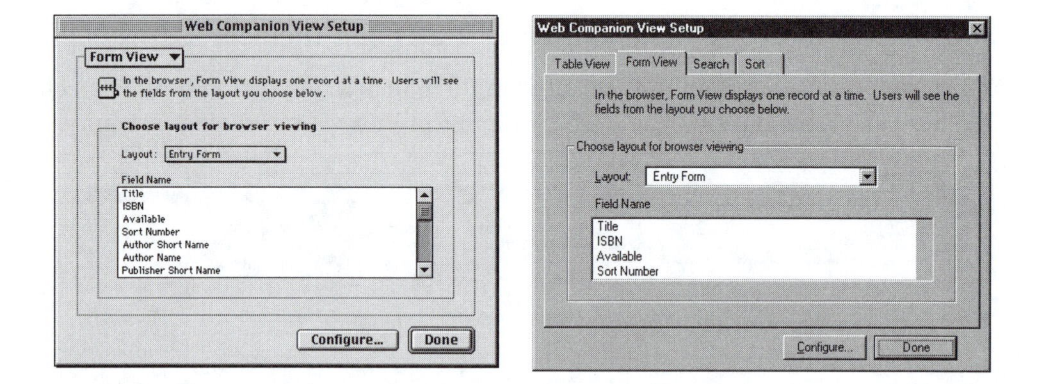

To specify the fields that will appear on the Search form, choose Search from the menu (Macintosh) or click the Search tab (Windows) in the Web Companion View Setup dialog box. Then choose an option from the Layout menu.

Setting Sort Options

Choose Sort from the menu (Macintosh) or click the Sort tab (Windows) in the Web Companion View Setup dialog box.

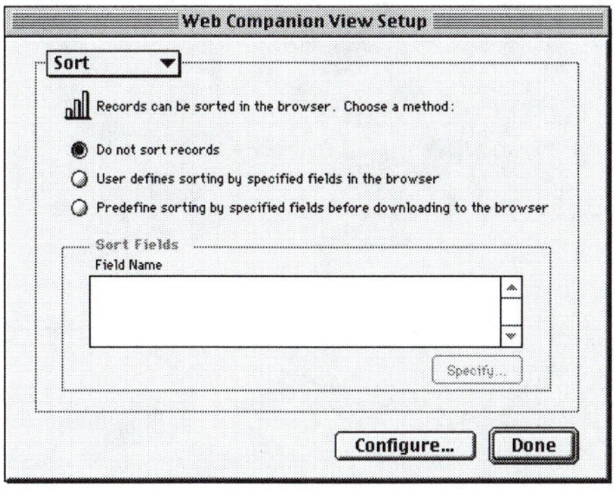

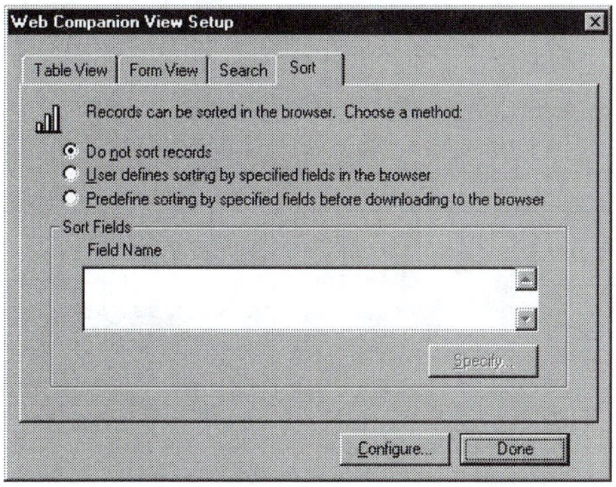

Select a radio button to determine how records can be sorted by a user viewing the database with a Web browser. You have three options:

- **DO NOT SORT RECORDS** disables record sorting. This is the default selection.
- **USER DEFINES SORTING BY SPECIFYING FIELDS IN THE BROWSER** enables the user to choose the fields by which he wants to sort the records.
- **PREDEFINE SORTING BY SPECIFIED FIELDS BEFORE DOWNLOADING TO THE BROWSER** sorts the records in the order you specify before the records appear in the Web browser. The user does not have any sort options.

If you select the first option, you're done. If you select either of the other options, click the Specify button. The Specify Sort Order (Macintosh) or Specify Sort (Windows) dialog box appears. This is the same dialog box you use to sort records in any other FileMaker Pro database.

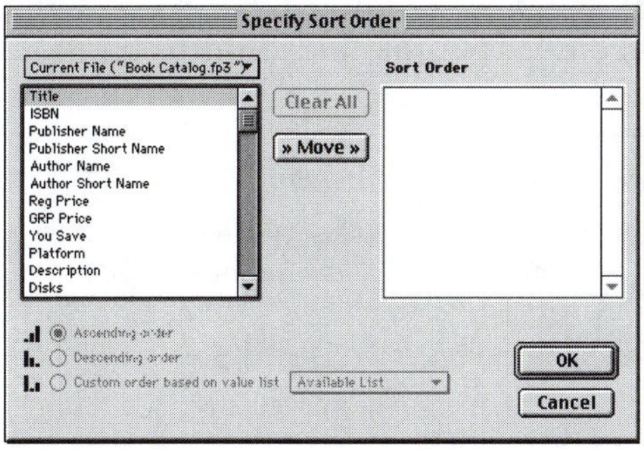

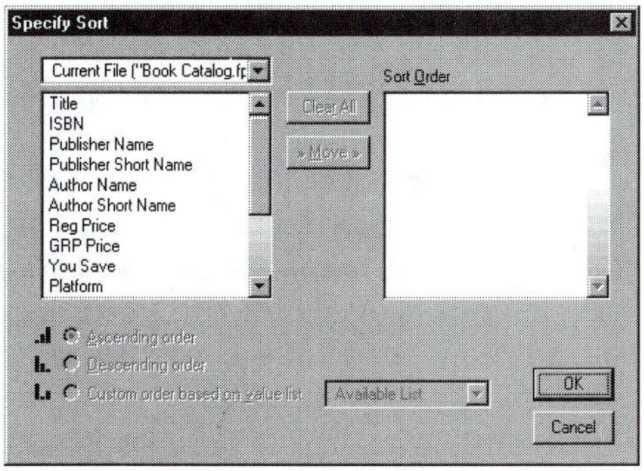

Use the dialog box to select the fields by which the user can sort or by which the records should automatically be sorted. Then click OK to save your settings. The order you selected appears in the Web Companion View Setup dialog box.

Saving Your Settings

Once you've enabled Web Companion sharing and set view options, click Done to dismiss the Web Companion View Setup dialog box and click OK to dismiss the File Sharing dialog box. Your settings are saved in the database file.

Accessing Published Data

If you've completed all of the steps in the previous section of this chapter, your database is now online. In this section, I tell you how to view, edit, and otherwise work with published data.

Opening a Database File

Launch your Web browser and use it to enter the IP address of the database Web server—the computer on which FileMaker Pro and the open database(s) are running. When you enter the URL, enter it in the format http://*xx.xx.xx.xx*/ where *xx.xx.xx.xx* is the IP address.

*If you specified a port number other than 80 in the Web Companion Configuration dialog box, a colon and that port number must be appended to the IP address in the URL. In that case, the URL will look something like this: http://*xx.xx.xx.xx*:591/, where* xx.xx.xx.xx *is the IP address of the database Web server. I tell you more about assigning port numbers in Chapter 3.*

The database Home page appears. If you chose (Built-in) from the Home Page menu in the Web Companion Configuration dialog box, all open database files are automatically listed as links.

To open one of the listed database files, click its link. It appears in Table View.

Browsing Records

Once a database file has been opened, you can browse its contents. Instant Web Publishing offers a number of standard Web page views for browsing records. It also enables you to search the database for specific records, display all of the records, and, if sorting is enabled, sort the records.

Browsing in Table View

Table View is the default view for a database. It displays a group of records at a time in a table, which is similar to a FileMaker Pro columnar report. Each row of the table represents a record and each column represents a field.

	Title	ISBN	Reg Price
1	The Macintosh Bible Guide to Word 6	1-56609-073-3	$24.95
2	The Macintosh Bible Guide to Excel 5	0-201-88373-2	$24.95
3	Excel for Windows 95: Visual QuickStart Guide	0-201-88372-4	$16.95
4	PageMill for Macintosh: Visual QuickStart Guide	0-201-88661-8	$15.95
5	The Macintosh Bible, Sixth Edition	0-201-88636-7	$29.95
6	America Online 3 for Macintosh: Visual QuickStart Guide	0-201-68807-7	$16.95

To switch to Table View from another view, click the Table View tab at the top of the Web page.

If you're using a Java-enabled browser, a Record Range icon and controls should appear near the top-left corner of the Web page.

Record range:

1-6

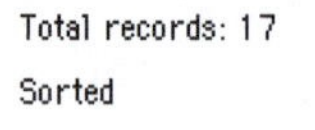

You can use this icon to view different groups of records. Here's how:

- To view the next group of records in the database, click the Next button (the down arrow) at the bottom of the Record Range icon.
- To view the previous group of records in the database, click the Previous button (the up arrow) at the top of the Record Range icon.
- To view a different group of records, drag the slider on the right side of the Record Range icon.
- To view a specific range of records, enter the range in the Record Range box and click the Enter button beside it.

There are also navigation buttons at the bottom of the Web page:

- To view the top of the page, click the Top button.
- To view the next group of records in the database, click the Next button.
- To view the previous group of records in the database, click the Back button.

Each time you change the range of records, your browser gets fresh database information from the server. It may take a moment or two for the information to appear, so be patient!

Browsing in Form View

Form View displays one record at a time. Each field and its contents is listed down the page.

There are two ways to switch to Form View:

- To switch from Table View or the Search form to Form View, click the Form View tab at the top of the Web page.
- To switch from Table View to Form View and display a specific record, click the number in the first column of the record's row.

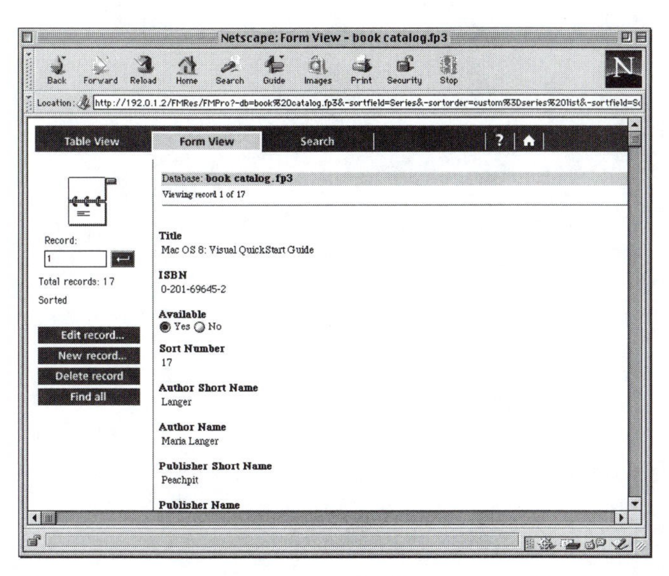

If you're using a Java-enabled browser, a Book icon and controls should appear near the top-left corner of the Web page. The Book should look familiar; it's very similar to the one that appears in the status panel in FileMaker Pro.

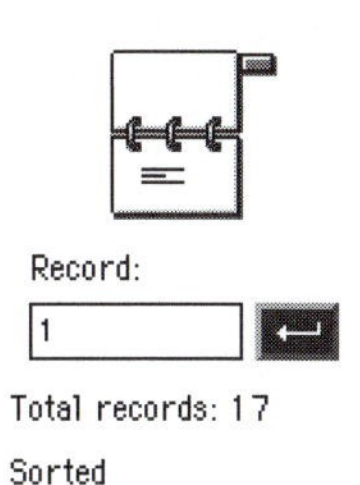

As you probably guessed, you can use the Book icon to switch from record to record while in Form view. Here's how:

- To view the next record in the database, click the bottom page of the Book icon.
- To view the previous record in the database, click the top page of the Book icon.
- To quickly switch to a different record, drag the slider on the right side of the book.
- To switch to a specific record, enter the record number in the Record box and click the Enter button beside it.

There are also navigation buttons at the bottom of the Web page:

- To view the top of the page, click the Top button.
- To view the next record in the database, click the Next button.
- To view the previous record in the database, click the Back button.

Searching for Records

You can use the Search form to search for records matching criteria that you specify. The results of the search appear in Table View.

To switch to the Search form, click the Search button at the top of the Web page.

To perform a search, begin by choosing an option from the Type menu beside the field for which you want to enter criteria. You have two options:

- **CONTAINS** finds records that contain the entry in the Criteria box.
- **DOES NOT CONTAIN** finds records that do not contain the entry in the Criteria box.

Next, enter the information for which you want to search in the Criteria box for the field in which you expect to find it.

TIP

You can include standard FileMaker Pro search operators in the Criteria box. Clicking the Search Tips button opens a Web page with additional information about searching and using operators.

If you enter information into more than one Criteria box, select one of the Match radio buttons:

- **MATCH ALL WORDS ON PAGE (AND)** tells the search engine to display only those records for which all search criteria match. This is the same as entering multiple search criteria in a FileMaker Pro Find request.
- **MATCH ANY WORD ON PAGE (OR)** tells the search engine to display any records for which any of the search criteria match. This is similar to creating multiple FileMaker Pro Find requests.

TIP

If you make a mistake along the way, you can click the Clear Fields button. This resets the Search form.

When you're satisfied with the criteria you've entered and the other settings on the Search form, click the Start Search button. A moment later, the results of your search appear in Table View. The number of records found appears beneath the Record Range icon.

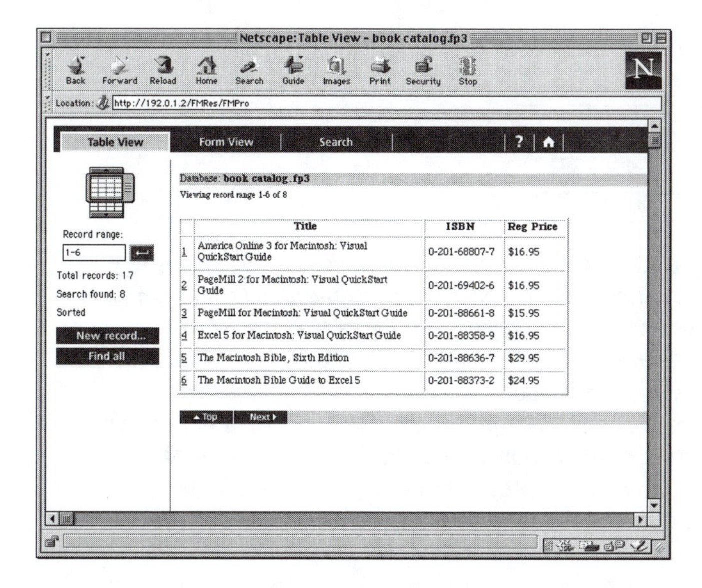

	Title	ISBN	Reg Price
1	America Online 3 for Macintosh: Visual QuickStart Guide	0-201-68807-7	$16.95
2	PageMill 2 for Macintosh: Visual QuickStart Guide	0-201-69402-6	$16.95
3	PageMill for Macintosh: Visual QuickStart Guide	0-201-88661-8	$15.95
4	Excel 5 for Macintosh: Visual QuickStart Guide	0-201-88358-9	$16.95
5	The Macintosh Bible, Sixth Edition	0-201-88636-7	$29.95
6	The Macintosh Bible Guide to Excel 5	0-201-88373-2	$24.95

If no records match your search criteria, the Web browser window displays a No Records Found graphic. Click the Search again button to return to the Search form or click the Find all button to find all records and return to Table View.

Finding All Records

When you're finished working with the records found as a result of a search, you may want to display all records again. To do so, click the Find all button, which appears on the left side of the Web page window in Table and Form Views.

Sorting Records

If sorting is enabled in the Web Companion Views Setup dialog box, a Sort button appears on the left side of the Web page window in Table and Form Views. To sort the records, click this button. The Sort form appears.

Sort

Records to sort: 17

Select field name(s) and sort order to define your sort, then click **Start sort.**

Start sort

Back to view

Revert

Sort by	Field name	Sort order
1.	-None-	Ascending
2.	-None-	Ascending
3.	-None-	Ascending
4.	-None-	Ascending

NOTE

If you've been paying close attention to the illustrations throughout this chapter, you may have noticed that the Sort option in the Web Companion Views Setup dialog box was set to Predefined sorting for the Macintosh illustrations and User defines sorting for the Windows illustrations. That's why a Sort button appears only in the Windows illustrations, which are always Unsorted, and why the Macintosh illustrations are always sorted. I did this on purpose to show how the sorting option affects the way pages appear. In the illustrations in the Sorting Records section, however, User defines sorting is selected in both Macintosh and Windows files.

Select a field from the Field Name menu in the first line. The menu displays all field names you specified in the Web Companion View Setup dialog box.

Next, select an option from the Sort order menu on the same line. Your options include:

- **ASCENDING** sorts from A to Z, low number to high number, or early date or time to late date or time, depending on the type of field.
- **DESCENDING** sorts from Z to A, high number to low number, or late date or time to early date or time, depending on the type of field.
- **VALUE LIST NAME** sorts in the order of items in a specific value list. A menu option will appear for every value list in the database.

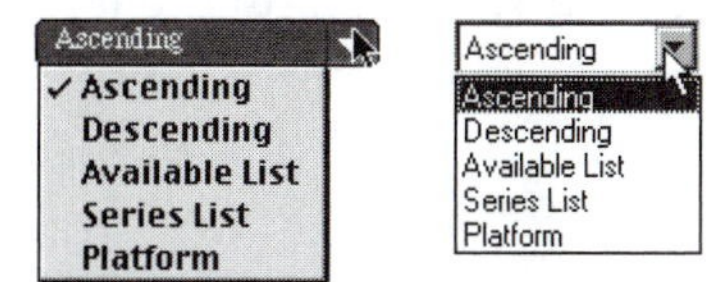

If desired, choose a field name and sort order for other lines on the Sort form. A line will appear for each field you specified in the Web Companion View Setup dialog box. This enables you to perform nested sorts, just like you can with FileMaker Pro.

If you mess up and want to start over, click the Revert button to reset the Sort form. If you change your mind and don't want to sort records at all, click the Back to view button to go back to the previous view of the database.

When you're satisfied with your choices on the Sort form, click the Start sort button. The records are sorted and appear in Table View. The word Sorted appears above the Sort button on the left side of the window.

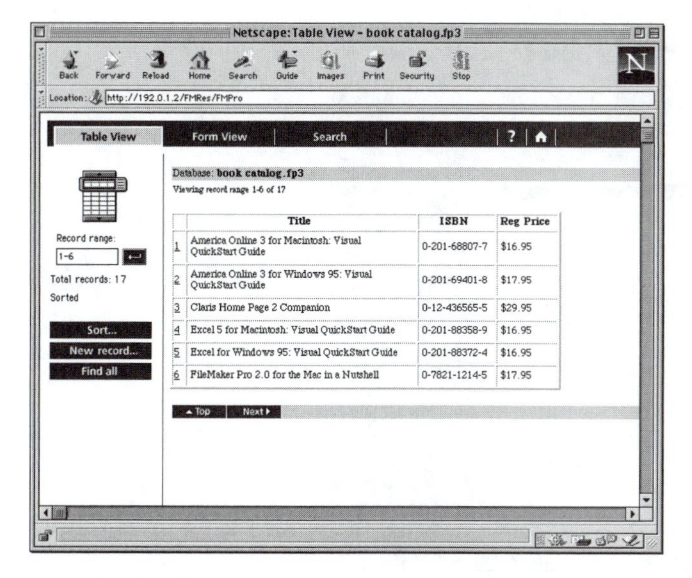

NOTE

Sorting the records with a Web browser does not change the sort order of the records in the database or the way it appears to other users accessing the database with a Web browser.

Unsorting Records

To unsort records, follow the steps for sorting records in the previous section, but do not choose any sort fields. When you click the Start sort button, the records are unsorted—returned to the order in which they were entered into the database. The word Unsorted appears above the Sort button on the left side of the Table View page.

Modifying the Database

Databases published on the Web using Instant Web Publishing can also be modified. Users can add, edit, or delete records.

Editing commands can be disabled using FileMaker Pro access privileges or the Web Security database. If a feature is disabled, the button that is normally used to access it does not appear on Web pages. I tell you more about security features in Chapter 3.

Adding Records

To add a record to the database, click the New record button on the left side of the Table View or Form View window. A New Record form appears. It uses the Form View layout but enables you to enter information into blank fields.

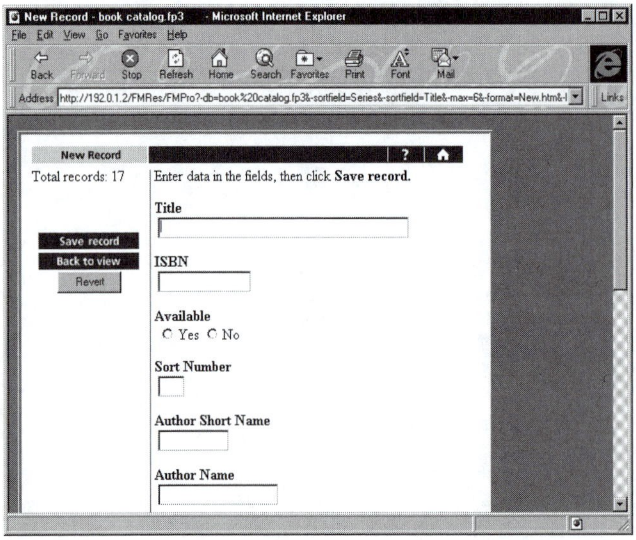

Enter the information that you want to include in the new record. You may have to use the scroll bars to see and enter information into every field. You can edit mistakes as you make them using standard editing techniques. If you make a lot of mistakes and want to start over, click the Revert button to reset the form. If you change your mind about creating a new record, click the Back to view button to go back to the previous view of the database.

You cannot enter information into container, calculation, summary, or global fields.

When you're finished entering information, click the Save record button. The information is entered into the FileMaker Pro database and appears on screen in Form View.

Editing Records

To modify the information in a database record, begin by viewing the record that you want to modify in Form View. Then click the Edit record button. The Edit Record form appears. It's just like the New Record form, but it is already filled in with the existing information for the current record.

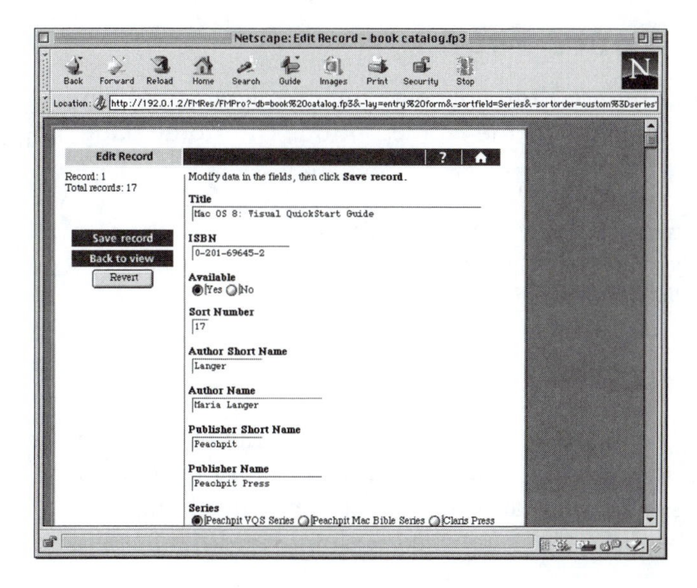

Using standard editing techniques, change the fields that you want to modify. If you make mistakes and want to start over, click the Revert button to reset the form. If you change your mind about editing the record, click the Back to view button to go back to the previous view of the database.

When you're finished editing information, click the Save record button. The record is modified in the FileMaker Pro database to reflect your changes and appears on screen in Form View.

Deleting Records

To delete a record, begin by viewing the record that you want to delete in Form View. Then click the Delete record button. A confirmation page appears. Click

Delete to delete the record or click Cancel if you change your mind and want to keep the record.

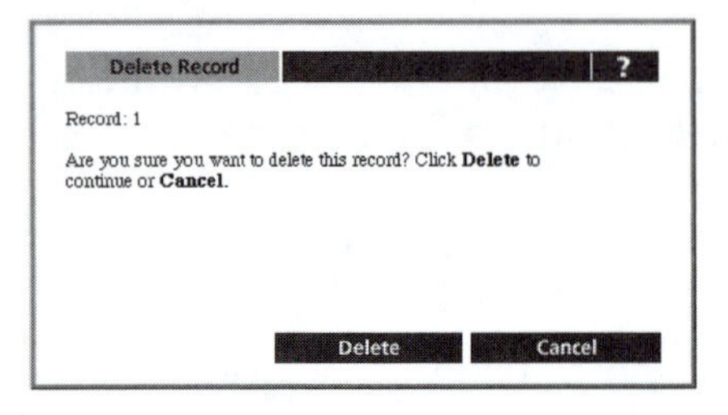

If you click Delete, the record is removed from the FileMaker Pro database. The record immediately before it appears on screen in Form View.

Returning to the Home Page

You can go back to the database Home page at any time while working with a database file. To do so, click the Home button. The Home page reappears.

TIP

Since the Home page is automatically reloaded each time you click the Home button at the top of the Web page, it will automatically reflect any changes in the list of available database files.

Getting Help

FileMaker Pro's Instant Web Publishing feature includes its own online help system. To access it, click the Help button at the top of the Web page. A separate browser window appears. It contains information on browsing and editing database files published with Instant Web Publishing.

TIP

The Help button displays a different part of the Help page depending on the Web page you are viewing when you click it. For example, if you click the Help button while in Form View, you'll go to the part of the Help page that discusses Form View.

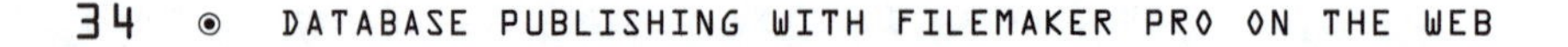

CHAPTER 2

Custom Web Publishing

For flexible database Web publishing solutions, FileMaker Pro version 4's new Custom Web Publishing feature is tough to beat. In this chapter, I tell you what Custom Web Publishing is, why you might or might not want to use it, and how you set it up. Along the way, I explain the two most important components of Custom Web Publishing: format files and Claris Dynamic Markup Language (CDML) tags.

NOTE

In this chapter, I work with a file named Guest Register.fp3, which is a deluxe guest book database. If you'd like to work with the same database file, look for it at http://www.gilesrd.com/fmproweb/.

Overview

As the name suggests, Custom Web Publishing enables you to create a custom Web publishing solution for database files. With it, you have complete control over the appearance and content of the Web pages that let users browse and interact with your databases. There is a price for all this power, however. In order to use Custom Web Publishing, you must know exactly what each page should do and how to enter the commands that will communicate your desires to FileMaker Pro's Web Companion plug-in.

NOTE

If you've used Lasso to publish FileMaker Pro databases on the Web, Custom Web Publishing should look very familiar to you. That's because Filemaker, Inc. purchased some of Blue World Communication's Lasso technology and incorporated much of it into FileMaker Pro version 4's Web Companion. I tell you more about Lasso in Chapter 5.

How It Works

Custom Web Publishing displays Web pages that enable users to browse, search, create, modify, and delete records in a FileMaker Pro database. These Web pages are created by combining HyperText Markup Language (HTML) and Claris Dynamic Markup Language (*CDML*) in special HTML documents called *format files*.

CDML Defined

CDML is a collection of tags, similar in many respects to HTML, that can be interpreted by Web Companion. They provide the instructions that Web Companion needs to interact with a FileMaker Pro database. There are about 90 of these tags, each designed to perform a specific task. You can find a complete list of them in Appendix B.

Format Files Defined

A format file is a plain text document that combines HTML with CDML. It provides Web Companion with information on how to format a Web page, as well as instructions that Web Companion needs to locate, display, change, add, or delete database records.

What's interesting about a format file is that although Web Companion uses it to display database information on a Web page, the source code for the resulting Web page is not the same as the format file. This is because Web Companion substitutes information from the database file to generate a Web page on the fly based on the format file.

TIP

Having trouble understanding what a format file is? Try this analogy: A format file is like a word processing document prepared for a mail merge—the final document is based on the original (the format file), but contains information from another source (the database file). Taking that analogy a step further, CDML commands in a format file are similar to mail merge commands—they provide instructions but never appear in the final document.

Benefits

Custom Web Publishing has several benefits over Instant Web Publishing, which I discuss in Chapter 1:

- **Custom Appearance.** With Custom Web Publishing, you have complete control over how information appears on Web pages. In addition, you can include other Web page elements like images, background patterns, and JavaScripts.
- **Custom Accessiblity.** Because Custom Web Publishing requires individual format files (and thus, Web pages) for specific tasks, you can control what fields and layouts are accessible to users. Simply provide a different set of URLs for different users.
- **Ability to Run Scripts.** Custom Web Publishing solutions can run scripts, either automatically or as the result of a user clicking a button or link. This makes it possible to perform predefined searches or sorts.

Drawbacks

Custom Web Publishing has some drawbacks, too. Consider these when deciding whether this technique is right for you:

- **No Instant Solution.** Creating a custom solution takes time. Although FileMaker Pro comes with a number of "canned solutions" (check the Web folder), it still takes time to customize them for your own use. I hope you get paid by the hour.
- **HTML + CDML.** As if HTML didn't have enough tags, to take advantage of Custom Web Publishing, you have to deal with an additional 90 CDML tags. While CDML isn't difficult to learn, it's just something to make your job a bit tougher.
- **Consistency Depends on You.** If you want consistent appearance and functionality from one page to the next, you must include consistent elements in the Custom Web Publishing format files. That's not difficult either, but it is an additional responsibility.

Author's Choice

The method I'd pick to publish a database really depends on the type of data that I need to publish. If it's just a quick list that I need to get online, I'd probably use Instant Web Publishing. But if it's something that I *cared* a lot about, I'd use Custom Web Publishing. That's the only way I'd get the information to look and work exactly the way I want it to.

A Closer Look at Format Files

Custom Web Publishing format files perform two functions:

- Provide a framework for the appearance of the Web page generated by Web Companion to display information from a database file.
- Provide instructions that can be interpreted by Web Companion to perform specific tasks with a database file.

They do this by combining text, standard HTML tags, and CDML tags. HTML determines appearance, displays static content, and offers standard Web interactivity while CDML enables database interactivity and displays dynamic content.

In this section, I tell you more about format files and explain how HTML and CDML determine their function.

Types of Format Files

There are several types of format files, each designed to perform a specific task. Although not all types are required to interact with a database, most complete Custom Web Publishing solutions include at least one of each type of format file:

- **New** enables the user to create a new record for the database.
- **Search** enables the user to search for records that match criteria. The criteria can be specified by the user, preset in the format file, or determined by a script.
- **Results** displays a list of records. It is usually used after a search.
- **Detail** displays information for one record at a time. It is often used to get more information about a record in a results list.
- **Edit** enables the user to edit the contents of a specific record.
- **Delete** enables the user to delete a record.
- **Reply** notifies the user that a task has been successfully completed. There are three types of replies. **New reply** appears when a record has been successfully added. **Edit reply** appears when a record has been successfully edited. **Delete reply** appears when a record has been successfully deleted.

There are no rules governing how to create or use the various format files. In fact, there's nothing to stop you from incorporating multiple functionality in one format file. For example, why not create a detail format file that appears as a reply when a record is added but offers options to edit or delete the newly added record? Once you master the basics, you can do all kinds of things with format files.

The Role of HTML in a Format file

The primary components of a format file are HTML elements and text. In fact, it's safe to say that a format file is nothing more than a highly specialized HTML file. HTML elements like these determine the appearance and part of the functionality of the format file:

- **HTML Formatting Tags** determine the appearance and position of text on the Web page. They make it possible to organize information in tables, make headings bold, or change text justification.
- **HTML Graphic Elements**, such as GIF or JPEG graphics, animated GIFs, AIFF sound files, Java Applets, and QuickTime movies, help ensure consistency with other Web pages on your site or make them stand out.
- **HTML HyperLink Tags** provide links to other pages and can activate embedded CDML tags. I tell you about embedding CDML tags in links later in this chapter.
- **HTML Form and Input Tags** enable users to enter information and begin Web Companion action. I tell you more about form-related tags later in this chapter.

When creating format files, you might find it useful to start by creating an HTML document that incorporates the text, images, and formatting you want the user to see. Then insert the CDML tags that will make the file interact with FileMaker Pro Web Companion and your open database files.

Static vs. Dynamic Forms

Remember my discussion of static vs. dynamic Web publishing back in the Introduction of this book? (Don't tell me that you skipped the Introduction; the introductions in my books are just as important as the numbered chapters!) The concept of static vs. dynamic pages is also important when discussing Custom Web Publishing.

Much of the interaction between a user and a database file is done with forms. With Custom Web Publishing, a form can be either static or dynamic:

- **Static forms** contain only HTML commands. Web Companion isn't put to work until the user clicks the Submit button, which may contain a CDML command. Static forms appear quickly because they don't need to access the database file for information.
- **Dynamic forms** contain a mixture of HTML and CDML commands. While the HTML commands are used to format the Web page and its elements, the CDML commands are used to obtain information from the database file. A good example is a form with a pop-up menu that is populated with items

from a value list within the database file. Dynamic forms appear more slowly because Web Companion must obtain data from the database and generate an HTML document based on the format file and data before the page can appear.

TIP

Use static forms whenever a form doesn't require information from a database file. This helps speed up access to pages on your site.

A Closer Look at CDML

CDML is what makes a format file a format file. It enables communication between the user and Web Companion, which, in turn, communicates with FileMaker Pro database files.

Types of CDML Tags

CDML tags fall into three broad categories:

- **Action tags** perform a specific action in FileMaker Pro. For example, the **-Delete** tag deletes a record in the FileMaker Pro database.
- **Variable tags** specify options for action tags. For example, the **-DB** tag specifies the name of the database with which the user will interact.
- **Replacement tags** are placeholders for data from the FileMaker Pro database. When the information is retrieved, the replacement tags are replaced with data. For example, the **[FMP-Field: Name]** tag is replaced with data from the Name field in the FileMaker Pro database.

You can find a complete list of CDML tags in Appendix B.

CDML Tag Syntax

Like HTML, CDML has its own syntax. Syntax is like English grammar, but a lot less forgiving. If you have poor grammar, most people can still figure out what you're trying to say. But if you make a CDML syntax error, Web Companion either won't work or it won't work the way you expect it to.

Fortunately, FileMaker Pro comes with the CDML Tool, which automatically generates properly formatted CDML code for you, based on menu selections you make for your database. I tell you more about that later. But since there's more to CDML syntax than what you'll find in the CDML Tool, I'll explain CDML syntax here.

Punctuation

CDML tags use several types of punctuation that aren't normally used in HTML:

- HYPHEN OR DASH (-) begins all action and variable tags. Two examples are **-Edit** (an action tag) and **-Format** (a variable tag). A hyphen or dash also appears after the characters *FMP* in replacement tags. An example is **[FMP-Field]**.
- SQUARE BRACKETS (**[ ]**) surround all replacement tags. An example is **[FMP-Field]**.
- COLON (**:**) appears between the text of a replacement tag and the name of the item it specifies. Two examples include **[FMP-Field: First Name]** (which specifies a field named First Name) and **[FMP-Portal: Accounts]** (which specifies a relationship named Accounts).
- SPACE CHARACTERS ( ) can appear between a colon and the name of the item specified by the tag (check the previous example). They can also appear within file names.

Space characters appearing in URLs should be encoded as **%20** *(the ISO Latin-1 equivalent of a space) before being read by a Web browser. For best results, avoid using spaces after colons or in file, layout, and field names. If you must include spaces in item names, make sure you or your Web authoring program make the necessary encoding to* **%20** *for each space in a URL.*

- COMMA (**,**) appears within a replacement tag to separate items from various types of encodings. An example is **[FMP-Field: Comments, BR]** (which includes the **BR** parameter for the field named Comments).
- AMPERSAND (**&**) appears between CDML name/value pairs when they appear in a link. An example is **<A HREF="FMPro?-DB=Guest%20Register.fp3&-Format=entries.htm&-SortField=Date&-SortOrder=Descend&-Max=10&-FindAll">Show Entries</A>** (which sets up a link that displays up to ten records from the file named Guest Register.fp3, sorted in descending order by the Date field, using the format file named entries.htm).
- QUESTION MARK (**?**) appears after FMPro at the beginning of any link that utilizes CDML tags. Check the previous example.

Case Sensitivity

CDML tags are not case sensitive. That means **-FindAll** is the same as **-FINDALL**, **-findall**, or **-fInDaLl**. I tend to capitalize the first letter of each tag so they stand out a little, but it really doesn't matter.

Links vs. Form Actions

Many CDML tags can be used two different ways in a format file: as a link or as part of a form action. The method you choose depends on your needs for the situation. Let me explain.

Using CDML in a Link

You can create a link in a Web page that, when clicked, interacts with Web Companion and a FileMaker Pro document. Here are a few examples to help you understand the kinds of things you can accomplish with this:

- Create a link that displays all records (or a predefined set of records) on a results page.
- Create a link that deletes, duplicates, or displays detail for the currently displayed record.
- Create a link that runs a script.
- Create a link that sends an e-mail message with predefined content to a predetermined address.

The main limitation of this is that the user cannot provide any additional information that could be used by the CDML commands. All instructions must be included in the CDML code that goes into the link. That means this method cannot be used to add or update a record with user input.

Constructing the link isn't difficult once you know what you want the link to do and what CDML tags it requires. Generally speaking, all CDML links require the following:

- HTML anchor (**A**) and reference (**HREF**) tags, which are required to create a link.
- **FMPro?** tells the Web server that the link will be handled by FileMaker Pro Web Companion.
- **-DB=*database name*** tells Web Companion which database file to use.
- **-Format=*format file name*** tells Web Companion which format file to use after completing the action.
- ***-action tag name*** tells Web Companion what action to perform.

These are the minimum requirements for a link containing CDML commands. The action you need to perform may require (or allow) more tags.

Here's an example that displays the ten most recently added records from a database file:

```
<A HREF="FMPro?-DB=Guest%20Register.fp3&-Format=entries.htm&-
SortField=Date&-SortOrder=Descend&-Max=10&-FindAll">View Guest
Register</A>
```

This example uses each of the required components, with **-FindAll** as the action tag. It also includes the **-SortField** and **-SortOrder** variable tags to include sorting instructions. Note that each name/value pair in the CDML code is separated by an ampersand.

Using CDML in a Form Action

The other, more common way to use CDML is in a form action. This method requires that you create a form containing the fields with which you want users to work. The action is incorporated into a Submit button on the form. Here are some examples of the kinds of things you can do with CDML in a form action:

- Enable users to create new database records based on information they enter.
- Enable users to modify existing database records based on information they enter.
- Enable users to search for records based on criteria they enter.
- Perform any of the actions you can perform with CDML in a link.

The only limitations to this method are those imposed by Web Companion itself. Perhaps that's why it's used in the CDML Tool, which I discuss in detail later in this chapter.

Constructing the form isn't difficult, either, especially if you use a Web authoring tool like Claris Home Page, Adobe PageMill, or Microsoft FrontPage. Simply create the form, then substitute CDML tags to indicate field names and other options. At a minimum, all CDML forms require the following:

- HTML form (**FORM**) tags, including the action (**FMPro**) and method (**post**).
- HTML input (**INPUT**) tag that includes **name="-DB" value="*database name*"** tells Web companion which database file to use. The type of input is usually set to "hidden".
- HTML input (**INPUT**) tag that includes **name="-Format" value="*format file name*"** tells Web companion which format file to use after completing the action. The type of input is usually set to "hidden".
- HTML input (**INPUT**) and/or selection (**SELECT**) fields. For input, use only HTML. For editing existing values, combine with CDML replacement tags to display current field contents.

◉ HTML submit button (**INPUT type="submit"**) tag that includes **name=** ***-action tag name*** tells Web companion what action to perform when the button is clicked.

These are the minimum contents. What you include depends on what you want to display on and accomplish with the page.

Here's an example of a form that displays information and enables the user to modify fields:

```
<FORM action="FMPro" method="post">
<INPUT type="hidden" name="-DB" value="Guest Register.fp3">
<INPUT type="hidden" name="-Format" value="editreply.htm">
First Name: <INPUT type="text" name="First Name" value="[FMP-Field:First
Name]"> <BR>
Last Name: <INPUT type="text" name="Last Name" value="[FMP-Field:Last
Name]"> <BR>
Comments: <INPUT type="textarea" name="Comments" value="[FMP-
Field:Comments]"> <BR>
Would you like to be on our mailing list? <INPUT type="radio" name="Mail
List" value="[FMP-Field:Mail List]"><P>
<INPUT type="submit" name="-Edit" value="Update Record">
```

By combining HTML form input tags with CDML replacement tags, you can display current settings while enabling the user to change them. The submit button determines what action is performed—in this case, editing (or updating) the record to incorporate the changes.

Tools for Creating Format Files

Although you can create a format file by typing HTML and CDML tags in any text editor or word processor, that isn't necessarily the best way. (It certainly isn't any fun, especially if you don't like typing brackets.) Fortunately, Filemaker, Inc. offers some tools to help you create format files. Here's the scoop.

The CDML Reference

The CDML Reference is a FileMaker Pro file that provides detailed information about CDML commands, including sample syntax. Although this file isn't a tool for creating format files, it's certainly an excellent resource for learning what each of the CDML tags are for and seeing syntax examples that show how they can be used.

The CDML Reference file comes with FileMaker Pro version 4. Find it in the Web Tools folder inside the FileMaker Pro 4.0 folder.

The CDML Tool

The CDML Tool is another FileMaker Pro file that comes with FileMaker Pro version 4. But rather than simply provide information, the CDML Tool can generate CDML code based on selections in its window. It also offers templates you can use to form the basis of CDML files you create with a text editor.

I think the CDML Tool is the most useful utility that Filemaker, Inc. provides with FileMaker Pro for creating format files. Take a closer look at it with me and you'll see why.

Begin by opening the CDML Tool (Macintosh) or CDML Tool.fp3 (Windows) file. You can find it in the Web Tools folder inside the FileMaker Pro 4.0 folder. After the initial appearance of a splash screen, the CDML Tool window should look like this:

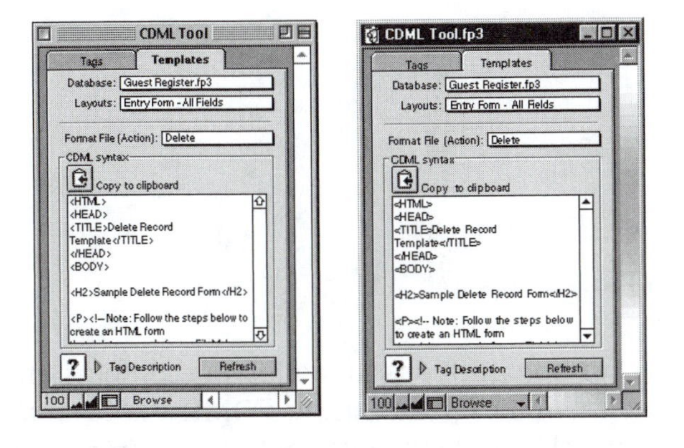

TIP

You must have at least one Database file open to use the CDML Tool. Otherwise, its menus will be empty. If you open a database after opening the CDML Tool, click the Refresh button in the CDML Tool window so the database appears on its Database menu.

Templates Tab

The Templates tab of the CDML Tool window is what appears first. It contains templates to create standard format files. Here's how it works.

Start by choosing a database from the Database menu. Click the Refresh button in the bottom of the window to collect that database's information for the Layouts menu. Next, choose the type of format file that you want to create from the Format File (Action) menu. Then, from the Layouts menu, choose a layout containing the fields that you want to use in the format file.

TIP

If you make choices from these menus in the order in which they appear (which, if you ask me, is the logical way to do it), your Layouts menu options may disappear. If that happens, click the Refresh button to display them again. You may need to choose the desired layout again, too.

The CDML syntax in the scrolling window is automatically modified to include information from your choices. Click the Copy to clipboard button to put a copy of the CDML syntax on the clipboard. Then switch to your favorite HTML editing tool, create a new document, and paste the CDML syntax in.

```
untitled
<HTML>
<HEAD>
<TITLE>Delete Record Template</TITLE>
</HEAD>
<BODY>

<H2>Sample Delete Record Form</H2>

<P><!--Note: Follow the steps below to create an HTML form
that deletes records from a FileMaker Pro database. An angle bracket and two hyphens indicate comments; comments are not displayed by the Web
browser.-->


<P><!--STEP 1. SPECIFY THE FORM ACTION
The form action is already set to "FMPro." When submitting
this form, the Web server is notified to pass this format file to
FileMaker Pro 4.0 for processing.-->
<P><FORM ACTION="FMPro" METHOD="post">


<P><!--STEP 2. SPECIFY THE DATABASE
If you've chosen a database in the CDML Tool, the database name should already be
specified within the Database CDML tag. If the database name has not been specified or
is incorrect, delete the database name specified in the value section of the
CDML database tag below and type the database name within the quotation marks.-->
<P><INPUT TYPE="hidden" NAME="-DB" VALUE="Guest Register.fp3">


<P><!--STEP 3. SPECIFY THE LAYOUT
If you've chosen a database and layout in the CDML Tool, the layout name should
already be specified within the Layout CDML tag. If the layout name has not been
specified or is incorrect, delete the layout name specified in the Value section of the
CDML Layout tag below and type the appropriate database name within the quotation marks.-->
<P><INPUT TYPE="hidden" NAME="-lay" VALUE="Entry Form - All Fields">


<P><!--STEP 4. SPECIFY THE FILENAME FOR RESPONSE FILE
```

This is where it gets a little ugly. Your next step is to modify the contents of the template to include field names and other options using CDML tags. The template provides instructions within HTML comments, but in my opinion, the instructions aren't always clear. Fortunately, some of the information required in the file—such as the **FORM** and **-DB** tags—are already correctly entered. You must enter the remaining tags yourself. That's where the Tags tab of the CDML Tool can help.

Tags Tab

Click the Tags tab of the CDML window to display its options. You can click the Tag Description triangle at the bottom of the window to display a brief description of a selected tag.

This window enables you to generate CDML code on a tag-by-tag basis. Choose a database from the Database menu. If necessary, click the Refresh button to repopulate the other menus with information from the database.

Next, choose a type of CDML tag from the Category menu. You'll notice that there are more than the three types discussed above. This is because the CDML Tool can combine tags to create complete code for a specific function.

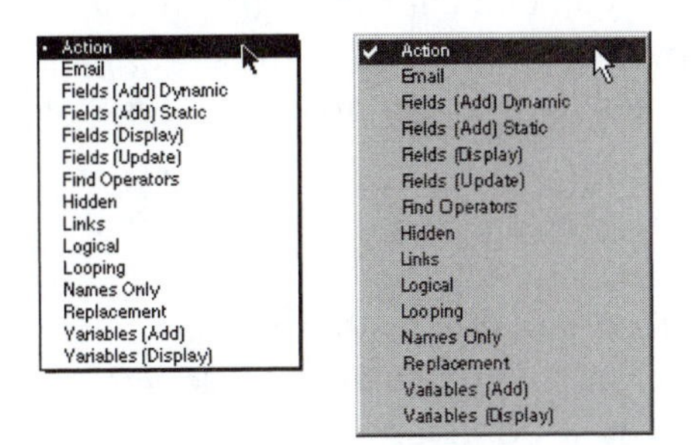

Click the Refresh button to populate the Tags menu for the category you selected. Then choose the tag that you want from the Tags menu. The options that appear depend on the Category menu choice. Here are two examples:

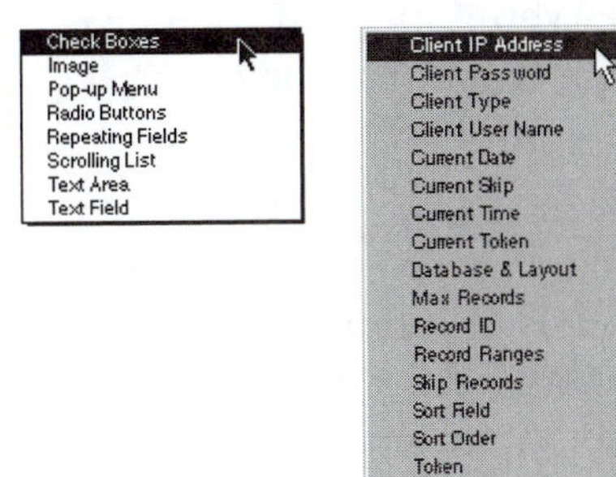

Depending on the tag you selected, you may be finished. But if the tag requires a field, click the Refresh button to populate the Fields, Parameter, and Value List menus for the tag. Then choose an option from the Field menu and if desired (or applicable), from the Parameter and/or Value List menus. Click the Refresh button one more time for good measure and the CDML code for the tag you chose should appear in the CDML syntax window.

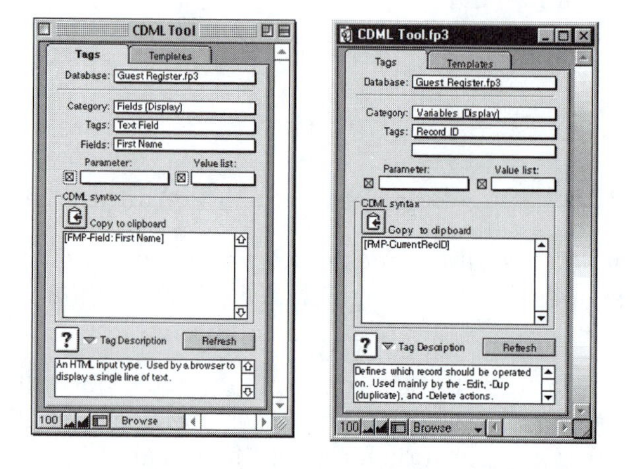

Once you've got the CDML code you need, you can click the Copy to clipboard button, switch to the document in which you want to paste the code, position the insertion point, and paste it in. No brackets to type, no typos. Just a lot of window switching and mousing around.

Putting it All Together

Although the two tabs of the CDML Tool can be used separately, they're designed to work together. If you read the comments in the templates you create with the CDML Tool's Template tab, you'll be given instructions to create code with the CDML Tool's Tags tab. With a little practice, I think you'll agree that it works well.

Using the CDML Tool with WYSIWYG Web Authoring Tools

The CDML Tool also works with WYSIWYG Web authoring tools like Claris Home Page, Adobe PageMill, and Microsoft FrontPage. You may not get exactly what you bargained for, however.

The main problem is the way these programs treat commands that they don't recognize—especially CDML commands that they've never seen before. Even if you paste a template or CDML code into the HTML editing mode of the program, the foreign code might be stripped out. This is something to keep in mind and watch out for if you use a WYSIWYG Web authoring program.

TIP

If you're worried about your Web authoring program messing up CDML tags you insert, try this: Create your Web page using the Web authoring program of your choice. Save the resulting HTML file. Now quit the Web authoring program and use a plain text editor to open the HTML file you created. Use the CDML Tool to create the CDML tags you need to interact with Web Companion and paste them into the text file. Save changes to the file and you're done.

Claris Home Page 3

By far, the best WYSIWYG Web authoring tool for creating Custom Web Publishing solutions for FileMaker Pro is Claris Home Page version 3 or later. It not only accepts all CDML code you type or paste into a document, but its new FileMaker Connection Assistant and FileMaker Pro Libraries features make it downright easy to include CDML tags in HTML documents.

TIP

If you plan on creating more than just one or two Custom Web Publishing solutions, buy Claris Home Page. It's not expensive—FileMaker, Inc. offers a discount to FileMaker Pro owners—and its built-in FileMaker Pro connectivity tools make it an ideal tool for creating format files for use with FileMaker Pro's Custom Web Publishing feature. If you do buy Home Page, be sure to pick up a good book about it. Although its online documentation is very good, its printed documentation is the pits!

In this section, I tell you a little about the FileMaker Pro connectivity tools built into Claris Home Page version 3.

Using the FileMaker Connection Assistant

Claris Home Page version 3 includes a number of assistants that walk you through the process of creating one or more Web pages for a specific purpose. The FileMaker Connection Assistant is one of them. You provide information about the database and the kind of interactivity that you want and Home Page builds the format files for you. When you're finished, the Custom Web Publishing solution is ready to use.

Using the FileMaker Connection Assistant is easy. First, make sure the database file that you want to publish is running on your computer or another computer to which you have access over the network. Then switch to Home Page and choose New from the File menu to display the New dialog box. Use options in the dialog box to select the FileMaker Connection Assistant.

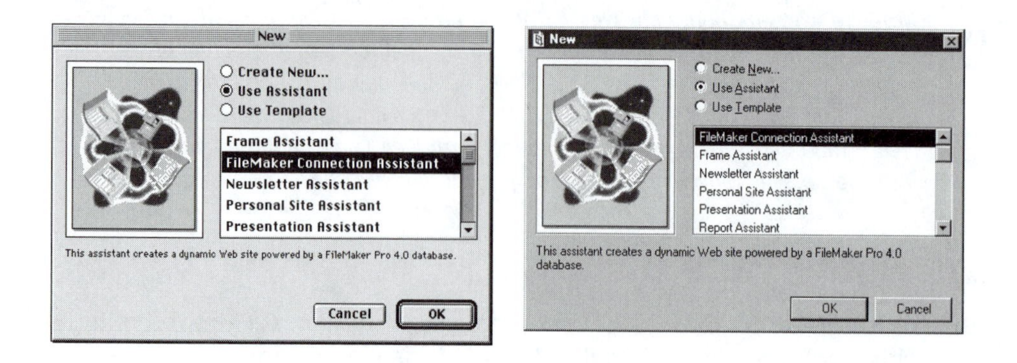

Click OK to continue. An Overview window appears next. It tells you what the assistant does. When you click the Next button, the Before You Begin window tells you some things you should know before you use the assistant. Read it and make sure you meet the requirements.

Click the Next button to continue. The Database Selection window appears next. This is where you tell FileMaker Connection Assistant which database you want to connect to. Enter the IP address of the computer on which the database is open and running; if it's running on your computer, simply click the This computer button. Then, if necessary, enter your User Name and Password in the appropriate boxes. Click the Connect to server button. A list of all available database files appears on the left. Select the one that you want to connect to.

When you click the Next button, the Layout Selection window appears. Use its menu to select the layout that contains all the database fields that you need to access for your Web publishing solution. The fields in that layout appear in the list below the menu.

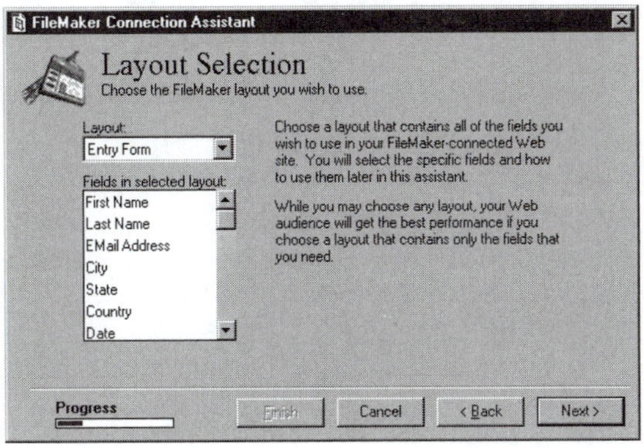

Click the Next button to continue. The Feature Selection window appears. Turn on the check boxes for the features that you want to include in your solution. The options that you select determine the format files that Home Page creates. They also determine which windows appear in the assistant. I've turned on all the check boxes so you'll see all the windows in these instructions.

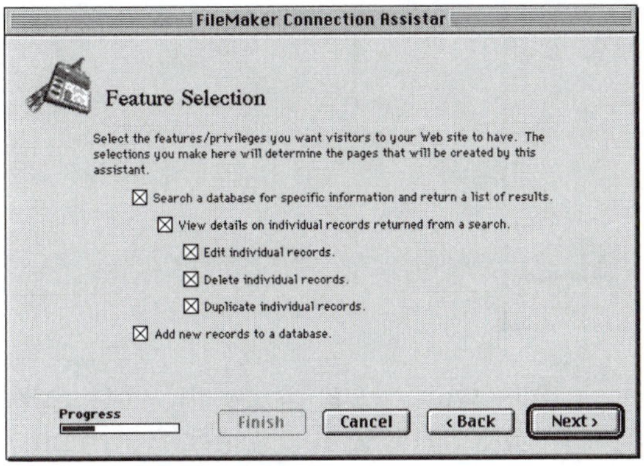

Click the Next button again. The Search Page window appears. This is where it gets interesting. Your job is to select the fields by which you want to allow users to search the database. Click the name of a field in the Fields list to select it, then click the Add button to add it to the Search page fields list. When a field name is selected, you can also use the options on the right side of the window to set the way you want it to appear and operate. The options you select are automatically included in the CDML tags that Home Page embeds in the format file—this saves you a lot of complex coding.

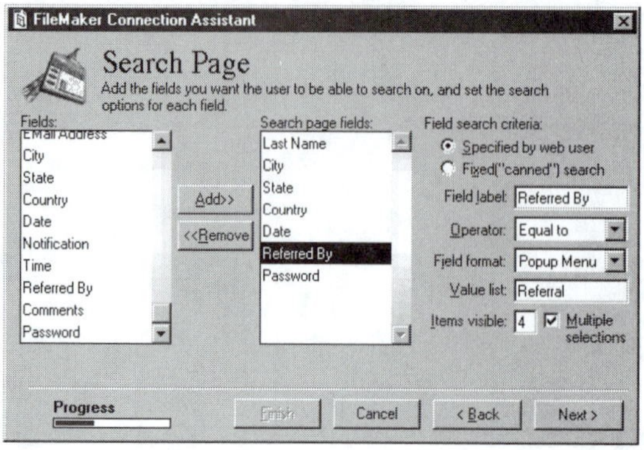

When you click the Next button, the Search Page Logical Operator window appears. Use it to select a logical operator option for multiple criteria searches.

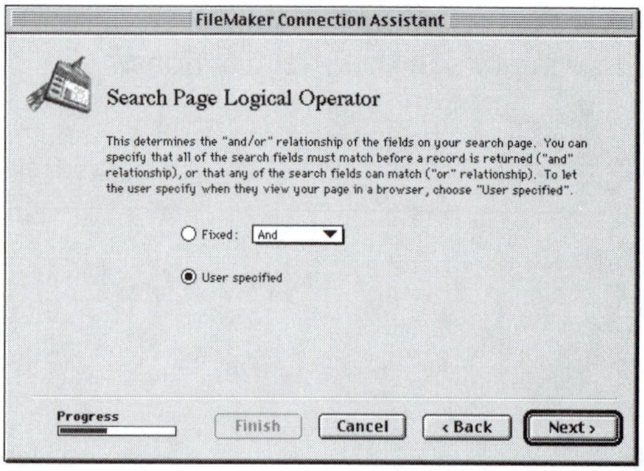

Click Next to go on. The Search Results window appears. It works like the Search Page window, but has fewer options. Use it to specify which fields should appear in a table of search results and how many records to display.

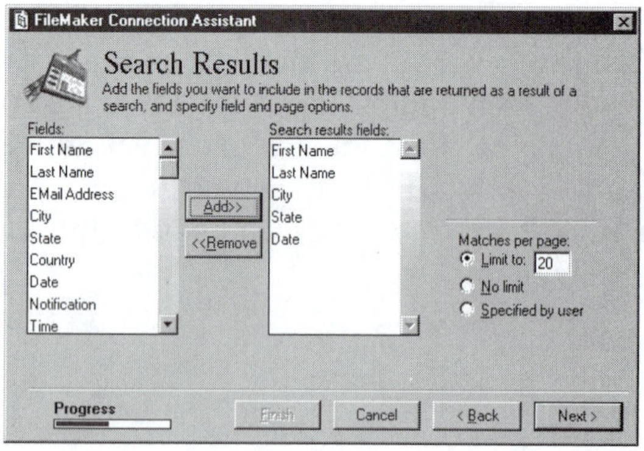

When you click the Next button again, the Sort Results window appears. Use it to select a sort option.

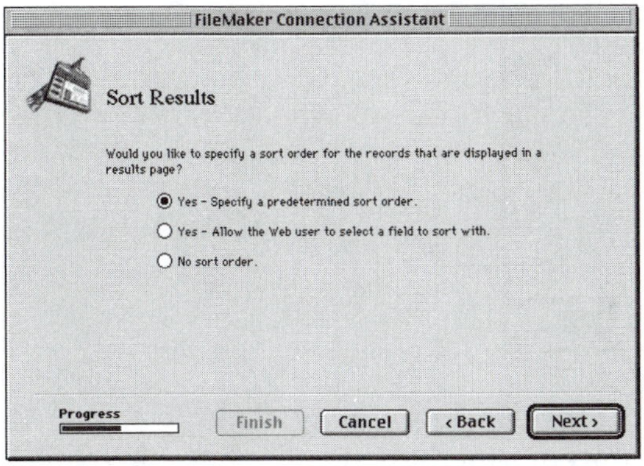

The option you select determines what window appears next:

- If you select the first option, the Predetermined sort order window appears. You can use it to set up a sort order to automatically apply to the data on the search results page.

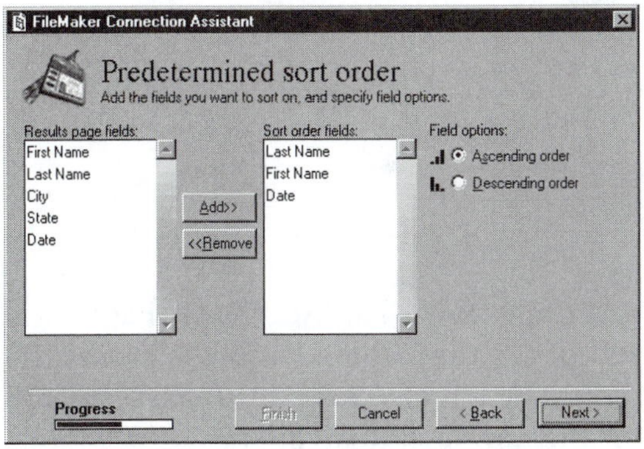

- If you select the second option, the Predetermined sort order window does not appear. Instead, the user is automatically given the option of sorting the results page contents by one of the fields that appears on the results page.
- If you select the third option, the contents of the results page appear in the same order in which they were entered into the database.

When you click the Next button, the Details Page window appears. Use it to select the fields and field options for the Details page—the page that appears when you click a link on the Search Results page.

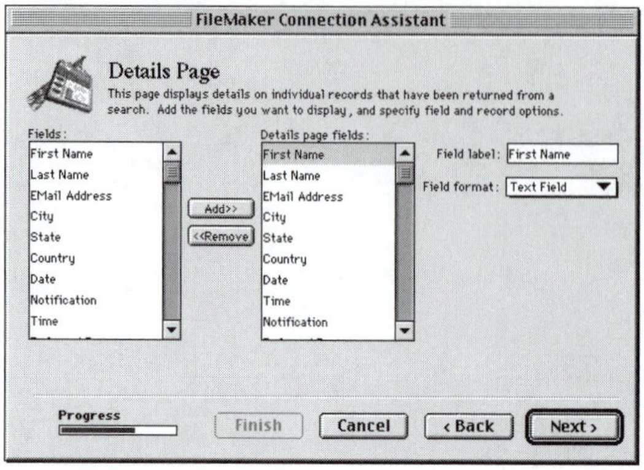

Clicking Next displays the New Record Page window, which you can use to select the fields and field options for entering new records into the database.

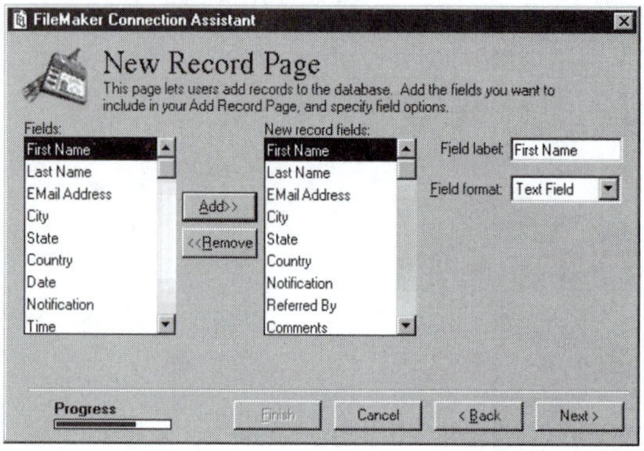

Click Next yet again. (You're almost done now.) The Additional Pages window appears. It tells you about the Web pages that Home Page will create to build the Custom Web Publishing solution "site." It also explains that the Site Editor window will automatically open for the new site. Read all this information, then click the Next button to go on.

The Style window appears next. Use it to select one of the predefined styles for the pages that Home Page creates. For some reason I don't quite understand, the style that you select is applied only to the format files, not to the default home page that is also created by Home Page. You can use the Customize button to modify colors while in the FileMaker Connection Assistant or wait until the pages have been created and customize them manually with Home Page.

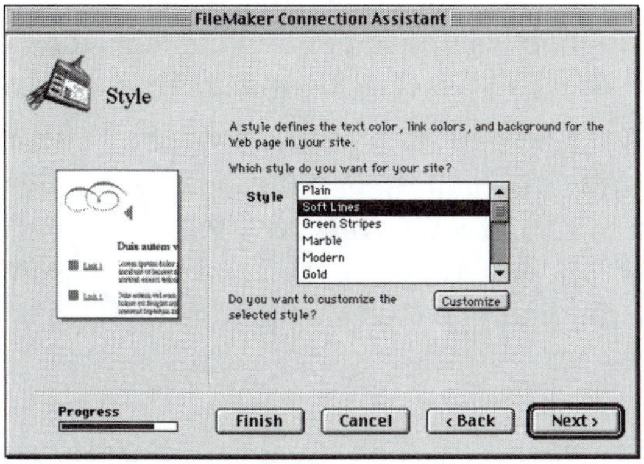

Click Next. The Final hints and suggestions window appears. (You're in the home stretch!) Read the information in the window—it explains what you need to do with the files that Home Page creates. When you're finished, click the Next button.

The Location window, which appears next, offers two buttons to select a location for the files: New Folder or Existing folder. Click the appropriate button, then use the dialog box that appears to either create or select a folder. After specifying a folder, the window displays the name of the folder and provides some additional instructions.

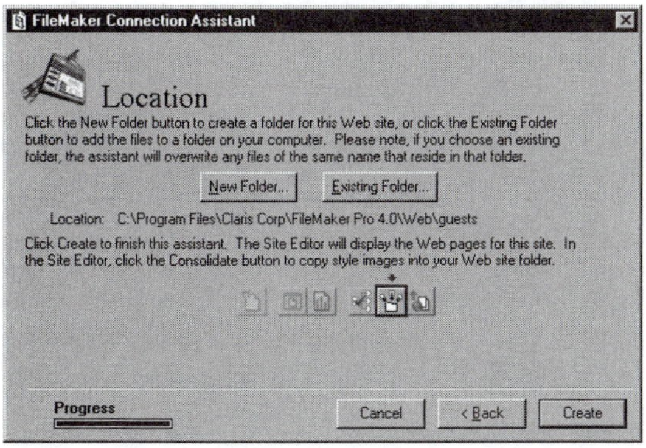

Click the Create button. Then wait while Home Page creates the format files you need for your Custom Web Publishing solution.

When it's done, the read_me.htm file appears in a Home Page document window. Read it. It includes important instructions for completing the site. When you're finished, you can click that window's close box or button.

The Site Editor window should also be open. Click the Consolidate button as instructed in the Location window. That copies all of the image files for the style that you selected in the Styles window into a folder within the site folder.

If desired, you can use Claris Home Page to modify the pages you created. When you're ready to test the solution, move the folder that contains the format files into the Web folder inside the FileMaker Pro folder. Then follow the instructions I provide near the end of this chapter for testing your solution.

As you've probably realized by now, the main benefit of using the FileMaker Connection Assistant is that you can build a Custom Web Publishing solution with little or no knowledge of HTML or CDML. To customize your solution, however, you need a good understanding of either Home Page or HTML.

FileMaker Pro Libraries

Claris Home Page's library feature enables you to create specially formatted files for storing Web page elements. Home Page version 3 comes with two library files designed specifically for use with FileMaker Pro:

- **FILEMAKER FORM LIBRARY** includes all of the CDML tags that you need to create format files that utilize HTML forms.
- **FILEMAKER REFERENCE LIBRARY** includes information about CDML tags—as well as the tags themselves—for building format files from scratch using Home Page.

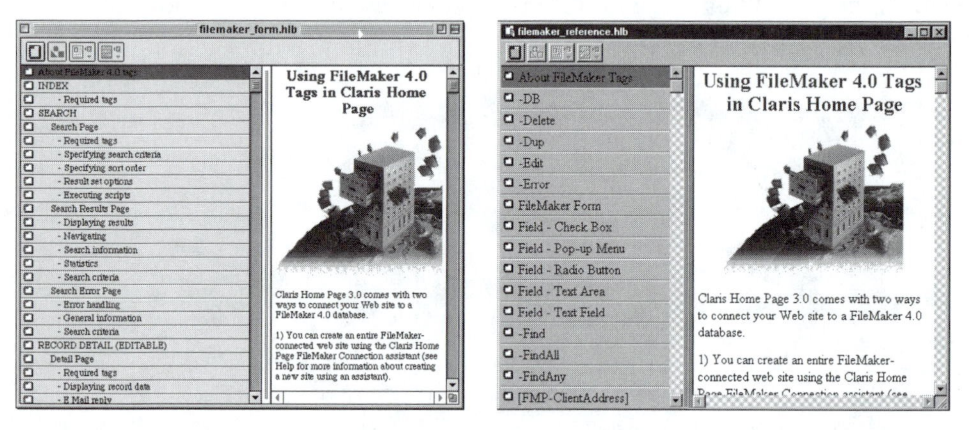

How you open a library depends on which version of Claris Home Page you have—Mac OS or Windows:

- To open a FileMaker Pro library on a Macintosh, choose the library name from the Window menu.
- To open a FileMaker Pro library on a Windows PC, choose the library name from the View menu.

Can someone please explain to me why the folks at the company formerly known as Claris couldn't make the interface for these two versions of the same program the same?

Once you've opened the library, you can drag format file components from the library window into a Home Page document window while in Edit Page mode. An icon for the CDML tag appears; you can double-click it to open the Home Page object editor and specify options.

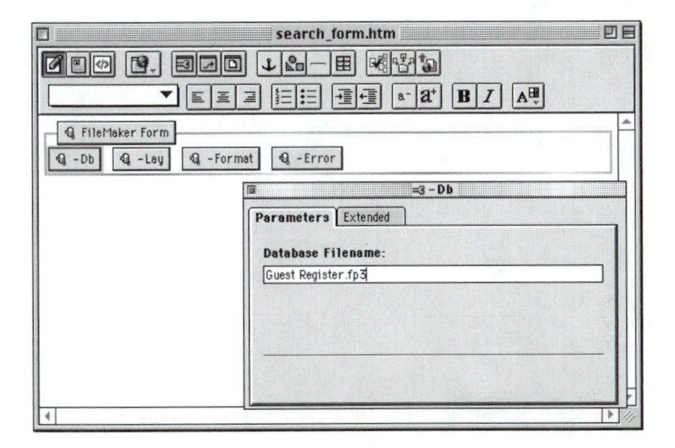

There are two main benefits to using FileMaker Pro Libraries to create format files in Home Page:

- Many of the library entries include all of the required CDML tags to perform an operation. This prevents you from omitting tags that you need.
- You can include whatever additional CDML tags you want—wherever you want them—to create a completely customized format file.

To use this feature, however, you still need a good understanding of Home Page and CDML.

Step-by-Step Setup

Ready to try building your own Custom Web Publishing solution? There's a lot of work involved, but I'm sure you'll agree that it's worth the effort when you see your database appear on the Web exactly the way you want it to.

In this section I outline the steps required to publish a database on the Web with Custom Web Publishing.

Enabling & Configuring the Web Companion Plug-In

Before your files can be published on the Web, you must enable and configure the Web Companion plug-in, which is part of FileMaker Pro. You do this with the Application Preferences and Web Companion Configuration dialog boxes.

TIP

You only need to follow these steps once, no matter how many databases you publish.

Enabling the Web Companion Plug-In

Start by choosing Application from the Preferences submenu under the Edit menu.

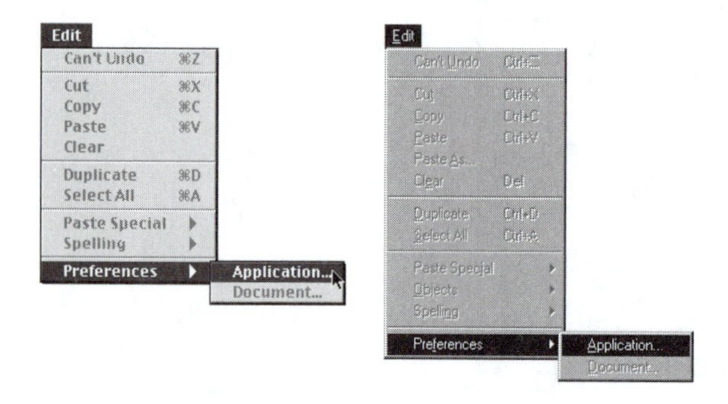

The Application Preferences dialog box appears. Choose Plug-Ins from the pop-up menu (Macintosh) or click the Plug-Ins tab (Windows). The dialog box changes to display a list of all plug-ins. The Web Companion plug-in should appear in the list—in fact, it may be the only item in the list. To enable it, simply turn on the check box beside it.

TIP

If the Web Companion plug-in does not appear in the Application Preferences dialog box, it was probably not installed with FileMaker Pro. Quit FileMaker Pro and use the FileMaker Pro installer to reinstall FileMaker Pro. When installing, choose the Easy (Macintosh) or Typical (Windows) Install option or, if you choose the Custom Install option, be sure to turn on the check box for Web Support. Restart your computer and try again. The Web Companion plug-in should be properly installed.

Disabling Instant Web Publishing

Although you can use Instant Web Publishing (which I discuss in Chapter 1) and Custom Web Publishing at the same time, you may prefer to use just Custom Web Publishing. If so, it's a good idea to turn off the Instant Web Publishing feature.

Select the Web Companion plug-in in the Application Preferences dialog box and click the Configure button. The Web Companion Configuration dialog box appears.

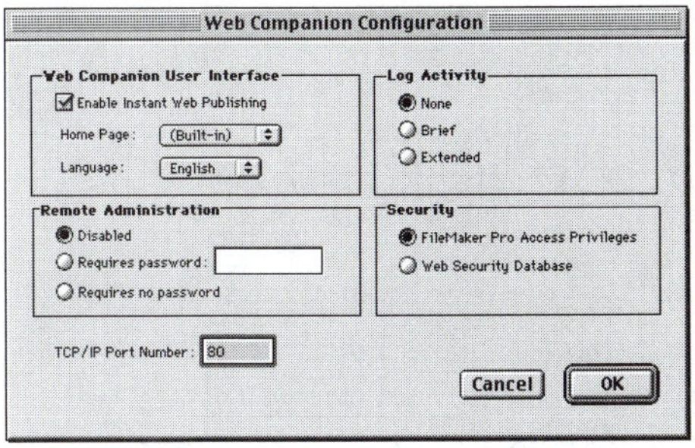

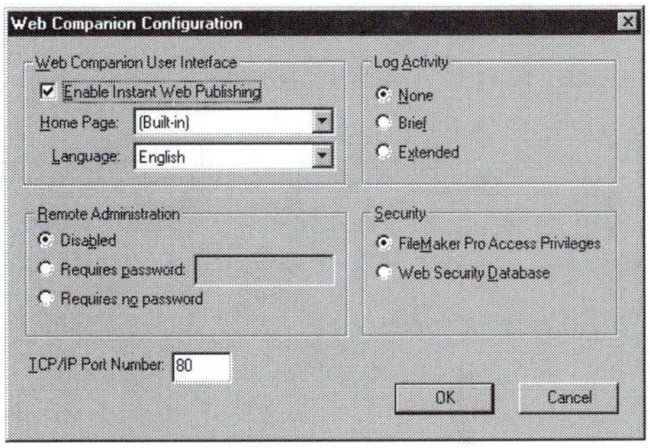

Turn off the Enable Instant Web Publishing check box. (It's turned on by default.)

Selecting the Custom Home Page

If you created your own custom Home page and saved it into the Web folder inside the FileMaker Pro 4.0 folder, you can configure Web Companion so it automatically displays your Home page to visitors. To do this, simply choose the name of the Home page that you created from the Home Page menu.

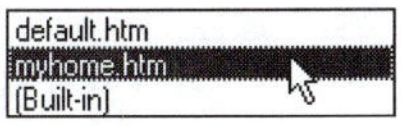

I tell you more about selecting a Home page in Chapter 3.

Setting Other Web Companion Configuration Options

The other options in the Web Companion Configuration dialog box apply to both Instant Web Publishing and Custom Web Publishing. I discuss them in Chapter 3, where I discuss a number of other options that apply to FileMaker Pro version 4's new Web publishing features.

Saving Your Settings

Once you've enabled and configured the Web Companion Plug-In, click OK to dismiss the Web Companion Configuration dialog box and click Done to dismiss the Application Preferences dialog box. Your settings are saved to the FileMaker and Web Companion preferences files.

Preparing a Database for Custom Web Publishing

Next, you need to prepare the database that you want to publish. This can be as easy as opening the database or it may require that you create new layouts with the fields that you want to appear in pages created by format files. It's also a good time to think about security and what privileges you want users to have.

Opening a Database

If you haven't already opened the database that you want to publish, choose Open from FileMaker's File menu. Use the dialog box that appears to locate and Open the database file.

WARNING

The database must be open for its contents to be published on the Web. If you close a database, it will no longer be available to users.

If a database will always be served from a computer, add an alias or shortcut for the database to the Startup Items Folder (Macintosh) or Startup Folder (Windows). This will automatically open the database every time you start the computer.

Creating Layouts

Generally speaking, it isn't usually necessary to create special layouts in your database file before publishing the file on the Web using Custom Web Publishing. There are, however, two instances in which you should consider doing so: when you're interested in improving performance and when you need to show related fields. Let me explain.

The **-Layout** variable CDML tag in a format file instructs the Web Companion to look for fields in a specific layout within the FileMaker Pro database file. In most instances, this tag is not required; if omitted, Web Companion looks for fields in Layout 0, an invisible layout that includes all database fields.

You can speed up the performance of Web Companion by including a **-Layout** tag for a layout that includes only the fields needed to display the format file. The performance boost is especially noticeable when displaying only a few fields from a database that has many fields.

Of course, you must use the **-Layout** tag to specify a layout that contains related fields if you want those fields to appear on a page generated by a format file. That's the only way to get those fields to appear in Custom Web Publishing.

Look at your database file and decide which combinations of fields you want to display on your Web pages. If necessary, create the layouts you need, keeping the above information in mind.

TIP

If you've been using the database for a while, it may already have all the layouts you need to publish it on the Web using Custom Web Publishing. In that case, you don't have to do a thing.

Setting Security Options

FileMaker Pro's built-in Web publishing features offer two ways to maintain security over your database:

- **FileMaker Pro Access Privileges**, when set, can also control access when the database is published on the Web.
- **The Web Security Database** is a separate database file that offers additional security for databases that are published on the Web.

I tell you more about both of these options in Chapter 3. If you decide to secure your database, be sure to set up security *before* making your database available to the public.

Creating & Saving Format Files

Up to this point, all setup tasks have been relatively simple and straightforward. Now comes the hard part—creating the format files that will make up your Custom Web Publishing solution.

Planning your Strategy

Before you begin churning out format files, take a moment to think about the kinds of format files that you'll need to build your Web publishing solution. Here are some tips:

- Since each format file performs a specific task, it's a good idea to use a task-oriented approach when planning your strategy. Refer to my discussion of format file types earlier in this chapter for ideas.
- Create a graphic representation or flow chart of the way format files will interact with each other (and the database). This will help you organize and link the files.
- Don't forget to create a database Home page that explains what the database is all about. This page might also offer links to other pages on your Web site (if applicable) in case visitors change their mind and decide they don't want to access the database after all.

TIP

For ideas on how your solution can work, be sure to check the examples in the last five chapters in this book, all of which can be downloaded from the book's companion Web site (http://www.gilesrd.com/fmproweb/.)

Creating a Project Folder

Although not required, it's a good idea to save all the files related to a specific Web publishing solution into the same folder. This project folder keeps your format files, standard HTML files, images, and database files together. It also keeps you Web folder neat!

The project folder can be anywhere on the FileMaker Pro Web server—the computer on which FileMaker Pro and the open database(s) are running. Unless security is a major concern, you may want to keep the project folder in the Web folder within the FileMaker Pro folder. I tell you more about security concerns in Chapter 3.

TIP

Use relative references in all the links for the format and standard HTML files you create. This makes the project folder portable—you can move it to any FileMaker Pro database server to relocate it or share it with a friend or work associate.

Creating the Format Files

This is where you put your HTML and CDML coding skills to the test. You must create each of the format files that make up your Custom Web Publishing solution.

For most people, this will be the most difficult part of Custom Web Publishing setup. But don't think of it as difficult. Think of it as a challenge and an opportunity to show off your creativity and problem-solving skills.

Here are some tips for creating format files:

- Use one or more of the tools I discuss earlier in this chapter to make the task easier.
- Whenever possible, base a new format file on an existing format file that does the same (or almost the same) thing.
- Start with the basics—format files that do the minimum that they need to. Once you get them working properly, add features to your heart's desire.

NOTE

I don't tell you exactly what to put in your format files in this chapter. Why? Because the contents of a format file vary depending on the needs of your specific Web publishing solution. Instead, I provide instructions on creating five Custom Web Publishing solutions in the last five chapters of this book. Refer to those examples and their completed files for help in creating your format files.

As you create your format files, be sure to save them into the project folder. If you use a Web authoring tool like Claris Home Page, Adobe PageMill, or

Microsoft FrontPage to create these files, relative links will be properly created and preserved.

Enabling Web Companion Sharing

The final step to publishing a database with Custom Web Publishing is enabling Web Companion Sharing. This is done individually for each FileMaker Pro database file that you want to publish on the Web.

Start by choosing Sharing from the File menu.

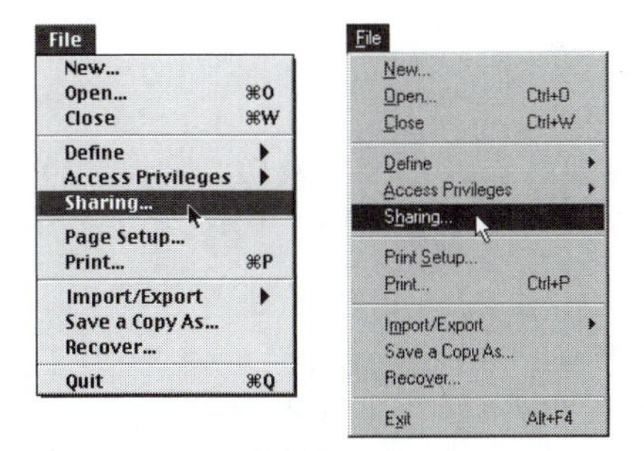

The File Sharing dialog box appears. In the Companion Sharing section of the dialog box, turn on the Web Companion check box.

Click OK. Your settings are saved with the file.

Accessing & Testing Your Custom Web Publishing Solution

If you've completed all the steps in the previous section of this chapter, your database is now online. In this section, I tell you how to access your Custom Web Publishing solution so you can test the appearance and functionality of its format files.

Opening the Database Home Page

Launch your Web browser and use it to enter the IP address of the database Web server—the computer on which FileMaker Pro and the open database(s) are running. When you enter the URL, enter it in the format http://*xx.xx.xx.xx*/ where *xx.xx.xx.xx* is the IP address.

If you specified a port number other than 80 in the Web Companion Configuration dialog box, a colon and that port number must be appended to the IP address in the URL. In that case, the URL will look something like this: http://xx.xx.xx.xx:591/, where xx.xx.xx.xx is the IP address of the database Web server. I tell you more about assigning port numbers in Chapter 3.

The database Home page you selected in the Web Companion Configuration dialog box appears.

If you used the FileMaker Connection Assistant feature of Claris Home Page, you'll have to point your Web browser to the folder that contains the default.htm file created by Home Page. That'll be inside the folder in which the solution's format files reside. For example, if the format files are in the guest folder within the Web folder on a computer with IP address 192.0.1.2, you'd open the following URL: http://192.0.1.2/guest/default.htm.

Testing Your Solution

This is the fun part. You get to try out all the links, buttons, and features that you included in the format files that make up your Custom Web Publishing solution. The goal is to make sure everything works the way it should.

Here's a checklist of the kinds of things you should look for:

- Do the pages appear the way they should? Look at text formatting and inserted images to make sure your HTML is correct.
- Are you able to successfully perform searches with the search format file(s) you created? Don't try just one search. Try a bunch. Then try a few with

intentional errors (like the accidental errors visitors will make) to see what happens.

- Do search results appear correctly? Check the formatting of listed items. Also check to be sure that the items that should appear do appear.
- Do links from results pages to detail pages work properly? Make sure the correct record appears.
- Are you able to successfully add records with a new format file? Check to make sure that you are warned when any fields that require entry are left blank.
- Are you able to successfully edit records with an edit format file? Make errors on purpose to see what happens.
- Are you able to successfully delete records with a delete format file? Is the correct record deleted?
- Do reply files appear when they should and look the way you intended?

Add items to this list to meet your specific needs. Then check to make sure everything is just the way it should be.

Troubleshooting Problems

The next part—fixing the problems you found—isn't fun. But if you did a good job creating format files and setting up Custom Web Publishing options, you shouldn't have too much troubleshooting to do.

Take each problem you find, one at a time, and think about what could have caused it. Whenever possible, try to narrow down the problem to a possible cause. I like to think that all causes fit into one of three categories:

- **HTML Coding Errors** normally result in formatting problems. Check the HTML code within the format file that created the problem page.
- **CDML Coding Errors** normally result in database communication problems or error messages. Check the CDML code within the format file that created the problem page.
- **Web Companion Setup Errors** normally result in error messages. Check the Web Companion and File Sharing setup.

Once you think you've got the problem fixed, access the database as instructed above and check the problem page or function again. If the problem is gone, move on to the next problem.

TIP

If a format file doesn't work properly but you have a similar format file that does work properly, compare the code in the two files to see what the differences are. One of those differences could be causing your problem. That's why it's a good idea to collect sample format files, like the ones that come with FileMaker Pro version 4 are available on the companion Web site for this book, http://www.gilesrd.com/fmproweb/.

CHAPTER 3

Web Companion Configuration & Security

In Chapters 1 and 2, I told you how to use FileMaker Pro version 4's two primary Web publishing features: Instant Web Publishing and Custom Web Publishing. In this Chapter, I expand on my discussion of those two topics by covering Web Companion Configuration and Security options that work with both of them.

Web Companion Configuration Options

The Web Companion Configuration dialog box, which I discuss briefly in Chapters 1 and 2, offers a number of options to control the way a database is published with Instant and Custom Web Publishing. Rather than discuss these options twice (once in each of those chapters), I tell you about them here.

To open the Web Companion Configuration dialog box, choose Web Companion from the Preferences submenu under the Edit menu.

TIP

The Web Companion option only appears on the Preferences submenu if Web Companion has been enabled. I tell you how to enable Web Companion in Chapters 1 and 2.

In the Web Companion View Setup dialog box that appears, click the Configure button. The Web Companion Configuration dialog box appears.

Web Companion User Interface Options

Web Companion User Interface options let you set the way users see and work with your Web pages.

Enabling or Disabling Instant Web Publishing

To enable or disable Instant Web Publishing, toggle the Enable Instant Web Publishing check box on or off. This check box is turned on by default.

Choosing a Home Page

You can use the Home Page menu to select the Home Page that will appear when a user points his Web browser to the IP address of the FileMaker Pro database Web server. By default, this menu offers two options:

- **(Built-in)** is the default choice. It creates a Home page on the fly from information stored within the Web Companion plug-in. This is the preferred choice for Instant Web Publishing since it automatically lists all open database files.

- **DEFAULT.HTM** is a sample Web page that ships with FileMaker Pro. You can find it in the Web folder inside the FileMaker Pro 4.0 folder. It includes links to sample Custom Web Publishing solutions.

If you're taking advantage of Custom Web Publishing, you'll probably want to create your own custom Web page for your published databases. To do so, create an HTML document using a Web page authoring tool like Claris Home Page, Adobe PageMill, or Microsoft Front Page. Be sure to include links to the appropriate format files that you created to publish your database. Save the file into the Web folder in the FileMaker Pro 4.0 folder. This adds the name of the file to the Home Page menu in the Web Companion Configuration dialog box so you can choose it.

Choosing a Language

You can use the Language menu to select the language in which you want pages published. Your selection affects the tabs, buttons, instructions, and even Help contents that appear on Web pages published with Instant Web Publishing.

Remote Administration

The remote administration feature lets you control database publishing from a computer other than the one on which FileMaker Pro and the databases reside. With this feature enabled, you can perform the following:

- Use HTTP **PUT** and **GET** commands to upload and download FileMaker Pro files to and from the Web folder inside the FileMaker Pro 4.0 folder. To learn more about these commands, check the documentation that came with your Web browser.
- Change the contents of FileMaker Pro files published on the Web.
- Change the contents of the Web Security database. I tell you more about the Web Security database later in this chapter.

To set the remote administration feature, select one of the three Remote Administration radio buttons:

- **Disabled** disables remote administration. This is the default setting.
- **Requires password** enables remote administration, but only if the proper password is provided. If you select this option, be sure to enter a password in the box beside it. To prevent your Web browser from confusing password characters with special HTML characters, your password should consist of letters, numbers, or a combination of the two; don't get fancy with spaces or other characters.
- **Requires no password** enables remote administration, but does not require a password. This means that *anyone* can remotely administer your published databases. I don't know about you, but I'd *never* leave my system wide open by selecting this option.

Log Activity

If desired, you can set up the Web Companion so that it automatically logs activity with database files. To set up this feature, select one of the three Log Activity radio buttons:

- **None** disables the activity log. This is the default setting.
- **Brief** creates a brief log of activity. It lacks most detail.
- **Extended** creates a much longer log of activity.

The text file created by Brief and Extended is called Web.log. On a Macintosh, you can find it in the Control Panels folder inside the System folder. On a Windows PC, you can find it in the FileMaker Pro 4.0 folder. You can open it with any text editor or word processor. Perhaps you'll find its contents more interesting than I did.

```
Web.log
9/29/97 11:25:14 AM 192.0.1.2 /
9/29/97 11:25:20 AM 192.0.1.2 /FMRes/FMPro
9/29/97 11:25:33 AM 192.0.1.2 /FMRes/enterBtnU.gif
9/29/97 11:25:36 AM 192.0.1.2 /FMRes/enterBtnD.gif
9/29/97 11:25:40 AM 192.0.1.2 /FMRes/FMPro
9/29/97 11:25:52 AM 192.0.1.2 /FMRes/FMPro
9/29/97 11:26:09 AM 192.0.1.2 /FMRes/FMPro
9/29/97 11:26:15 AM 192.0.1.2 /FMRes/bookTop.gif
9/29/97 11:26:19 AM 192.0.1.2 /FMRes/bookTopP.gif
9/29/97 11:26:20 AM 192.0.1.2 /FMRes/bookBtm.gif
9/29/97 11:26:22 AM 192.0.1.2 /FMRes/bookBtmP.gif
```

```
Web.log
9/29/97 11:29:08 AM 192.0.1.2 /
9/29/97 11:29:08 AM /
9/29/97 11:29:08 AM Got search argument.
9/29/97 11:29:08 AM ?
9/29/97 11:29:08 AM Sending reply.    Elapsed time: 16 millisec.
9/29/97 11:29:14 AM 192.0.1.2 /FMRes/HomeHelp.gif
9/29/97 11:29:14 AM /FMRes/HomeHelp.gif
9/29/97 11:29:14 AM Sending reply.    Elapsed time: 4 millisec.
9/29/97 11:29:14 AM 192.0.1.2 /FMRes/HomeHdr.gif
9/29/97 11:29:14 AM /FMRes/HomeHdr.gif
9/29/97 11:29:14 AM Sending reply.    Elapsed time: 4 millisec.
9/29/97 11:29:14 AM 192.0.1.2 /FMRes/ClrsLogo.gif
9/29/97 11:29:14 AM /FMRes/ClrsLogo.gif
9/29/97 11:29:14 AM Sending reply.    Elapsed time: 3 millisec.
9/29/97 11:29:14 AM 192.0.1.2 /FMRes/HomeBgrd.gif
9/29/97 11:29:14 AM /FMRes/HomeBgrd.gif
9/29/97 11:29:14 AM Sending reply.    Elapsed time: 3 millisec.
9/29/97 11:29:15 AM 192.0.1.2 /FMRes/HmTopBtn.gif
9/29/97 11:29:15 AM /FMRes/HmTopBtn.gif
9/29/97 11:29:15 AM Sending reply.    Elapsed time: 4 millisec.
9/29/97 11:29:16 AM 192.0.1.2 /FMRes/WebCmpn.gif
9/29/97 11:29:16 AM /FMRes/WebCmpn.gif
9/29/97 11:29:16 AM Sending reply.    Elapsed time: 4 millisec.
9/29/97 11:29:16 AM 192.0.1.2 /FMRes/HomeFter.gif
9/29/97 11:29:16 AM /FMRes/HomeFter.gif
9/29/97 11:29:16 AM Sending reply.    Elapsed time: 4 millisec.
9/29/97 11:29:16 AM 192.0.1.2 /FMRes/HomeSpcr.gif
9/29/97 11:29:16 AM /FMRes/HomeSpcr.gif
9/29/97 11:29:16 AM Sending reply.    Elapsed time: 4 millisec.
9/29/97 11:29:17 AM 192.0.1.2 /FMRes/HmHrSpcr.gif
9/29/97 11:29:17 AM /FMRes/HmHrSpcr.gif
9/29/97 11:29:17 AM Sending reply.    Elapsed time: 4 millisec.
9/29/97 11:29:24 AM 192.0.1.2 /FMRes/FMPro
9/29/97 11:29:24 AM Got search argument.
9/29/97 11:29:24 AM
-DB=Book%20Catalog.fp3&-Lay=Fields%20for%20Table%20View&-T
oken=25&-Format=TableVw.htm&-Error=Err.htm&-SortField=Series
&-SortOrder=Custom%3dSeries%20List&-SortField=Sort%20Number
&-SortOrder=Descend&-SortField=Title&-SortOrder=Descend&-SortF
ield=Publisher%20Short%20Name&-SortOrder=Descend&-Findall
9/29/97 11:29:24 AM Sending reply.    Elapsed time: 72 millisec.
```

TIP

In creating the above illustrations, I performed the same few activities twice. I noticed that the system response was much slower when Extended was selected—probably because Web Companion was busy writing text to the Web.log file while I was trying to get it to show me a database. You may want to perform your own tests before leaving this option turned on.

Security

Web Companion offers two ways to secure the database files you publish on the Web. Pick the one you want to use by selecting one of the two Security radio buttons:

- **FileMaker Pro Access Privileges** relies on the passwords and groups set up for the database file to determine what fields users can see or change and what modification tasks they can perform.
- **Web Security Database** gets security and access information from a special FileMaker Pro file that you maintain for the databases you publish.

I tell you about both of these options in detail a little later in this chapter.

TCP/IP Port Number

TCP/IP Port Number is the last option in the Web Companion Configuration dialog box. This option, which is set to 80 by default, does not need to be changed unless port 80 is in use by another application—such as Web server software that is running on the same computer. If you do need to change this number, change it to 591, which has been registered with the Internet Assigned Numbers Authority for use with FileMaker Pro. This will prevent any conflicts with other applications.

If you change the TCP/IP port number, users must append a colon and the port number to the IP address of the server in order to access FileMaker Pro database files. For example, if the database Web server's IP address is 192.0.1.2 and the TCP/IP port number is 591, users must point to http://192.0.1.2:591/. Otherwise the Web browser will access the application using port 80 rather than FileMaker Pro.

Security

Security is a major issue with any files available over a network. When the network is as big as the world—as it is with the Internet—security becomes even more important.

Throughout this part of the chapter, I work with the file named Associates.fp3, which is a database of employee information. If you'd like to work with the same database file, look for it at http://www.gilesrd.com/fmproweb/.

Overview

As I discuss briefly earlier in this chapter, the Web Companion offers two security methods: FileMaker Pro access privileges and the Web Security database. Each method has its own pros and cons.

FileMaker Pro Web Companion does not have SSL server capabilities. This means it is not able to handle secure transactions. If you're interested in using a FileMaker Pro database as part of a solution for doing commerce on the Web, consider using a secure Web server like WebSTAR SSL with one of the third-party CGIs or plug-ins that I discuss in Part II of this book.

If you're already familiar with access privileges and your database files already use them for protection, you may prefer using this method to protect the files when they are published on the Web. But if you want to set more complex security options for Web-published databases, you should consider using the Web Security database.

To choose the security method that you want to use, select its radio button in the Web Companion Configuration dialog box. I tell you how earlier in this chapter.

Just selecting a security method in the Web Companion Configuration dialog box isn't enough to secure your database. You still have to set up the security options for each individual database file that you publish.

Securing a Database with Access Privileges

FileMaker Pro's access privileges give you two kinds of control over database files:

- Using passwords, you can control the browsing and editing tasks that a user can perform with the file. For Web publishing, the tasks you would most likely want to control are the ability to add, delete, or modify records. You can also prevent a user who doesn't have a password from opening the file at all.
- Using groups, you can control the fields that a user can see when he opens the file.

Together, these two kinds of controls are normally enough for most Web publishing needs.

To set access privileges, you use commands under the Access Privileges submenu under the File menu. These commands open the Define Groups, Define Passwords, and Access Privileges dialog boxes.

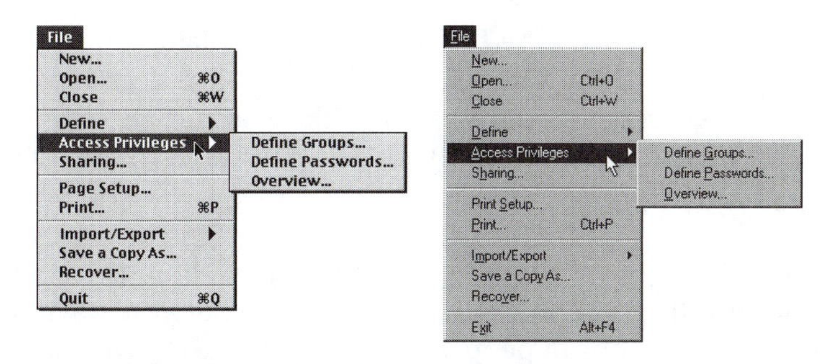

To change a file's existing access privileges, you must open the file with a password that has full access to the file. You'll know right away if you can't change privileges because the Access Privileges submenu will not appear on the File menu.

Although teaching you how to set up access privileges is beyond the scope of this book—it falls into the general FileMaker Pro knowledge prerequisite I discuss in the Introduction—the following sections provide a brief outline of the steps you need to follow.

Creating Groups

Choose Define Groups from the Access Privileges submenu under the File menu to display the Define Groups dialog box. In the Group Name box, enter a name for a group that you want to have full access to the file's fields and click the Create button. The name appears in the list. Now enter a name for a group that you want to have limited access to the file's fields and click the Create button. That name appears, too. If you want to set up different combinations of fields for different groups to access, follow these steps to create a group for each combination. When you're finished, the Define Groups dialog box might look something like this:

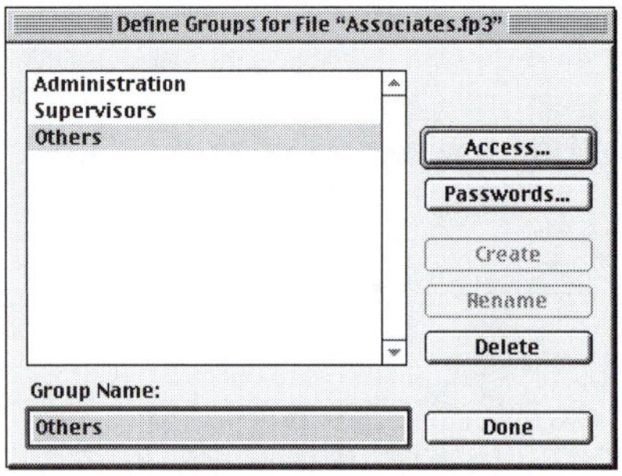

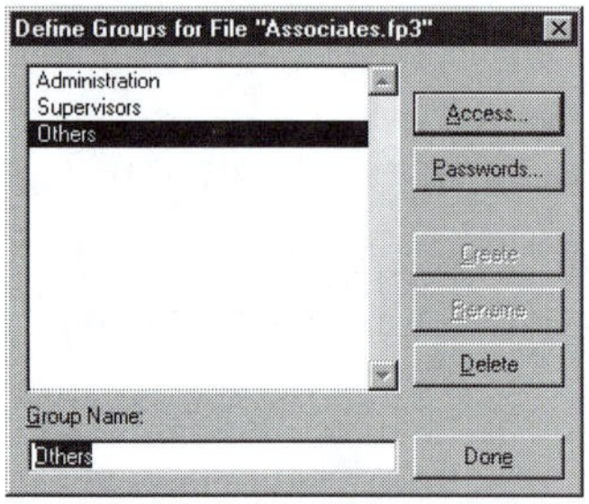

Creating Passwords

Click the Passwords button to display the Define Passwords dialog box. In the Password box, enter a password for the person who will have access to the entire file. Make sure the Access the entire file check box is turned on in the Privileges area. Then click the Create button to add the password to the list.

The next part can be done two ways:

- Create a password with appropriate Privileges check box settings for each person who will access the file. The trouble with that is that you may have hundreds, thousands, or millions of people accessing the file once it's on the Internet. I doubt whether you want to create a password for every single person.

Stinky Interface!

It's time for me to climb onto a soapbox.

I absolutely hate the interface that the folks at the company formerly known as Claris dreamed up for setting access privileges in FileMaker Pro. It's mind boggling and, on the surface, completely unintuitive. What were they thinking? Were they trying to confuse us? If so, they succeeded. Setting access privileges is, by far, the most difficult process for new users to grasp. And just try teaching it to someone!

- Create passwords for every combination of privileges you plan to grant to users. This makes much more sense when you expect the database to be accessed by many users.

Whichever method you choose, you create each password by entering the password in the Password box, setting the Privileges check boxes, and clicking Create. Here's the Define Passwords dialog box for my sample database:

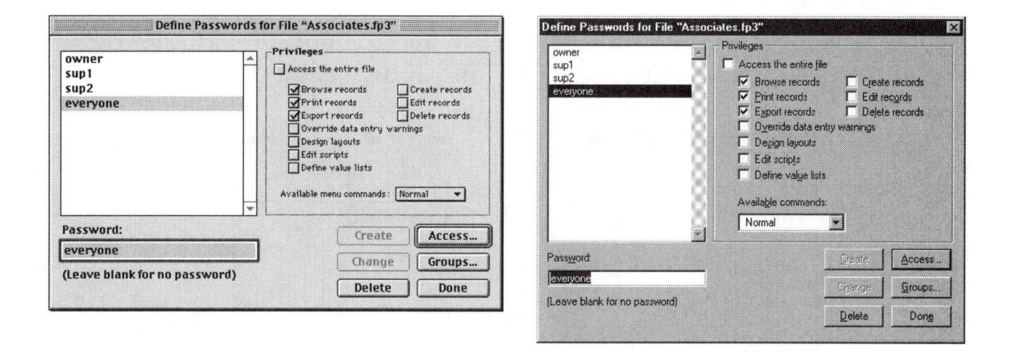

When creating passwords, don't leave the Password box empty to create a "no password" password. Doing so will prevent a password dialog box from appearing when users access the database from the Web. Although this won't create a security breech, it will prevent users with additional privileges from using those privileges.

To prevent a user with LAN access to a database from publishing the database on the Web, turn off Export privileges for his password. With Export privileges disabled, Web Companion cannot be be enabled in the Sharing dialog box. I tell you about enabling Web Companion and the Sharing dialog box in Chapters 1 and 2.

Assigning Passwords and Field Access to Groups

Click the Access button to display the Access Privileges dialog box. You use this dialog box to assign passwords and field access to groups.

Start by selecting the name of the group in the Groups column that will have full access to the database. Then make sure the bullet to the left of the full access password in the Passwords column is black—if it isn't, click it until it turns black. If more than one password applies to the group, click the bullet to the left of each applicable password so that it turns black. This assigns the password(s) to the group.

With the full access group still selected, make sure the bullets to the left of all the entries in the Layouts and Fields columns are black; if they're not, click them until they turn black. This makes all the layouts and fields accessible to the full access group.

Still with me? I hope so.

Click the name of the next group in the Groups list. (At this point, a dialog box may ask whether you want to save changes to access privileges; if so, click the Yes button.) Then click to turn the bullets beside the corresponding password(s) in the Passwords column black. (You will not be able to turn the full access password's bullet gray, so don't bother trying.) In the Fields column, click bullets to change the access privileges for the selected group.

Repeat this process for each group in the Groups list. Here's the Access Privileges dialog box with settings for one of my groups:

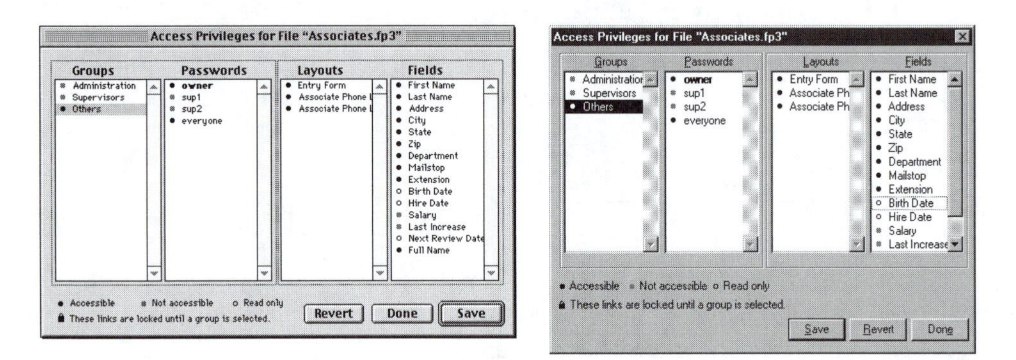

Changes to the access privilege settings in the Layouts column of the Access Privileges dialog box do not affect security over databases that are accessed over the Web. Why? Because FileMaker Pro's Web publishing features do not use FileMaker Pro layouts—just fields.

Saving Access Privilege Settings

You're almost done. All you need to do is save changes. Click the Save button and then the Done button in the Access Privileges dialog box. Then click the Done button in the Define Passwords dialog box. If you're asked to confirm that you know a password that lets you access the entire file, enter the full access password in the Confirm dialog box and click OK.

Securing a Database with the Web Security Database

The Web Security database lets you control whether individual users can perform the following operations on databases you publish on the Web:

- Browse specific records
- Access specific fields
- Search the database
- Modify records
- Add records
- Delete records
- Run scripts

What makes the Web Security database so powerful is its ability to limit access to specific records. This is something you can't do with access privileges. In addition, if your Custom Web Publishing files take advantage of scripts in a FileMaker Pro database, you must use the Web Security database to limit access to scripts.

NOTE *If you're a Lasso user, the Web Security database should be familiar to you. As I discuss in Chapter 2, FileMaker, Inc. purchased the Lasso technology so it could incorporate Custom Web Publishing features into FileMaker Pro version 4. Although not identical to the Lasso Security database, the Web Security database is very similar. I tell you about Lasso in Chapter 5.*

Opening the Web Security Database

The Web Security database is a FileMaker Pro file. You set privileges by making or changing entries in the database file.

To set up the Web Security database, begin by opening the file named Web Security.fp3. You'll find it in the Databases folder inside the Web Security folder in the FileMaker Pro 4.0 folder. It looks like this:

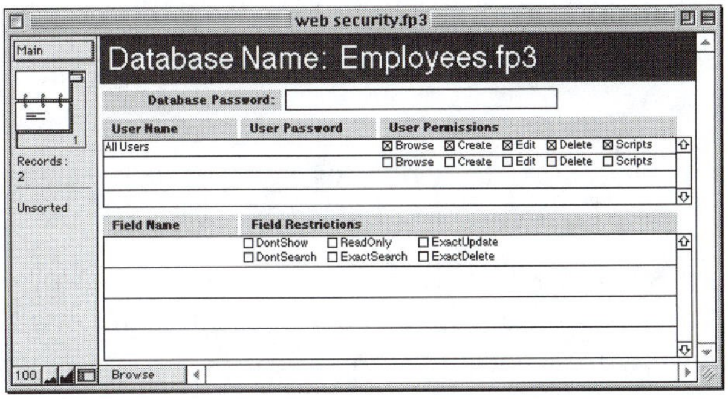

NOTE *Web_Fields_.fp3 and Web_Users_.fp3 are two other files in the Databases folder that are related to Web Security.fp3. It is not necessary to open these files; FileMaker Pro automatically opens and hides them when you open the Web Security database. Do not rename, delete, separate, or alter the structure of any of the files in the Databases folder.*

If Web Security Database is selected in the Web Companion Configuration dialog box, the Web Security database must be open when a user attempts to access a Web-published database. If it's not open, security is automatically disabled, preventing any user from accessing any file. FileMaker Pro will display an error message explaining the problem and offering two solutions: protect the database with access privileges or open the Web Security database. Until the problem is resolved, any user who attempts to access the database sees an error message with instructions in his browser window.

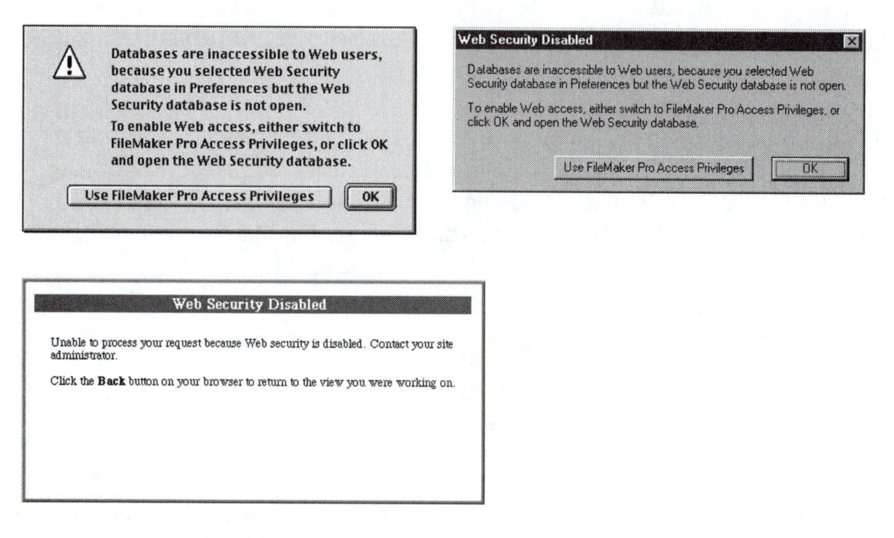

Reviewing Default Options

By default, the Web Security database is preconfigured with two records:

- **EMPLOYEES.FP3** is one of the sample Custom Web Publishing databases that comes with FileMaker Pro.
- **ALL DATABASES** is a special record that defines security settings for all databases that are not recorded by name in the Web Security database.

Both of these records are set so that all users have all user permissions and there are no field restrictions. They can be changed using the instructions I provide for defining names, passwords, permissions, field-level security, and record-level security below.

The user settings in the All Databases record override any settings for specific databases. By default, the All Databases record gives everyone full access to databases—this means the database will be completely unprotected! I highly recommend that you remove the All Users entry from the All Databases record—or delete the All Databases record entirely.

Creating a Database Record

Each database that you want to secure must have its own record in the Web Security database. To create a record for a database, choose New Record from the Mode menu or press Command-N (Macintosh) or Control-N (Windows).

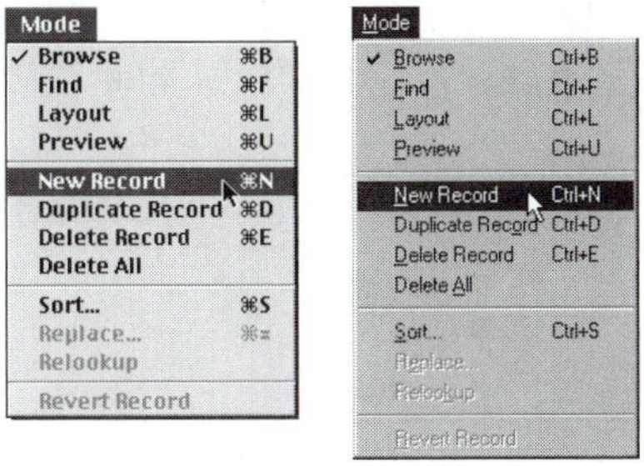

In the empty record that appears, enter the exact name of the database in the Database Name field at the top of the window.

If the database is protected with access privileges, enter the access privileges password in the Database Password field. The Web security database cannot grant more access to users than the access privileges granted by this password.

Defining Names, Passwords, and Permissions

The next step is to enter user names and their corresponding passwords and permissions.

Start by entering a user's name in the first User Name portal field. Then enter that user's password in the User Password field beside it. To prevent a Web browser from confusing password characters with special HTML characters, the password should consist of letters, numbers, or a combination of the two; don't use spaces or other characters.

Next, turn on check boxes to specify user security options. There are five check boxes that can be turned on in any combination:

- BROWSE allows the user to browse, search for, and display all records.
- CREATE allows the user to add new records to the database.
- EDIT allows the user to modify existing records, thus updating the database.
- DELETE allows the user to delete existing records.
- SCRIPTS allows the user to run scripts. This affects scripts that are run automatically as part of a format file or scripts that are run when the user clicks a button or link.

All of these permissions are subject to the field-level or record-level restrictions set on the lower half of the form.

Repeat this process for each user for which you want to enter permissions. Each time you enter a new user name in the User Name portal field, a new related record appears in the portal. To enter permissions for all users who do not have a password, enter All Users in the User Name field, leave the User Password field blank, and select the User Permissions that you want. When you're finished, the User area of the form might look something like this:

User Name	User Password	User Permissions
Maria Langer	owner	☒ Browse ☒ Create ☒ Edit ☒ Delete ☒ Scripts
John Aabbott	ocotillo	☒ Browse ☐ Create ☒ Edit ☐ Delete ☒ Scripts
All Users		☒ Browse ☐ Create ☐ Edit ☐ Delete ☒ Scripts
		☐ Browse ☐ Create ☐ Edit ☐ Delete ☐ Scripts

NOTE

In case you're wondering, the information you enter into the User Name, User Password, and User Permissions fields is stored in the Web_Users_.fp3 file. It is not necessary, however, for you to manually open or edit this file.

Defining Field-Level and Record-Level Security

In the Field area of the form, you define restrictions that limit the uses of specific fields. Start by entering the exact name of the field that you want to restrict in the first Field Name portal field.

Next, use the check boxes to specify the restrictions for that field. The first three check boxes provide field-level security:

- DONTSHOW prevents the field's contents from appearing.
- DONTSEARCH prevents a field from being used to search.
- READONLY prevents a field's contents from being changed.

The next three check boxes provide record-level security:

- EXACTSEARCH prevents records from being retrieved unless the user enters the exact value of this field. This means the user cannot use any operators other than equals (=) in the field.
- EXACTUPDATE prevents a record from being modified unless the user enters the exact value of this field.
- EXACTDELETE prevents a record from being deleted unless the user enters the exact value of this field.

NOTE

I think record-level security restrictions are fiendishly clever. They work by forcing the user to provide exactly matching information to search and view, modify, or delete a record. By including a field with a secret number or word and requiring a user to enter a record's word to work with the record, you protect the record.

Repeat this process for each field for which you want to set restrictions. When you're finished, the Field area of the form might look something like this:

Field Name	Field Restrictions		
Salary	☒ DontShow	☐ ReadOnly	☐ ExactUpdate
	☒ DontSearch	☐ ExactSearch	☐ ExactDelete
Last Increase	☒ DontShow	☐ ReadOnly	☐ ExactUpdate
	☒ DontSearch	☐ ExactSearch	☐ ExactDelete
Employee Number	☒ DontShow	☒ ReadOnly	☒ ExactUpdate
	☐ DontSearch	☐ ExactSearch	☒ ExactDelete
	☐ DontShow	☐ ReadOnly	☐ ExactUpdate
	☐ DontSearch	☐ ExactSearch	☐ ExactDelete

NOTE

The information you enter into the Field Name and Field Restrictions fields is stored in the Web_Fields_.fp3 file. It is not necessary, however, for you to manually open or edit this file.

Clearing a User or Field Entry

If you want to clear an entire User or Field entry, position the insertion point in any field within that entry and choose Delete Record from the Mode menu or press Command-E (Macintosh) or Control-E (Windows). Then click the Related button in the dialog box that appears to remove just that related record.

Do you want to delete the entire master record or just this one related record?

Master | Related | Cancel

FileMaker Pro

Do you want to delete the entire master record or just this one related record?

Master | Related | Cancel

Deleting Settings for an Entire Database

To remove a specific database from the Web Security database, display its record and choose Delete Record from the Mode menu or press Command-E (Macintosh) or Control-E (Windows). Then click the Delete or Master button in the dialog box that appears to remove the entire record.

Permanently delete this ENTIRE record?

Delete | Cancel

FileMaker Pro

Permanently delete this ENTIRE record?

Delete | Cancel

Using the Web Security Database with Instant Web Publishing

There are some special things to remember when using the Web Security database to secure databases published with Instant Web Publishing.

- Do not create an All Users entry. Doing so prevents the password dialog box from appearing when users access the database from the Web. Although this won't create a security breech, it will prevent users with additional privileges from using those privileges. For example, if an All Users entry has Create, Edit, and Delete permissions disabled, the New Record, Edit Record, and Delete Record buttons do not appear in the browser window.
- The Browse permission must be turned on for all users.
- The setting for the Scripts permission doesn't matter since scripts are not accessible in databases published with Instant Web Publishing.
- The ExactSearch, ExactUpdate, and ExactDelete restrictions must be turned off for all users. This means you cannot take advantage of record-level security.

TIP

In general, I don't recommend using the Web Security database to secure databases published with Instant Web Publishing. Since record-level security is not available, the Web Security Database offers very little additional security over access privileges.

Creating Custom Security Violation Pages

When a security violation occurs, one of two security violation pages appears:

- **DATABASE_VIOLATION.HTM** appears when a user attempts to access the database with the wrong User Name or User Password.
- **FIELD_VIOLATION.HTM** appears when a user attempts to access a field or record protected with Field Restrictions.

You can find both of these files in the Security folder inside the Web Security folder in the FileMaker Pro 4.0 folder. The default pages are very boring. See?

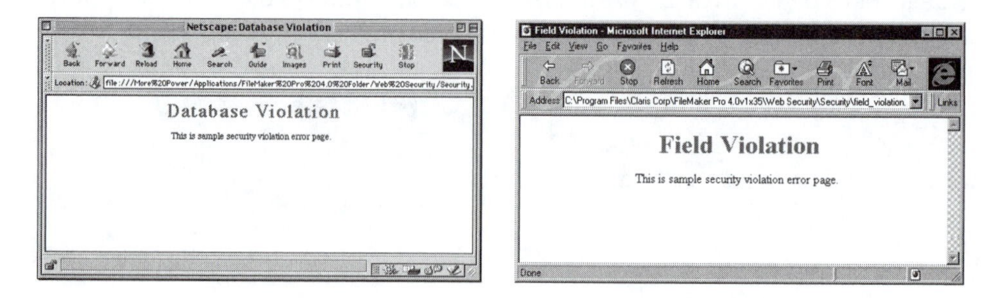

You can edit the security violation pages to provide more information and instructions to security violators. You can also include graphics and other formatting options so the security violation pages match the appearance of the other pages on your Web site.

There are two ways to modify the security violation pages:

- Open the HTML documents with a Web authoring tool like Claris Home Page, Adobe PageMill, or Microsoft FrontPage and modify the page using a WYSIWYG interface.
- Open the HTML documents with a text editor and modify the page's raw HTML code.

Guess which method I'd pick. I'll give you a hint: I hate typing angle brackets.

When you're finished making changes to the documents, be sure to save them. Do not change the file name and do not move the files out of the Security folder.

Accessing a Secured Database File

When a user attempts to access a secured database file with his browser, a password dialog box appears. How this dialog box looks depends on the browser and operating system. Here are two examples:

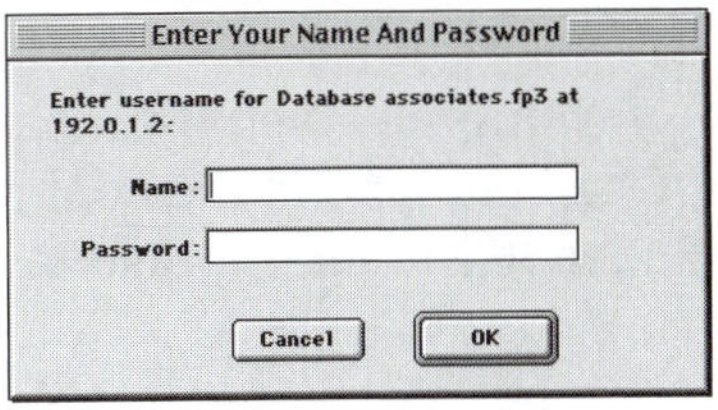

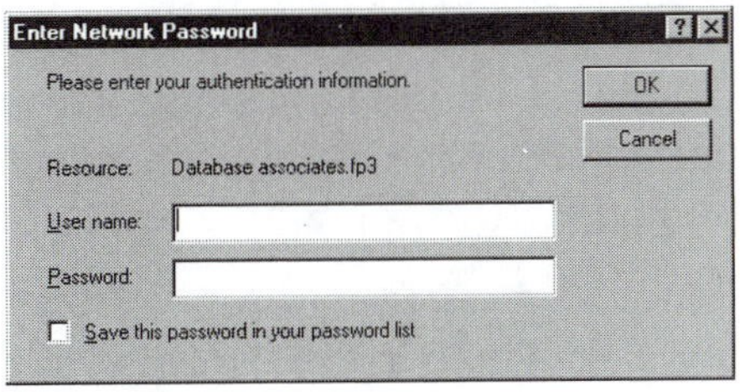

No password dialog box will appear if there are any settings that allow a user to access the database without a password.

To access the file, the user must enter valid login information in the appropriate box(es) and click OK. What the user enters depends on the security method selected in the Web Companion Configuration dialog box:

- If FileMaker Pro Access Privileges is selected, the user just needs to enter a valid password in the Password box. Anything entered into the Name or User Name box is ignored.
- If Web Security database is selected, the user must enter both a name and corresponding password.

If Custom Web Publishing is used, the user may be prompted for a name and password again, depending on the types of actions he tries to perform. If Instant Web Publishing is used, no additional password dialog boxes appear for the database.

Dealing with Security "Loopholes"

There are some minor security loopholes that can easily be patched—if you know what they are. If you're very concerned about security, be sure to read this section carefully.

Preventing Open Files from Appearing on the Home Page

If you use Instant Web Publishing, it may seem as if the built-in Home page lists any FileMaker Pro database file that is open on the database Web server. That isn't exactly true. There are three ways to prevent the files that you open on the database Web server from appearing on the built-in Home page:

- Disable Web Companion sharing for the file. You do this in the Sharing dialog box for the file. I tell you more about this in Chapters 1 and 2.
- Include an underscore character at the end of the file name before any dot-plus-three file extension. For example, a file named Web_Users_.fp3 will never appear on the built-in Home page. I guess that's why the folks at FileMaker, Inc. named that file that way.
- Disable Instant Web Publishing. You do this in the Web Companion Configuration dialog box, which I discuss in Chapter 1 and at the beginning of this chapter. This, of course, isn't a good idea if you plan to use Instant Web Publishing.

If you don't care whether the file is listed but you want to keep unauthorized users out, simply set tight security over the file as I discuss above.

Securing Related Files

On a related topic (no pun intended), if you open a database that has a relationship with another database, the other database also opens. There are two things about this to consider:

- If you don't want the related file to appear on the built-in Home page, use one of the techniques in the previous section to keep it private.
- Related fields that appear on layouts cannot be protected with access privileges or the Web Security database. Choose or design your layouts carefully!

Securing Other Files

A network-savvy hacker could find his way into the Web folder inside the FileMaker Pro folder. If you're concerned about a user downloading database or format files, keep the files out of the Web folder.

Remotely Administering the Web Security Database

If Remote Administration is enabled in the Web Companion Configuration dialog box, you can use Custom Web Publishing to change the settings in the Web Security database, even if you're at a computer other than the database Web server.

FileMaker Pro comes with all the Custom Web Publishing format files that you need to modify the contents of the Web Security database. These files are in the Security folder inside the Web Security folder inside the FileMaker Pro 4.0 folder. Before you can use Custom Web Publishing to remotely administer the Web Security database, you must copy the Security folder to the Web folder inside the FileMaker Pro 4.0 folder.

Use a Web browser to point to the IP address of the database Web server, followed by */Security/default.htm*. The Web Companion Security Administration page appears.

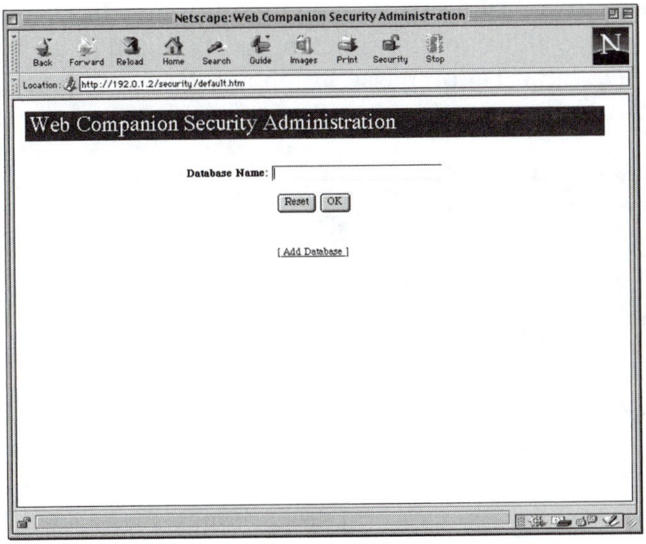

How you proceed depends on what you want to do.

To change the security settings for an existing database, enter the name of the database in the Database Name box and click the OK button. If remote administration requires a password, a Password dialog box appears. Enter Admin in the Name box and enter the remote administration password in the Password box. Then click the OK button. A window like the one below lets you view, change, and add settings for the database.

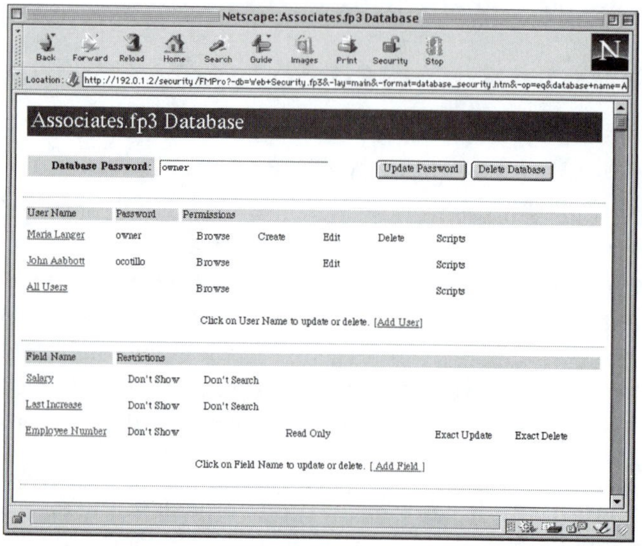

Netscape: Associates.fp3 Database

Location: http://192.0.1.2/security/FMPro?-db=Web+Security.fp3&-lay=main&-format=database_security.htm&-op=eq&database+name=A

Associates.fp3 Database

Database Password: owner [Update Password] [Delete Database]

User Name	Password	Permissions				
Maria Langer	owner	Browse	Create	Edit	Delete	Scripts
John Aabbott	ocotillo	Browse		Edit		Scripts
All Users		Browse				Scripts

Click on User Name to update or delete. [Add User]

Field Name	Restrictions				
Salary	Don't Show	Don't Search			
Last Increase	Don't Show	Don't Search			
Employee Number	Don't Show		Read Only	Exact Update	Exact Delete

Click on Field Name to update or delete. [Add Field]

To Add a database to the Web Security database file, click the Add Database link on the Web Companion Security Administration page. If remote administration requires a password, a Password dialog box appears. Enter Admin in the Name box and enter the remote administration password in the Password box. Then click the OK button. The Add Web Database window appears.

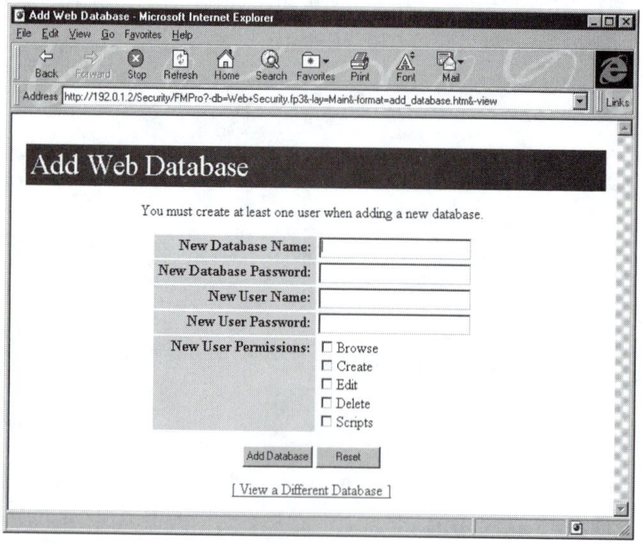

Add Web Database - Microsoft Internet Explorer

Address http://192.0.1.2/Security/FMPro?-db=Web+Security.fp3&-lay=Main&-format=add_database.htm&-view

Add Web Database

You must create at least one user when adding a new database.

New Database Name:
New Database Password:
New User Name:
New User Password:
New User Permissions: ☐ Browse ☐ Create ☐ Edit ☐ Delete ☐ Scripts

[Add Database] [Reset]

[View a Different Database]

Enter database name, database password, and user information for the database that you want to add and click the Add Database button. A window like the one below appears. It confirms the information that was added for the database.

Links in these windows display other pages that provide information and enable you to change, add, or remove settings. It's very straightforward and easy to understand.

TIP

If Instant Web Publishing is enabled, you can use it to open the Web Security database file. This, however, is probably the worst way to modify the file because it's slow and does not enable you to add or remove users or fields.

CHAPTER 4

Static Web Publishing

If the data in your databases doesn't change much and you have no need for interaction between the user and the database, consider static Web publishing. As I discuss in the Introduction, this type of Web publishing offers a quick and easy way to present just the information you want on a Web page.

TIP

Static Web publishing is especially useful if you cannot run FileMaker Pro or CGIs on the Web server.

There are two main techniques for creating static Web pages based on a database's contents: the Export to HTML Table option offered in FileMaker Pro version 4 and using calculation fields in any version of FileMaker Pro to generate HTML code. This chapter discusses both.

NOTE

Throughout this chapter, I work with the file named Book Catalog.fp3. If you'd like to work with the same database file, look for it at http://www.gilesrd.com/fmproweb/.

Export to HTML Table

With version 4 of FileMaker Pro, the programmers at FileMaker, Inc. included a special treat in the Export Records command. In addition to the usual collection of export formats, HTML Table is now an option. In this section, I tell you more about this option, including why and how you'd use it.

Overview

As anyone who's worked with a database knows, there's no better way to present related information than in a nice, neat table of columns and rows. Let's face it—FileMaker Pro's "columnar" reports are really nothing more than highly configurable, scrollable tables. Spreadsheets use tables, too.

HTML tables make it possible to present information in table format on Web pages. Since the information you want to present may already exist somewhere, Web authoring programs like Claris Home Page and Adobe PageMill can automatically create tables from tab-delimited text files or copied spreadsheet cells. Unfortunately, no Web authoring program lets you create tables directly from FileMaker Pro.

That changed with FileMaker Pro version 4. With its support of HTML Table format, FileMaker not only exports the data, but it includes of all the nasty HTML tags needed to make it look like a table when viewed with a Web browser.

Ah, Tables

I remember when Netscape began supporting HTML tags for tables. It wasn't long ago in human time, but in Internet time, it was ages ago. (I was still coding HTML in a word processor back then, learning just how much I could hate typing angle brackets.) When table tags were incorporated into HTML specifications, they changed the way Web pages looked, making it possible for Web authors to do real page layout with positioned graphics and text in a Web page. If you've been a Web author long enough to remember Web pages before tables, you know what a great, welcome change tables ushered in.

You see, not all tables look like grids. Take a look at some of the home pages for your favorite Web sites. See multiple columns of text? See images in the middle of the page with text or other images all around? Chances are, those pages were created using tables. Take away the borders and work some colspan and rowspan magic and anything is possible.

But I digress. Time to stop reminiscing and get back to work.

Exporting Data as an HTML Table

Exporting FileMaker Pro records as an HTML table is a two step process: prepare the data that you want to export and export the data to a file on disk.

Preparing the Data

By preparing the data, I mean gathering the records that you want to export and putting them in the desired order. You must do this before you export the data since you can't do it afterwards.

1. Use the Find command to locate the records that you want to export. These records become part of the found set. If you want to export all of the records, use the Find All command to put all records in the found set.
2. Use the Sort command to put the records in the found set in the desired sort order.

TIP

These are optional steps. If you want to include all of the data and you don't care what order it's in, you can skip this process.

Exporting the Data

To export data as an HTML table, start by choosing Export Records from the Import/Export submenu under the File menu.

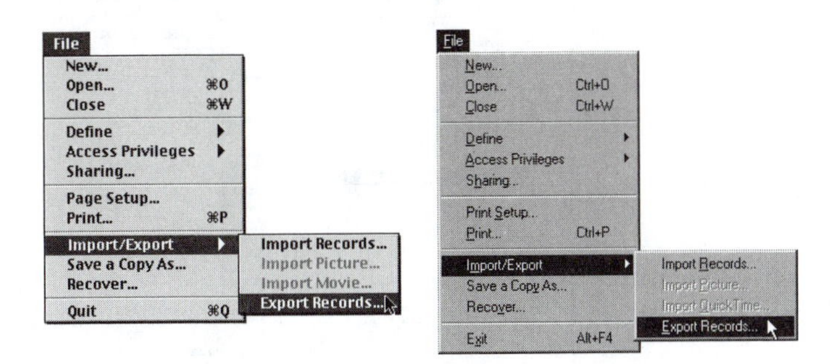

An export dialog box, which looks and works like a Save As dialog box, appears. Enter a name for the file in the Save As box (Macintosh) or File Name box (Windows). You may want to include the extension .html or .htm so the file is automatically recognized as a Web file by a Web browser. Then choose HTML table from the Type menu (Macintosh) or Save as Type menu (Windows) at the bottom of the dialog box.

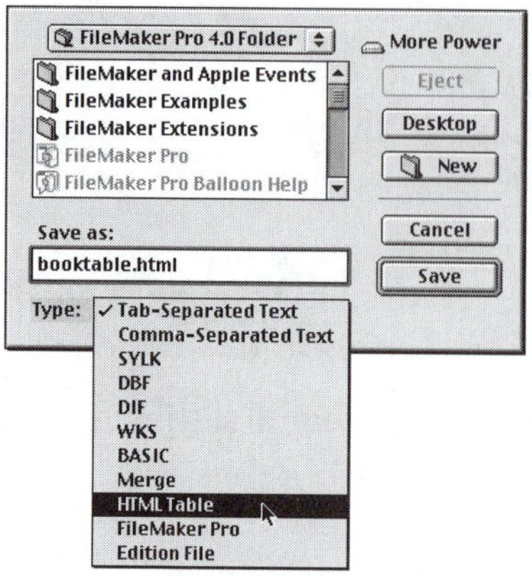

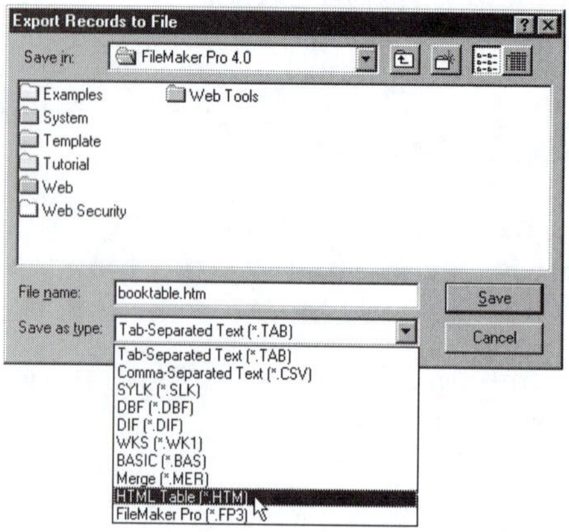

Click Save. The Export Field Order (Macintosh) or Specify Field Order for Export (Windows) dialog box appears. Use it to select the fields that you want to include in the table. When you're finished, the dialog box might look something like this:

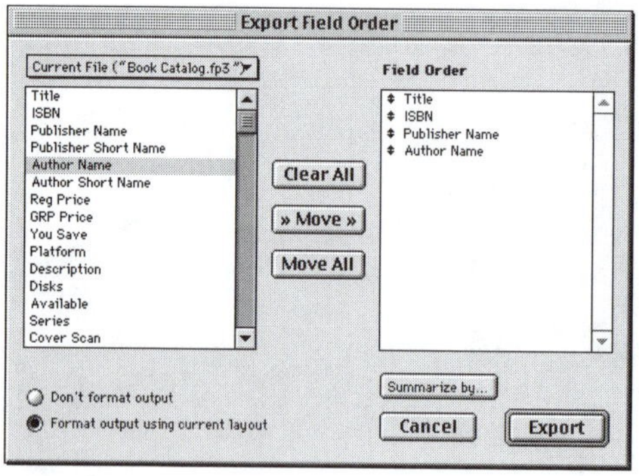

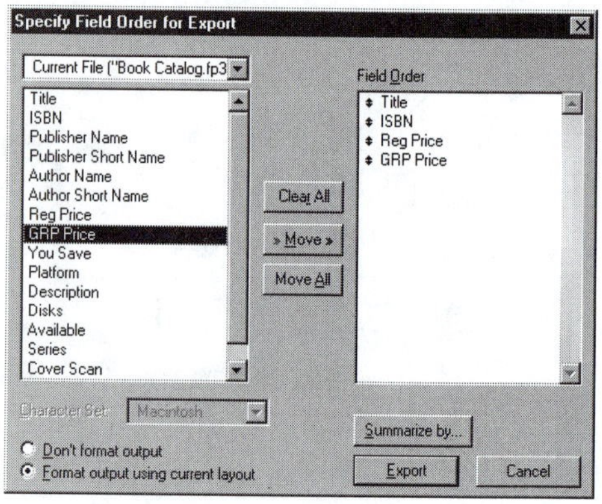

Click the Export button. The records are exported to the file and location you specified in the export dialog box.

Using Exported Data as a Web Page

Once the data has been exported as an HTML table, it's ready to use on the Web. See for yourself. Open it with your browser. My two tables look like this:

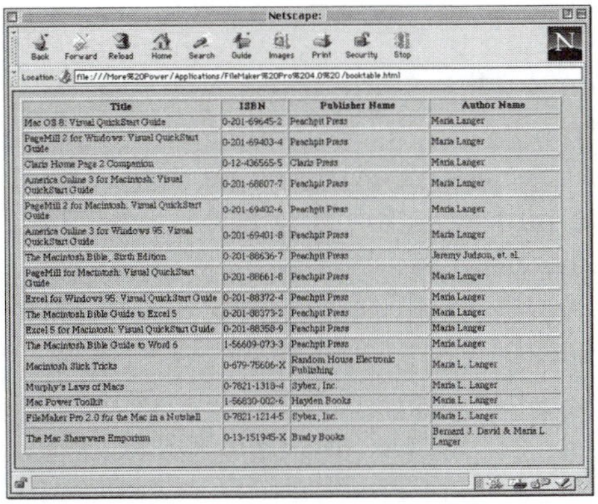

Title	ISBN	Publisher Name	Author Name
Mac OS 8: Visual QuickStart Guide	0-201-69645-2	Peachpit Press	Maria Langer
PageMill 2 for Windows: Visual QuickStart Guide	0-201-69403-4	Peachpit Press	Maria Langer
Claris Home Page 2 Companion	0-12-436565-5	Claris Press	Maria Langer
America Online 3 for Macintosh: Visual QuickStart Guide	0-201-68807-7	Peachpit Press	Maria Langer
PageMill 2 for Macintosh: Visual QuickStart Guide	0-201-69402-6	Peachpit Press	Maria Langer
America Online 3 for Windows 95: Visual QuickStart Guide	0-201-69401-8	Peachpit Press	Maria Langer
The Macintosh Bible, Sixth Edition	0-201-88636-7	Peachpit Press	Jeremy Judson, et. al
PageMill for Macintosh: Visual QuickStart Guide	0-201-88661-8	Peachpit Press	Maria Langer
Excel for Windows 95: Visual QuickStart Guide	0-201-88372-4	Peachpit Press	Maria Langer
The Macintosh Bible Guide to Excel 5	0-201-88373-2	Peachpit Press	Maria Langer
Excel 5 for Macintosh: Visual QuickStart Guide	0-201-88358-9	Peachpit Press	Maria Langer
The Macintosh Bible Guide to Word 6	1-56609-073-3	Peachpit Press	Maria Langer
Macintosh Slick Tricks	0-679-75606-X	Random House Electronic Publishing	Maria L. Langer
Murphy's Laws of Macs	0-7821-1318-4	Sybex, Inc.	Maria L. Langer
Mac Power Toolkit	1-56830-002-6	Hayden Books	Maria L. Langer
FileMaker Pro 2.0 for the Mac in a Nutshell	0-7821-1214-5	Sybex, Inc.	Maria L. Langer
The Mac Shareware Emporium	0-13-151945-X	Brady Books	Bernard J. David & Maria L Langer

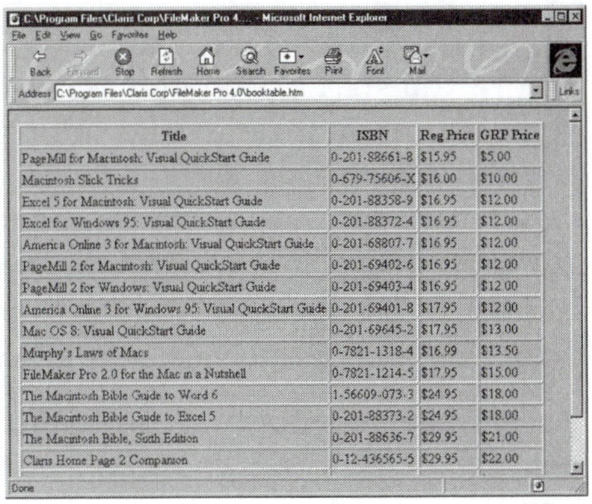

Title	ISBN	Reg Price	GRP Price
PageMill for Macintosh: Visual QuickStart Guide	0-201-88661-8	$15.95	$5.00
Macintosh Slick Tricks	0-679-75606-X	$16.00	$10.00
Excel 5 for Macintosh: Visual QuickStart Guide	0-201-88358-9	$16.95	$12.00
Excel for Windows 95: Visual QuickStart Guide	0-201-88372-4	$16.95	$12.00
America Online 3 for Macintosh: Visual QuickStart Guide	0-201-68807-7	$16.95	$12.00
PageMill 2 for Macintosh: Visual QuickStart Guide	0-201-69402-6	$16.95	$12.00
PageMill 2 for Windows: Visual QuickStart Guide	0-201-69403-4	$16.95	$12.00
America Online 3 for Windows 95: Visual QuickStart Guide	0-201-69401-8	$17.95	$12.00
Mac OS 8: Visual QuickStart Guide	0-201-69645-2	$17.95	$13.00
Murphy's Laws of Macs	0-7821-1318-4	$16.99	$13.50
FileMaker Pro 2.0 for the Mac in a Nutshell	0-7821-1214-5	$17.95	$15.00
The Macintosh Bible Guide to Word 6	1-56609-073-3	$24.95	$18.00
The Macintosh Bible Guide to Excel 5	0-201-88373-2	$24.95	$18.00
The Macintosh Bible, Sixth Edition	0-201-88636-7	$29.95	$21.00
Claris Home Page 2 Companion	0-12-436565-5	$29.95	$22.00

If you're like me, you'll agree that the tables are nice, but argue that they don't cut it as completed pages. There's no heading, title, graphics, links to other pages—none of the things that users expect when they surf the Web. No problem. You can open the exported file with your favorite Web authoring tool and add the finishing touches you think it needs.

Generating HTML with Calculation Fields

Exporting data as an HTML table is the newfangled way to get finished static Web pages out of FileMaker Pro. But it's not the only way. Lots of people—including me—have been using calculation fields to create Web pages for years. If you think you've got the stomach for it, read on and I'll tell you how.

Overview

Calculation fields aren't just for numbers. They're for text, too. That's why FileMaker Pro includes a whole range of text operators and functions in the Specify Calculation dialog box that appears when you define a calculation field.

To create a calculation field that generates HTML code, you need two things:

- **Knowledge of HTML.** There's no getting around this one. If you don't know HTML, you can't use calculation fields to create HTML code.
- **Understanding of FileMaker's Text Operators and Functions.** At a minimum, you must understand how to use the concatenation symbol (&) and quotes to combine fields and literal text.

By combining the contents of database fields with HTML tags, you can create a single field that generates an HTML "entry" for a record. Exporting that field creates an HTML document that contains entries for all exported records.

Before You Start

Before you start, it's a good idea to spend a little time thinking about how you want to present the database information. By far, it's easiest to create a calculation that simply lists selected fields for each record. With a little extra effort, you can include field names to identify data and links to e-mail addresses or URLs in the database. If you've never done anything like this before, it's a good idea to start with something simple, even if you had more complex layouts in mind. I provide a moderately easy example here.

As you get comfortable with the HTML generation process, you can get fancier. For example, you may want to have FileMaker Pro generate an HTML table for your data. (If you're using version 4 of FileMaker, do yourself a favor and use the Export to HTML Table feature I discuss above.) In that case, you need to include some additional tags before and after the table row entries to define the beginning and end of the table. If you want to generate individual pages of data, you need to use the Find command to select the records for each page and export each page separately with a different name.

> **Scripting Can Help!**
>
> Once you've written the calculation fields, you can go a step further and create scripts that organize, sort, and export the completed HTML files for you. This is especially useful if your solution is complex and requires a lot of Find, Sort, and Export commands.

NOTE

Generating HTML with calculation fields can get quite complex. For example, to create the Mac Companies Database you can find at http://www.gilesrd.com/mcd/, I use three databases and over 30 scripts. The solution took a long time to create, but now it can automatically generate 27 Web pages with over 700 entries in less than 3 minutes.

Creating the Calculation Field

In the following example, I create a calculation field in my Book Catalog.fp3 file that generates HTML code for entries that look like this in a browser window; note that the Publisher name field includes a link to the publisher's Web site:

Netscape:

Back Forward Reload Home Search Guide Images Print Security Stop

Location: file:///More%20Power/booklist.html

Mac OS 8: Visual QuickStart Guide

by Maria Langer

Peachpit Press
0-201-69645-2
Retail Price: 17.95

Mac OS 8 is finally here! This 304-page book, which is part of Peachpit Press's popular Visual QuickStart Series, gets you up and running with Mac OS 8 quickly. Follow step-by-step instructions with plenty of illustrations. For veteran or brand new Mac OS users.

PageMill 2 for Windows: Visual QuickStart Guide

by Maria Langer

Peachpit Press
0-201-69403-4
Retail Price: 16.95

Through step-by-step instructions and plenty of illustrations, learn how to use Adobe's hot Web publishing tool, PageMill 2.0. Covers all of PageMill's features and provides a wealth of information not included in the PageMill manual, including an HTML reference written specifically for PageMill users.

Claris Home Page 2 Companion

by Maria Langer

Claris Press
0-12-436565-5
Retail Price: 29.95

Creating the Field

To begin, choose Fields from the Define submenu under the File menu or press Command-Shift-D (Macintosh) or Control-Shift-D (Windows).

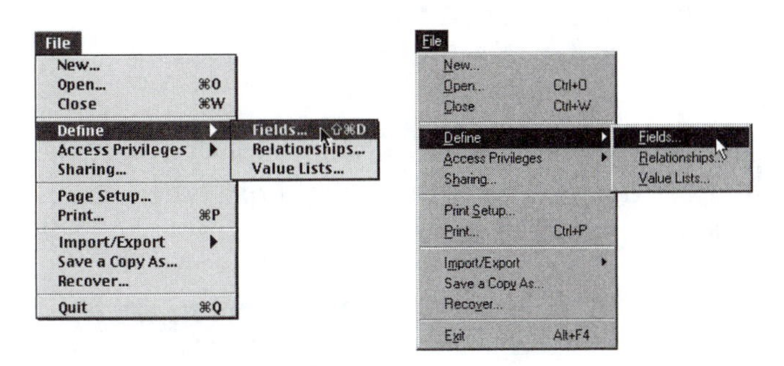

In the Define Fields dialog box that appears, enter a name for the new field in the Field Name box and select the Calculation radio button or press Command-C (Macintosh only).

Define Fields for “Book Catalog.fp3”

17 field(s) · View by: custom order

Field Name	Type	Options
Title	Text	Indexed
ISBN	Text	
Publisher Name	Text	
Publisher Short Name	Text	
Publisher Web Site	Text	
Author Name	Text	
Author Short Name	Text	Indexed
Reg Price	Number	
GRP Price	Number	
You Save	Calculation	= If(1-(GRP Price / Reg Price)=0,"n/a",(1-(GRP Price
Platform	Text	Indexed, Auto-enter Data, By Value List
Description	Text	
Disks	Text	
Available	Text	Indexed, Auto-enter Data
Series	Text	Auto-enter Data, By Value List
Cover Scan	Container	
Sort Number	Number	Auto-enter Serial

Field Name: HTML

Type: Text ⌘T, Number ⌘N, Date ⌘D, Time ⌘I, Container ⌘O, ◉ Calculation ⌘C, Summary ⌘S, Global ⌘G

Create · Options... · Save · Duplicate · Delete · Done

Define Fields for "Book Catalog.fp3"

17 field(s) · View by: custom order

Field Name	Type	Options
Publisher Web...	Text	
Author Name	Text	
Author Short N...	Text	Indexed
Reg Price	Number	
GRP Price	Number	
You Save	Calculati...	= If(1-(GRP Price / Reg Price)=0,"n/a",
Platform	Text	Indexed, Auto-enter Data, By Value List
Description	Text	
Disks	Text	
Available	Text	Indexed, Auto-enter Data
Series	Text	Auto-enter Data, By Value List
Cover Scan	Container	
Sort Number	Number	Auto-enter Serial

Field Name: HTML

Type: Text, Number, Date, Time, Container, ◉ Calculation, Summary, Global

Create · Options... · Save · Duplicate · Delete · Done

Defining the Calculation

Click the Create button to display the Specify Calculation dialog box. Now the fun begins. Click buttons, double-click field names, and type text (including the dreaded angle brackets) to enter the following calculation in the box:

**"<H2>" & Title & "</H2>by " & Author Name & "<P><A HREF=http://" & Publisher Web Site & ">" & Publisher Name & "</A>
" & ISBN & "
Retail Price: " & Reg Price & "<P>" & Description & "<P><HR WIDTH=50%>"**

When you're finished clicking and typing, be sure to choose Text from the Calculation result is menu near the bottom of the dialog box. When you're finished, the dialog box should look a lot like this:

Specify Calculation

Current File (“Book Catalog.fp3”) · Operators · View: all by name

Fields: Title, ISBN, Publisher Name, Publisher Short Name, Publisher Web Site, Author Name, Author Short Name, Reg Price

Buttons: & / "" * ¶ - () +

Operators: = ≠ > < ≥ ≤ and or

Functions: Abs (number), Atan (number), Average (field...), Case (test1, result1 [, test2, re, Choose (test, result0 [, result1, Cos (number), Count (field...), DatabaseNames

HTML =

"<H2>" & Title & "</H2>by " & Author Name & "<P><A HREF=http://" & Publisher Web Site & ">" & Publisher Name & "</A>
" & ISBN & "
Retail Price: " & Reg Price & "<P>" & Description & "<P><HR WIDTH=50%>"

Calculation result is: Text

☐ Repeating field with a maximum of 2 values

☑ Do not evaluate if all referenced fields are empty

Storage Options... · Cancel · OK

Specify Calculation

Current File ("Book Catalog.fp · Operators · View: all by name

Fields: Title, ISBN, Publisher Name, Publisher Short Name, Publisher Web Site, Author Name, Author Short Name, Reg Price

Buttons: & / "" * ¶ - () +

Operators: = <> > < >= <= and or

Functions: Abs (number), Atan (number), Average (field...), Case (test1 , result1 [, test2 , , Choose (test , result0 [, result, Cos (number), Count (field...), DatabaseNames

HTML =

"<H2>" & Title & "</H2>by "& Author Name & "<P><A HREF=http://" & Publisher Web Site & ">" & Publisher Name & "</A>
" & ISBN & "
Retail Price: " & Reg Price & "<P>" & Description & "<P><HR WIDTH=50%>"

Calculation result is: Text

☐ Repeating field with a maximum of 2 values

☑ Do not evaluate if all referenced fields are empty

Storage Options... · OK · Cancel

Analyzing the Calculation

The calculation above may seem like a big mess. It is. Before I continue, here's a line-by-line explanation to help you understand just what this calculation does:

"<H2>" & Title & "</H2> incorporates heading level 2 tags around the Title field. Since a new paragraph must begin after the close of a heading, the following line can start right after it.

by " & Author Name & "<P> inserts the word "by" followed by a space and the contents of the Author Name field and ends the paragraph.

**<A HREF=http://" & Publisher Web Site & ">" & Publisher Name & "</A>
"** inserts the Publisher Name field as a link to the Publisher Web Site field and ends the line.

**& ISBN & "
** inserts the ISBN field and ends the line.

Retail Price: " & Reg Price & "<P>" inserts the words "Retail Price:" followed by a space and ends the paragraph.

& Description & "<P> inserts the contents of the Description field and ends the paragraph.

<HR WIDTH=50%>" inserts a horizontal rule that's 50 percent of the page width.

More about Quotes

If you know your HTML, then you know that the HTML code generated in this example isn't 100 percent legal. Technically, the URL for the HREF should be enclosed within double quotes. In this example, it works fine without them. Other times, it may not.

There are two ways to include double quotes in HTML code that you enter in the Specify Calculation dialog box:

- Enter two double quotes for every one double quote that you need to display. FileMaker Pro evaluates two double quotes as a single double quote. Sound confusing? It can be. But it works.
- Create a Global field that contains a quote character and enter that field each time you need to enter a quote. I find this less confusing, but it introduces a new problem if the database file is hosted by FileMaker Pro Server—the global field may not be properly updated. To fix this problem, create a startup script with the following command: **Paste Literal [Select, "quote" , """].**

One more thing about quotes...if you know you're going to use a database's information on the Web, be sure to turn off Smart Quotes. This prevents the four different curly quote characters (', ', ", and ") from appearing as what I call balloon characters (Ô, Ó, Ò, and Õ) in browser windows. To turn off Smart Quotes, choose Document from the Preferences submenu under the Edit menu. Then turn off the Use smart quotes check box and click Done.

The most important thing to remember is that all literal text must be included within quotation marks and that literal text must be joined to field names with concatenation symbols. If you screw up, FileMaker Pro may tell you—it depends on how badly you screwed up. Even if FileMaker Pro doesn't tell you, you should see the results of an error when you view the HTML code with your browser.

Saving the Calculation Field

When you're satisfied with the calculation, click the OK button in the Specify Calculation dialog box. (If you made an error, this is where FileMaker Pro will let you know.) Then click the Done button in the Define Fields dialog box. The new field is now saved with the rest of the database.

Exporting the Records

You've done the difficult part. The rest is much easier.

Exporting the HTML code calculated for FileMaker Pro records is a two step process: prepare the data that you want to export and export the HTML code to a file on disk.

Preparing the Data

Gather the records that you want to export and put them into the desired sort order. You must do this before you export the data since you can't do it afterwards.

1. Use the Find command to locate the records that you want to export. These records become part of the found set. If you want to export all of the records, use the Find All command to put all records in the found set.
2. Use the Sort command to put the records in the found set in the desired sort order.

TIP

These are optional steps. If you want to include all of the data and you don't care what order it's in, you can skip this process.

Exporting the HTML Code

To export the HTML code, choose Export Records from the Import/Export submenu under the File menu. In the export dialog box that appears, enter a name for the file in the Save As box (Macintosh) or File Name box (Windows). You may want to include the extension .html or .htm so the file is automatically recognized as a Web file by a Web browser. Then choose Tab-Separated Text from the Type menu (Macintosh) or Save as Type menu (Windows) at the bottom of the dialog box and click Save.

Do not select HTML Table in the FileMaker Pro version 4 export dialog box. Doing so will create a table filled with raw HTML code. Not a pretty picture, I assure you.

The Export Field Order (Macintosh) or Specify Field Order for Export (Windows) dialog box appears next. Use it to select only the calculation field that you created to generate the HTML code. Click the Export button. The records are exported to the file and location you specified in the export dialog box.

Checking (and Troubleshooting) Your Work

Unless you're incredibly sure of your HTML and concatenation skills, you should check the finished page by opening it with your Web browser. How does it look? Did you get the code right? If you screwed up, this is where you'll see it.

Troubleshooting a problem puts your HTML knowledge to the test. First you have to figure out what's wrong with the code. Then you have to find and fix the problem in the calculation field's definition. Finally, re-export the field and check it again.

Using Exported Data as a Web Page

Once the data has been exported, it's ready to use on the Web. If you want to add a heading, title, or other Web page elements, simply open the exported file with your favorite Web authoring tool and add the finishing touches you want.

Third Party Solutions

Macintosh users have additional options for publishing FileMaker Pro version 3 and version 4 databases on the Web using Macintosh Web server software and third party CGIs or plug-ins. Unfortunately none of these options are available for Windows PC users.

This part of the book discusses three popular third party FileMaker Pro Web publishing solutions. Its three chapters are:

Chapter 5: Lasso

Chapter 6: Tango for FileMaker

Chapter 7: WEB•FM

CHAPTER 5

Lasso

Blue World Communications' Lasso product line enables you to create flexible database Web publishing solutions for FileMaker Pro version 3 or 4. In this chapter, I tell you about each of the Lasso products, why you might or might not want to use them, and how you set them up. Along the way, I explain the two important concepts used by Lasso Web publishing: format files and Lasso Dynamic Markup Language.

If you're a Windows PC user...

You may notice the lack of Windows instructions and illustrations in this chapter. That's because Lasso only works on Mac OS systems. If you're interested in Lasso, please do read on. But be prepared to buy a Mac OS computer if you decide you want to implement a Lasso solution for your database Web publishing needs.

NOTE

In this chapter, I work with a file named Web Solutions.fp3, which is a database of Web sites and pages that publish FileMaker Pro databases on the Web using a variety of methods. If you'd like to work with the same file, look for it at http://www.gilesrd.com/fmproweb/.

Lasso vs FileMaker Pro Web Companion

As I mention in Chapter 2, Claris purchased some of Blue World Communications' Lasso technology and incorporated it into FileMaker Pro version 4's Web Companion plug-in. Does that mean that Lasso and Web Companion Web publishing features are the same? They're close, but no cigar.

Although there are many similarities between FileMaker Pro's Custom Web Publishing and Web publishing using Lasso, the two solutions are not the same. Here's a partial list of the differences, many of which show clear advantages of Lasso over FileMaker Pro.

- Lasso works with both FileMaker Pro version 3 and version 4. FileMaker Pro's built-in Web Publishing features are only available in FileMaker Pro version 4.
- Lasso works with SDK versions of FileMaker Pro databases. FileMaker Pro's built-in Web Publishing features do not support SDK databases.
- Lasso supports additional tags and commands not included in FileMaker Pro. These include the Inline command for processing multiple database routines in a single form submission, the log command to log access information to a separate database, more complex if/else comparisons, and Apple Event support.
- Lasso's CGI or plug-in works directly with any Macintosh Web server that supports CGIs or plug-ins. FileMaker Pro does not work as a server CGI or plug-in but relies on its own internal Web publishing capabilities.
- Lasso's CGI or plug-in is compatible with SSL Web servers, which make secure Web transactions possible. FileMaker Pro does not support secure transactions.
- Lasso includes a set of Java classes that enable you to call FileMaker Pro from Java applets. FileMaker Pro Web Companion does not.
- New features in Lasso version 2.5 include additional tags, support for FileMaker Pro's CDML tags, and the ability to store format files in FileMaker Pro database fields.

What does this mean to you? If you're already a Lasso user, you have access to features not available to FileMaker Pro version 4 users. If you're not a Lasso user and prefer to depend on FileMaker Pro version 4's built-in Web publishing features, you have an easy upgrade path to Lasso if you find that you need the additional features it offers.

You can learn more about Lasso at http://www.blueworld.com/.

One more thing...this chapter is similar in content to Chapter 2. But like Lasso and FileMaker Pro Custom Web Publishing, Chapters 2 and 5 are not exactly the same. If you're interested in using Lasso, be sure to read this chapter thoroughly to understand the differences.

Overview

Lasso enables you to build custom Web publishing solutions for database files. With it, you can create Web pages that enable users to browse, search, create, modify, or delete records in a FileMaker Pro database. Lasso gives you complete control over how pages look and interact with the database. To tap into its power, you must know exactly what each Web page should do and how to enter the commands that will communicate your desires to Lasso and FileMaker Pro.

Lasso Products

There are four individual Lasso products:

- **LASSO CGI** is an asynchronous CGI that works with Web server software to link FileMaker Pro database files to Web pages.
- **LASSO PLUG-IN** is a WebSTAR API-compatible plug-in that works with Web server software to link FileMaker Pro database files to Web pages.
- **LASSO SERVER** is a specialized HTTP server, designed to publish FileMaker Pro databases. It includes most of the functionality of the Lasso CGI and Plug-In versions but does not require Web server software.
- **FM LINK** is an application that enables you to drag pre-coded Lasso tags from a palette to a Lasso format file.

You do not need to use all of these products. Instead, choose either Lasso CGI, Lasso Plug-In, or Lasso Server. FM Link, which comes with all versions of Lasso, is not required to use Lasso, but as I discuss later in this chapter, its a useful tool for creating Lasso format files.

NOTE

Lasso Tag Converter, which also comes with Lasso, is a BBEdit plug-in that converts format files created for previous versions of Lasso or for FileMaker Pro Custom Web Publishing to a format compatible with the current version of Lasso. To use this plug-in, you must have BBEdit version 4.0 or later; a demo version of BBEdit is included with Lasso.

More about the Lasso CGI and Plug-In

Lasso CGI and Lasso Plug-In are shipped together in one package. You can choose the one you want to use depending on your needs. There are two differences between the CGI and plug-in versions:

- The CGI supports the [timeout] Lasso command tag. The plug-in does not support this tag. Instead, it uses the CGI timeout value set for the Web server as its timeout value.

- The CGI allows a maximum of 24K of data to be passed to the Web server in a form. The plug-in allows almost any amount of data to be passed to the Web server in a form; the amount is limited by the Web server's memory and capabilities.

More about the Lasso Server

The Lasso Server includes the functionality of the Lasso CGI and plug-in, so it doesn't include either the CGI or plug-in component. Although it does not require Web server software, it is not designed to replace a full-featured Web server package. Because it is optimized to work with FileMaker Pro, however, its performance in serving up FileMaker Pro database files is far superior to using Web server software with the Lasso CGI or plug-in.

> **Author's Choice**
>
> Still can't figure out which Lasso product to use for a Lasso-based solution? Let my two cents guide you.
>
> - If you need to publish a complete Web site on a Mac OS system, choose Lasso plug-in with regular Web server software like WebSTAR. This gives you all the Web server features you need while enabling you to publish your FileMaker Pro databases.
> - If you're only interested in publishing FileMaker Pro databases and you don't already have Web server software, go with Lasso Server. It's optimized to work with FileMaker Pro and doesn't have a lot of standard Web server features you might never need.

How It Works

Lasso displays Web pages that enable users to browse, search, create, modify, and delete records in a FileMaker Pro database. These Web pages are created by combining HyperText Markup Language (HTML) and commands called *Lasso Dynamic Markup Language (LDML) tags* in special HTML documents called *format files.*

LDML Tags Defined

LDML tags, which are similar in many respects to HTML, are commands that can be interpreted by Lasso. They provide the instructions that Lasso needs to interact with FileMaker Pro and open FileMaker Pro databases. There are about 200 of these tags, each designed to perform a specific task. I tell you more about LDML tags later in this chapter. You can find a complete list of them in Appendix C.

Format Files Defined

A format file is a plain text document that combines HTML with LDML tags. It provides Lasso with information on how to format a Web page, as well as instructions that Lasso needs to locate, display, change, add, or delete database records.

What's interesting about a format file is that although Lasso uses it to display database information on a Web page, the source code for the resulting Web page is not the same as the format file. This is because Lasso substitutes information from the database file to generate a Web page on the fly based on the format file.

Having trouble understanding what a format file is? Try this analogy: A format file is similar to a word processing document that you might prepare for a mail merge—the final document is based on the original (the format file), but contains information from another source (the database file). Taking that analogy a step further, the LDML tags in a format file are similar to mail merge commands—they provide instructions but never appear in the final document.

Benefits & Drawbacks

The main benefit of using a Lasso product to publish a database on the Web is its sheer power and flexibility. You have complete control over the appearance and functionality of the Web pages, the database access and interaction features you offer visitors, and the processing of information. Because Lasso offers more features than FileMaker Pro Web Companion, you can create Web publishing solutions that are more powerful and flexible than those you can create with FileMaker Pro alone.

As for drawbacks, the most important one is the time and effort required to create and test a complete solution. Although Blue World includes sample solutions that can be modified to meet your needs, you'll still need the time and the knowledge required to modify them. I think it's safe to say that Lasso tags can't be learned overnight—it'll take trial and error and a lot of patience to create format files that do just what you want. But once you know how to create format files for FileMaker Pro's built-in Custom Web Publishing feature, you're only a step away from doing the same with Lasso.

A Closer Look at Format Files

Lasso format files perform two functions:

- Provide a framework for the appearance of the Web page generated by Lasso to display information from a database file.
- Provide instructions that can be interpreted by Lasso to perform specific tasks with a database file.

Lasso format files do this by combining text, standard HTML tags, and LDML tags. HTML determines appearance, displays static content, and offers standard

Web interactivity. LDML tags enable database interactivity and display dynamic content.

In this section, I tell you more about format files and explain how HTML and LDML tags determine their function.

Types of Format Files

There are several types of format files, each designed to perform a specific task. Although not all types are required to interact with a database, most complete Lasso Web publishing solutions include at least one of each type of format file:

- **Add** enables the user to create a new record for the database.
- **Update** enables the user to modify the contents of existing records.
- **Search** enables the user to search for records that match criteria. The criteria can be specified by the user, preset in the format file, or determined by a script.
- **Search Results** displays a list of records found as the result of a search. It can include options to update or delete a single record.
- **Detail** displays information for one record at a time. It is often used to get more information about a record in a results list and can include options to update, delete, or duplicate the record.
- **Reply** notifies the user that a task has been successfully completed. There are three types of replies. **Add Reply** appears when a record has been successfully added. **Update Reply** appears when a record has been successfully edited. **Delete Reply** appears when a record has been successfully deleted. **Duplicate Reply** appears when a record has been successfully duplicated.
- **Error** displays a custom message when the user makes a data entry error or submits an invalid request. **Add Error** appears when an error occurs when attempting to add a record. **No Results Error** appears when no records are found as the result of a search. Error format files are optional since Lasso includes default error pages.

There are no rules governing how to create or use the various format files. If desired, you can incorporate more than one function in one format file. For example, you can create a detail format file that appears as a reply when a record is added but offers options to edit or delete the newly added record. Once you master the basics, you can do all kinds of things with format files.

The Role of HTML in a Format File

The primary components of a format file are HTML elements and text. In fact, it's safe to say that a format file is nothing more than a highly specialized HTML file. HTML elements like these determine the appearance and part of the functionality of the format file:

- **HTML Formatting Tags** determine the appearance and position of text on the Web page. They make it possible to organize information in tables, make headings bold, or change text justification.
- **HTML Graphic Elements**, such as GIF or JPEG graphics, animated GIFs, AIFF sound files, Java Applets, and QuickTime movies, help ensure consistency with other Web pages on your site or make them stand out.
- **HTML HyperLink Tags** provide links to other pages and can activate embedded LDML tags. I tell you about embedding LDML tags in links later in this chapter.
- **HTML Form and Input Tags** enable users to enter information and begin Lasso action. I tell you more about form-related tags later in this chapter.

TIP

When creating format files, you might find it useful to start by creating an HTML document that incorporates the text, images, and formatting you want the user to see. Then insert the LDML tags that will enable the file to interact with Lasso and your open database files.

Directing Actions to Lasso

All instructions to Lasso are accomplished as part of a Lasso action. This is a tag or command that tells the Web server to pass a request to Lasso for processing.

How you specify a Lasso action depends on two things:

- What version of Lasso you are using: CGI, plug-in, or Server. I discuss the different Lasso versions earlier in this chapter.
- Whether the action is part of an HTML link (a URL) or HTML form (a **FORM** action). I tell you about the differences between URL-embedded actions and form actions later in this chapter.

In this section, I discuss all commonly used methods for specifying Lasso actions.

Specifying the Lasso Action for the CGI

The first time you send a request to Lasso, you must include the relative path from the format file to the Lasso CGI. For example, if the Lasso.acgi file is in the

Web server folder and the format file is in a folder within that folder, the Lasso action for a form would be specified as:

```
<FORM action="../Lasso.acgi" method="POST">
other form tags
</FORM>
```

The same Lasso action specified in a URL would be:

```
<A HREF="../Lasso.acgi?other Lasso tags">Text to Click</A>
```

Here's an example where the Lasso.acgi file is in the cgi-bin folder and the format file is within a folder inside the Web server folder:

```
<FORM action="../cgi-bin/Lasso.acgi" method="POST">
other form tags
</FORM>
```

or

```
<A HREF="../cgi-bin/Lasso.acgi?other Lasso tags">Text to Click</A>
```

TIP

If you really want to, you can use absolute paths that include the server name and complete path to the Lasso.acgi. But if you ever rename the server or any of the folders or move the format file to another server, the path will be invalid and the request to Lasso won't work.

TIP

You can make it a lot easier to reference the Lasso.acgi file by placing an alias of it in the same folder as the format files. Then no pathnames are ever necessary.

Subsequent requests to Lasso can be performed without the path. Just reference the Lasso.acgi file, like this:

```
<FORM action="Lasso.acgi" method="POST">
other form tags
</FORM>
```

or

```
<A HREF="Lasso.acgi?other Lasso tags">Text to Click</A>
```

Specifying the Lasso Action for the Plug-In or Server

Specifying the Lasso action is much easier when you're using the plug-in or server version of Lasso. The path to the action is not necessary. Here's an example:

```
<FORM action="action.Lasso" method="POST">
other form tags
</FORM>
```

The same Lasso action specified in a URL would be:

```
<A HREF="action.Lasso?other tags">Text to Click</A>
```

NOTE

The word action *can be replaced with any word you like. The Web server refers to the suffix; anything before the period is ignored.*

Pre-Lasso & Post-Lasso Modes

In the Introduction to this book, I discuss the concept of static and dynamic Web pages. This concept—which is referred to as the *mode* by Lasso—also applies to Lasso. Since the mode becomes important when creating format files for a Lasso Web publishing solution, let me take a moment or two to explain it.

Pre-Lasso vs. Post-Lasso Pages and Forms

When working with a Lasso-based Web publishing solution, a Web page or form can be served either without or with a Lasso action. Lasso refers to this as *Pre-Lasso* (not served by Lasso) or *Post-Lasso* (served by Lasso) pages and forms.

- **PRE-LASSO** pages contain mostly HTML commands. Lasso isn't put to work until the user clicks a link or the Submit button on a form, either of which may utilize LDML tags. Pre-Lasso pages and forms are static—they always look the same because all the information is included in the format file (a standard HTML file) that displays them. These pages appear quickly because they don't need to access the database file for information.
- **POST-LASSO** pages contain a mixture of HTML and Lasso tags. While the HTML tags are used to format the Web page and its elements, the LDML tags are used to obtain information from the database file. A good example is a form that includes editable fields that are already filled in with information from the database. Post-Lasso pages and forms are dynamic—the way they appear depends on the information gathered from the database before the page's HTML code is generated. These pages appear more slowly because Lasso must obtain data from the database and generate an HTML document based on the format file and data before the page can appear.

TIP

Use pre-Lasso or static pages or forms whenever a page or form does not require information from a database file. This helps speed up access to pages on your site.

Display vs. Update

Post-Lasso forms can be further separated into two categories: *display* or *update*.

- **Post-Lasso Display** pages or forms display the contents of FileMaker Pro fields gathered by Lasso as part of a link or form action. Fields appear on a Web page based on a specific format file. They cannot be modified.
- **Post-Lasso Update** forms also display the contents of FileMaker Pro fields gathered by Lasso as part of a link or form action. The fields, however, appear in form elements like text boxes or text areas on Web pages based on a specific format file. Because they appear in form elements, they can be modified. In fact, the Submit button on a Post-Lasso Update form normally includes the **-update** tag.

A Closer Look at LDML Tags

LDML tags are what make a format file a format file. They enable communication between the user and Lasso, which in turn, communicates with FileMaker Pro database files.

Types of LDML Tags

LDML tags fall into five broad categories. Here's a discussion of each type, along with a quick list of its tags.

Action Tags

Action tags perform a specific action with FileMaker Pro. For example, the **-findall** tag finds all of the records in the FileMaker Pro database. Here's a list of the action tags in Lasso version 2.5:

-add
-delete
-duplicate
-findall
-image
-nothing
-random
-scripts
-search
-show
-update

Command Tags

Command tags specify options for action tags. For example, the **-layout** tag specifies the name of the FileMaker Pro layout to be used to display fields. Here's a list of the command tags in Lasso version 2.5:

-adderror
-database
-deletereply
-doscript.post
-doscript.post.back
-doscript.pre
-doscript.pre.back
-doscript.presort
-doscript.presort.back
-duplicatereply
-emailbcc
-emailcc
-emailformat
-emailfrom
-emailhost
-emailsubject
-emailto
-lassopassword
-lassousername
-layout
-logicalop
-maxrecords
-noresult
-opbegin
-opend
-operator
-recid
-reqfieldmissing
-required
-response
-skiprecords
-sortfield
-sortorder
-timeout
-token

Substitution Tags

Substitution tags are placeholders for data from the FileMaker Pro database, visitor's browser, or HTTP stream from the server. When the information is obtained, the replacement tags are replaced with data. For example, the **[field: Company]** tag is replaced with data from the Company field in the FileMaker Pro database. Here's a list of the substitution tags in Lasso version 2.5; tags that include an ellipsis (...) require additional information, such as an item name:

[begnum]
[client_addr]
[client_ip]
[client_password]
[client_type]
[client_username]
[content_type: ...]
[cookie: ...]
[database_name]
[decode_url: ...]
[detail_link: ...]
[encode_breaks: ...]
[encode_html: ...]
[encode_raw: ...]
[encode_smart: ...]
[encode_url: ...]
[next_url]
[nfound]
[nshown]
[option: ...]
[post_inline: ...]
[prev_url]
[recid_value]
[referrer_url]
[response_file_path]
[server_date]
[server_day]
[server-time]
[setcookie: ...]
[set_var:...]
[skiprecords_value]
[string_concatenate: ...]

[endnum]
[field: ...]
[field_name: ...]
[form_param: ...]
[image: ...]
[include: ...]
[inline_result]
[lasso_action]
[lasso_process: ...]
[logicalop_value]
[math-add: ...]
[math-div: ...]
[math-mod: ...]
[math-mult: ...]
[math-round: ...]
[math-sub: ...]
[maxrecords_value]
[string_countfields: ...]
[string_extract: ...]
[string_findposition: ...]
[string_getfield: ...]
[string_insert: ...]
[string_length: ...]
[string_lowercase: ...]
[string_remove: ...]
[string_removeleading: ...]
[string_removetrailing: ...]
[string_replace: ...]
[string_uppercase: ...]
[token_value]
[total_records]
[var: ...]

Container Tags

Container tags are specialized substitution tags. They require an opening and closing tag element which are used to enclose HTML or other Lasso substitution tags. For example, the **[record]...[/record]** tag is used to display information from the enclosed fields for every record in the database or found set. Here's a list of the container tags in Lasso version 2.5; tags that include an ellipsis (...) within the brackets require additional information, such as an item name:

[db_names] ... [/db_names]
[event: ...] ... [/event]
[header] ... [/header]
[html_comment] ... [/html_comment]
[if: ...] ... [/if]
[inline: ...] ... [/inline]
[lay_names: ...] ... [/laynames]
[log: ...] ... [/log]
[loop: ...] ... [/loop]
[next] ... [/next]
[portal: ...] ... [/portal]
[prev] ... [/prev]
[record] ... [/record]
[referrer] ... [/referrer]
[repeating: ...] ... [/repeating]
[search_args] ... [/search_args]
[sort_args] ... [/sort_args]
[valuelist: ...] ... [/valuelist]
[while: ...] ... [/while]

Sub-Container Tags

Sub-container tags are specialized subtitution tags that can be used only between the opening and closing tag elements of container tags. Like container tags, they also have their own opening and closing tag elements. For example, **[loop_count] ... [/loop_count]** keeps track of the number of times commands have looped within the **[loop: ...] ... [/loop]** tag structure. Here's a list of the sub-container tags in Lasso version 2.5; tags that include an ellipsis (...) require additional information:

```
[checked] ... [/checked]
[db_name] ... [/db_name]
[else] ... [/else]
[else: if: ...] ... [/else]
[event_errorstring] ... [/event_errorstring]
[event_result] ... [/event_result]
[event_resultcode] ... [/event_resultcode]
[lay_name] ... [/lay_name]
[list_value] ... [/list_value]
[loop_count] ... [/loop_count]
[repeat_value] ... [/repeat_value]
[repetition] ... [/repetition]
[search_field] ... [/search_field]
[search_op] ... [/search_op]
[search_value] ... [/search_value]
[selected] ... [/selected]
[sort_field] ... [/sort_field]
[sort_order] ... [/sort_order]
```

LDML Syntax

Like HTML, LDML has its own syntax. Syntax is like English grammar, but a lot less forgiving. If you have poor grammar, most people can still figure out what you're trying to say. But if you make a LDML syntax error, Lasso either won't work or it won't work the way you expect it to.

Fortunately, Lasso comes with FM Link, which automatically generates properly formatted LDML tags for you, based on menu selections you make for your database. I tell you more about that later. But since there's more to Lasso syntax than what you'll find in FM Link, I'll explain Lasso syntax here.

Punctuation

Lasso tags use several types of punctuation that aren't normally used in HTML:

- HYPHENS (**-**) preceed all LDML action and command tags. An example is **-findall**. There is one exception to this rule: when using a tag within another tag, omit the hyphen for the embedded tag.
- SQUARE BRACKETS (**[ ]**) surround all substitution, container, and sub-container tags. An example is **[field: "First Name"]**. There is one exception to this rule: when using a tag within another tag, omit the brackets for the embedded tag.
- COLON (**:**) appears between a tag name and the value of the item it specifies. An example is **[field: "First Name"]**, which specifies a field named First Name.
- SPACE CHARACTERS (   ) can appear between a colon and a value (check the previous example). They can also appear within field and file names in some instances.

Space characters appearing in URLs should be represented as a plus sign (+) or encoded as 20% (the ISO Latin-1 equivalent of a space) before being read by a Web browser. For best results, avoid using spaces after colons or in file, layout, and field names. If you must use a space in an item name, make sure that you or your Web authoring program convert each space that appears in a URL to a + or encode it as %20.

- AMPERSAND (**&**) appears between LDML tag name/value pairs when they appear in a link. An example is **<A HREF="action.Lasso?-database=Web+Solutions.fp3&-response=entries.htm&-sortfield=Date&-sortorder=descending&-maxrecords=50&-findall"> Show Entries </A>** (which sets up a link that, when clicked, displays up to 50 records from the file named Web Solutions.fp3, sorted in descending order by the Date field, using the format file named entries.htm).
- QUESTION MARK (**?**) appears after action.Lasso or Lasso.acgi at the beginning of any link that utilizes LDML tags. Check the previous example.

Case Sensitivity

LDML tags are not case sensitive. That means **-findall** is the same as **-FINDALL**, **-FindAll**, or **-fInDaLl**..

URL-Embedded Actions vs. Form Actions

Many LDML tags can be used two different ways in a format file: as an action embedded in a URL for a link or as a form action. The method you choose depends on your needs for the situation. Let me explain.

Embedding LDML Tags in a URL

You can create a link in a Web page that, when clicked, interacts with Lasso and a FileMaker Pro document. Here are a few examples to help you understand the kinds of things you can accomplish with this:

- Create a link that displays all records (or a predefined set of records) on a results page.
- Create a link that deletes, duplicates, or displays detail for the currently displayed record.
- Create a link that runs a script.
- Create a link that sends an e-mail message with predefined content to a predetermined address.

The main limitation of this is that the user cannot provide any additional information that could be used by the LDML tags. All instructions must be included in the LDML tag code that goes into the URL. That means this method cannot be used to add or update a record with user input.

Constructing the link isn't difficult once you know what you want the link to do and which LDML tags it requires. Generally speaking, all URL-embedded LDML tags require the following components:

- HTML anchor (**A**) and reference (**HREF**) tags, which are required to create a link.
- **Lasso.acgi?** (for lasso CGI) or **action.Lasso?** (for Lasso plug-in or Lasso Server) tells the Web server that the URL will be handled by Lasso. I tell you more about directing actions to Lasso earlier in this chapter.
- **-database=*database name*** tells Lasso which database file to use.
- **-response=*format file name*** tells Lasso which format file to use after completing the action.
- ***-action tag name*** tells Lasso which action to perform.

These are the minimum requirements for a URL containing Lasso tags. The action you need to perform may require (or allow) more tags.

Here's an example that displays the 50 most recently added records from a database file, using the Lasso plug-in or Lasso Server to interact with FileMaker Pro:

```
<A HREF="action.Lasso?-database=Web+Solutions.fp3&-response=entries.html
&-sortfield=Date&-sortorder=descending&-maxrecords=50&-findall">
Show Entries</A>
```

This example uses each of the required components, with **-findall** as the action tag. It also includes the **-sortfield** and **-sortorder** command tags to include sorting instructions. Note that each name/value pair in the Lasso URL is separated by an ampersand.

Using Lasso Tags in a Form Action

The other, more common way to use Lasso tags is in a form action. This method requires that you create a form containing the fields with which you want users to work. The action is incorporated into a Submit button on the form. Here are some examples of the kinds of things you can do with Lasso tags in a form action:

- Enable users to create new database records based on information they enter.
- Enable users to modify existing database records based on information they enter.
- Enable users to search for records based on criteria they enter.
- Perform any of the actions you can perform with Lasso tags embedded in a URL.

The only limitations to this method are those imposed by Lasso itself.

Constructing the form isn't difficult, either, especially if you use a Web authoring tool like Claris Home Page, Adobe PageMill, or Microsoft FrontPage. Simply create the form, then add or substitute Lasso tags to indicate field names and other options. At a minimum, all Lasso forms require the following components:

- HTML form (**FORM**) tags that includes **action="Lasso.acgi"** (for the CGI version) or **action="Action.Lasso"** (for the plug-in or server version) and **method="POST"**. I tell you more about directing actions to Lasso earlier in this chapter.
- HTML input (**INPUT**) tag that includes **name="-database" value="*database name*"** tells Web companion which database file to use. The type of input is usually set to **"hidden"**.
- HTML input (**INPUT**) tag that includes **name="-response" value="*format file name*"** tells Web companion which format file to use after completing the action. The type of input is usually set to **"hidden"**.
- HTML input (**INPUT**) and/or selection (**SELECT**) fields. For input, use only HTML. For editing existing values, combine with Lasso substitution tags to display current field contents.
- HTML submit button (**INPUT type="submit"**) tag that includes **name="*-action tag name*"** tells Lasso what action to perform when the button is clicked.

These are the minimum contents. What you include depends on what you want to display on and accomplish with the page.

Here's an example of a form that displays information and enables the user to modify fields:

```
<FORM action="Action.Lasso" method="POST">
<INPUT type="hidden" name="-database" value="Web Solutions.fp3">
<INPUT type="hidden" name="-response" value="updatereply.htm">
Site Name: <INPUT type="text" name="Site Name" value="[field:First
Name]"> <BR>
Site URL: <INPUT type="text" name="Site URL" value="[field:Site Home Page
URL]"> <BR>
Description: <INPUT type="textarea" name="Description"
value="[field:Description]"> <BR>
<INPUT type="submit" name="-update" value="Update Record">
```

By combining HTML form input tags with Lasso substitution tags, you can display current settings while enabling the user to change them. The submit button determines what action is performed—in this case updating the record to incorporate the changes.

Using FM Link

Although you can create a format file by typing HTML and LDML tags in any text editor or word processor, that isn't necessarily the best way. (It certainly isn't any fun, especially if you don't like typing brackets.) Fortunately, Lasso comes with FM Link, an application designed specifically to create format files.

FM Link offers two methods to create format files:

- **Templates** contain all of the HTML and LDML tags to make up a complete format file. You drag the template name from the FM Link window into an empty document window in your HTML editing application. Then modify the template's contents to create your own custom format file. The main benefit of using a template is that it includes most of the HTML and Lasso tags you need for a specific type of format file. The main drawback is that you must properly modify the generic information to meet your specific needs; if you make an error, the resulting format file won't work properly.
- **Lasso Commands** are customized LDML tags that are based on selections you make. Use FM Link to select options based on your database and a function that you want to perform. Then drag the name of the tag to your HTML document to insert the code. The main benefit of using Lasso commands is that most HTML and LDML tags are completely customized with information from your database. The main drawback is that you must know which HTML and LDML tags must be included to make the format file work; if you leave one out, the resulting format file won't work properly.

> **Author's Choice**
>
> The templates feature is nice, but I don't recommend using it. The instructions that template files include aren't as explicit as they should be to walk a beginner through the process of creating a custom format file from a template. If you want to learn about how format files work, you'd be better off looking at examples like the ones that come with Lasso. These examples work—the template files don't work unless you correctly edit them for your database and Web publishing needs.
>
> I prefer building my format files from scratch, using the Lasso commands feature of FM Link. This enables me to create a custom format file without having to deal with additional template code that I may or may not need to include or modify. It also lets me decide exactly what I want in my format file—without worrying about what a template creator thinks it should include.

In this section, I explain how to use FM Link to create a Lasso format file.

Opening FM Link

Since FM Link works with open FileMaker Pro database files, it's a good idea to begin by opening the database for which you want to create the format file. Then locate and open the FM Link application. It should be in the FM Link folder that was installed when you installed Lasso.

A splash screen with information about FM Link appears briefly. Then the FM Link window appears, displaying its Databases tab. It should look something like this:

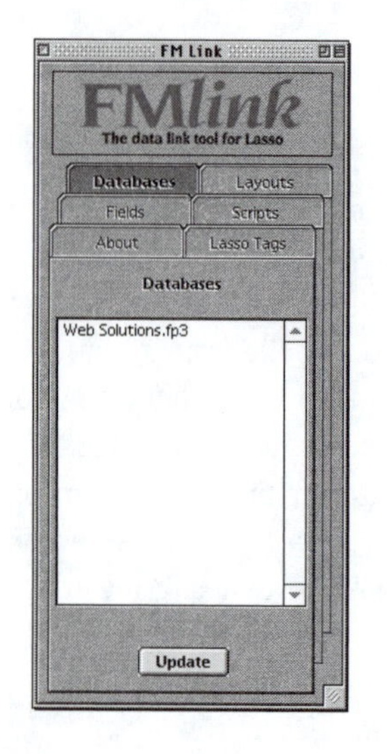

TIP

If you open a database file after opening FM Link, click the Update button at the bottom of the Databases tab to list and access the newly opened database.

Using a Template

To create a format file based on a template, click the Lasso Tags tab in the FM Link window. A scrolling list of Lasso commands appears. Scroll down to the bottom of the list. A list of 13 templates appears beneath a TEMPLATES heading.

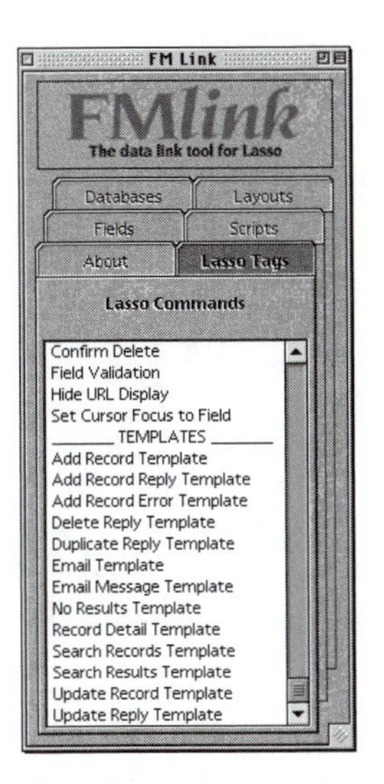

To learn more about what a template does, double-click it. The Help Window appears. It displays the name of the template, a window containing all of its tags, and a scrolling window that describes what the template does.

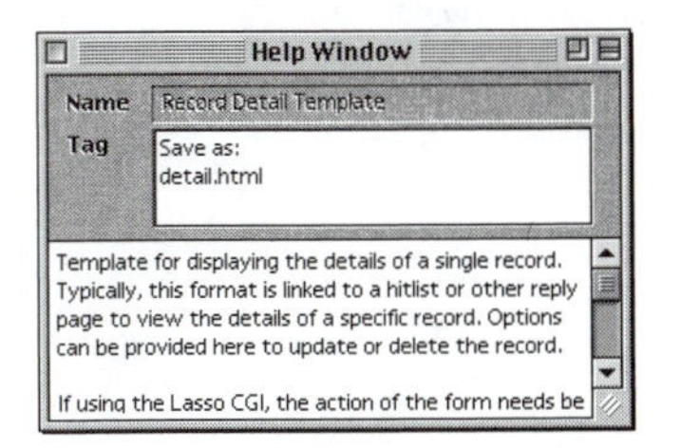

To use a template, drag its name from the FM Link window into an empty document window for your favorite HTML editing application. The template's contents are copied into the window for you to edit.

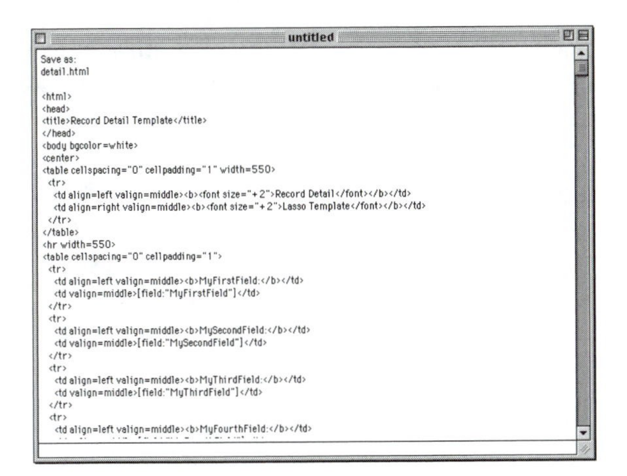

```
untitled
Save as:
detail.html

<html>
<head>
<title>Record Detail Template</title>
</head>
<body bgcolor=white>
<center>
<table cellspacing="0" cellpadding="1" width=550>
 <tr>
  <td align=left valign=middle><b><font size="+2">Record Detail</font></b></td>
  <td align=right valign=middle><b><font size="+2">Lasso Template</font></b></td>
 </tr>
</table>
<hr width=550>
<table cellspacing="0" cellpadding="1">
 <tr>
  <td align=left valign=middle><b>MyFirstField:</b></td>
  <td valign=middle>[field:"MyFirstField"]</td>
 </tr>
 <tr>
  <td align=left valign=middle><b>MySecondField:</b></td>
  <td valign=middle>[field:"MySecondField"]</td>
 </tr>
 <tr>
  <td align=left valign=middle><b>MyThirdField:</b></td>
  <td valign=middle>[field:"MyThirdField"]</td>
 </tr>
 <tr>
  <td align=left valign=middle><b>MyFourthField:</b></td>
```

Now the fun begins—and yes, I do mean that sarcastically. Your job is to go through the entire template and replace the generic names of databases, layouts, fields, response files, and other items with real names from your database. Comments in the template tell you a little about the changes you need to make. Because the template is designed to be used with any kind of database, it won't exactly meet your needs and will require a lot of editing. Knock yourself out. If you make a mistake or neglect to change something, you'll know because the format file won't work properly when you try it.

Building a Format File from Scratch

The other way to create a format file is to build it from scratch using LDML tags that FM Link can automatically code for you. It isn't that difficult—try it and see.

Follow the instructions in this section to create a format file for Web Solutions.fp3 that enables a visitor to edit database information in a form on a Web page. You'll learn many of the format file creation skills you'll use over and over every time you create a format file.

NOTE

As I mention at the beginning of this chapter, you can get the file named Web Solutions.fp3 from this book's companion Web site, http://www.gilesrd.com/fmproweb/. But you don't have to use that file. Pick a file of your own and substitute your file's information for the selections here.

Entering Required HTML Code

Remember, a format file is a specialized HTML file. That means it needs the **HTML**, **HEAD**, and **BODY** tags you'd find in any other HTML document.

There are two ways to enter these tags:

- Manually type them into a document window of your favorite HTML editing application.
- Open a new document window in a WYSIWYG Web page authoring program like Claris Home Page, Adobe PageMill, or Microsoft FrontPage and switch to the HTML editing mode. The program enters it for you.

untitled

```
<html>
<head>

</head>
<body>

</body>
</html>
```

WARNING

WYSIWYG Web authoring programs don't work as well with FM Link as plain text editors. I tell you more about the possible problems you may encounter later in this chapter.

Saving the File

I like to save my files as I work with them. (You should, too.) Take a moment right now to save the file. Choose Save from the File menu to display the Save As dialog box. Since this format file will enable users to update information on the page, give it a name like update.html. Save it into a folder with the other format files for this Web publishing solution.

TIP

Once you save the file, you can use the Command-S shortcut to save changes to the file at the end of each section in this little tutorial.

Specifying a Database and Layout

Switch to FM Link and position it so that you can see it and your HTML document. If the Databases tab of FM Link is not displayed, click it. Then double-click the name of the database with which Lasso will communicate—for this example, Web Solutions.fp3. The Layout tab should appear automatically, with the name of the database displayed in the window. If it doesn't, click it to display it.

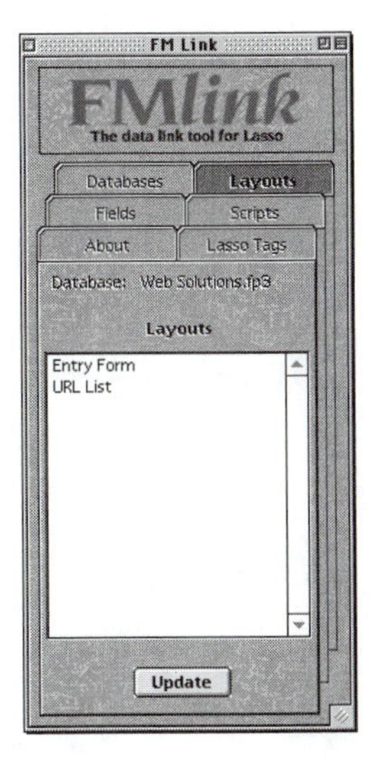

The Layouts tab displays all of the layouts in the database you selected. Double-click the name of a database layout that includes all of the fields that Lasso will display on a Web page. For this example, double-click Entry Form. The Fields tab should appear next. If it doesn't, click it to display it.

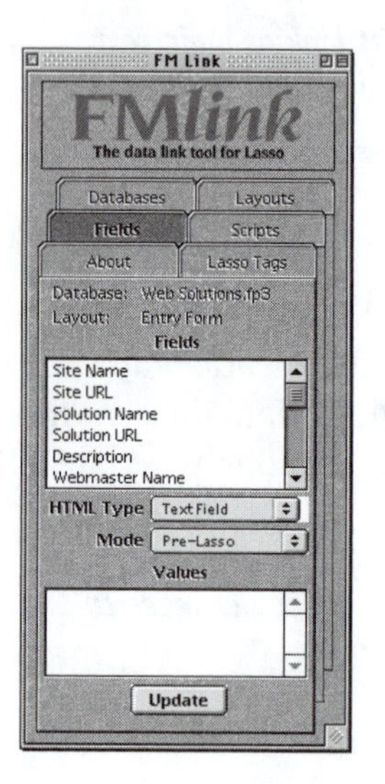

TIP

If any of the Databases, Layouts, or Fields tabs are empty, click the Update button to refresh their contents. If that doesn't work, click the Databases tab and follow the instructions in this section to select a database and layout again.

Using the Lasso Tags Tab

Click the Lasso Tags tab to display a list of Lasso Commands in a scrolling window. Tags are organized by function to make them easy to find.

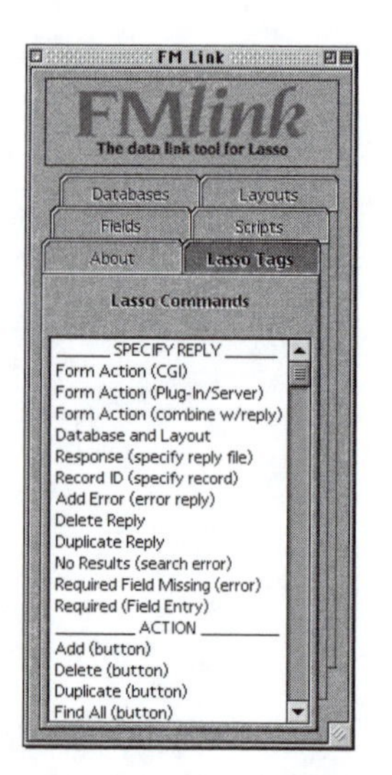

To learn more about a command, double-click it. The Help Window appears. It displays the name of the command, a window containing all of its code, and a scrolling window that describes what the command does.

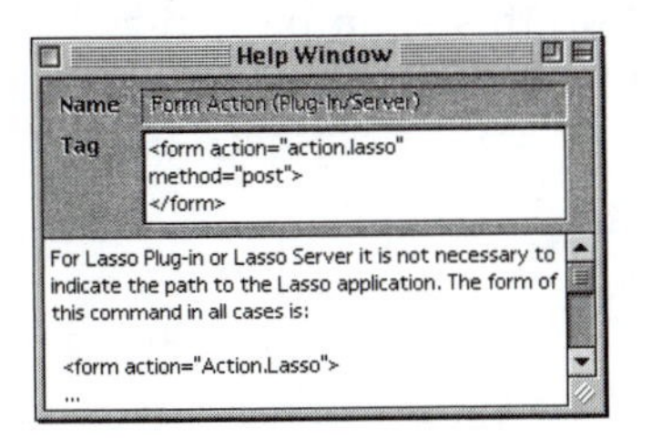

To use a tag, drag its name from the scrolling list and into the HTML document window. Its code appears at the insertion point.

Entering Required Form Tags

Since this format file will display a form, it needs tags that define the form and provide information that Lasso needs to display and work with database information. Add these one at a time to the body section of the HTML document.

The first tag to enter is the **FORM** container tag, which includes the form action instructions. Make sure the Lasso Tags tab is displayed; if it isn't, click it to display it. Then drag either the Form Action (CGI) or the Form Action (Plug-In/Server) command name from the FM Link window to the HTML document window, right after the **<BODY>** tag. On my system, I dragged the Form Action (Plug-In/Server) command since I'm using the server version of Lasso. When you're finished, it looks like this:

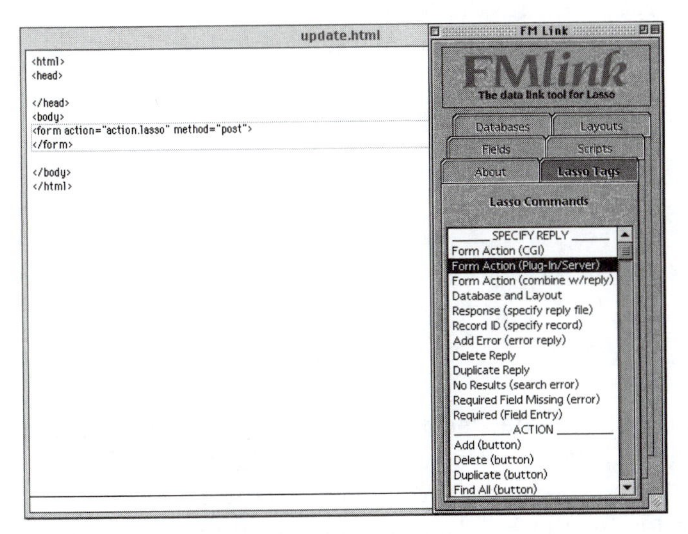

Next, enter a hidden **INPUT** tag that specifies the database and layout Lasso will access. Drag the command named Database and Layout from the FM Link window to the HTML document window, within the **FORM** container tag. Two tags are added. Switch to the HTML editing application and replace **YourDBName** with the name of the database (in this example, Web Solutions.fp3)

and **YourLayoutName** with the name of the layout (in this example, Entry Form). Do not delete the quotes. When you're finished, it looks like this:

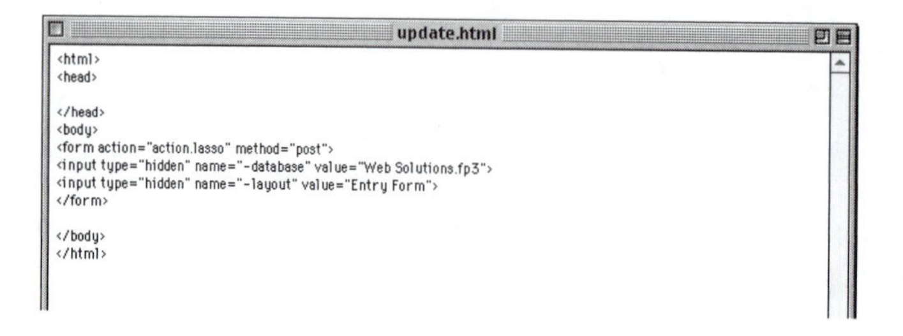

update.html

```
<html>
<head>

</head>
<body>
<form action="action.lasso" method="post">
<input type="hidden" name="-database" value="Web Solutions.fp3">
<input type="hidden" name="-layout" value="Entry Form">
</form>

</body>
</html>
```

The next tag to enter is a hidden **INPUT** tag that specifies the response file name—that's the format file that should be used when the user clicks the Submit button on this form. Switch back to FM Link and drag the command named Response (specify reply file) from the FM Link window to the HTML document window, within the **FORM** container tag. Then switch to the HTML editing application and replace **Pathto/YourFileName.html** with the name of the response file. If the file is (or will be) located in a different folder than the Lasso CGI, plug-in, or Server application (whichever you're using), be sure to include the relative path to the file from Lasso. Do not delete the quote marks.

For my example, I plan to create a format file named updatereply.html that will appear when a user finishes updating a record. This file will be in a folder within the Lasso folder, so the path includes the name of the folder. If you're following along with me, when you're finished, the format file might look like this:

update.html

```
<html>
<head>

</head>
<body>
<form action="action.lasso" method="post">
<input type="hidden" name="-database" value="Web Solutions.fp3">
<input type="hidden" name="-layout" value="Entry Form">
<input type="hidden" name="-response" value="solutions/updatereply.html">
</form>

</body>
</html>
```

Finally, a hidden **INPUT** tag with the **-recid** command tag must be included so that Lasso knows which FileMaker Pro record it should display and update. Switch to FM Link and drag the command named Record ID (specify record) from the FM Link window to the HTML document window, within the **FORM** container tag. This tag is used as is; no editing is required.

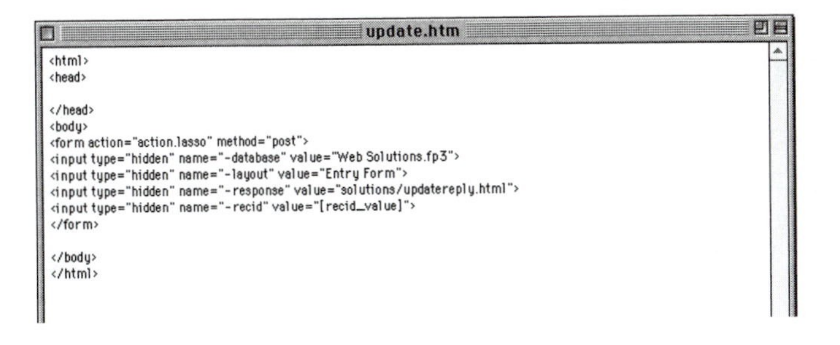

```
<html>
<head>

</head>
<body>
<form action="action.lasso" method="post">
<input type="hidden" name="-database" value="Web Solutions.fp3">
<input type="hidden" name="-layout" value="Entry Form">
<input type="hidden" name="-response" value="solutions/updatereply.html">
<input type="hidden" name="-recid" value="[recid_value]">
</form>

</body>
</html>
```

Adding Form Fields with Database Information

The next step is to add form fields that will display and enable a user to edit database information. This example uses plain text fields and a text area to display the database's seven fields.

Click the Fields tab in the FM Link window. Select the first field with which you want to work—in this case, Site Name. Choose a type of field from the HTML Type menu. If the field is formatted as a Standard field in the selected layout within FileMaker Pro, your only choices will be Text Field or Text Area, as shown here:

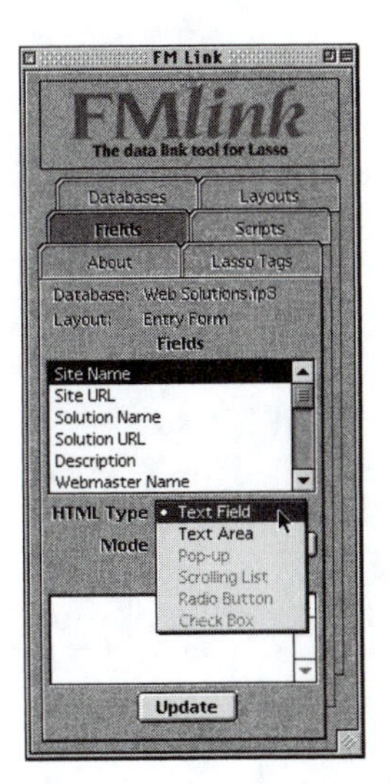

If the field is formatted as a Pop-up list, a Pop-up menu, Check boxes, or Radio buttons in the selected layout within FileMaker Pro, you'll have the same choices in the HTML Type menu. Here's an example from another database:

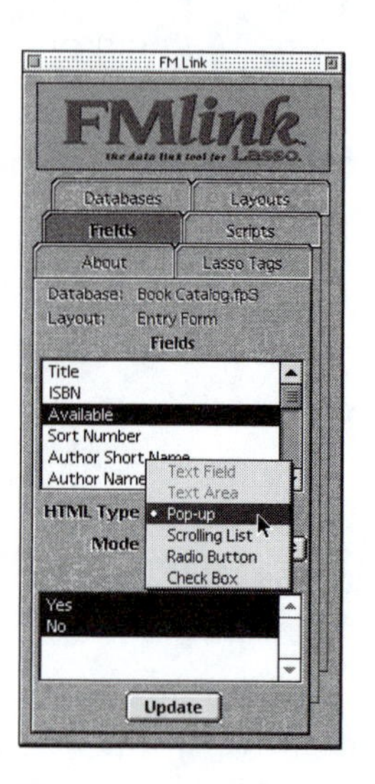

Then choose an option from the Mode menu. In this example, the field will display information from the database (post-Lasso) and enable the user to modify (update) it, so I chose Post-Lasso (Update).

When your selections are complete, drag the name of the field from the FM Link window to the HTML document, within the **FORM** container.

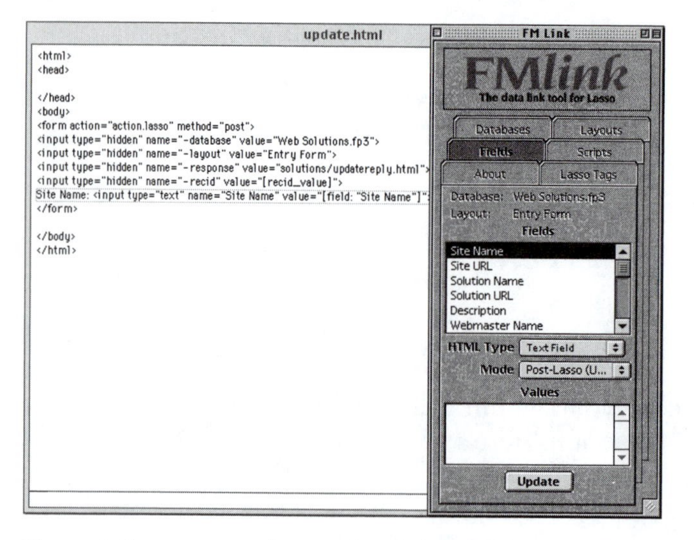

Repeat these steps for each of the fields that you want to include in the form. FM Link automatically includes all necessary information for each tag. It even provides a text label before the form field to identify the field on the Web page.

You might want to include HTML **<P>** tags after each field to put them on separate lines. When you're finished, the HTML document might look like this:

```
update.html
<html>
<head>

</head>
<body>
<form action="action.lasso" method="post">
<input type="hidden" name="-database" value="Web Solutions.fp3">
<input type="hidden" name="-layout" value="Entry Form">
<input type="hidden" name="-response" value="solutions/updatereply.html">
<input type="hidden" name="-recid" value="[recid_value]">
Site Name: <input type="text" name="Site Name" value="[field: "Site Name"]"><P>
Site URL: <input type="text" name="Site URL" value="[field: "Site URL"]"><P>
Solution Name: <input type="text" name="Solution Name" value="[field: "Solution Name"]"><P>
Solution URL: <input type="text" name="Solution URL" value="[field: "Solution URL"]"><P>
Description: <textarea name="Description" rows=4 cols=40 wrap="soft">[field: "Description"]</textarea><P>
Webmaster Name: <input type="text" name="Webmaster Name" value="[field: "Webmaster Name"]"><P>
Webmaster Email: <input type="text" name="Webmaster Email" value="[field: "Webmaster Email"]"><P>
</form>

</body>
</html>
```

Inserting Reset and Submit Buttons

The final required ingredients for this format file are the Reset and Submit buttons found on all Web page forms.

Click the Lasso Tags tab in the FM Link window to display the list of Lasso Commands again. Scroll the list so you can see the commands in the ACTION section. Drag the command named Reset (button) from the FM Link window into the HTML document, within the **FORM** container. Then drag the command named Update (button) from the FM Link window into the HTML document, also within the **FORM** container. When you're finished, the HTML document should look like this:

```
update.html
<html>
<head>

</head>
<body>
<form action="action.lasso" method="post">
<input type="hidden" name="-database" value="Web Solutions.fp3">
<input type="hidden" name="-layout" value="Entry Form">
<input type="hidden" name="-response" value="solutions/updatereply.html">
<input type="hidden" name="-recid" value="[recid_value]">
Site Name: <input type="text" name="Site Name" value="[field: "Site Name"]"><P>
Site URL: <input type="text" name="Site URL" value="[field: "Site URL"]"><P>
Solution Name: <input type="text" name="Solution Name" value="[field: "Solution Name"]"><P>
Solution URL: <input type="text" name="Solution URL" value="[field: "Solution URL"]"><P>
Description: <textarea name="Description" rows=4 cols=40 wrap="soft">[field: "Description"]</textarea><P>
Webmaster Name: <input type="text" name="Webmaster Name" value="[field: "Webmaster Name"]"><P>
Webmaster Email: <input type="text" name="Webmaster Email" value="[field: "Webmaster Email"]"><P>
<input type="reset" value="Clear Entries"> <input type="submit" name="-update" value="Update Record">

</form>

</body>
</html>
```

Getting Fancy

As you probably realize, the example format file created here has the bare minimum number of components to get the job done. There's no fancy formatting or graphics—heck, there isn't even a title on the page. Here's what the format file looks like with information from the database when viewed with Netscape Navigator:

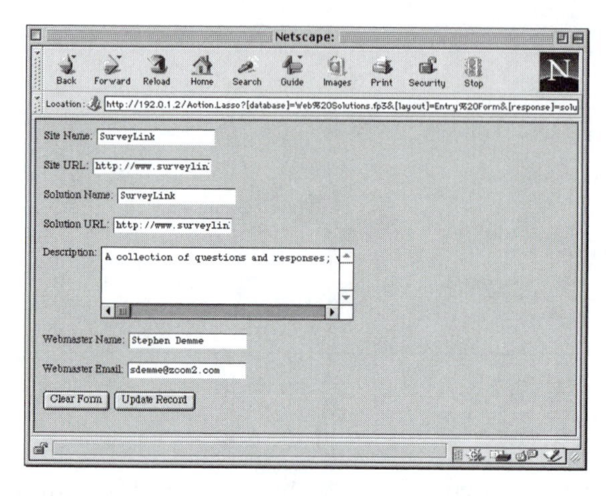

You might want to use your HTML editing skills to improve the appearance of the page or add information or instructions for the user. You can tackle that on your own.

Using FM Link with WYSIWYG Web Authoring Tools

Although I illustrate FM Link with a plain text editor, it also works with WYSIWYG Web authoring tools like Claris Home Page, Adobe PageMill, and Microsoft FrontPage. You may not get exactly what you bargained for, however. It's important to be aware of potential problems if you decide to use a WYSIWYG Web authoring tool to create Lasso format files.

There are three problems you may encounter, depending on the program you use:

- Some programs do not allow you to drag tags from FM Link into the program's document window. You may be able to get around this by changing the selected settings on FM Link's Drag menu or by using a different editing mode in the Web authoring program.
- Some programs change or strip out LDML tags after you insert them. This is because these programs don't know how to treat commands they don't recognize. Although this problem is going away as Web authoring programs evolve, you should check the LDML tags in HTML editing mode or with a plain text editor.
- Some programs insert line breaks in the middle of LDML tags, making the tags impossible for Lasso to understand. This has to do with word-wrap features built into some Web authoring programs. Use HTML editing mode or a plain text editor to make sure there are no line breaks or paragraph breaks within angle brackets marking HTML code that includes LDML tags.

If you're worried about your Web authoring program messing up LDML tags you insert, try this: Create your Web page using the Web authoring program of your choice. Save the resulting HTML file. Now quit the Web authoring program and use a plain text editor to open the HTML file you created. Use FM Link to create the LDML tags you need to interact with Lasso and paste them into the text file. Save changes to the file and you're done.

Step-by-Step Setup

Ready to try building your own Lasso Web Publishing solution? Here are the steps you'll need to follow to get your database online with Lasso.

Installing & Registering Lasso

Before your files can be published on the Web, you must install the Lasso product of your choice. Quit your Web server application (if applicable), insert the Lasso disk in your computer, and follow the appropriate instructions below for the Lasso product you've selected.

You only need to follow these steps once for only one of the Lasso products, no matter how many databases you publish.

Installing and Registering the Lasso CGI

Follow these steps:

1. Copy the following items from the Lasso CGI folder to either your Web server folder or the cgi-bin folder within your Web server folder:
   - Lasso.acgi file
   - LassoCommonCode file
   - Lasso Modules folder
   - Lasso Startup Items folder
   - Lasso Security folder

Installing the Lasso CGI and its files in the Web server folder makes it easier to specify a pathname for the CGI in format files. It also makes it easier to switch to the plug-in version in the future, since the path to the plug-in is the same as the server software.

2. Copy the FM Link and User Guide folders to any location on your hard disk.

3. Launch the Lasso.acgi application. Enter your serial number in the dialog box that appears and click OK. Then quit the Lasso.acgi program to store the serial number within the program and relaunch it.

Lasso CGI is now ready to use.

Installing and Registering the Lasso Plug-In

Follow these steps:

1. Copy the Lasso Plug-in file from the Lasso Plug-in folder to the Plug-ins folder inside your Web server folder.
2. Copy the following items from the Lasso Plug-in folder to your Web server folder:
   - LassoCommonCode file
   - Lasso Modules folder
   - Lasso Startup Items folder
   - Lasso Security folder
3. Copy the FM Link and User Guide folders to any location on your hard disk.

Relaunch your Web server software. It should automatically load the Lasso plug-in; the server's status window will list Lasso among the initialized plug-ins.

The first time Lasso receives a request, it displays a registration page. Enter your Lasso serial number and click the Register button. A confirmation page appears. Then quit your Web server software to store the serial number in the application and relaunch it. The Lasso Plug-in is now ready to use.

Installing and Registering the Lasso Server

Follow these steps:

1. Create a new folder on your hard disk to act as the Web serving or "root" folder.
2. Copy the following items from the Lasso Server folder to your Web serving folder:
   - Lasso Server file
   - LassoCommonCode file
   - Lasso Modules folder
   - Lasso Startup Items folder
   - Lasso Security folder
3. Copy the FM Link and User Guide folders to any location on your hard disk.

4. Launch the Lasso Server application. Enter your Lasso serial number in the dialog box that appears and click OK.
5. Copy the site's Home page to the Web serving folder. Rename it default.html.

The Lasso Server is now ready to use.

Preparing a Database for Publishing with Lasso

Next, you need to prepare the database that you want to publish. This can be as easy as opening the database or it may require that you create new layouts with the fields that you want to appear in pages created by format files.

Opening a Database

If you haven't already opened the database that you want to publish, now's the time. Double-click the database's document icon or choose Open from FileMaker Pro's File menu and use the Open dialog box that appears to locate and open the database file.

WARNING

The database must be open for its contents to be published on the Web. If you close a database, it will no longer be available to users on the Web.

Creating Layouts

Lasso's **-layout** tag instructs Lasso to look for fields in a specific layout within the FileMaker Pro database file. This tag is not required; if omitted, Lasso looks for fields in Layout 0, an invisible layout that includes all database fields.

Generally speaking, therefore, it isn't usually necessary to create special layouts in your database file before publishing the file on the Web using Lasso. It is necessary, however, if you want to use Lasso's **-layout** tag, which is necessary to accomplish three things:

- You must use the **-layout** tag to specify a layout with a specially formatted field if you want to use special field formatting in a Lasso format file. For example, if you want to display a field as Radio buttons, you must use the **-layout** tag to specify a layout that displays the field as something other than a Standard field.
- You must use the **-layout** tag to specify a layout that contains related fields if you want those fields to appear on a page generated by a format file.
- You can speed up the performance of Lasso by including a **-layout** tag for a layout that includes only the fields needed to display the format file. The performance boost is especially noticeable when displaying only a few fields from a database that has many fields.

Look at your database file and decide which combinations of fields you want to display on your Web pages. If necessary, create the layouts you need, keeping the above information in mind.

TIP

If you've been using the database for a while, it may already have all the layouts you need to publish it on the Web using Lasso. In that case, you don't have to do a thing.

Creating & Saving Format Files

Up to this point, all setup tasks have been relatively simple and straightforward. Now comes the hard part—creating the format files that will make up your Lasso Web publishing solution.

Planning your Strategy

Before you begin churning out format files, take a moment to think about the kinds of format files that you'll need to build your Web publishing solution. Here are some tips:

- Since each format file performs a specific task, it's a good idea to use a task-oriented approach when planning your strategy. Refer to my discussion of format file types earlier in this chapter for ideas.
- Create a graphic representation or flow chart of the way format files will interact with each other (and the database). This will help you organize and link the files.
- Don't forget to create a database Home page that explains what the database is all about and provides links to the appropriate format files that make up your Web publishing solution. This page might also offer links to other pages on your Web site (if applicable) in case visitors change their mind and decide they don't want to access the database after all.

Creating a Project Folder

Although not required, it's a good idea to save all the files related to a specific Web publishing solution into the same folder. This project folder keeps your format files, standard HTML files, images, and database files together. It also keeps your Web server folder neat!

The project folder can be anywhere on the server computer or on any computer accessible via AppleTalk. Unless security is a major concern, you may want to keep the project folder in the Web server folder. I tell you more about security later in this Chapter.

Use relative references in all the links for the format and standard HTML files you create. This makes the project folder portable—you can move it to any server to relocate it or share it with a friend or work associate.

Creating the Format Files

This is where you put your HTML and LDML coding skills to the test. You must create each of the format files that make up your Lasso Web publishing solution and save them into the project folder.

Here are some tips for creating format files:

- Use FM Link, which I discuss in detail earlier in this chapter, to make the task easier.
- Whenever possible, base a new format file on an existing format file that does the same (or almost the same) thing.
- Start with the basics—format files that do the minimum that they need to. Once you get them working properly, add features to your heart's desire.

Lasso Security

Lasso comes with its own security system, which you can configure using the Lasso Security database. Lasso Security offers both field- and record-level security controls over FileMaker Pro databases published with Lasso on an individual user basis.

The Web Security database in FileMaker Pro version 4 is almost identical to the Lasso Security database that comes with Lasso. This is part of the technology that Claris purchased from Blue World. I tell you about Claris's Web Security database in Chapter 3.

In this section, I tell you how to set up Lasso's security system to secure your database files, access secured databases, and handle security "loopholes" that you might encounter.

Setting Up Security

To set up security, you must launch and configure the Lasso Security database. Here are the details.

Locating the Security Files

The security system works with two folders full of files that were installed when you installed Lasso:

- **Lasso Startup Items folder** contains three FileMaker Pro database files that store security settings. Lasso automatically opens these files when it launches and stores their settings in RAM.
- **Security folder** contains a number of preconfigured Lasso format files. Although it isn't necessary to change these files, they must be in the proper location on the Web server for the security system to work properly.

Do not delete or move any of the files within the Security folder.

Opening the Lasso Security Database

The Lasso Security database is a FileMaker Pro file. You set privileges by making or changing entries in the database file.

To set up the Lasso Security database, begin by opening the file named Lasso_Security.fp3. You'll find it in the Lasso Startup Items folder. When opened, it looks like this:

Lasso_Fields.fp3 and Lasso_Users.fp3 are two other files in the Databases folder that are related to Lasso_Security.fp3. It is not necessary to open these files; FileMaker Pro automatically opens and hides them when you open Lasso_Security.fp3. Do not rename, delete, separate, or alter the structure of any of these files.

Lasso_Security.fp3 must be open for Lasso's security system to work.

Reviewing Default Settings

By default, the Lasso Security database is preconfigured with four records:

- **ALL DATABASES** is a special record that defines security settings for all databases that are not recorded by name in the Lasso Security database. It is set so that the user named Admin has all user permissions and there are no field restrictions.
- The other three records provide settings for sample databases that come with Lasso.

The user settings in the All Databases record override any settings for specific databases. Do not create an entry in the All Databases record that gives all permissions to All Users. Doing so will give everyone full access to all databases, leaving all databases completely unprotected!

Specifying an Admin Password

Display the record for All Databases. It should be the first record in Lasso_Security.fp3 file. Click in the Password portal field to the right of the Admin user name. Enter a password for the database administrator. This User Name/Password combination gives complete access to all databases published on the Web using Lasso.

Specifying Settings for a Database Record

Each database that you want to secure must have its own record in the Web Security database.

To create a record for a database, choose New Record from the Mode menu or press Command-N. In the empty record that appears, enter the exact name of the database in the Database Name field at the top of the window.

Defining Names, Passwords, and Permissions

The next step is to enter user names and their corresponding passwords and permissions.

Start by entering a user's name in the first UserName portal field. Then enter that user's password in the Password field beside it. To prevent a Web browser from confusing password characters with special HTML characters, the password should consist of letters, numbers, or a combination of the two; don't use spaces or other characters.

Next, turn on check boxes to specify user security options. There are six check boxes that can be turned on in any combination:

- **ADMIN** establishes the user as the database administrator. This check box overrides all other user privileges and any field restrictions set for the database. It also allows the user to use the Lasso Remote Security Administration feature to change security settings for the database.
- **SEARCH** allows the user to search for and display records.
- **ADD** allows the user to add new records to the database.
- **UPDATE** allows the user to modify existing records, thus updating the database.
- **DELETE** allows the user to delete existing records.
- **SCRIPTS** allows the user to run scripts. This affects scripts that are run automatically as part of a format file or scripts that are run when the user clicks a button or link.

All of these permissions are subject to the field-level or record-level restrictions set on the lower half of the form.

Repeat this process for each user for which you want to enter permissions. Each time you enter a new user name in the User Name portal field, a new related record appears in the portal. To enter permissions for all users who do not have a password, enter All Users in the User Name field, leave the Password field blank, and select the Permissions that you want. When you're finished, the User area of the form might look something like this:

UserName	Password	Permissions
Maria Langer	owner	☒ Admin ☒ Search ☒ Add ☒ Update ☒ Delete ☒ Scripts
John Aabbott	123xyz	☐ Admin ☒ Search ☒ Add ☒ Update ☒ Delete ☒ Scripts
All Users		☐ Admin ☒ Search ☒ Add ☒ Update ☐ Delete ☐ Scripts
		☐ Admin ☐ Search ☐ Add ☐ Update ☐ Delete ☐ Scripts

In case you're wondering, the information you enter into the User Name, Password, and Permissions fields is stored in the Lasso_Users.fp3 file. It is not necessary, however, for you to manually open or edit this file.

Defining Field-Level and Record-Level Security

In the Field area of the form, you define restrictions that limit the uses of specific fields. Start by entering the exact name of the field that you want to restrict in the first Field Name portal field.

Next, use the check boxes to specify the restrictions for that field. Three check boxes provide field-level security:

- **DontShow** prevents the field's contents from appearing.
- **DontSearch** prevents a field from being used to search.
- **ResponseField** allows the field to be used as a response to a Lasso action.

Three check boxes provide record-level security:

- **ExactSearch** prevents records from being retrieved unless the user enters the exact value of this field. This means the user cannot use any operators other than equals (=) in the field.
- **ExactUpdate** prevents a record from being modified unless the user enters the exact value of this field.
- **ExactDelete** prevents a record from being deleted unless the user enters the exact value of this field.

Record-level security restrictions work by forcing the user to provide exactly matching information to search and view, modify, or delete a record. By including a field with a secret number or word and requiring a user to enter a record's word to work with the record, you protect the record.

Repeat this process for each field for which you want to set restrictions. When you're finished, the Field area of the form might look something like this:

Field Name	Restrictions					
Site URL	☐ DontShow	☐ DontSearch	☐ ExactSearch	☐ ExactUpdate	☒ ExactDelete	☐ ResponseField
Solution URL	☐ DontShow	☐ DontSearch	☐ ExactSearch	☒ ExactUpdate	☒ ExactDelete	☐ ResponseField
Webmaster Email	☒ DontShow	☐ DontSearch	☐ ExactSearch	☐ ExactUpdate	☐ ExactDelete	☐ ResponseField
	☐ DontShow	☐ DontSearch	☐ ExactSearch	☐ ExactUpdate	☐ ExactDelete	☐ ResponseField

The information you enter into the Field Name and Restrictions fields is stored in the Lasso_Fields.fp3 file. It is not necessary, however, for you to manually open or edit this file.

Clearing a User or Field Entry

If you want to clear an entire User or Field entry, position the insertion point in any field within that entry and choose Delete Record from the Mode menu or press Command-E. Then click the Related button in the dialog box that appears to remove just that related record.

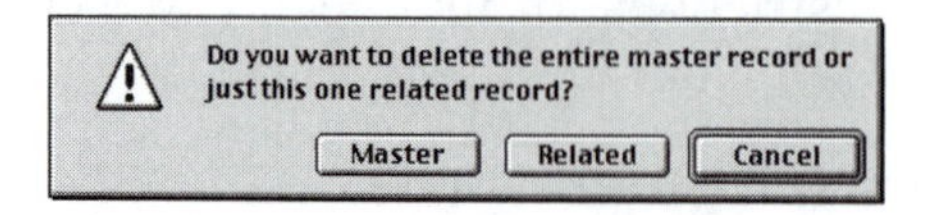

Deleting Settings for an Entire Database

To remove a specific database from the Lasso Security database, display its record and choose Delete Record from the Mode menu or press Command-E. Then click the Delete or Master button in the dialog box that appears to remove the entire record.

Permanently delete this ENTIRE record?

Delete | Cancel

Relaunching the CGI or Server

Changes in the Lasso Security database do not take affect until they are read into Lasso. This means quitting and restarting either the CGI or the server software as follows:

- If you're using the Lasso CGI, quit and relaunch the CGI.
- If you're using the Lasso plug-in, quit and relaunch the Web server software.
- If you're using the Lasso Server application, quit and relaunch Lasso Server.

NOTE

This step is not necessary if you modify the Lasso Security database using the Remote Administration feature. I tell you more about that later in this Chapter.

Creating Custom Security Violation Pages

When a security violation occurs, one of two security violation pages appears:

- DATABASE_VIOLATION.HTML appears when a user attempts to access the database with the wrong User Name or User Password.
- FIELD_VIOLATION.HTML appears when a user attempts to access a field or record protected with Field Restrictions.

You can find both of these files in the Security folder. They're very boring. See for yourself:

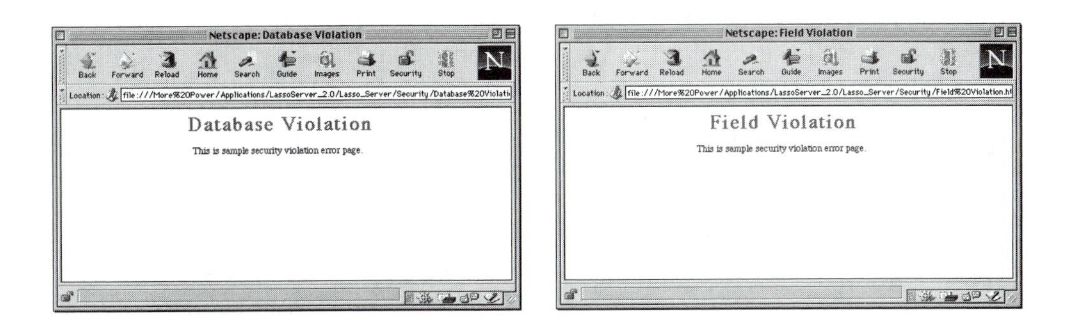

If desired, you can edit the security violation pages to provide more information and instructions to security violators. You can also include graphics and other formatting options so the security violation pages match the appearance of the other pages on your Web site. Since these are standard HTML files, you can edit them with your favorite Web authoring tool or any text editor. Just be sure to save them with the same names in the same location on disk.

Accessing a Secured Database File

When a user attempts to access a secured database file with his browser, a password dialog box appears. How this dialog box looks depends on the browser and operating system. Here are two examples:

Enter Your Name And Password
Enter username for database WEB SOLUTIONS.FP3 at 192.0.1.2:
Name:
Password:
Cancel OK

Enter Network Password
Please enter your authentication information.
Resource: Web Solutions.fp3
User name:
Password:
Save this password in your password list
OK Cancel

WARNING

No password dialog box will appear if there are any settings that allow a user to access the database without a password.

To access the file, the user must enter a name and corresponding password in the appropriate boxes and click OK.

Dealing with Security "Loopholes"

There are two minor security loopholes that can easily be patched—if you know what they are. Here's a quick discussion of each.

- Related fields that appear on layouts and are displayed with format files cannot be protected with the Lasso Security database. Choose or design your layouts carefully!
- A network-savvy hacker can find his way into the Web serving folder. If you're concerned about a user downloading database or format files, keep those files out of the Web serving folder.

TIP

One way to prevent a FileMaker Pro file from being downloaded from a location within the Web server folder is to establish a Web server realm or Web server action to deny serving any files with the .fp3 extension. This is not necessary for Lasso Server, which is internally configured to deny access to .fp3 files.

TIP

Another way to prevent a Lasso format file from being served by Web server software like WebSTAR is to change the file's creator code to WWWΩ *(Ω is the character that is generated by typing Option-Z). You can change a program's creator code with a program like ResEdit or FileTyper.*

Remotely Administering the Lasso Security Database

The Security folder includes a number of format files that enable you to modify the contents of the Lasso Security database from another computer.

Use a Web browser to point to the IP address or domain name of the database Web server, followed by /Security/default.html. The Lasso Security Administration page appears.

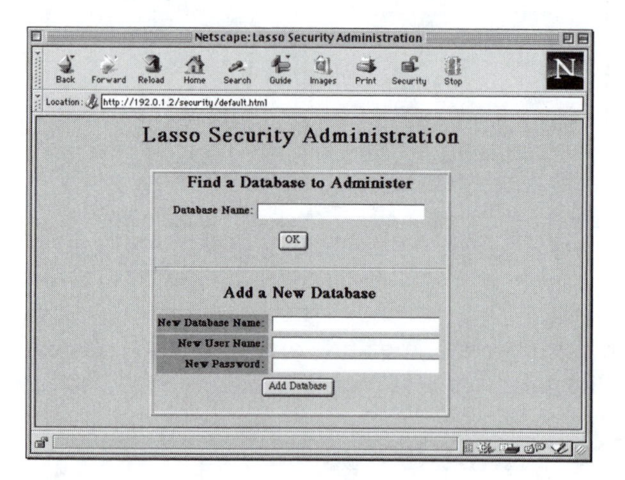

How you proceed depends on what you want to do.

Changing Settings for a Database in the Lasso Security Database

To change the security settings for a database that is already included in the Lasso Security database, enter the name of the database in the Database Name box and click the OK button. If a password prompt appears, enter the name and password for the user with Admin permissions for Lasso_Security.fp3 and click OK. A window like the one below lets you view, change, and add settings for the database.

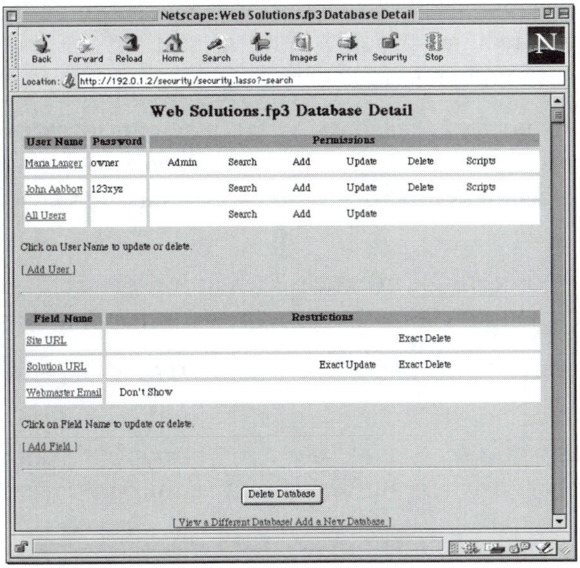

Adding a Database to the Lasso Security Database

To Add a database to the Lasso Security database, enter the Database name and the name and password of the database's administrator in the appropriate edit boxes at the bottom of the Lasso Security Administration page. Click the Add Database button. If a password prompt appears, enter the name and password for the user with Admin permissions for Lasso_Security.fp3 and click OK. The Add Lasso Database Permissions window appears. It confirms that the database has been added and enables you to enter additional permissions for the file.

Accessing & Testing Your Lasso Web Publishing Solution

If you've completed all of the steps in the Step-by-Step Setup section of this chapter, your database is now online. In this section, I tell you how to access your Lasso Web publishing solution so you can test the appearance and functionality of its format files.

Start by launching your Web browser and using it to point to the URL for the database Home page. Then start testing. You'll have to try out all of the links, buttons, and other features that you included in the format files that make up your Web publishing solution. The goal is to make sure everything works the way it should.

Here's a checklist of the kinds of things you should look for:

- Do the pages appear the way they should? Look at text formatting and inserted images to make sure your HTML is correct.
- Are you able to successfully perform searches with the search format file(s) you created? Don't try just one search. Try a bunch. Then try a few with intentional errors (like the accidental errors visitors will make) to see what happens.
- Do search results appear correctly? Check the formatting of listed items. Also check to be sure that the items that should appear do appear.
- Do links from results pages to detail pages work properly? Make sure the correct record appears.
- Are you able to successfully add records with a new format file? Check to make sure that you are warned when any fields that require entry are left blank.
- Are you able to successfully edit records with an edit format file? Make errors on purpose to see what happens.
- Are you able to successfully delete records with a delete format file? Is the correct record deleted?
- Do reply files appear when they should and look the way you intended?

Add items to this list to meet your specific needs. Then check to make sure everything is just the way it should be.

If you find a problem, you have to troubleshoot it. Take each problem you find, one at a time, and think about what could have caused it. Whenever possible, try to narrow down the problem to a possible cause. I like to think that all causes fit into one of three categories:

- **HTML Coding Errors** normally result in formatting problems. Check the HTML code within the format file that created the problem page.
- **LDML Coding Errors** normally result in database communication problems or error messages. Check the LDML tags within the format file that created the problem page.

- **Lasso Setup Errors** normally result in error messages. Check to make sure that Lasso is properly installed and running.

Once you think you've got the problem fixed, access the database as instructed above and check the problem page or function again. If the problem is gone, move on to the next problem.

If a format file doesn't work properly but you have a similar format file that does work properly, compare the code in the two files to see what the differences are. One of those differences could be causing your problem. That's why it's a good idea to collect sample format files, like the ones that come with Lasso.

CHAPTER 6

Tango for FileMaker

Everyware Development Corp.'s Tango for FileMaker products enable you to build database Web publishing solutions for FileMaker Pro version 3 or 4. In this chapter, I tell you about the Tango for FileMaker products, why you might or might not want to use them, and how you set them up. Along the way, I tell you how to use Tango Editor to create query documents that enable interaction between a Web site visitor and a FileMaker Pro database file.

If you're a Windows PC user...

You may notice the lack of Windows instructions and illustrations in this chapter. That's because Tango for FileMaker only works on Mac OS systems. Everyware does, however, develop similar products for use with other database applications on Windows PC systems. Check Everyware's Web site, http://www. everyware.com/ for details.

If you're interested in using Tango with FileMaker Pro, please read on. But be prepared to buy a Mac OS computer if you decide you want to implement a Tango for FileMaker solution for your database Web publishing needs.

NOTE

In this chapter, I work with a file named Web Solutions.fp3, which is a database of Web sites and pages that publish FileMaker Pro databases on the Web using a variety of methods. If you'd like to work with the same file, look for it at http://www.gilesrd.com/fmproweb/.

Overview

Tango for FileMaker (hereafter simply referred to as Tango) enables you to create custom Web publishing solutions for database files. With it, you can display Web pages that enable users to browse, search, create, modify, or delete records in a FileMaker Pro database. Tango gives you a great deal of control over how pages look and interact with the database. It also offers an easy-to-use interface for creating the query documents that enable communication between the Web visitor and FileMaker Pro.

NOTE

Everyware Development's Tango Enterprise for Mac offers the same FileMaker Pro connectivity features as Tango for FileMaker, plus the ability to connect to Everyware's Butler application and other ODBC-compliant databases. It looks and works the same as Tango for FileMaker.

Tango for FileMaker Products

The Tango for FileMaker package has three main components:

- **Tango Server Plug-In** is a WebSTAR API-compatible plug-in that works with Web server software to link FileMaker Pro database files to Web pages. The plug-in's file name is *Tango Server*; if you are using WebSTAR as your Web server, it is automatically installed in the Plug-Ins folder inside the WebSTAR folder.
- **Tango CGI** is an asynchronous CGI that works with Web server software to link FileMaker Pro database files to Web pages. The CGI's file name is *Tango.acgi*; it is automatically installed in the root level of your Web server folder.
- **Tango Editor** is an application that enables you to create Tango query documents. Tango Editor is automatically installed in the root level of your Web server folder.

Although the Tango plug-in and CGI are shipped together in the Tango package, you don't need to use both of them. Instead, choose just one.

What's the difference? Which one should you choose? Well, it's like this: The plug-in loads when you start the Web server software and, in effect, becomes part of the Web server. It's capable of faster data transfer rates and better performance. For this reason, you should use the plug-in version if your Web server software supports WebSTAR plug-ins.

How it Works

Tango displays Web pages that enable users to interact with a FileMaker Pro database file. These Web pages are generated by Tango *query documents*, which include (among other things) HTML and commands called *Tango meta tags*.

Tango Meta Tags Defined

Tango meta tags, which are similar to HTML, are commands that can be interpreted by Tango. They provide the instructions that Tango needs to interact with a FileMaker Pro database. There are 47 of these tags, each designed to perform a specific task. You can find a complete list of them in Appendix D.

Query Documents Defined

A query document is a special type of document file that combines HTML with Tango meta tags and other Tango instructions. Each query document handles a number of operations for interacting with a FileMaker Pro database file, automatically generating a complete series of forms and responses on Web pages.

What I find interesting about query documents is that each one displays several Web pages—not just one. A query document handles all aspects of a logical series of operations. This reduces the amount of logical thinking and planning that you have to do to create a Tango Web publishing solution.

Benefits & Drawbacks

The main benefit of using Tango is its combination of an easy-to-use interface for creating query documents with flexibility. Tango gives you control over most aspects of the appearance, contents, and functionality of the Web pages it displays to visitors. The Tango Editor makes it easy to build query documents that not only handle the display of Web pages, but the underlying logic of branching from page to page. This approach makes it very easy to create custom database Web publishing solutions. In fact, it's possible to create a Tango Web publishing solution without typing a single HTML or Tango meta tag!

Tango does not, however, offer as much power and flexibility as FileMaker Pro version 4's Web Companion or Blue World Communication's Lasso, which I discuss in Chapters 2 and 5. These two products have nearly twice the number of commands and enable you to create completely custom solutions. In addition, although using the Tango Editor's builders for creating query documents is relatively straightforward and easy to understand, editing query documents without the builders to provide additional HTML and Tango meta tag instructions can be downright baffling. Unfortunately, this is the best way to tap into the underlying power of Tango.

A Closer Look at Query Documents

Tango query documents, which can only be created or modified with Tango Editor, perform several functions:

- Provide a framework for the appearance of Web pages generated by Tango to display forms for interacting with a database file or information from a database file.
- Provide instructions that can be interpreted by Tango to perform specific tasks with a database file.
- Provide instructions that can be interpreted by Tango to branch logically from one Web page to another.

Query documents do this by combining text, standard HTML tags, and Tango meta tags. These components are written by Tango Editor when you select options, drag fields, or enter additional HTML or Tango meta tags within Tango Editor windows and dialog boxes.

Types of Query Documents

There are two main types of query documents:

- **Search Query Documents** enable a Web site visitor to enter database criteria on a search form. When the form is processed, the search query document displays a record list page that displays all of the found records in a list layout. Clicking a hyperlink for one of the records displays a record detail page which can enable the user to modify one or more record fields. The search query document includes HTML and Tango meta tags for generating all three Web pages—search form, record list page, and record detail page—as well as other instructions for branching from page to page and handling errors.
- **New Record Query Documents** enable a Web site visitor to enter information to create a new record. The new record query document includes HTML and Tango meta tags for generating the new record entry page and response page, as well as other instructions for branching from page to page and handling errors.

Within each type of query document, you can specify fields, formatting information, and interaction instructions that define the appearance and functionality of the Web pages that Tango creates.

Query Document Contents

Although the Tango Editor can automatically assemble query document components, it's a good idea to know what they are, especially if you plan to edit them.

Each query document contains a number of instructions called *actions*. Some actions, in turn, can include *action attributes*, which provide further information about how the actions work.

Tango Actions

Each Tango action performs a specific function that enables interaction between a user and a FileMaker Pro database. There are two types of actions: *database actions* and *other actions*.

Database actions perform specific functions on database records. There are four database actions:

- SEARCH enables the user to enter criteria and search for records.
- INSERT enables the user to enter information that is added to the database as a new record.
- UPDATE enables the user to change existing values for a database record.
- DELETE enables the user to delete database records.

Other actions handle the flow of Tango-generated Web pages and display information. There are five other actions:

- APPLE EVENT sends an Apple Event to another application and retrieves the results.
- BRANCH uses a comparison to determine which action to perform next.
- DIRECT TO DATABASE runs a FileMaker Pro scriptmaker script.
- STOP ends the execution of the query document and sends generated HTML to the Web server.
- NO OPERATION performs no action, but enables you to display HTML documents or assign values to global variables.

Action Attributes

An action attribute is a set of additional instructions that can be included as part of a Tango action. Action attributes usually include HTML, Tango meta tags, or both.

There are five possible action attributes:

- **Results HTML** is an HTML document that displays a query action's results when data is returned. An example is a Web page that appears when items are found as a result of a search action.
- **No Results HTML** is an HTML document that displays a query action's results when no data is returned. An example is a Web page that appears when no items are found as a result of a search action.
- **Error HTML** is an HTML document that appears when Tango encounters an error while processing a query document.
- **Global Assignments** enable you to assign specific values to global variables used in the Tango query document.
- **Data Source** enables you to specify a data source (or FileMaker Pro database) for a specific action. This enables you to perform an action with a different data source than the one used for the rest of the query document.

A Closer Look at Tango Meta Tags

Tango meta tags enable communication between the user and Tango, which in turn, communicates with FileMaker Pro database files. Tango Editor automatically inserts meta tags into query documents when you use Tango Editor's builders. If desired, you can further customize the appearance and functionality of the Web pages Tango generates by manually inserting meta tags into query documents using Tango Editor's query editing capabilities.

Tango version 2.1 includes 47 meta tags. Here's a quick list of them. Tags that include an ellipsis (...) require additional information, such as a text string, file name or path, URL, item name, or parameter.

<@ABSROW>
<@ACTIONRESULT ...>
<@ASCII ...>
<@CALC ...>
<@CGI>
<@CHAR ...>
<@CGIPARAM ...>
<@CGIPATH>
<@COL ...>
<@COLUMN ...>
<@CURRENTDATE>
<@CURRENTTIME>
<@CURRENTTIMESTAMP>
<@CURROW>
<@DBMS>
<@LOCATE ...>
<@LOWER ...>
<@LTRIM ...>
<@MAXROWS>
<@NUMROWS>
<@OMIT ...>
<@POSTARG ...>
<@QUERYDOC>
<@QUERYPATH>
<@RANDOM ...>
<@RESULTS>
<@ROWS> ... </@ROWS>
<@RTRIM ...>
<@SEARCHARG ...>
<@STARTROW>

```
<@ERROR ...>
<@ERRORS> ... </@ERRORS>
<@GLOBAL ...>
<@IF ...> ... [<@ELSE> ... ] </@IF>
<@IFEMPTY ...> ... [<@ELSE> ... ] </@IF>
<@IFEQUAL ...> ... [<@ELSE> ... ] </@IF>
<@INCLUDE ...>
<@KEEP ...>
<@LENGTH ...>
<@TOTALROWS>
<@TRIM ...>
<@UPPER ...>
<@URLENCODE ...>
<@USERREFERENCE>
<@USERREFERENCEARGUMENT>
<@USERREFERENCECOOKIE>
<@VERSION>
```

TIP

You may notice that there is no meta tag for fields. That's because Tango refers to fields as columns. To display the contents of a field, you use the **<@COLUMN ...>** *tag.*

Using Tango Editor to Create Query Documents

Tango Editor offers two ways to create Tango query documents:

- **Query Document Builder** offers an easy to use, graphic user interface for creating both types of query documents. You specify fields and interaction options in a query builder file, then tell Tango Editor to build the query document with all of the necessary components. This is the easiest way to create query documents.
- **Query Document Editor** enables you to open a query document and edit its actions and action attributes. It also offers a graphic user interface, but to use it, you must have a good understanding of Tango's actions, attributes, and meta tags. This is the best way to add features to a Tango Web publishing solution that go beyond the features offered by the query document builder.

In this section, I provide step-by-step instructions for using Tango Editor to create a search query document and a new record query document using the query document builder. I also show you how to open and examine the contents of query documents using Tango Editor's query document editor.

Starting Tango Editor

Locate and double-click the Tango Editor application icon. The Tango Editor splash screen appears briefly and Tango is ready to use.

If you have never used Tango before, a serial number dialog box like the one below appears. Enter your Tango Editor serial number and click OK. If you don't have a serial number, you can click the Test Drive! button to use Tango Editor for up to two hours.

Please enter your Tango Editor serial number:

Test Drive! Cancel OK

Setting Tango Editor Options

The first time you use Tango, it's a good idea to set several options that will affect the query documents you create. These fall into two categories: preferences, which you'll probably set just once, and data sources, which you might modify each time you create a new Web publishing solution.

Setting Preferences

Choose Preferences from the Edit menu.

The Preferences dialog box appears. You can use it to change a number of options that affect the way Tango Editor creates query documents and displays HTML on screen.

Preferences

WWW Server Address:
The address of your Web server (e.g.: www.everyware.com)
www.yourserver.com

CGI Calling Method:
Normal
Tango CGI path relative to the Web server root directory (e.g.: /Tango/Tango.acgi):
/Tango/Tango.acgi
Action/Plug-In
Action suffix (e.g.: qry): qry
Display URLs for generated query documents

HTML/SQL Editing Font:
Font: Geneva Size: 9

Cancel OK

It's vital that the following preferences are properly set for your system and Web publishing solution:

- **WWW Server Address** is the address of your Web server. Enter the URL for your Web server. It can be a domain name (such as www.peachpit.com) or an IP address (such as 192.0.1.2).
- **CGI Calling Method** is the method in which actions are directed to Tango. If you're using the Tango CGI, select the Normal radio button and enter the path from the Web server's root directory to the Tango.acgi file. If you're using the Tango Server plug-in, select the Action/Plug-In radio button and make sure the Action suffix edit box contains qry.

The other options are not as important. You can leave them set as is.

When you're finished setting your preferences, click the OK button to dismiss the preferences dialog box and save your settings.

Selecting Data Sources

A data source is the FileMaker Pro database with which the query document will interact. To create a query document with the Tango Editor, you must first specify its data source in the Data Sources dialog box.

Begin by choosing Data Sources from the Edit menu.

The Data Sources dialog box appears. It lists all of the data sources that you have previously selected. If you haven't selected any yet, it looks like this:

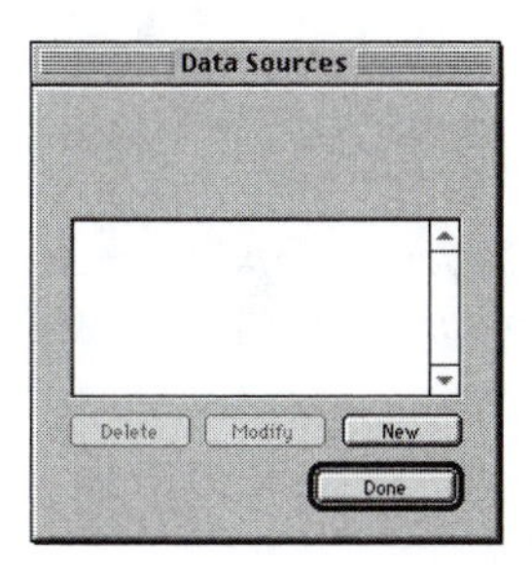

To add a data source to the Data Sources list, click the New button. The FileMaker Application dialog box appears.

FileMaker Application

Any FileMaker application
Named FileMaker application: Choose...
Networked FileMaker application: Choose...
Zone:
Machine:
FileMaker:
Cancel OK

Select one of its radio buttons to specify the copy of FileMaker Pro with which you want to open the data source database:

- **ANY FILEMAKER APPLICATION** opens the data source with the first copy of FileMaker Pro that Tango Editor finds.
- **NAMED FILEMAKER APPLICATION** opens the data source with a specific copy of FileMaker Pro. If you select this option, you must click the Choose button and use the Open dialog box that appears to locate and select a specific copy of FileMaker Pro. Then click Open to accept your selection.
- **NETWORKED FILEMAKER APPLICATION** opens the data source with a copy of FileMaker Pro that is accessible over the network. If you select this option, you must click the Choose button and use the dialog box that appears to select the Macintosh and Program to which you want to link. Then click OK to accept your selections.

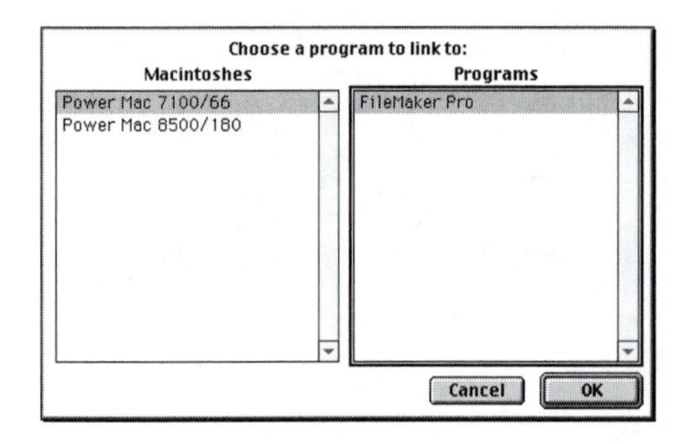

Program Linking must be turned on in the File Sharing control panel of the host computer to open a data source with a copy of FileMaker Pro on that computer.

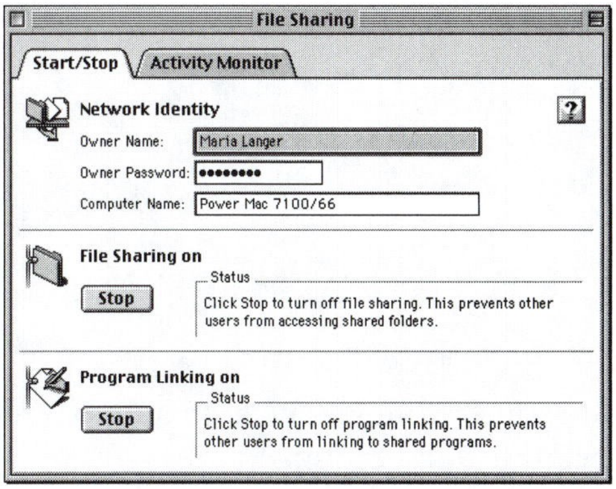

Click OK in the FileMaker Applications dialog box to accept your settings and dismiss the dialog box. The Opened Databases dialog box appears next. It lists all of the opened database files.

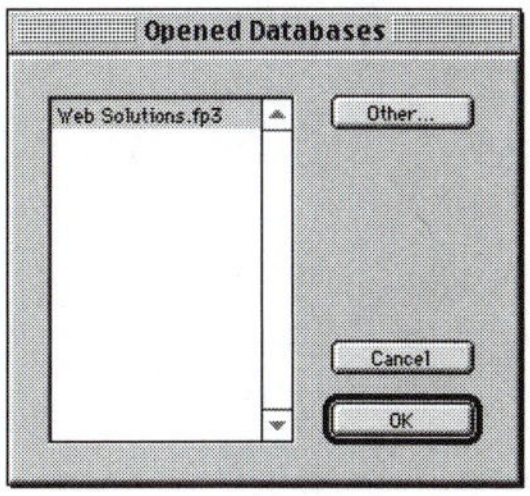

To display another database in the dialog box, click the Other button. Then use the Open dialog box that appears to locate and open the database that you want to display. It appears in the list.

To use an open database as a data source, select its name in the list and click OK. The Modify Data Source dialog box appears next. The only change you can make is to the name of the data source, which, by default, is the same as the database.

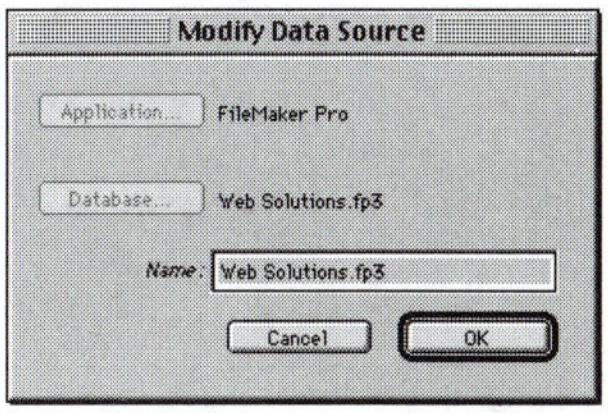

Make changes as desired, then click the OK button. The name of the data source appears in the Data Sources window.

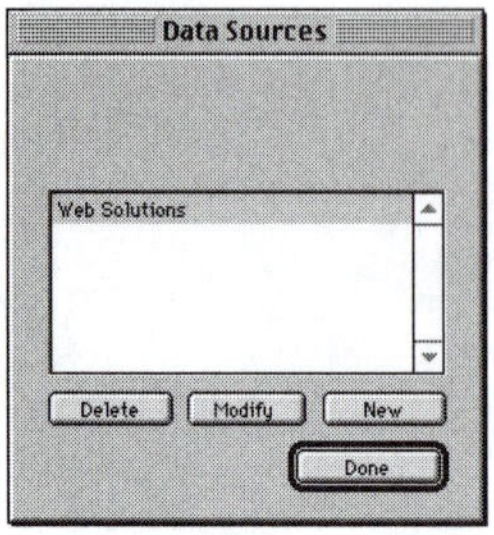

You can repeat these steps for each data source that you want to add to the Data Sources list. When you're finished, click the Done button.

Creating a Query Builder File

As I mention earlier in this chapter, query builder files offer the easiest way to create query documents. To create a query builder file, select New from the File menu or press Command-N.

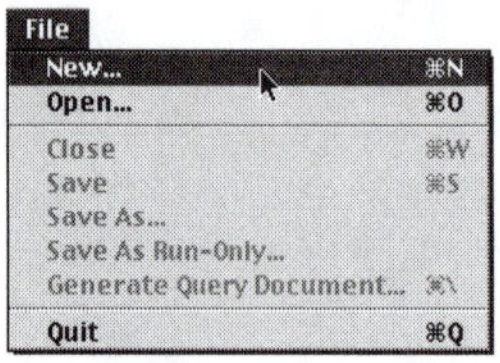

The New Document dialog box appears.

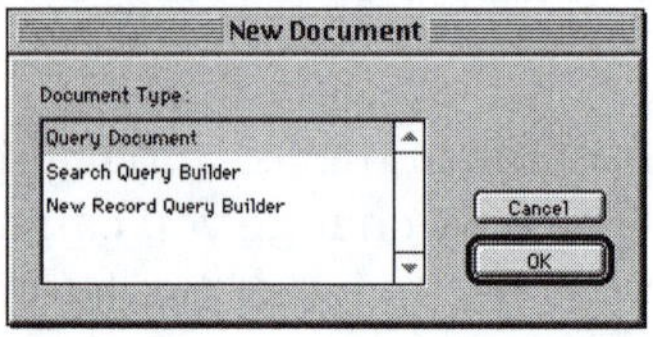

Specifying the Type of File

The New Document dialog box offers three options.

- To build a query document from scratch (without using the builder), select Query Document.
- To build a search query builder file, select Search Query Builder.
- To build a new record query builder file, select New Record Query Builder.

If you want to follow along with me, select Search Query Builder because that's the first type of query builder file I show you. Then click OK.

Selecting the Data Source

The Data Source Selection dialog box appears next. It should list all of the data sources you selected earlier.

Click the name of the data source that you want to use to select it. If the database is password protected, enter its password in the Password edit box; otherwise, leave the box blank. Then click OK.

A Database palette and an Untitled Builder window appear. They should look something like this:

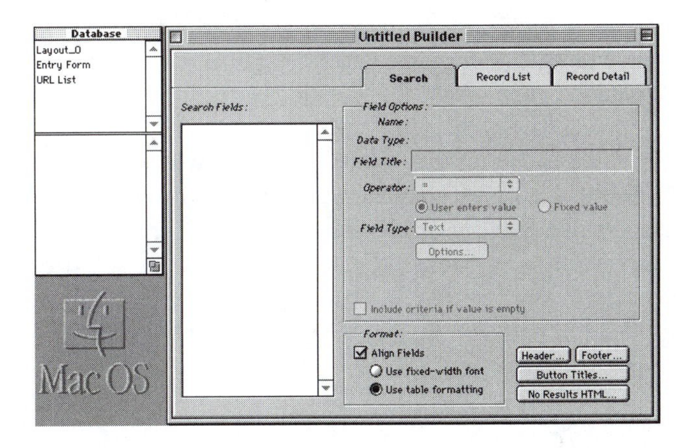

Saving the File

At this point, it's a good idea to save the file. Choose Save As from the File menu and use the Save As dialog box that appears to save the file.

TIP

You may want to include a three-character file extension to help identify the type of builder file. If so, use .sbd for a search builder document and .nbd for a new record builder document.

TIP

Once you've saved the file, you can use the Command-S shortcut to save the builder file after each of the following sections.

Using the Database Palette

The Database palette displays all of the layouts in your database, including Layout_0, an invisible layout that includes all database fields. When you select one of the layouts, a list of that layout's fields appears in the bottom half of the palette.

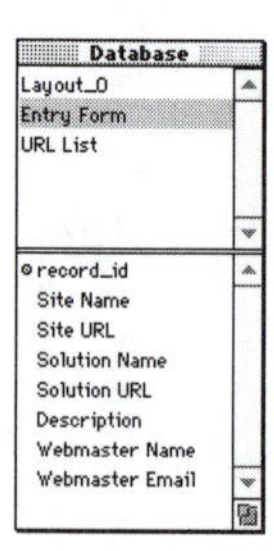

NOTE

The field name with a blue bullet beside it is the one that is unique for every record in the database. Tango refers to this as the Record Identifier. *In most cases, this will be the invisible record_id field.*

To use the Database palette, select the layout containing the field that you want to use, then drag the field from the palette to the appropriate builder or editor list window. You can drag fields in the order in which you want them to appear or drag them into specific locations on the list. You can even drag to change the order of fields that are already in the list. If you change your mind about a field you added to the list, click it once to select it, press the Delete key, and click OK in the delete confirmation dialog box that appears. It's as simple as that.

Specifying Search Options

The first part of a search query builder file is the Search tab, which is illustrated on the previous page. You use it to specify fields and options for a search form.

Specifying Fields

Start by dragging the fields that you want to appear on the search form from the Database palette to the Search Fields list box as I explain above. When you're finished, the Search tab might look something like this:

Setting Field Options

For each field, you can specify a number of options that vary slightly depending on the type of field. To set a field's options, begin by clicking its name to select it. Then set field options as follows:

- **Field Title** is the text that identifies the field on the Web page. You can change it to anything you like, but you should make sure it's something that adequately identifies the field to the user.
- **Operator** is the search operator used in the search form. Select an option from the pop-up menu. To enable the user to select the operator, choose User Enters.

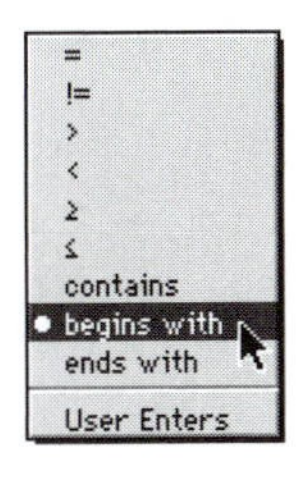

TIP

If you choose any of the first six operators—= (equals), != (does not equal), > (greater than), > (less than), ≥ (greater than or equal to), or ≤ (less than or equal to)—you can use the Include criteria if value is empty check box to determine whether the field should be included in the search criteria even if it is empty.

- **User enters value**, when selected, allows the user to enter a value in the search field. (This is the default selection.) It offers the following additional options:

  - **Field Type** determines the appearance of the field. Use the pop-up menu to make your choice. The default option is Text.

    If you choose Pop-up Menu, Selection List, or Radio Buttons, the Description Values dialog box automatically appears. Use it to specify the options that should appear and the option selected by default (if any). When you're finished adding option names and values, click OK.

    If you choose Checkbox, the Description Values dialog box also automatically appears, although it looks different. Use it to specify the field's value if the check box is selected and to specify whether the check box should be selected by default. When you're satisfied with your settings, click OK.

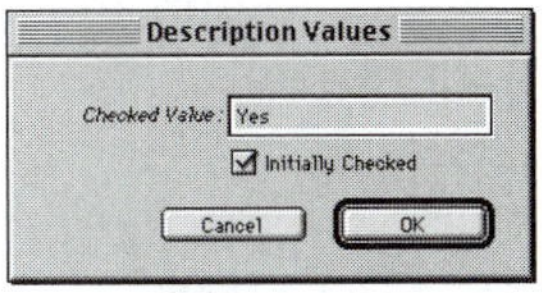

- **OPTIONS** displays the Description Attributes or Description Values (see above) dialog box. Use the Description Attributes dialog box to enter a default value for the field; specify the field width, maximum length, and height; and indicate whether the field should appear as a scrolling field. When you're satisfied with your settings, click OK.

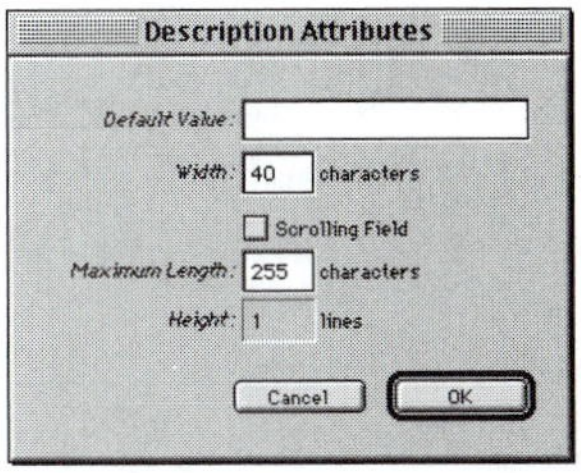

◉ **FIXED VALUE** lets you specify a value that should automatically appear in the field on the search form. When you select this radio button, the Field Options area changes to offer different options.

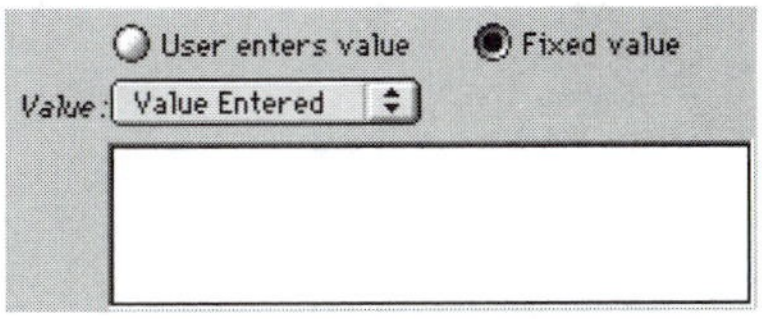

- **VALUE** is a pop-up menu that you can use to select one of a dozen or so values obtained by Tango from the Web server. To enter a specific value, choose Value Entered, which is the default choice.

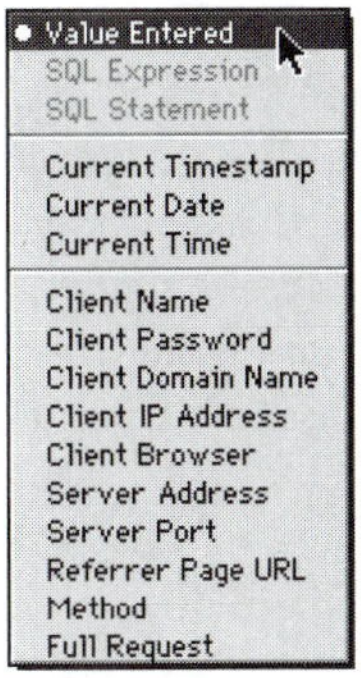

- If you choose Value Entered from the Value pop-up menu, enter the value in the edit box beneath the menu.

Setting Format Options

You can use the Format area of the Search tab to select search form formatting options. If you turn on the Align Fields check box (which is turned on by default), you can select a radio button to specify whether the fields should be aligned using a fixed-width font or table formatting (which is selected by default).

Specifying a Header or Footer

If desired, you can further customize the search page by including information above or below the search form fields and buttons. Click the Header (for before) or Footer (for after) button. The Header HTML or Footer HTML dialog box appears.

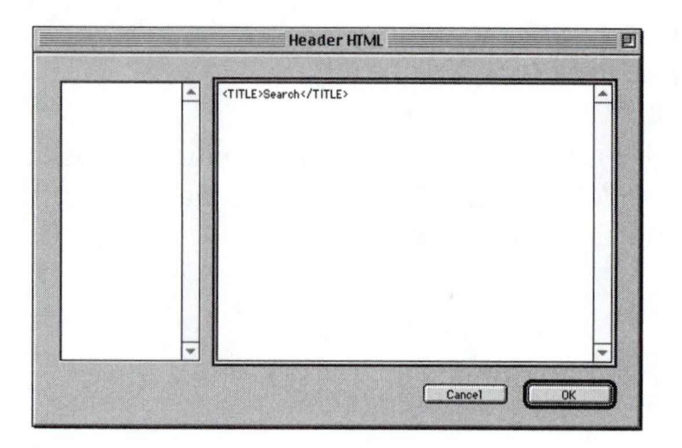

Enter the HTML for the header or footer of the document. You can include just about any HTML tags you like to insert formatted text, horizontal rules, images, Java Applets, or other HTML elements. You can also use Tango meta tags to include information from the database or Web server. When you're finished, click OK.

TIP

You can use the HTML Snippets command under the Edit menu to build a library of HTML and Tango meta tags to use in headers and footers. These tags appear in a list on the left side of HTML editing dialog boxes (such as the Header HTML, Footer HTML and No Results HTML dialog boxes) and can be dragged into position in the HTML editing window. This makes it quicker and easier to compose headers and footers and to keep their contents consistent from one page to another.

Setting Button Titles

To change the text that appears on search form buttons, click the Button Titles button. The Button Titles dialog box appears.

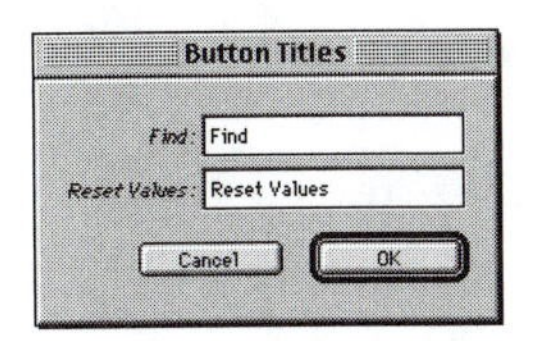

Enter the text that you want to appear on each button and click OK.

Customizing the No Results HTML

You can also customize the Web page that appears when no records match the user's entered search criteria. To do so, click the No Results HTML button. The No Results HTML dialog box appears.

Edit the contents of the large scrolling list to include whatever HTML you want to display. When you're finished, click OK.

Specifying Record List Options

The next step to creating a search query builder file is to specify the fields and options for the record list page that appears to display the results of a search. You do this on the Record List tab of the search query builder dialog box.

Specifying Fields and Sort Order

Start by dragging the fields that you want to appear on the record list from the Database palette to the Display Fields list box. I provide instructions for dragging fields in the Using the Database Palette section a little earlier in this chapter.

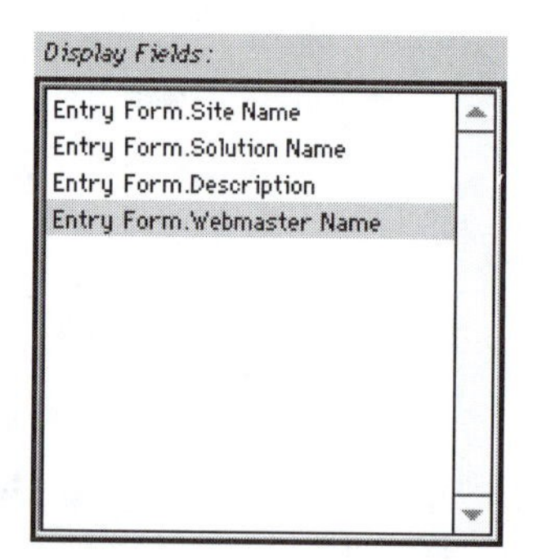

Next, drag the field(s) by which you want to sort records from the Database palette to the Order By list box. If desired, click the triangle to the left of the field name to change the sort order from ascending (the default) to descending.

Setting Field Options

For each field, you can set a variety of options that affect the way the field appears and functions. To set a field's options, begin by clicking its name to select it. Then set field options as follows:

- FIELD CONTAINS HTML, when turned on, tells Tango to interpret the field's contents as HTML rather than plain text.
- LINK TO RECORD DETAIL, when turned on, turns the field into a hyperlink to the Record Detail page.
- FIELD TITLE is the text that identifies the field on the Web page. You can change it to anything you like, but you should make sure it's something that adequately identifies the field to the user.

Setting Maximum Matches Options

You can also specify the maximum number of matches that appear on a record list page.

- To limit the number of matches, select the Limit To radio button (which is selected by default) and enter or edit the number of records to display in the edit box beside it. You can then toggle the Show Multiple Pages If Limit Exceeded check box to determine whether excess matches should be displayed on linked pages.
- To allow all matches to display, select the No Maximum radio button.

Setting Format Options

Tango Editor's builder offers two formats for record list pages:

- STANDARD displays the search results with each field on a new line. You can click the Options button to set other formatting options in the Standard Options dialog box:
    - SHOW COLUMN TITLES displays field names. This option is turned on by default.
    - HORIZONTAL RULE BETWEEN RECORDS displays a horizontal rule between each record's group of fields. This option is also turned on by default.

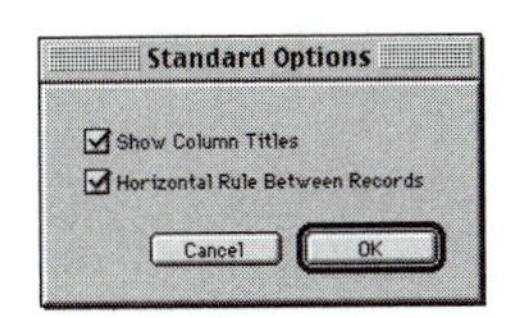

- **TABLE**, which is the default selection, displays the search results in a table, with each record in a different row. You can click the Options button to set other formatting options in the Table Options dialog box:
  - **HEADER ROW** puts the field names in a row at the top of the table. This option is turned on by default.
  - **TABLE BORDER WIDTH** lets you choose the width of the table's border from a pop-up menu. The default choice is 1.

Specifying a Header or Footer

If desired, you can further customize the record list page by including information above or below the search form fields and buttons. Click the Header (for before) or Footer (for after) button. The Header HTML or Footer HTML dialog box appears. I explain how to enter HTML in this dialog box a little earlier in this chapter.

Specifying Record Detail Options

The last step to creating a search query builder file is to specify the fields and options for the record detail page that appears when the user clicks a link on the record list page. You do this on the Record Detail tab of the search query builder dialog box.

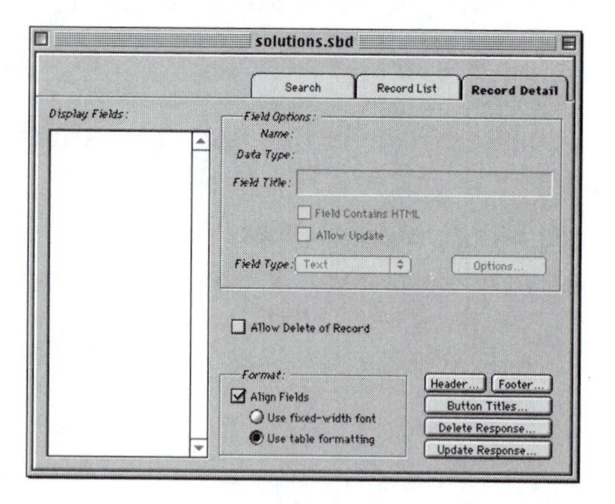

Specifying Fields

Start by dragging the fields that you want to appear on the record detail page from the Database palette to the Display Fields list box. I provide instructions for dragging fields in the Using the Database Palette section a little earlier in this chapter.

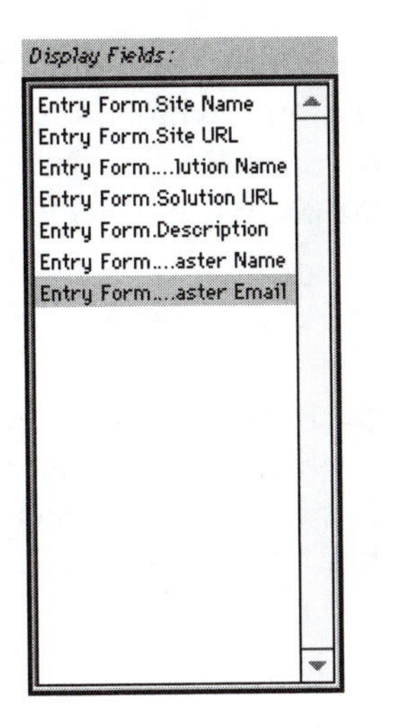

Setting Field Options

For each field, you can set a variety of options that affect the way the field appears and functions. To set a field's options, begin by clicking its name to select it. Then set field options as follows:

- FIELD TITLE is the text that identifies the field on the Web page. You can change it to anything you like, but you should make sure it's something that adequately identifies the field to the user.
- FIELD CONTAINS HTML, when turned on, tells Tango to interpret the field's contents as HTML rather than plain text.
- ALLOW UPDATE, when turned on, enables the user to change the field's contents. It also puts an update button on the page to process an update request, thus changing the record. If you turn on the Allow Update check box, the Field Type pop-up menu and Options button beneath it can be used. They work just like the Field Type pop-up menu and Options button I discuss in the Specifying Search Options section earlier in this chapter.

Allowing a Record to be Deleted

If you want the user to be able to delete a record, turn on the Allow Delete of Record check box. This puts a Delete button on the Record Detail page. Clicking the button deletes the record.

Setting Format Options

You can use the Format area of the Record Detail tab to select record detail page formatting options. If you turn on the Align Fields check box (which is turned on by default), you can select a radio button to specify whether the fields should be aligned using a fixed-width font or table formatting (which is selected by default).

Specifying a Header or Footer

If desired, you can further customize the record detail page by including information above or below the search form fields and buttons. Click the Header (for before) or Footer (for after) button. The Header HTML or Footer HTML dialog box appears. I explain how to enter HTML in this dialog box a little earlier in this chapter.

Setting Button Titles

To change the text that appears on record detail form buttons, click the Button Titles button. The Button Titles dialog box appears.

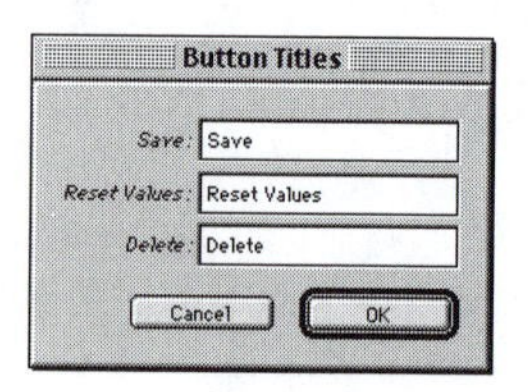

Enter the text that you want to appear on each button and click OK.

Customizing the Delete Response and Update Response Pages

You can also customize the Web pages that appear when a user deletes or updates a record. To do so, click the Delete Response or Update Response button. The Delete Response HTML or Update Response HTML dialog box appears.

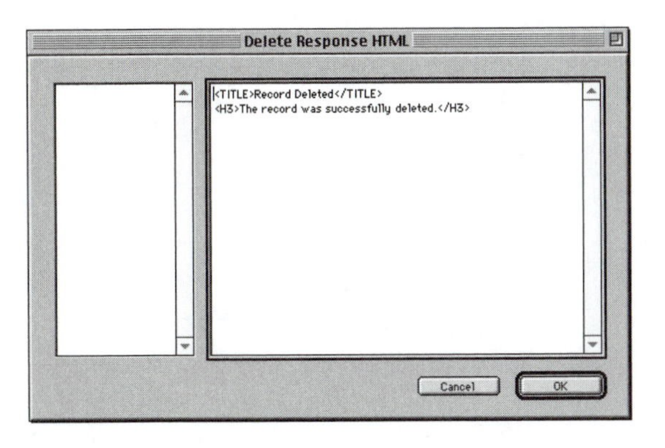

Edit the contents of the large scrolling list to include whatever HTML you want to display. When you're finished, click OK.

If you do not allow users to update records, you do not need to display (or edit) the update response page. The same is true for the delete response page if you do not allow users to delete records.

Specifying New Record Options

When you select New Record Query Builder in the New Document dialog box and specify a data source as instructed earlier in this chapter, the New Record Query dialog box appears. You use this dialog box to create a new record query builder file by specifying fields and setting options.

Specifying Fields

Start by dragging the fields that you want to appear on the new record page from the Database palette to the Fields list box. I provide instructions for dragging fields in the Using the Database Palette section a little earlier in this chapter.

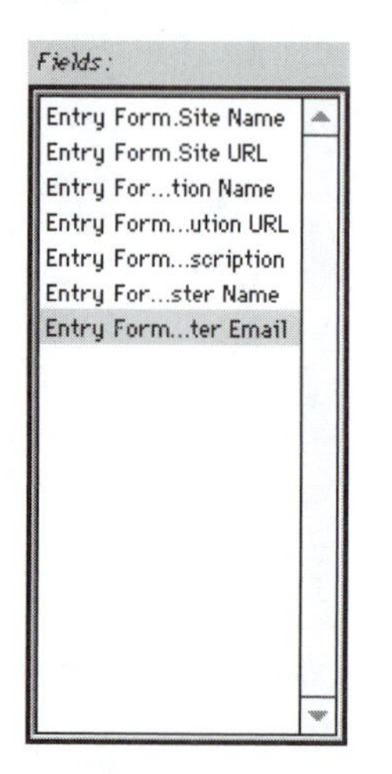

Setting Field Options

For each field, you can set a variety of options that affect the way the field appears and functions. To set a field's options, begin by clicking its name to select it. Then set field options as follows:

- FIELD TITLE is the text that identifies the field on the Web page. You can change it to anything you like, but you should make sure it's something that adequately identifies the field to the user.
- VALUE radio buttons let you specify whether the user should enter the value or you provide a fixed value. I explain these options and the additional options related to each in the Specifying Search Options section earlier in this chapter.
- REQUIRED, when turned on, requires the user to enter a value in the field.

Setting Format Options

You can set new record page formatting options in the Format areas. If you turn on the Align Fields check box (which is turned on by default), you can select a radio button to specify whether the fields should be aligned using a fixed-width font or table formatting (which is selected by default).

Specifying a Header or Footer

If desired, you can further customize the record detail page by including information above or below the search form fields and buttons. Click the Header (for before) or Footer (for after) button. The Header HTML or Footer HTML dialog box appears. I explain how to enter HTML in this dialog box a little earlier in this chapter.

Setting Button Titles

To change the text that appears on new record form buttons, click the Button Titles button. The Button Titles dialog box appears.

Enter the text that you want to appear on each button and click OK.

Customizing the New Record Response Page

You can also customize the Web page that appears when a user adds a record. To do so, click the New Record Response button. The New Record Response HTML dialog box appears.

Edit the contents of the large scrolling list to include whatever HTML you want to display. If desired, you can include fields listed on the left side of the dialog box by dragging them into the HTML. This inserts Tango meta tags that display field contents. When you're finished, click OK.

Generating a Query Document

Creating a search query builder file or new record query builder file isn't the same as creating a search query document or new record query document. Builder files are in a special format that enables you to edit them with the builder's interface. To use the options you selected with Tango, you must generate a regular query document file.

Fortunately, generating a query document is both fast and easy. Start by activating the window containing the builder file on which you want to base the query document. Then choose Generate Query Document from the File menu or press Command-\.

A Save As dialog box appears. Use it to name and save the query document.

If using the Tango Server plug-in, be sure to name the query document with the .qry extension; otherwise, your Web server may not recognize it as a Tango query document.

When you click the Save button, a dialog box like the one below may appear (this depends on whether the Display URLs for generated query documents check box is turned on in the Preferences dialog box).

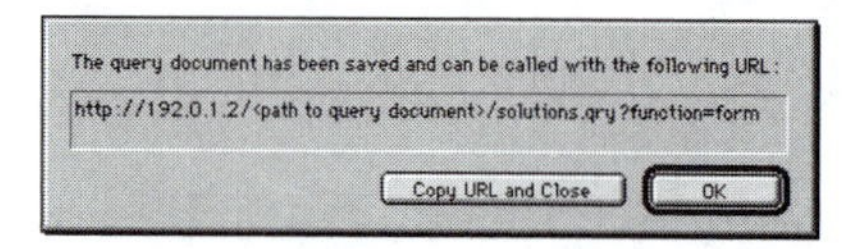

- To copy the URL to the clipboard and close the dialog box, click the Copy URL and Close button.
- To simply dismiss the dialog box, click OK.

If you copy the URL to the Clipboard, you can paste it into the location box of a Web browser, provide missing path information, and press Return to view the first Web page displayed by the query document. I tell you more about testing Tango Web publishing solutions near the end of this chapter.

Working with the Query Document Editor

Tango Editor also enables you to open existing query documents for editing or create new query documents without the builder. In each case, you work with the query document in the query document editor.

I don't provide detailed instructions for using the query document editor. If I did, I wouldn't have much room to discuss anything else. The query builder I discuss earlier in this section is enough to get you started creating Tango query documents. You can explore the query document editor on your own.

Creating a New Query Document

Choose New from the File menu. In the New Document dialog box that appears, select Query Document and click OK.

A Data Source Selection dialog box appears next. Use it to select the default data source for the query document and click OK. An Actions palette and untitled query window appear.

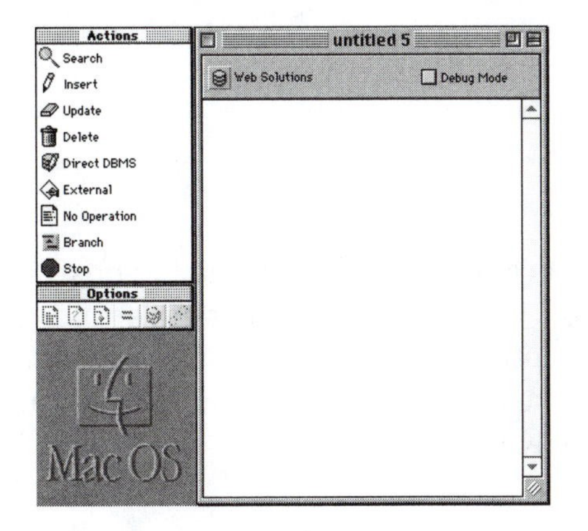

To create a query document from scratch, drag actions from the Actions palette to the query document window. If necessary, double-click actions in the query document window to display and edit options. You can also click buttons on the Options palette or choose commands from the Options menu to specify attributes for a selected action. When you're finished, choose Save As from the File menu to save the query document and it's ready to use.

TIP

If you do decide to build a query document from scratch, base it on an existing query document. This will help ensure that your new query document includes all necessary components.

Opening an Existing Query Document

Choose Open from the File menu or press Command-O.

File
New... ⌘N
Open... ⌘O
Close ⌘W
Save ⌘S
Save As...
Save As Run-Only...
Generate Query Document... ⌘\
Quit ⌘Q

Use the Open dialog box that appears to locate and open the query document with which you want to work. It appears in the query document window.

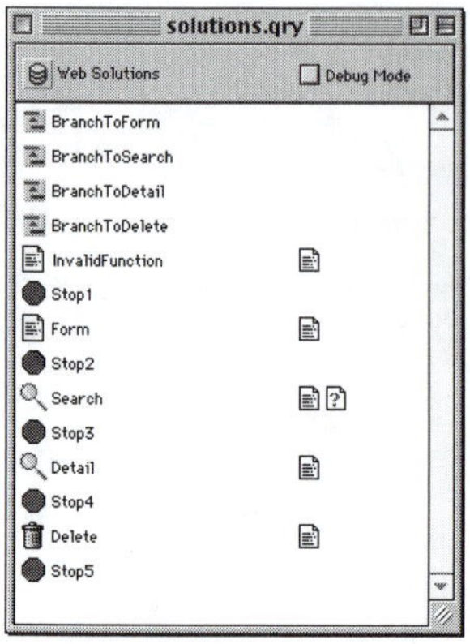

To edit query document actions, double-click them and use the dialog boxes that appear to enter or change options. You can also select an action and then choose one of the commands under the Options menu to edit an action's attributes. When you're finished, choose Save from the File menu or press Command–S. The query document is ready to use.

Step-by-Step Setup

Ready to try building your own Tango Web publishing solution? Here are the steps you'll need to follow to get your database online with Tango.

Installing Tango

Before your files can be published on the Web, you must install Tango.

TIP

You only need to follow these steps once, no matter how many databases you publish.

Installing Tango Components

If necessary, quit your Web server application. Launch the TangoFM Installer application on the Tango CD. Use the Easy Install option to install Tango components. If StarNine's WebSTAR software is installed, Tango is automatically installed in the WebSTAR folder. If desired, you can use the Install Location pop-up menu to select a different disk or folder. When the installation process is finished, restart your computer.

Entering the Tango Serial Number

Locate and double-click the Tango.acgi application icon. A serial number dialog box appears.

Please enter your Tango serial number:

Test Drive! | Cancel | OK

Enter your Tango Server serial number and click OK. If you plan to use the Tango Server plug-in, choose Quit from the File menu to quit the Tango CGI. Otherwise, leave the Tango CGI running.

If you don't register the Tango Server plug-in by launching the Tango CGI, the plug-in runs in test drive mode.

About Test Drive Mode

If you do not have a Tango serial number, you'll have to use Tango in Test Drive mode. Click the Test Drive! button when prompted for a serial number. Tango will process requests for only two hours before it must be restarted. For obvious reasons, this is not the best way to use Tango.

Launching the Web Server

To use the Tango Server plug-in or CGI, your Web server software must be running. If it is not already running, launch it. If you're using the Tango Server plug-in, it will load into the Web server so it's ready to use.

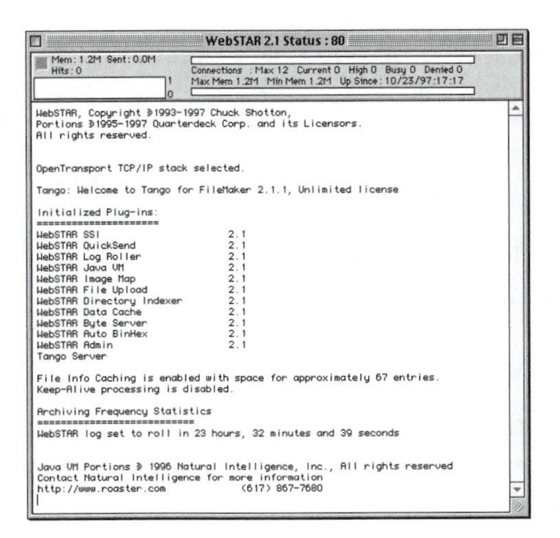

Opening the Data Source

If you haven't already opened the database that you want to publish, now's the time. Double-click the database's document icon or choose Open from FileMaker Pro's File menu and use the Open dialog box that appears to locate and open the database file.

WARNING

The database must be open for its contents to be published on the Web. If you close a database, it will no longer be available to users.

Creating & Saving Query Documents

Use Tango Editor to create the query documents that make up your Web publishing solution. I discuss using Tango Editor in detail earlier in this chapter. When you're finished creating the query documents, save them somewhere within your Web serving folder.

TIP

I recommend that you depend on the query builder feature to create your query documents until you're familiar with the way Tango query documents work. Then use the query editing feature to fine-tune and add features to your query documents, thus expanding the capabilities of your Web publishing solution.

Adding a Link to a Query Document on another Web Page

To access a Tango query document, you must include a link to the query document on a Web page. This is done by referencing the document's URL as follows:

http://*web address/path to query document/*querydocument.qry?function=form

For example, the query document that I create earlier in this chapter would be referenced as follows:

http://192.0.1.2/solutions/solutions.qry?function=form

The IP address in this example could just as easily be replaced with a web address domain name such as www.peachpit.com. The path to the query document is the path from the Web serving folder to the query document—not from the root directory of the Web server computer's hard disk.

Remember, the URL must be specified as a link—you can't just enter the URL in a Web page and expect it to work. The complete HTML code for a link would be something like this:

```
<A HREF="http://192.0.1.2/solutions/solutions.qry?function=form"> Search
Our Database</A>
```

Accessing & Testing Your Tango Web Publishing Solution

If you've completed all of the steps in the previous section of this chapter, your database is now online. In this section, I tell you how to access your Tango Web publishing solution to test the appearance and functionality of its query documents.

Testing Your Solution

Launch your Web browser and use it to point to the URL for the Web page that contains a link to the Tango query document. Click the link and start testing. You'll have to try out all the links, buttons, and other features that you included in the query documents that make up your Web publishing solution. The goal is to make sure everything works the way it should.

If you used Tango Editor's builder to create your query documents, it's unlikely that you'll encounter any errors. After all, the builder assembled all of the actions and attributes that went into the query documents. You're more likely to encounter content or appearance problems related to choices you made while using the builder—for example, inadequately sized fields, incorrect search operators, or missing fields. If you edited any of the HTML in response files, problems could be more serious.

Using Debug Mode

Tango Editor's Debug Mode option can display information about actions, results, globals, and other query document contents in the Web browser window when the query document is accessed. This can help you locate the source of problems and better understand how query documents work.

Enabling Debug Mode

To enable debug mode, use Tango Editor to open the query document that you want to debug. Then turn on the Debug Mode check box in the query document's editing window. Save the query document and close its window.

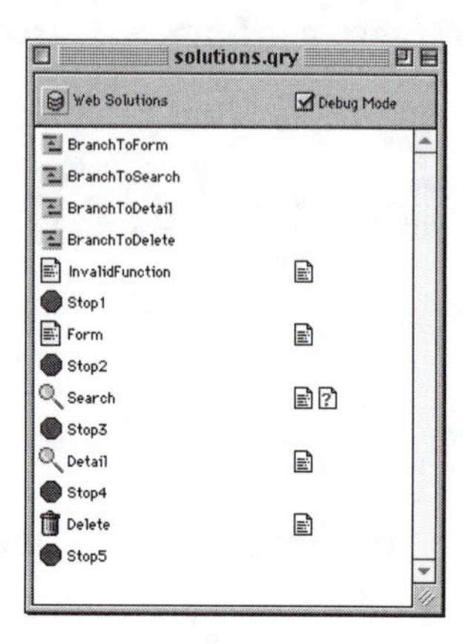

Viewing Debugger Information

When you access the query document for which you turned on Debug Mode, a list of actions and other query document information appears at the bottom of the Web browser window.

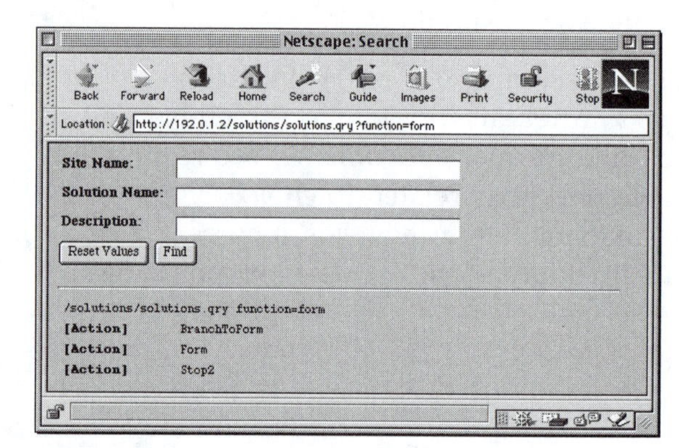

Troubleshooting Problems

If you find a problem, you have to troubleshoot it. Use Tango Editor to open the query builder file on which the query document is based and check all settings that could have caused the problem. If you edited any HTML, be sure to check it for syntax errors or missing Tango meta tags. Then use the Generate Query Document command to regenerate the query document. Or, if you're more familiar with Tango operations, open the query document with Tango Editor and edit it using the query document editor.

Once you think you've fixed the problem, access the query document as instructed above and check the problem page or function again. If the problem is gone, move on to the next problem.

CHAPTER 7

WEB•FM

Web Broadcasting Corporation's WEB•FM enables you to build database Web publishing solutions for FileMaker Pro version 3 or 4. In this chapter, I tell you about WEB•FM and related products, why you might or might not want to use them, and how you set them up. Along the way, I tell you how to create the calculation fields in FileMaker Pro that WEB•FM uses to display database information on the Web.

If you're a Windows PC user...

You may notice the lack of Windows instructions and illustrations in this chapter. That's because WEB•FM only works on Mac OS systems. If you're interested in using WEB•FM, please read on. But be prepared to buy a Mac OS computer if you decide you want to implement a WEB•FM solution for your database Web publishing needs.

NOTE

In this chapter, I work with a file named Web Solutions.fm, which is a database of Web sites and pages that publish FileMaker Pro databases on the Web using a variety of methods. If you'd like to work with the same file, look for it at http://www.gilesrd.com/fmproweb/.

Overview

WEB•FM enables you to create custom Web publishing solutions for database files. With it, you can display Web pages that enable users to browse, search, create, modify, or delete records in a FileMaker Pro database. WEB•FM gives you control over how pages look and interact with the database, but the level of control varies depending on your knowledge of HTML and FileMaker Pro calculations.

WEB•FM & Related Products

Web Broadcasting offers several products that enable you to publish FileMaker Pro database information on the Web:

- **WEB•FM** is a WebSTAR API-compatible plug-in that works with Web server software to link the textual information in FileMaker Pro database files to Web pages.
- **WEB•FM SDK** is a WebSTAR API-compatible plug-in that works with Web server software to link the textual information in FileMaker Pro runtime applications to Web pages.
- **PICT•FM** is a WebSTAR API-compatible plug-in that provides "on-the-fly" conversions of images stored in a FileMaker Pro database file to JPEG format so they can be displayed on Web pages. PICT•FM works with any FileMaker Pro Web publishing solution—not just Web Broadcasting's products.
- **TAG•FM** is a free, standalone application that helps you create HTML documents for use with WEB•FM.
- **LOG•FM** is a Web server log analysis and real-time statistics tool for WebSTAR API-compatible Web servers that is based on the FileMaker Pro runtime database engine.

These products are available separately from Web Broadcasting. You can get more information and evaluation copies from the Web Broadcasting Web site: http://macweb.com/.

This chapter concentrates on WEB•FM and TAG•FM.

How it Works

WEB•FM displays Web pages that display information from FileMaker Pro database files based on instructions in an HTML document that includes WEB•FM commands and variables as part of a link or form. The HTML that generates the resulting Web pages is stored within specially named FileMaker Pro calculation fields.

Benefits & Drawbacks

The main benefit of using WEB•FM is performance: WEB•FM is both fast and able to handle a large number of transactions. By completely rewriting the WEB•FM code in C for version 3.0, the folks at Web Broadcasting made it possible to perform database searches in less than a second. Because the HTML for displaying database information resides within the FileMaker Pro database, FileMaker Pro handles the burden of generating HTML. WEB•FM simply sends the HTML for the appropriate records to the Web server, which in turn, sends it to the user's Web browser. This helps make WEB•FM's response time fast. WEB•FM can also handle the traffic of Web sites with tens of thousands of database transactions per day.

The main drawback of using WEB•FM is the amount of knowledge you must have to build a WEB•FM Web publishing solution. Not only must you know the WEB•FM commands, variables, and other codes, but you must have a solid understanding of HTML and FileMaker Pro calculation fields. Clearly, WEB•FM is not for the Web publishing novice!

WEB•FM & HTML

WEB•FM uses HTML in two ways:

- HTML documents on the Web server provide WEB•FM with instructions to query FileMaker Pro databases.
- HTML code in FileMaker Pro database fields provide WEB•FM with instructions to display the results of queries on Web pages.

When I say HTML, I mean a combination of text, HTML tags, and special commands and variables that are read and understood by WEB•FM.

The Role of HTML

HTML elements like these determine the appearance and part of the functionality of the Web pages with which WEB•FM works:

- **HTML Formatting Tags** determine the appearance and position of text on the Web page. They make it possible to make headings bold, specify text justification, and set text and page background colors.
- **HTML Graphic Elements**, such as GIF or JPEG graphics, animated GIFs, AIFF sound files, Java Applets, and QuickTime movies, help ensure consistency with other Web pages on your site or make them stand out.
- **HTML HyperLink Tags** provide links to other pages and can activate embedded WEB•FM commands. I tell you about embedding WEB•FM commands in URLs later in this chapter.
- **HTML Form and Input Tags** enable users to enter information and begin WEB•FM action. I tell you more about form-related tags later in this chapter.

TIP

When creating HTML documents to work with WEB•FM, you might find it useful to start by creating an HTML document that incorporates the text, images, and formatting that you want the user to see. Then insert the WEB•FM commands and variables that will enable the file to interact with WEB•FM and your database files.

Directing Actions to WEB•FM

All instructions to WEB•FM are accomplished as part of a WEB•FM action. This is a command that tells the Web server to pass a request to WEB•FM for processing.

How you specify a WEB•FM action depends on whether the action is part of an HTML form (a **FORM** action) or an HTML link (a URL). I tell you about the differences between form actions and URL-embedded actions later in this chapter.

Specifying the WEB•FM Action in a Form

To process a form request with WEB•FM, you must include the name of the database file in the **FORM** tag, like this:

```
<FORM method="POST" action="Database+Name.fm">
other form tags
</FORM>
```

If desired, you can also include the desired WEB•FM command so you don't have to include it in the code for the form's Submit button. The resulting **FORM** tag may look like this:

```
<FORM method="POST" action="Database+Name.fm$CommandName">
other form tags
</FORM>
```

TIP

If you include the WEB•FM command in the FORM tag, you cannot have multiple Submit buttons that perform different commands.

Specifying the WEB•FM Action in a URL

You can also direct an action to WEB•FM within a URL, like this:

<A HREF="*Database+name*.fm?*other tags*">*Text to Click*</A>

More about the .fm File Name Suffix

Although you are not required to include the .fm suffix in the FileMaker Pro file name, including it helps the Web server recognize that the request is for a database file to be processed by WEB•FM. I recommend including it. Either way, it is not necessary to name the file with the suffix even if you use the suffix in the form action or URL.

TIP

Including the .fm suffix in a FileMaker Pro database name enhances security over the file when it is stored inside the Web serving folder. I tell you more about that later in this chapter.

A Closer Look at WEB•FM Codes

WEB•FM recognizes a variety of special codes which are used to specify the way WEB•FM works:

- **Basic Commands** tell WEB•FM how to interact with a FileMaker Pro database.
- **INPUT Variables** customize the way WEB•FM interacts with a FileMaker Pro database.
- **Reserved Field Names** identify fields in a FileMaker Pro database that are used to display information on Web pages generated by WEB•FM.
- **Substitution Tokens** provide information from the Web server or user's browser for use on Web pages displayed by WEB•FM.

In this section, I tell you more about all of these codes. I also provide information about code syntax that is unique to WEB•FM.

Basic Commands

WEB•FM recognizes eight commands for working with FileMaker Pro database files. Most of these commands are similar to commands within FileMaker Pro. For example, Find performs a find request based on criteria entered into a form or included in a URL. Here's a list of the commands in WEB•FM version 3.1:

Add	**FindUser**
Delete	**Random**
Find	**Retrieve**
FindAll	**Update**

INPUT Variables

WEB•FM recognizes twelve INPUT variables to customize the way WEB•FM interacts with a FileMaker Pro database file. They're called INPUT variables because they're usually included as part of an HTML INPUT tag in a form, although they can be included in a URL. Some variables are required for some commands while others are strictly optional. Here's a list of the variables in WEB•FM version 3.1:

DoScript	**Layout**
Error	**Max**
Field	**Operator**
Footer	**Sort**
Header	**SortOrder**
HTML	**Value**

Reserved Field Names

WEB•FM works by displaying HTML and other information that is stored within a database's fields. To properly display this information, WEB•FM requires that you reserve certain field names within FileMaker Pro for use with WEB•FM. Here's a quick list of the reserved names. I tell you more about them later in this chapter.

detail	**header**
error	**html**
footer	**www**

Two of these fields *must* be created in the FileMaker Pro database file(s) that you want to publish on the Web: **html**, which displays a "hitlist" of found records, and **detail**, which displays detailed information about a specific record. I tell you more about these fields, including how to create them, later in this chapter. The other fields are optional; if you omit them, WEB•FM displays default data whenever they should be used.

Substitution Tokens

A token is a placeholder for the substitution of dynamic information. There are two types of tokens: outgoing and incoming. Here's a brief discussion of each.

Outgoing Tokens

An outgoing token is one generated by your Web server. It can be information residing on the server computer, such as **[date]** (the current date), or information generated by WEB•FM, such as **[max]** (the maximum number of records displayed). Here's a list of outgoing tokens; tokens that include an ellipsis require additional information, such as text or additional tokens.

[date]	**[prev] ... [/prev]**
[end]	**[range]**
[fields]	**[RedID]**
[found]	**[start]**
[max]	**[values]**
[next] ... [/next]	

Incoming Tokens

An incoming token is one generated by the user's Web browser. An example is **[domain]** (the user's domain name). Here's a list of incoming tokens:

[browser]	**[password]**
[cookie]	**[referrer]**
[domain]	**[username]**

WEB•FM Code Syntax

Like HTML, WEB•FM has its own syntax. Syntax is like English grammar, but a lot less forgiving. If you have poor grammar, most people can still figure out what you're trying to say. But if you make a WEB•FM syntax error, WEB•FM either won't work or it won't work the way you expect it to.

Fortunately, WEB•FM syntax is straightforward and not much different from HTML syntax, which you need to know anyway to use WEB•FM. Here are the details.

TIP *To make your WEB•FM coding a bit easier, you may want to download TAG•FM from Web Broadcasting's Web site: http://macweb.com/. This little application, which is free, can create bits of HTML code for you to drag into your favorite HTML editing application. I tell you more about using TAG•FM later in this chapter.*

Punctuation

WEB•FM recognizes some punctuation that isn't normally used in HTML:

- **SQUARE BRACKETS ([ ])** surround all tokens. An example is **[date]**.
- **SPACE CHARACTERS (   )** can appear within field and layout names—but only when they are part of a form-related tag.

TIP

Space characters appearing in URLs must be represented as a plus sign (+) or encoded as %20 (the ISO Latin-1 equivalent of a space) before being read by a Web browser. For best results, avoid using spaces in file, layout, and field names. If you must include spaces in item names, make sure you or your Web authoring program convert each space in a URL to a + or encode it as %20.

- **QUESTION MARK (?)** appears after the name of the database (and, optionally, the WEB•FM command) at the beginning of any link that utilizes a WEB•FM command. An example is **<A HREF="*Database+name.fm?other tags*">*Text to Click*</A>**
- **DOLLAR SIGN ($)** appears between the name of the database and the WEB•FM command, when the command is included in a **FORM** tag or URL. An example is **<A HREF="Web+Solutions.fm$FindAll?HTML=html">Show Entries</A>** (which sets up a link that, when clicked, displays all records from the file named Web Solutions.fm, using the HTML code in the field named html).
- **AMPERSAND (&)** appears between WEB•FM ***name=value*** pairs when they appear in a link. An example is **<A HREF="Web+Solutions.fm$FindAll?HTML=html&max=10&Footer=footer&Sort=Last+Name">Show Entries</A>** (which sets up a link that, when clicked, displays up to 10 records from the file named Web Solutions.fm, sorted by the Last Name field, using the HTML code in the field named html with the field named footer).

Case Sensitivity

WEB•FM codes are not case sensitive. That means **FindAll** is the same as **FINDALL**, **findall**, or **fInDaLl**. I try to follow the capitalization used in the WEB•FM documentation, although it really isn't very consistent.

URL-Embedded Actions vs. Form Actions

Many WEB•FM codes can be used two different ways in an HTML file: as an action embedded in a URL for a link or as a form action. The method you choose depends on your needs for the situation.

- Use embedded actions to create a link that instructs WEB•FM to display FileMaker Pro database information based on commands, variables, and tokens that you provide.
- Use a form action to instruct WEB•FM to display FileMaker Pro database information based on information entered by a user in a form.

Embedding WEB•FM Actions in a URL

Constructing a link isn't difficult once you know what you want the link to do and what WEB•FM commands, variables, and tokens it requires. Generally speaking, all URL-embedded WEB•FM actions require the following:

- HTML ANCHOR **(A)** AND REFERENCE **(HREF)** TAGS, which are required to create a link.
- ***database+name*.fm?** tells the Web server that the URL involves a FileMaker Pro database and will be handled by WEB•FM.

These are the minimum requirements for a URL to work with WEB•FM. WEB•FM will utilize default values for other required commands or variables, such as the **Find** command or **HTML** variable. Other commands may require more tags.

Here's an example that displays the 50 most recently added records from a database file, using WEB•FM to interact with FileMaker Pro:

```
<A HREF="Web+Solutions.fm$FindAll?Sort=Date&SortOrder=descending&max=
50">Show Entries</A>
```

This example uses each of the required components, with FindAll as the command. It also includes the **Sort** and **SortOrder** variables to include sorting instructions. Note that each ***name=value*** pair in the URL is separated by an ampersand.

Using WEB•FM with a Form Action

Constructing a form isn't difficult, either, especially if you use a Web authoring tool like Claris Home Page, Adobe PageMill, or Microsoft FrontPage. Simply create the form, then add or substitute WEB•FM commands and variables to indicate the database name, command to use, and other options. At a minimum, all WEB•FM forms require the following:

- HTML FORM **(FORM)** TAG that includes **action="Database+Name.fm"** and **method="post"**.
- HTML INPUT **(INPUT)** AND/OR SELECTION **(SELECT)** FIELDS. This is pure HTML that displays form fields for entering search criteria or new record data.

- HTML SUBMIT BUTTON (**INPUT TYPE="SUBMIT"**) TAG that includes **name=*command*** tells WEB•FM what command to perform when the button is clicked.

These are the minimum contents. What you include depends on what you want to display on and accomplish with the page.

Here's an example of HTML that displays a search form:

```
<FORM action="Web Solutions.fm" method="post">
Site Name: <INPUT type="text" name="Site Name" value=""> <BR>
Site URL: <INPUT type="text" name="Site URL" value=""> <BR>
Description: <INPUT type="textarea" name="Description" value=""> <BR>
<INPUT type="submit" name="Find" value="Search for Sites">
```

Using TAG•FM to Create HTML Documents

TAG•FM is a free drag-and-drop application available at the Web Broadcasting Corporation Web site: (http://macweb.com/). You can use it to help you create the HTML documents that make up your WEB•FM Web publishing solution. Here's how.

Opening a Database File with TAG•FM

To use TAG•FM, the layout and field information for the FileMaker Pro database that you want to use must be read into it. You do this by opening the database with TAG•FM.

Drag the database's document icon onto the TAG•FM application icon. A splash screen appears briefly. Then the TAG•FM window appears. The name of the database that you dragged should appear in the Database pop-up menu at the top of the window.

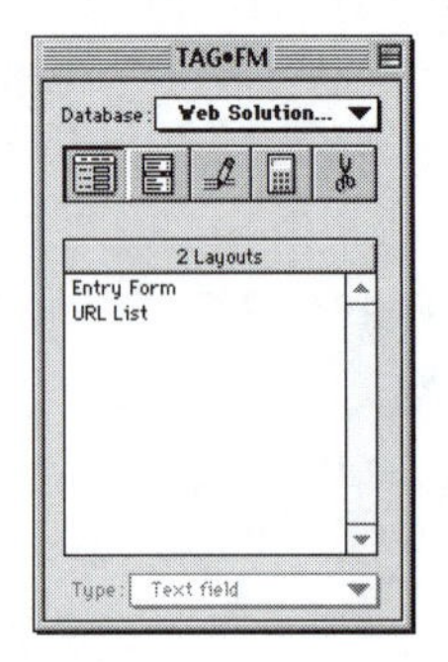

Setting Preferences

Before you use TAG•FM for the first time, check its Drag Options preference settings to make sure they're properly set for your Web authoring program. Begin by choosing Preferences from the Edit menu.

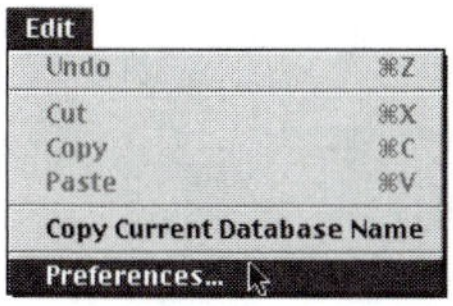

The Preferences dialog box appears.

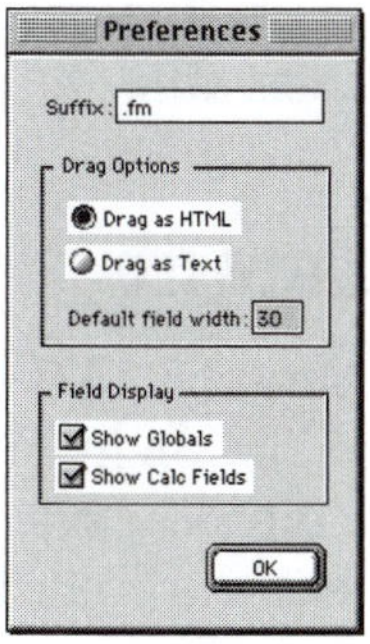

- If you use a WYSIWYG Web authoring tool like Claris Home Page, Adobe PageMill, or Microsoft FrontPage, select the Drag as HTML radio button.
- If you use a text-based Web authoring tool like BBEdit or SimpleText, select the Drag as Text radio button.

Click OK to accept your setting and dismiss the Preferences dialog box.

About the TAG•FM Window

The TAG•FM window includes five buttons you can use to access WEB•FM codes for your database. From left to right, they are:

- LAYOUTS, which is illustrated in the TAG•FM window on the previous page, displays a list of all layouts in the database file.
- ALL FIELDS displays a list of all fields in the database file.
- RESERVED FIELD NAMES displays a list of all WEB•FM basic commands and INPUT variables. I tell you about commands and variables earlier in this chapter.

- ◉ **FILEMAKER CALCULATIONS** displays a list of all FileMaker Pro status functions and possible values for the special www field that I tell you more about later in this chapter.
- ◉ **PREFORMATTED HTML SNIPPETS** displays a list of most outgoing tokens. I tell you about tokens earlier in this chapter, too.

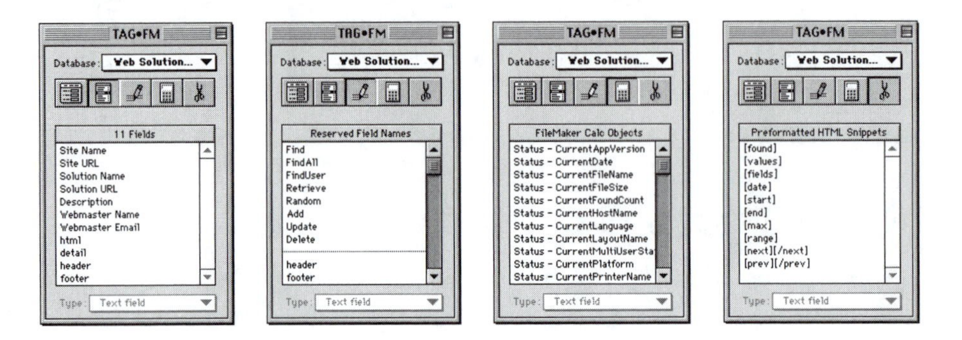

Adding WEB•FM Codes to an HTML Document

To add WEB•FM codes to an HTML document, begin by clicking the TAG•FM button for the item that you want to use. If necessary, choose an option from the Type pop-up menu—this is used to specify a field type. Click the item once to select it, then click it again and drag it into the HTML document. As you drag, a TAG•FM screen appears briefly. When you release the mouse button to complete the drag, the appropriate information appears.

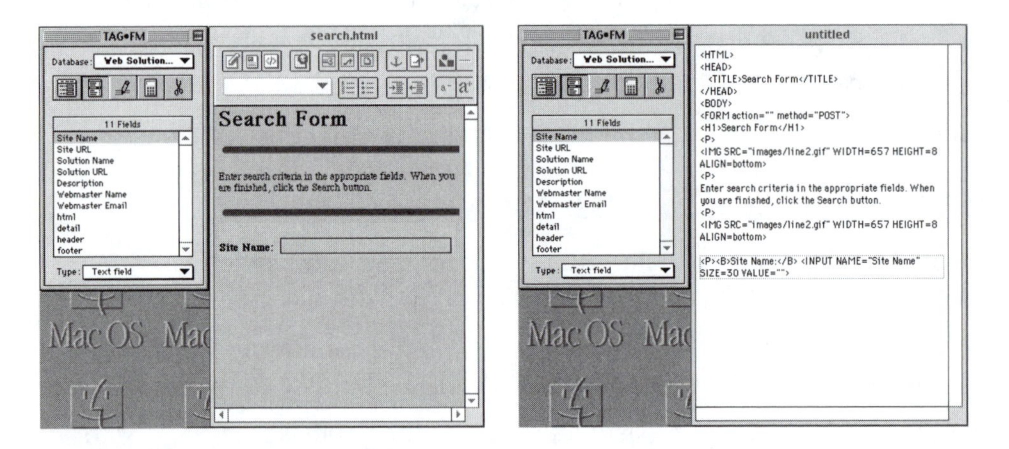

Continue building the HTML document using a combination of TAG•FM items and your Web authoring program's commands and features. Here's a simple form I created with TAG•FM and Claris Home Page, along with the underlying HTML code.

```
<HTML>
<HEAD>
  <TITLE>Search Form</TITLE>
</HEAD>
<BODY>
<FORM action="Web Solutions.fm" method="POST">
<H1>Search Form</H1>
<P><IMG SRC="images/line2.gif" WIDTH=657 HEIGHT=8 ALIGN=bottom>
<P>Enter search criteria in the appropriate fields. When you are
finished, click the Search button.
<P><IMG SRC="images/line2.gif" WIDTH=657 HEIGHT=8 ALIGN=bottom>
<P><B>Site Name:</B> <INPUT TYPE="text" NAME="Site Name" VALUE=""
SIZE=30>
<P><B>Solution Name:</B> <INPUT TYPE="text" NAME="Solution Name"
VALUE="" SIZE=30>
<P><B>Description:</B> <TEXTAREA NAME="Description" ROWS=3
COLS=33></TEXTAREA>
<P><CENTER><INPUT TYPE="submit" NAME="FIND"
VALUE="Search"><INPUT TYPE="reset" VALUE="Clear Entries"></CENTER>
</FORM>
</BODY>
</HTML>
```

When using TAG•FM to create a form, be sure to include the name of the FileMaker Pro file as the form action. This may require that you switch to your Web authoring tool's HTML editing mode or use one of its commands or other features to specify a form action.

Other Ways to Use TAG•FM

Although TAG•FM can make a fine complement to your favorite Web authoring program, it can also be used in the following ways:

- Drag items from the TAG•FM window into FileMaker Pro's Specify Calculation dialog box when creating calculations for the html and header fields.
- Drag items from the TAG•FM window into FileMaker Pro fields when creating HTML for the header, footer, and error fields.
- Use the Export Claris Home Page Library command under the edit menu to save all TAG•FM items in a Claris Home Page Library file. You can then use the library file instead of TAG•FM to create HTML documents in Claris Home Page.

Step-by-Step Setup

Ready to try building your own WEB•FM Web publishing solution? Here are the steps you'll need to follow to get your database online with WEB•FM.

Installing WEB•FM

Before your files can be published on the Web, you must install WEB•FM.

TIP

You only need to follow these steps once, no matter how many databases you publish.

Installing the WEB•FM Plug-In

Quit your Web server application and launch the WEB•FM Installer application on the WEB•FM Installer disk. Use the Easy Install option to install WEB•FM components. When the installation is finished, quit the installer application and eject the disk.

Open the WEB•FM folder on your hard disk. Locate the WEB•FM plug-in file and drag it into your Web server's Plug-Ins folder. Now launch your Web server software. The WEB•FM plug-in should be listed among the loaded plug-ins in the server's status window.

```
WebSTAR 2.1 Status : 80
Mem: 1.2M Sent: 0.0M
Hits: 0
Connections :Max 12  Current 0  High 0  Busy 0  Denied 0
Max Mem 1.2M  Min Mem 1.2M  Up Since: 11/03/97 15:51

WebSTAR, Copyright ©1993-1997 Chuck Shotton,
Portions ©1995-1997 Quarterdeck Corp. and its Licensors.
All rights reserved.

OpenTransport TCP/IP stack selected.

Initialized Plug-ins:
======================
WEB•FM                          3.1 PPC
WebSTAR SSI                     2.1
WebSTAR QuickSend               2.1
WebSTAR Log Roller              2.1
WebSTAR Java VM                 2.1
WebSTAR Image Map               2.1
WebSTAR File Upload             2.1
WebSTAR Directory Indexer       2.1
WebSTAR Data Cache              2.1
WebSTAR Byte Server             2.1
WebSTAR Auto BinHex             2.1
WebSTAR Admin                   2.1

File Info Caching is enabled with space for approximately 67 entries.
Keep-Alive processing is disabled.

Archiving Frequency Statistics
==============================
WebSTAR log set to roll in 24 hours, 0 minutes and 0 seconds


Java VM Portions © 1996 Natural Intelligence, Inc., All rights reserved
Contact Natural Intelligence for more information
http://www.roaster.com              (617) 867-7680
```

Entering the WEB•FM Serial Number

Open the database file named pi_admin.fm, which is located in the WEB•FM folder. It's a FileMaker Pro file with a number of layouts, each with its own "tab." When it first appears, its General tab should be showing, like this:

Enter your WEB•FM serial number and your company name in the appropriate fields.

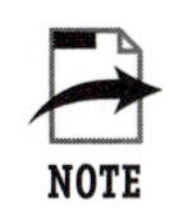

If you are using a demo version of WEB•FM, you won't have a serial number. Go on to the next step.

Entering an Administrator Username and Password

Click the Security tab. The pi_admin.fm window changes to display the Security tab's fields:

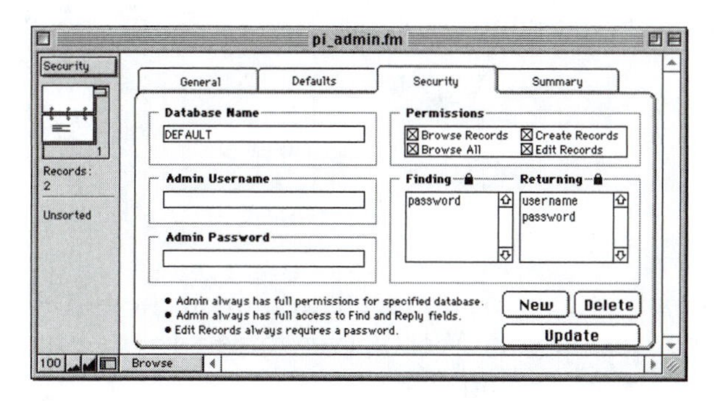

Enter a username and password in the appropriate fields for the DEFAULT database record. Then switch to the second record, which is for the PI_ADMIN.FM database, and enter a username and password in the appropriate fields.

Normally, you will enter the same username and password for both records. I tell you more about setting up security later in this chapter.

Don't skip this step! Doing so might prevent you from accessing the databases you publish with WEB•FM.

Saving Your Preferences

How you save the information you entered depends on whether you are using a PowerPC-based Web server or a 680x0 Macintosh Web server. Follow the appropriate steps for your server:

- For a PowerPC Web server, click the Update button. A dialog box like the one below appears.

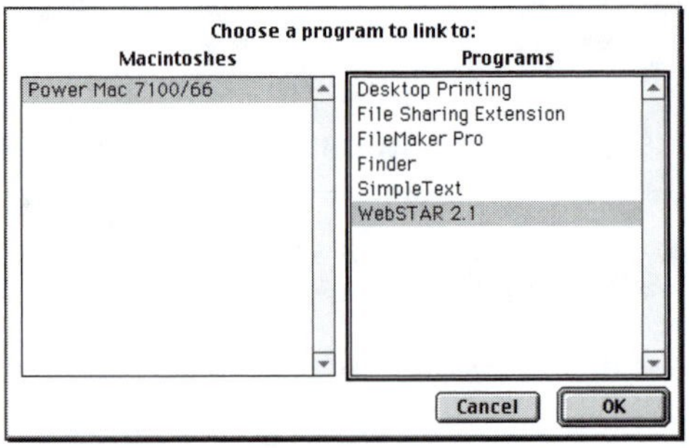

  Select your Web server application from the list on the right side of the dialog box and click OK. When a dialog box appears to confirm that WEB•FM has been successfully updated, click its OK button to dismiss it.

- For a 680x0 Macintosh Web server, choose Export from the Script menu or press Command-3.

  Use the Save As dialog box that appears to locate and open the FM Prefs folder in the Plug-Ins folder inside your Web server folder. Then click the Save button to save the WEB•FM Settings file.

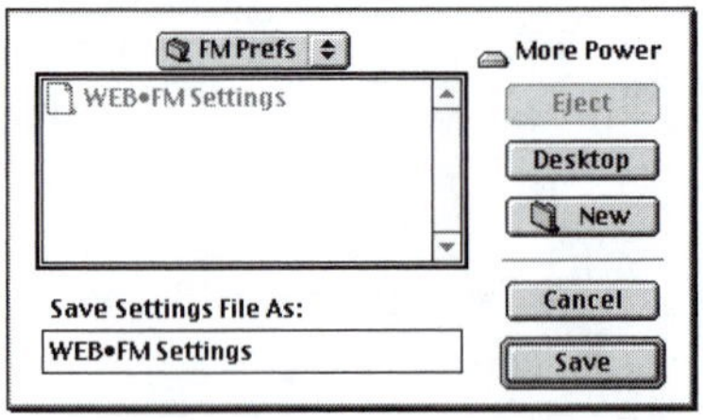

  When a confirmation dialog box asks whether you want to replace the existing WEB•FM Settings file, click the Replace button.

When you are finished, close the pi_admin.fm file and restart your Web server software.

Preparing the FileMaker Pro Database File

WEB•FM displays information based on the contents of special calculation and global fields in the FileMaker Pro database file that you want to publish. This means you need to spend some time preparing the database file for publication.

Opening the FileMaker Pro Database File

If you haven't already opened the database that you want to publish, now is the time. Double-click the database's document icon or choose Open from FileMaker Pro's File menu and use the Open dialog box that appears to locate and open the database file.

The database must be open for its contents to be published on the Web. If you close a database, it will no longer be available to users via the Web.

About Required Fields

At a bare minimum, you must create two calculation fields in your FileMaker Pro database:

- **HTML** is a calculation field containing HTML code that displays basic information for the record. This HTML code is used by WEB•FM to display a hitlist of found items. The field's code usually contains a link to detailed information for each specific record.
- **DETAIL** is a calculation field containing HTML code that displays most or all fields for the record. This HTML code is used by WEB•FM to display detailed information about a specific record.

Creating Required Fields with TAG•FM

You can use TAG•FM to create the two required fields for you. Start by dropping the database file's icon onto the TAG•FM application icon to open it with TAG•FM. Then Choose Auto Web-Enable Database from the File menu.

File
Update Database List... ⌘=
Auto Web-Enable Database...
Export Claris® Home Page™ Library...
Convert File... ⌘O
Convert Clipboard...
Quit ⌘Q

A dialog box like the one below appears, explaining what TAG•FM will attempt to do and warning you not to click or type anything until it's finished.

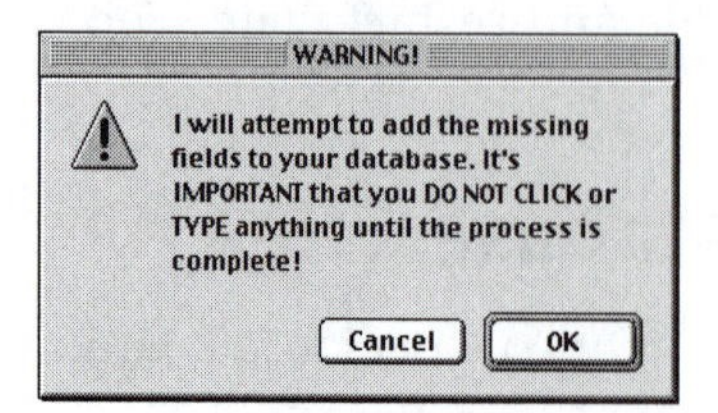

Click OK. Then wait while TAG•FM runs a script that creates both fields. When it's finished, a dialog box like the one below tells you. Click OK to dismiss it.

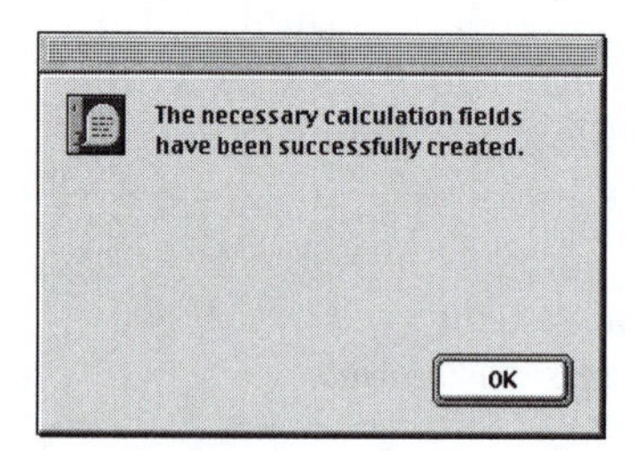

Here are the two calculations that TAG•FM created in my Web Solutions.fm database:

html=

```
"<LI><A HREF=" & """" & "Web+Solutions.fm$RETRIEVE?&value=[recID]
&field=recid&html=detail" & """" & ">" & Site Name & "</A><P>"
```

The html calculation field created by TAG•FM that is shown here has a slight error that will cause an error message to appear when a link is clicked if it is not corrected. After the command **RETRIEVE** *there is a question mark and an ampersand. The ampersand must be removed. I tell you how in a moment.*

detail=

```
"<HTML>
<HEAD>
<TITLE>Detail</TITLE>
</HEAD>
<BODY>" &
"Site Name:" & Site Name &
"Site URL:" & Site URL &
"Solution Name:" & Solution Name &
"Solution URL:" & Solution URL &
"Description:" & Description &
"</BODY>
</HTML>"
```

And here's how they appear when viewed as part of my WEB•FM Web publishing solution:

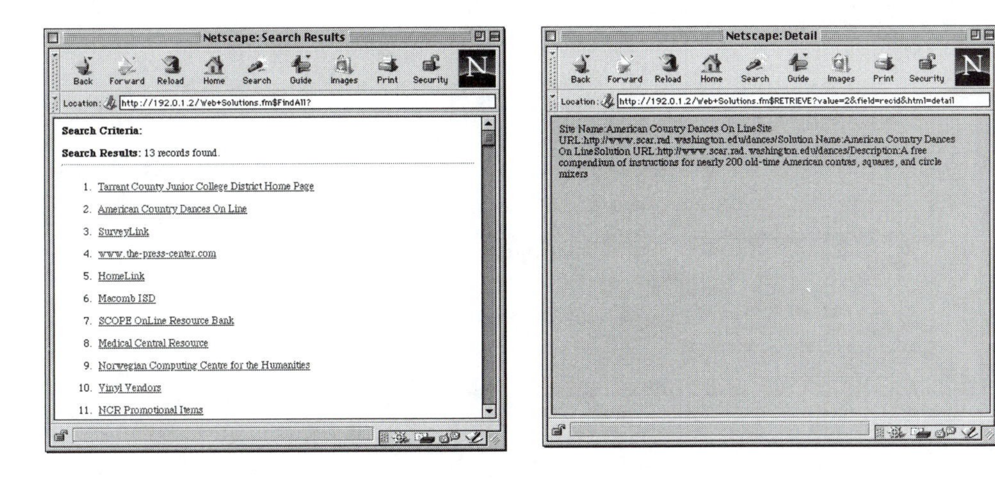

Although the hitlist page looks fine, the detail page definitely needs some work. To fix it up, you need to edit it in the Specify Calculation dialog box.

Creating or Editing Required Fields Manually

If FileMaker Pro is not the active application, switch to it. Then choose Fields from the Define menu under the File menu or press Command-Shift-D.

The Define Fields dialog box appears.

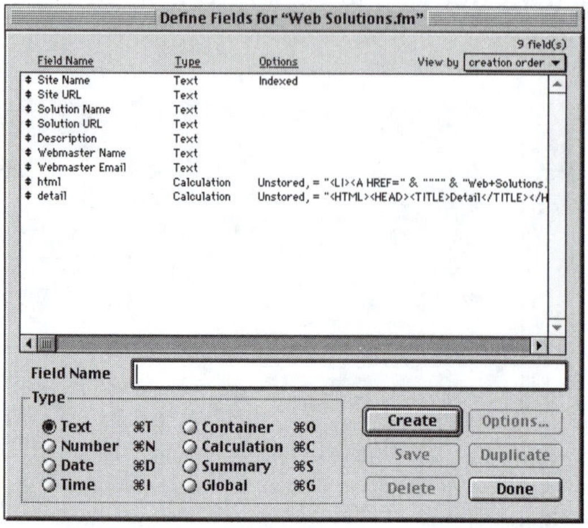

- To create one of the required fields, enter its name in the Field Name edit box. Select the Calculation radio button or press Command-C. Then click the Create button.
- To edit a required field that you already created manually or with TAG•FM, double-click the name of the field that you want to edit.

The Specify Calculation dialog box appears. Use it to concatenate field names with literal text to create a legal HTML string.

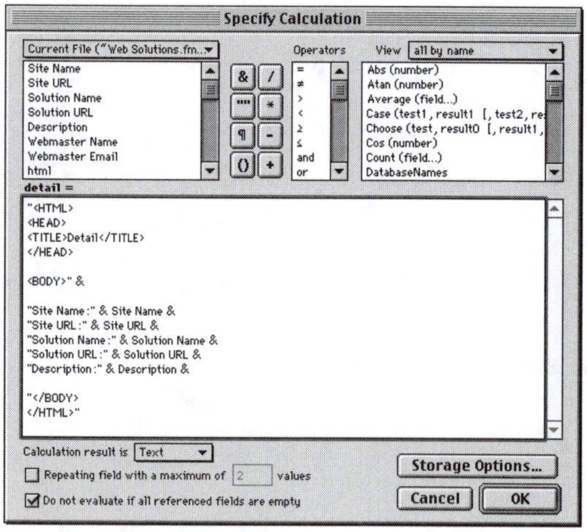

- To specify a calculation for a new field, use the scrolling lists and buttons at the top of the window, along with your keyboard to enter a calculation. If you're not sure what to enter, consult the examples above and below. You can always modify them later on.

- To edit a calculation for an existing field, use the scrolling lists and buttons at the top of the window, along with your keyboard, to edit the calculation.

Teaching you how to create calculations in FileMaker Pro is beyond the scope of this book. If you're not sure how to use the Specify Calculation dialog box, consult the documentation that came with FileMaker Pro or a more basic book about using FileMaker Pro.

If you're editing fields created by TAG•FM, there are two things to check and edit:

- Make sure there's only one punctuation mark—a question mark (**?**) after the **RETRIEVE** command in the html field's calculation.
- Include a **
** or **<P>** tag after each line of the detail field's calculation to put each field on a separate line.

When you're finished, the calculations in the Specify Calculation window may look like this:

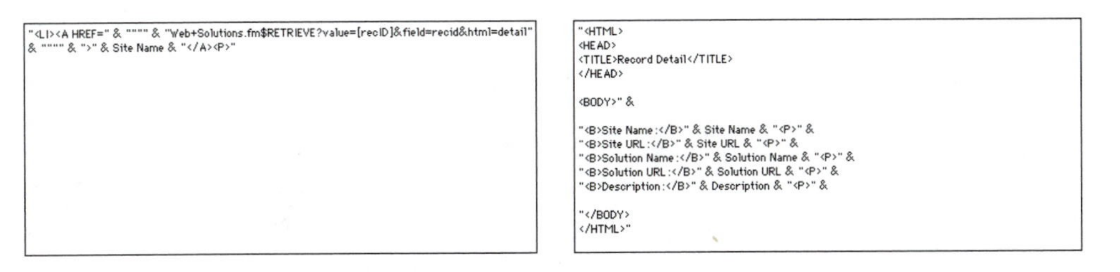

```
"<LI><A HREF=" & """" & "Web+Solutions.fm$RETRIEVE?value=[recID]&field=recid&html=detail"
& """" & ">" & Site Name & "</A><P>"
```

```
"<HTML>
<HEAD>
<TITLE>Record Detail</TITLE>
</HEAD>

<BODY>" &

"<B>Site Name:</B>" & Site Name & "<P>" &
"<B>Site URL:</B>" & Site URL & "<P>" &
"<B>Solution Name:</B>" & Solution Name & "<P>" &
"<B>Solution URL:</B>" & Solution URL & "<P>" &
"<B>Description:</B>" & Description & "<P>" &

"</BODY>
</HTML>"
```

Although the hitlist page does not change (the only edit was to correct a link), the detail page now looks like this:

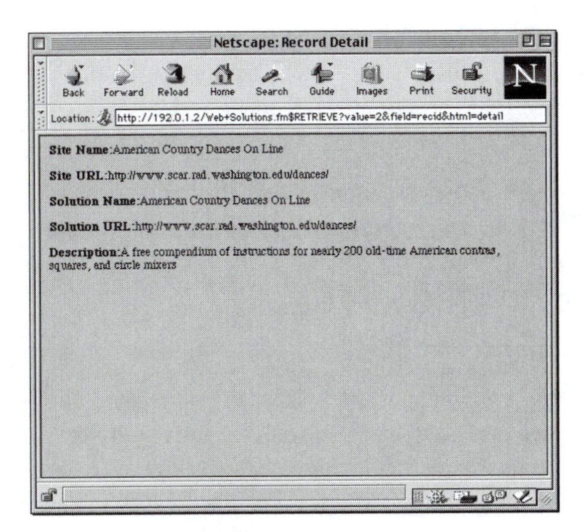

TIP

To improve performance, click the Storage Options button in the Specify Calculation dialog box for the detail field and any other calculation field that you create other than the html field. In the Storage Options dialog box that appears, select the Off radio button for Indexing and turn on the Do not store calculation results check box. Then click OK.

Storage Options for Field “detail”

Indexing and storing the results of a calculation improves performance of some operations like finds at the cost of increased file size and time spent indexing.

Indexing: On / Off — Automatically turn indexing on if needed

Do not store calculation results -- calculate only when needed

Default language for indexing and sorting text: English

Cancel OK

When you are finished specifying a calculation, click the OK button to dismiss the Specify Calculation dialog box. When you are finished creating or editing fields, click the Done button to dismiss the Define Fields dialog box.

Those Pesky Quotes

One of the most confusing things about entering calculations that generate HTML code is the use of double quotes. The problem is, FileMaker Pro’s Specify Calculation dialog box recognizes double quote characters as the beginning or end of literal text strings. That makes it a bit tricky to tell FileMaker Pro that you want it to display a double quote rather than end a string.

There are two ways to include double quotes in HTML code that you enter in the Specify Calculation dialog box:

- Enter two double quotes for every one double quote that you need to display. FileMaker Pro evaluates two double quotes as a single double quote. Sound confusing? It can be. But it works. This is the method that TAG•FM uses; that’s why there are so many double quotes in the examples above.
- Create a Global field that contains a quote character and enter that field each time you need to enter a quote. I find this less confusing, but it introduces a new problem if the database file is hosted by FileMaker Pro Server—the global field may not be properly updated. To fix this problem, create a startup script with the following command:

  Paste Literal [Select, “quote” , “"”]

One more thing about quotes...if you know you’re going to use a database’s information on the Web, be sure to turn off Smart Quotes before entering data. This prevents the four different curly quote characters (‘, ’, “, and ”) from appearing as what I call balloon characters (Ô, Ó, Ò, and Õ) in browser windows. To turn off Smart Quotes, choose Document from the Preferences submenu under the Edit menu. Then turn off the Use smart quotes check box and click Done.

Creating Optional Fields

If desired, you can also create the following fields to further customize your WEB•FM Web publishing solution:

- **HEADER** is a global field containing HTML code for WEB•FM to display at the top of each Web page.
- **FOOTER** is a global field containing HTML code for WEB•FM to display at the bottom of each page.
- **ERROR** is a global field containing HTML code for WEB•FM to display when a command cannot be completed—for example, if no records are found as a result of a search.
- **WWW** is a global field that should be formatted with 20 empty repetitions. It gathers certain HTTP request parameters sent by the user's Web browser.

Here's an example of the page created with the html field with a custom header field:

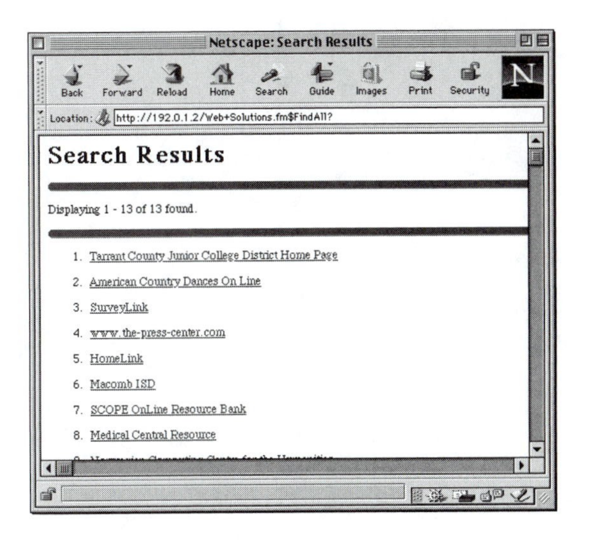

NOTE

If you don't create the header, footer, or error fields, WEB•FM will supply default header, footer, or error HTML code as needed.

To create any of these fields, start by choosing Fields from the Define submenu under FileMaker Pro's File menu or pressing Command-Shift-D to display the Define Fields dialog box. Enter the name of the field in the Field Name edit box and select the Global radio button or press Command-G. Click the Create button. In the Options for Global Field dialog box that appears, choose Text from the Data Type pop-up menu. If you're creating the www field, be sure to specify 20 repetitions.

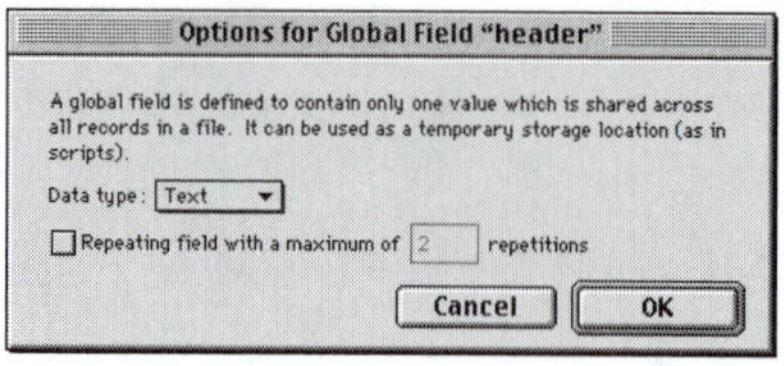

Click OK to accept your settings and return to the Define Fields dialog box. When you're finished creating fields, click the Done button to dismiss the Define Fields dialog box.

If necessary, use the Field tool in Layout mode to add the newly created field(s) to a layout. For the www field, be sure to use the Field Format dialog box to display all 20 repetitions.

Next, switch to Browse mode and display a layout that includes the field(s) that you created. Click in a field and enter the desired HTML code. In the following illustration, I've entered the HTML for the header in the above example:

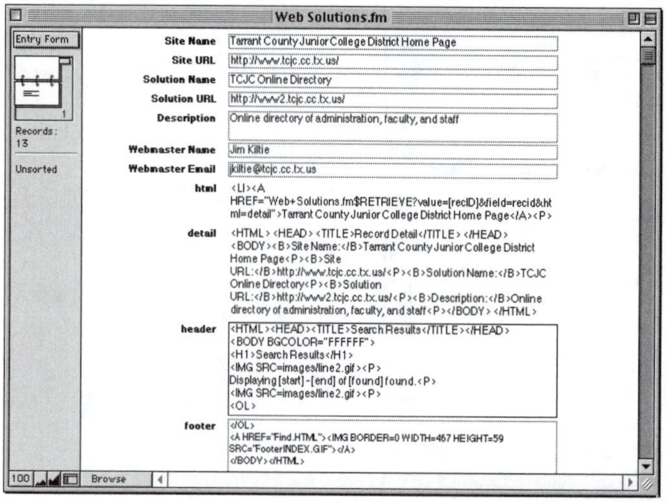

TIP

Hate typing HTML code? I do, too. Fortunately, you can create the header, footer, or error fields without typing a single angle bracket. Just use your favorite Web authoring tool—Claris Home Page, Adobe PageMill, Microsoft FrontPage, etc.—to create the HTML code that you want to use. Then switch to HTML editing mode, select and copy the HTML code you created, switch to FileMaker Pro, and paste the HTML code into the appropriate field.

Creating Security-Related Fields

Finally, for security purposes, you should consider creating two more fields: username and password. These two fields, which can be text or global fields, are required for updating or deleting records.

WARNING

If you do not create username and password fields for your database, the user must provide the Admin password to modify or delete a record in the database.

TIP

If you create the username and password fields as text fields, you can specify a different username and password for each record, thus providing record-level security for your database file. I tell you more about WEB•FM security later in this chapter.

Creating Layouts

By default, WEB•FM looks for database fields in Layout 0, an invisible layout created and maintained by FileMaker Pro that includes all database fields. The **Layout** INPUT variable, which is optional, tells WEB•FM to look for fields in a specific layout. There are three instances when you should use this variable:

- You must use the **Layout** variable to specify a layout that includes a specially formatted number, date, or time field if you want to use that field's formatting on a Web page.
- You must use the **Layout** variable to specify a layout that includes related fields if you want WEB•FM to access those fields.
- You can speed up the performance of WEB•FM by using the **Layout** variable to specify a layout that includes only the fields WEB•FM needs to access. The performance boost is especially noticeable when accessing only a few fields in a database that has many fields.

Look at your database file and decide which combinations of fields WEB•FM will access. If necessary, create the layouts you need, keeping the above information in mind.

TIP

If you've been using the database for a while, it may already have all of the layouts that you need to publish it on the Web using WEB•FM. In that case, you don't have to do a thing.

Creating & Saving HTML Documents

WEB•FM displays database information based on HTML in the required html and detail fields discussed earlier in this chapter. It also relies on HTML documents that include WEB•FM commands and variables to query the database and display information. You must create these HTML documents to complete your WEB•FM Web publishing solution.

Planning your Strategy

Before you begin churning out HTML files, take a moment to think about the things you want to accomplish with your Web publishing solution. Here are some tips:

- Each HTML file should perform at least one specific task. For example, you may want to create one HTML file that has a link or button to display all records and another HTML file that enables users to search based on criteria entered for specific fields. Keep these tasks in mind when deciding what files you need.
- Create a graphic representation or flow chart of the way HTML files will interact with each other (and the database). This will help you organize and link the files. You can find sample flowcharts in the last five chapters of this book.
- Don't forget to create a database Home page that explains what the database is all about and provides links to the appropriate HTML files that make up your Web publishing solution. This page might also offer links to other pages on your Web site (if applicable) in case visitors change their mind and decide they don't want to access the database after all.

Creating a Project Folder

Although not required, it's a good idea to save all of the files related to a specific Web publishing solution into the same folder. This project folder keeps your HTML files, images, and database files together. It also keeps your Web server folder neat!

TIP

Use relative references in all of the links for the HTML files you create. This makes the project folder portable—you can move it to any server to relocate it or share it with a friend or work associate.

Creating the HTML Files

This is where you put your HTML and WEB•FM coding skills to the test. You must create each of the HTML files that make up your WEB•FM Web publishing solution and save them into the project folder.

Here are some tips for creating format files:

- Use TAG•FM, which I discuss earlier in this chapter, to make the task easier.
- Whenever possible, base a new HTML file on an existing HTML file that does the same (or almost the same) thing.

- Start with the basics—HTML files that do the minimum that they need to. Once you get them working properly, add features to your heart's desire.

WEB•FM Security

WEB•FM includes a number of security options to help protect your database files from unauthorized access. You can use them in addition to the security features offered by your Web server software.

Naming Files with the .fm Suffix

By default, the .fm suffix identifies files that should be acted upon by WEB•FM. This means that anytime a file with a .fm suffix is requested from the Web server, the Web server software lets WEB•FM serve the database.

What does this mean to you? It means that any FileMaker Pro file in your Web serving folder that is named with the .fm suffix is safe from outside intruders. If you do not want to use the .fm suffix to name FileMaker Pro files, be sure to store those files outside of your Web serving folder.

Securing the Admin Database

The Admin database file (the file named pi_admin.fm) is what gives you control over security on individual FileMaker Pro files. For this reason, it's important to secure it from unauthorized access. Here are several methods for keeping the Admin database safe:

- Don't store the Admin database on the Web serving computer. Instead, open the Admin database on another and administer WEB•FM using program linking. You can turn on program linking with the File Sharing control panel.

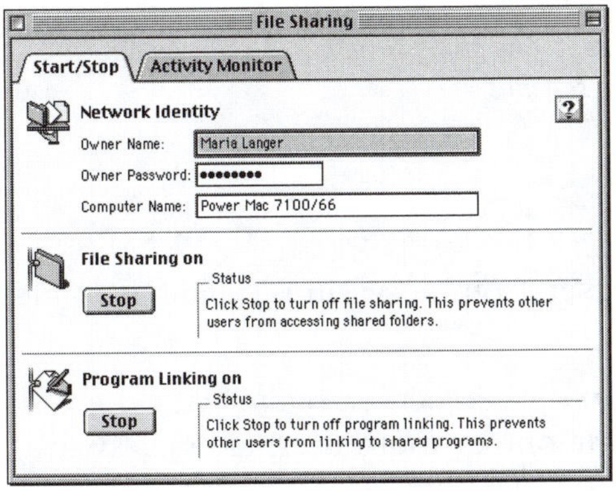

- Password protect the Admin database. To do so, open the pi_admin.fm database and choose Change Password from the File menu. In the Change Password dialog box that appears, enter WEB•FM in the Old password edit box and the password of your choice in the other two edit boxes. Click OK. You will then be prompted for a password each time you open the pi_admin.fm file.

- Define a Web server realm with pi_admin as the match string and add a Web server password that allows access to the realm.

Securing Your Database Files

WEB•FM offers four levels of security over the database files you publish on the Web: database, task, field, and record. Here are the details.

NOTE

When working with WEB•FM security, keep one thing in mind: A valid Admin password can override any permissions settings.

Database-Level Security

Database-level security prevents a user from accessing a database unless he enters the correct password.

To set database-level security, set up a Web server realm with the database name as the match string. Then create one or more username/password combinations to control who has access to the database.

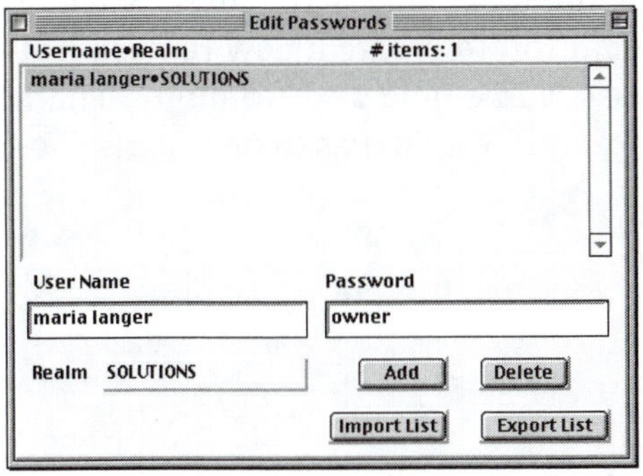

When a user attempts to access a secured database file, a password dialog box like the one below appears. The user must enter a correct username and password for the database file's Web server realm in the appropriate edit boxes to work with the database file.

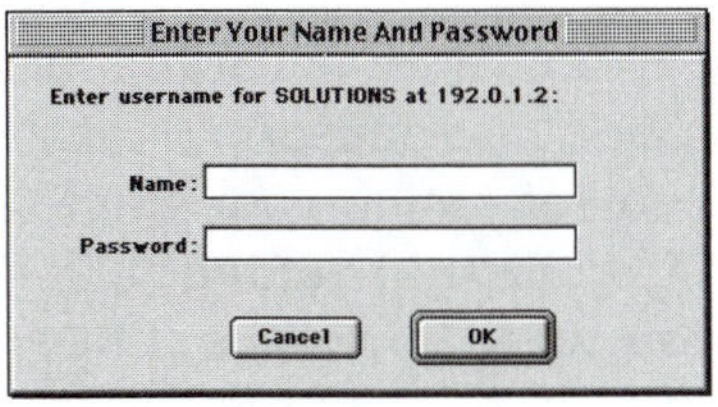

Task-Level Security

Task-level security enables or disables certain tasks for a database. There are four permissions, each responsible for one or more WEB•FM commands:

- BROWSE RECORDS, when turned on, enables the Find, Retrieve, and Random commands.
- BROWSE ALL, when turned on, enables the FindAll command.
- CREATE RECORDS, when turned on, enables the Add command.
- EDIT RECORDS, when turned on, enables the Update, Delete, and FindUser commands.

To set task-level security, begin by opening the Admin database (the file named pi_admin.fm). If necessary, click the Security tab. Then do one of the following:

- To change the permissions for all databases that are not specifically listed in the Admin database, display the record for the DEFAULT database. Toggle permissions check boxes as desired.
- To change the permissions for a specific database already included in the Admin database, display the record for the database. Set permissions check boxes as desired.

- To set the permissions for a specific database that is not already included in the Admin database, click the New button to create a new record. Enter the name of the database in the Database Name field and Admin username and password in the Admin Username and Admin Password fields. Then set permissions check boxes as desired.

Permissions
☒ Browse Records ☐ Create Records
☒ Browse All ☐ Edit Records

How you save the permissions you entered depends on whether you are using a PowerPC-based Web server or a 680x0 Macintosh Web server:

- For a PowerPC Web server, click the Update button. Select your Web server application from the list on the right side of the dialog box that appears and click OK. When a confirmation dialog box appears to confirm that WEB•FM has been successfully updated, click its OK button to dismiss it.
- For a 680x0 Macintosh Web server, choose Export from the Script menu or press Command-3. Use the Save As dialog box that appears to locate and open the FM Prefs folder in the Plug-Ins folder inside your Web server folder. Then click the Save button to save the WEB•FM Settings file. When a confirmation dialog box asks whether you want to replace the existing WEB•FM Settings file, click the Replace button.

Field-Level Security

Field-level security disables access to certain database fields. There are two possible settings:

- **Finding** prevents users from searching the specified field.
- **Returning** prevents users from seeing a specified field.

To set field-level security, begin by opening the Admin database (the file named pi_admin.fm). If necessary, click the Security tab. Then do one of the following:

- To change field-level security for all databases that are not specifically listed in the Admin database, display the record for the DEFAULT database. Enter the field name(s) in the Finding and/or Returning scrolling lists as desired.
- To change field-level security for a specific database already included in the Admin database, display the record for the database. Enter the field name(s) in the Finding and/or Returning scrolling lists as desired.
- To change field-level security for a specific database that is not already included in the Admin database, click the New button to create a new record. Enter the name of the database in the Database Name field and

Admin username and password in the Admin Username and Admin Password fields. Enter the field name(s) in the Finding and/or Returning scrolling lists as desired.

Finding: Site URL, Webmaster, Name
Returning: Site URL, Solution URL, Webmaster, Email

TIP

Be sure to press the Return key after each field name you enter in the Finding and Returning scrolling lists.

Follow the instructions in the previous section to save your settings.

Record-Level Security

Record-level security prevents users from modifying (updating) or deleting existing records. It works by requiring the user to provide a username and password that corresponds to the ones in the username and password fields for the record within the database. I tell you about creating these two fields earlier in this chapter.

WARNING

If you do not create username and password fields for your database, the user must provide the Admin password to modify or delete a record in the database.

Accessing & Testing Your WEB•FM Web Publishing Solution

If you've completed all of the steps in the Step-by-Step setup section of this chapter, your database is now online. In this section, I tell you how to access your WEB•FM Web publishing solution so you can test the appearance and functionality of its HTML files.

Start by launching your Web browser and using it to point to the URL for the database Home page. Then start testing. You'll have to try out all of the links, buttons, and other features that you included in the HTML files that make up your Web publishing solution. The goal is to make sure everything works the way it should.

Here's a checklist of the kinds of things you should look for:

- Do the pages appear the way they should? Look at text formatting and inserted images to make sure your HTML is correct.
- Are you able to successfully perform searches with the search form HTML file(s) you created? Don't try just one search. Try a bunch. Then try a few with intentional errors (like the accidental errors visitors will make) to see what happens.
- Do search results appear correctly? Check the HTML calculated in the html field. Also check to be sure that the items that should appear do appear.
- Do links from the page created by the html field to pages created by the detail field work properly? Make sure the correct records appear.
- Are you able to successfully add records?
- Are you able to successfully edit records? Make errors on purpose to see what happens.
- Are you able to successfully delete a record? Is the correct record deleted?
- Do error pages appear when they should and look the way you intended?

Add items to this list to meet your specific needs. Then check to make sure everything is just the way it should be.

If you find a problem, you have to troubleshoot it. Take each problem you find, one at a time, and think about what could have caused it. Whenever possible, try to narrow down the problem to a possible cause. I like to think that all causes fit into one of three categories:

- HTML Coding Errors normally result in formatting problems. Check the HTML code within the calculation field or HTML file that displayed the problem page.
- WEB•FM Coding Errors normally result in error messages. Check the WEB•FM commands, variables, reserved field names, and tokens you used in the calculation field or HTML file that displayed the problem page.
- WEB•FM Setup Errors also normally result in error messages. Check to make sure that WEB•FM is properly installed and loaded into the Web server software.

Once you think you've got the problem fixed, access the database as instructed above and check the problem page or function again. If the problem is gone, move on to the next problem.

TIP

If a calculation field or HTML file doesn't work properly but you have a similar one that does work properly, compare the two to see what the differences are. One of those differences could be causing your problem. That's why it's a good idea to collect sample files, like the ones that come with WEB•FM.

III

Real-Life Database Publishing Examples

As shown in the previous chapters of this book, database Web publishing solutions can vary in complexity from simple to extremely complex. There's no right or wrong answer—each solution is unique depending on the Web publishing requirements. The best way to learn how to create a Web publishing solution is to study existing solutions and apply their techniques to your needs.

This part of the book provides real-life examples of Web publishing solutions using FileMaker Pro version 4's Web Companion. Its five chapters are:

Chapter 8: Basic Data Publishing

Chapter 9: Including Graphics in Published Data

Chapter 10: Making Published Data Interactive

Chapter 11: Performing Calculations

Chapter 12: Handling Transactions

CHAPTER 8

Basic Data Publishing

The most basic database Web publishing requirement is to simply make the information in a database file available on the Web. That's what the examples in this chapter do.

This chapter illustrates a number of methods for publishing the contents of a database file on the Web. In each example, the information is simply made available for Web visitors to browse.

TIP

Don't skip this chapter just because your own needs are more complex. If you've never published database information on the Web before, this is a great example to get you started. Remember, you must learn to walk before you can run!

NOTE

You can download the solution files for this chapter from the companion Web site for this book, http://www.gilesrd.com/fmproweb/. That's also where you can find links to some of these solutions.

About the Database

Contacts.fp3 is a simple database that provides name and contact information for individuals. The Web publishing requirement is to put the contact information online so others can access it.

In this section, I provide some specifics about Contacts.fp3 for the folks who want to create it from scratch or explore the copy that they download from the book's companion Web site.

Database Fields

The database has the following fields:

FIELD NAME	TYPE	DESCRIPTION
recid	text	unique, auto-enter, non-modifiable serial number
Name	text	contact's first and last name
Title	text	contact's job title
Company	text	contact's company name
Address	text	contact's street or P.O. box address
City	text	contact's city
State	text	contact's state
Zip	text	contact's zip
Phone	text	contact's phone number
Extension	text	contact's phone extension
Email	text	contact's e-mail address

This list of fields excludes any fields created as part of a Web publishing solution. Fields created for a solution are discussed in the section about the solution.

Database Layouts

The database has one layout called Record View. This layout presents all fields in a simple but relatively nice-looking data-entry form.

Database Records

To publish a database, it must have some records. The database available on the book's companion Web site has two records—you can see them in the previous illustration. If you're creating the database from scratch, make sure you create at least two records for it.

Exporting to an HTML Table

Exporting to an HTML table is the quickest and easiest static Web publishing technique. I provide step-by-step instructions in Chapter 4; here are a few specifics for exporting the data in Contacts.fp3.

TIP

If you use this method repeatedly to generate updated versions of a Web page, consider creating a FileMaker Pro script that will perform the export for you. It can be a big timesaver, especially if you use the Find and Sort commands before exporting the data.

Preparing the Database for Export

Start by using the Find and Sort commands to browse only those records that you want to export in the order in which you want to export them.

In our example, there are only two records—we want to export them both. You may also want to sort by the Name or Company field. To sort by last name, there must be a separate last name field; this simple database only has one name field, enabling you to sort by first name only.

Exporting the Records

Use the Export Records command to set up the export. In the Export Field Order (Macintosh) or Specify Field Order for Export (Windows) dialog box, add the following fields to the Field Order list: Name, Title, Company, Phone, and Email. Then click the Export button to create the HTML table.

Checking (and Troubleshooting) Your Work

When the export is complete, you can open the resulting file with your favorite Web browser to see how it will look to the world. Here's how our solution looks:

Name	Company	Title	Phone	Email
Andy Knasinski	NRG Software, LLC	Partner	414-545-0353	ajk@nrgsoft.com
Maria Langer		Author/Consultant		MariaL1@aol.com

If the file doesn't appear with HTML table formatting, repeat the export. Make sure you choose HTML Table from the menu at the bottom of the Export to File dialog box. (Choosing something else will not properly format the document.) It should work. After all, FileMaker Pro is doing the hard part—writing all the HTML code to display database contents in table cells.

Improving the Appearance of the Exported Table

If desired, open the exported file with your favorite Web authoring tool. You can then customize the appearance of the Web page FileMaker Pro created to add a title, graphics, and other HTML elements. Here are the same two tables after a little customization with Claris Home Page:

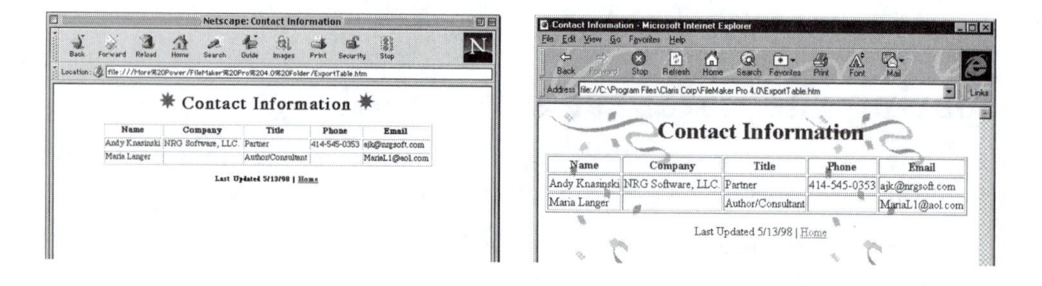

Publishing the Page

To make the page available on the Internet or your company intranet, you must copy the HTML document to the appropriate directory of your Web server. Then add links to the document on other pages or distribute the page's URL so visitors can find it.

Exporting Calculation Fields

Creating and exporting calculation fields that generate HTML code is a bit more difficult but much more flexible. As I explain in the second half of Chapter 4, it requires a solid understanding of HTML, as well as a clear idea of how you want your Web pages to look. And of course, you must understand how to concatenate text in the Specify Calculation dialog box.

Our solution looks like this:

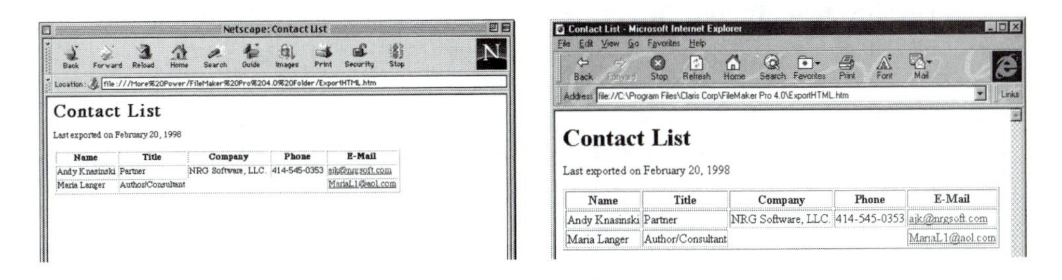

In this section, I tell you all about the calculation fields and how you can use them to create the HTML document.

Creating the Calculation Fields

The solution uses three calculation fields that are exported for each record. Here's the information for each field, including a summary of its purpose, the formula, and notes that explain what each part of the formula does. Use the Define Fields and Specify Calculation dialog box to create each of these calculation fields.

TIP

It's a good idea to use Return and Space characters within complex formulas to help keep them straight in your mind as you create them. These three formulas are good examples. FileMaker Pro ignores Returns and Spaces unless they are enclosed within double quote characters.

header html

This calculation field determines whether the record being exported is the first record. Then:

- If it is the first record, the field provides HTML tags needed to start an HTML document and an HTML table within it.
- If it isn't the first record, the field is left blank.

Here's the formula for this field, along with my comments. The formula code is in **bold, sans serif type**; my comments are in this type. Don't enter my comments into the formula.

```
If(Status(CurrentRecordNumber)=1,
```

This tells FileMaker Pro to see if the current record is the first record.

```
"<HTML>¶
<HEAD><TITLE>Contact List</TITLE></HEAD>¶
<BODY BGCOLOR=""FFFFFF"">¶
<H1>Contact List</H1>¶
```

```
Last exported on " & MonthName(Today) & " " & Day(Today) & ", " &
Year(Today) & "¶
<P>¶
<TABLE BORDER=1>¶
<TR><TH>Name</TH><TH>Title</TH><TH>Company</TH><TH>Phone</TH><TH>
E-Mail</TH></TR>¶"
```

If the record is the first record in the database, FileMaker Pro creates HTML code for the beginning of an HTML document titled Contact List. The document displays a heading and the current date at the top of the page followed by the beginning of a table with field names as headings in the first row.

```
,"")
```

If the current record is not the first record, FileMaker Pro leaves the field blank.

When you're finished entering the formula, check it for accuracy. Then choose Text from the Calculation result is menu at the bottom of the dialog box. Click the Storage Options button. In the Storage Options dialog box, turn on the Do not store calculation results check box and click OK.

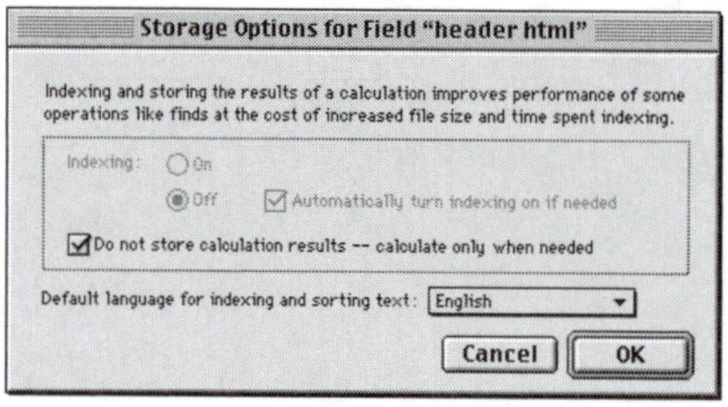

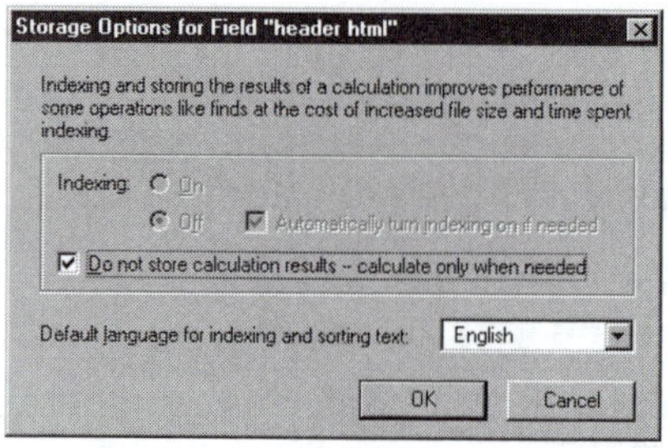

If you fail to turn on the Do not store calculation result check box, the header html code may appear for incorrect records.

Click OK in the Specify Calculation dialog box to save the formula.

record html

The record html field creates HTML code that displays the fields in table cells. This field is calculated for every single record of the database.

Here's the **formula** and my comments:

```
"<TR>¶
<TD>"&Name&"</TD>¶
<TD>"&Title&"</TD>¶
<TD>"&Company&"</TD>¶
<TD>"&Phone&If(Extension≠""," Ext. "&Extension,"")&"</TD>¶
```

```
<TD>"&If(Email≠"","<A HREF=""mailto:"&Email&""">"&Email&"</A>","")&"</TD>¶
</TR>¶"
```

This tells FileMaker Pro to create HTML that displays the contents of certain fields in cells of a table row.

When you're finished entering the formula, check it, choose Text from the Calculation result is menu, and click OK.

footer html

The footer html field determines whether the record being exported is the last record. Then:

- If it is the last record, the field provides all the tags needed to end the table and the HTML document.
- If it isn't the last record, the field is left blank.

Here's the **formula** for footer html, along with my comments:

```
If(Status(CurrentRecordNumber)=Status(CurrentRecordCount),
```

This tells FileMaker Pro to check if the current record is the last record in the database.

```
"</TABLE>¶
</BODY>¶
</HTML>"
```

If the current record is the last record, FileMaker Pro creates the HTML code to end the table, the document body, and the HTML document itself.

```
,"")
```

If the current record is not the last record, FileMaker Pro leaves the field blank.

When you're finished entering the formula, check it for accuracy. Then choose Text from the Calculation result is menu at the bottom of the dialog box. Click the Storage Options button and turn on the Do not store calculation results in the Storage Options dialog box. Click OK to save your setting, then click OK to save the formula.

If you do not turn on the Do not store calculation result check box, the footer html code may appear for incorrect records.

Exporting the Records

Creating the calculation fields is the hard part. Exporting them to an HTML document is much easier. I tell you exactly how in Chapter 4, but here are some additional specifics for this example.

Use the Export Records command to export as a Tab-separated text file (not an HTML Table!). When you specify the fields to export, select the header html, record html, and footer html calculation fields you created, in that order. When you click the Export button, the HTML document is created.

Checking (and Troubleshooting) Your Work

Open the exported file with your favorite Web browser to check your work.

If the file doesn't look like the examples shown at the beginning of this section, go back to FileMaker Pro and check your formulas. If you make any changes, you'll have to re-export the records and reload the file into your Web browser to check it again.

Publishing the Page

To make the page available on the Internet or your company intranet, you must copy it to the appropriate directory of your Web server. Then add links to the page on other pages or distribute the URL for the page so visitors can find it.

Instant Web Publishing

Instant Web Publishing, which I discuss in Chapter 1, offers an easy way to publish FileMaker Pro databases using FileMaker Pro Web Companion's Web serving capabilities. Here's how you can get Contacts.fp3 on the Web using Instant Web Publishing.

NOTE

The instructions for this solution assume that you have properly installed FileMaker Pro, enabled and configured the Web Companion Plug-In for Instant Web Publishing, and turned on Web Companion Sharing in the File Sharing dialog box. I provide detailed instructions for completing all of these tasks in Chapter 1.

Moving the File to the Web Folder

To publish a database using Instant Web Publishing, the database file must be in the Web folder inside the FileMaker Pro folder of the computer that will act as the database Web server.

If Contacts.fp3 is open, close it. Then move it to the Web folder. Double-click its icon to open it again.

Creating a New Layout

Instant Web Publishing creates Web pages (or views) by displaying fields that exist on specific layouts within the database file. The example database only has one layout; to display different fields in different views, there must be a layout for each view.

Our example displays only two views—Table and Form views. The existing layout is fine for the Form view, but it contains far too many fields for the Table view. A new layout is required.

Switch to layout mode and create a new columnar report layout named Contact List. Include the following fields on the layout: Name, Company, Phone, and Email. When you're finished, the layout might look like this in Browse mode:

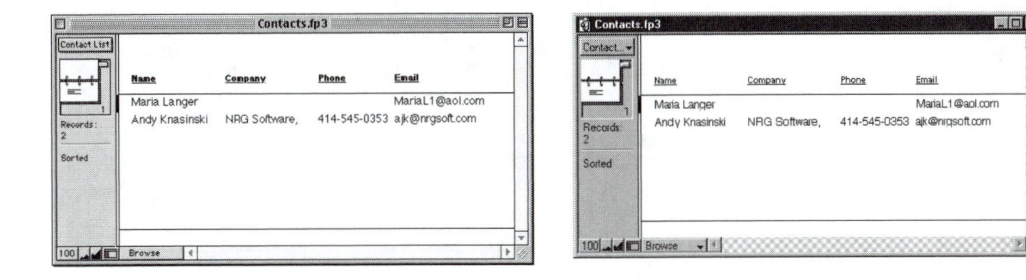

Setting Up Views

To display the correct fields on Web pages, you must specify which layout should be used for each view. You do this in the Web Companion View Setup dialog box. I provide step-by-step instructions for setting up views in Chapter 1; here are some specifics for this example:

- For Table View, choose Contact List from the Layout menu.
- For Form View, choose Record View from the Layout menu.
- For Search choose either of the defined layouts from the Layout menu. (We chose Contact List.)

Although searching is not required for this solution, it cannot be disabled for Instant Web Publishing. That's why you need to specify an appropriate layout for the Search page.

- For Sort, select the last radio button, then set the sort order by Company.

Here's what the Web Companion View Setup dialog box should look like:

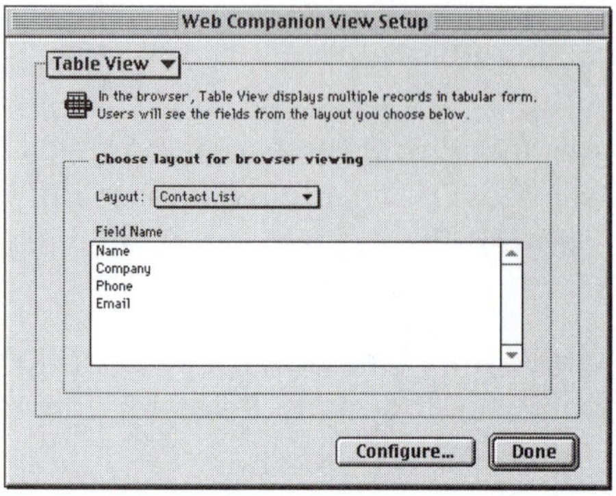

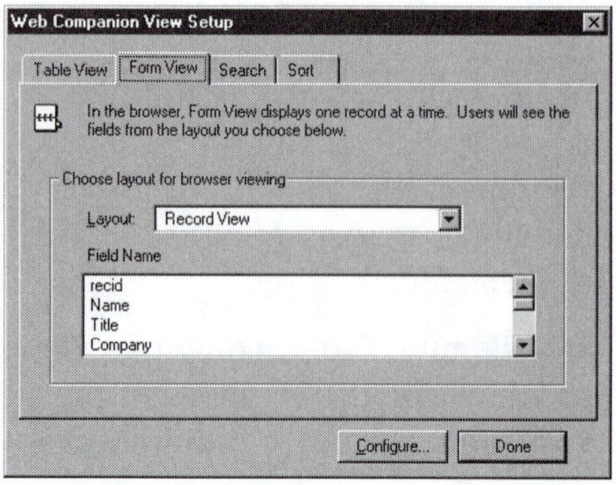

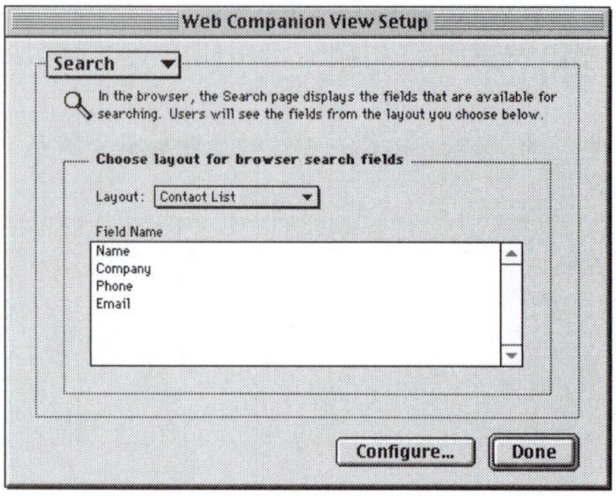

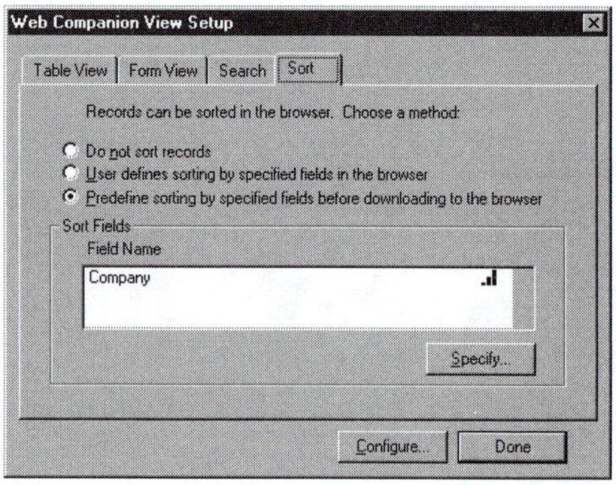

Checking the Instant Web Publishing Solution

To check your Instant Web Publishing solution, fire up your favorite Web browser and point it to the IP address of the database Web server. FileMaker Pro Web Companion's built-in home page should list the file. Click its link to check your work. Here's what the Table and Form views look like in our solution:

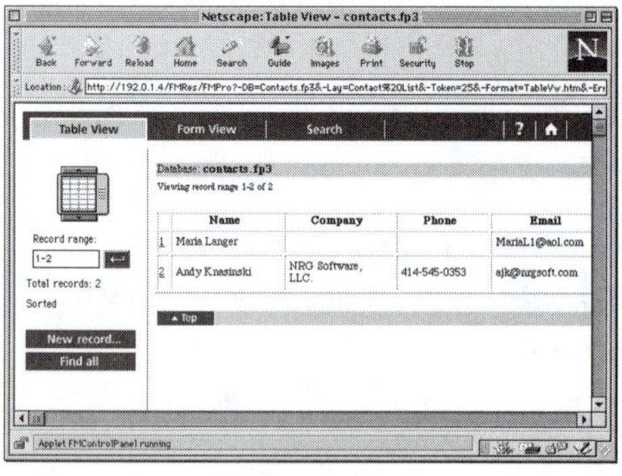

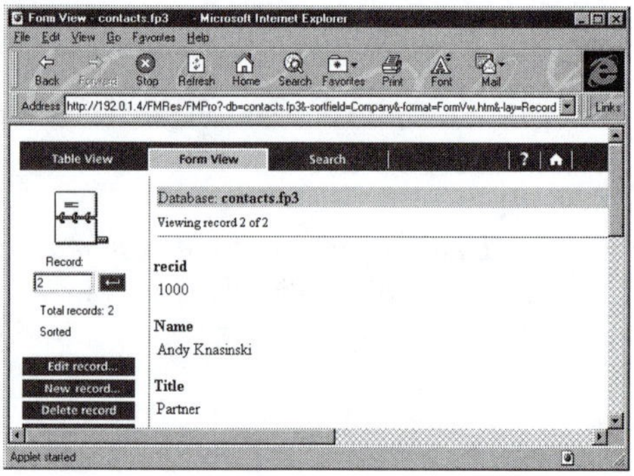

There isn't much room for error here. The only thing you can screw up is the view setup. If the wrong fields appear or the fields appear in the wrong order, check the layouts selected in the Web Companion View Setup dialog box, then look at the actual layouts themselves. Remember, fields appear on a page in the order in which they appear on a layout—you may have to rearrange the fields on the layout—or create a whole new layout—to get them to appear the way you want in Instant Web Publishing.

Custom Web Publishing

For complete control over the appearance of Web pages that you publish using FileMaker Pro Web Companion, you must use Custom Web Publishing, which I discuss in Chapter 2. This requires knowledge of both HTML and CDML and the ability to create format files.

Here's what the two Web pages of our solution look like when viewed with Web browser software:

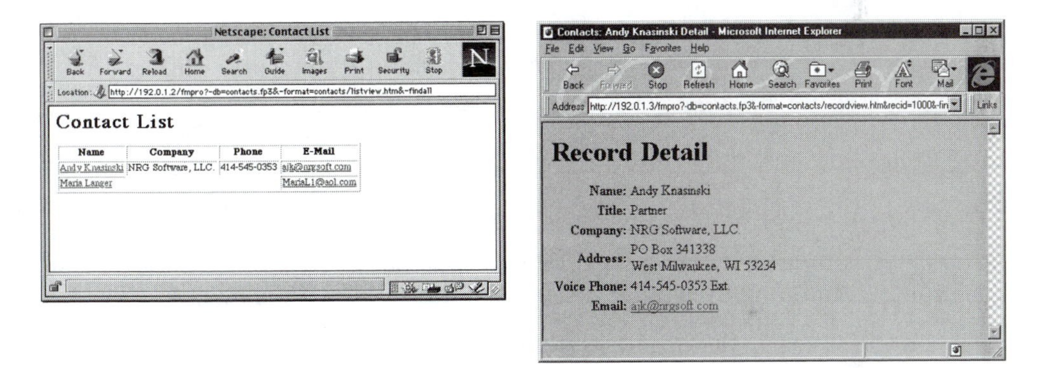

In this section, I provide instructions for creating this solution with FileMaker Pro's built-in Custom Web Publishing.

The instructions for this solution assume that you have properly installed FileMaker Pro, enabled and configured the Web Companion Plug-In for Custom Web Publishing, and turned on Web Companion Sharing in the File Sharing dialog box. I provide detailed instructions for completing all of these tasks in Chapter 2.

Creating a Project Folder in the Web Folder

This example includes a number of format files that will be stored in a "project folder" inside the Web folder in the FileMaker Pro folder. The database file will be stored with them.

Create a folder named contacts inside the Web folder. If the database file is open, close it. Then move it into the contacts folder. Double-click its icon to open it.

Creating the Format Files

This solution requires three format files that provide HTML and CDML commands for FileMaker Pro Web Companion.

Here's the information for each format file, including a discussion of its purpose, the HTML and CDML code within it, and notes that explain what each part of the code does. The code is in **bold, sans serif type**; my comments are in this type. Don't enter my comments in the format files!

TIP

Chapter 2 offers suggestions for using the CDML Tool that comes with FileMaker Pro or Claris Home Page to create format files. This is the best alternative to manually typing in the code for each format file.

default.htm

The default home page, default.htm, includes a link that, when clicked, displays the listview.htm format file with data from the database. In a real-life situation, the default home page would probably include many links besides this one.

Here's the **code** for default.htm, along with my comments:

```
<HTML>
<HEAD><TITLE>Contacts</TITLE></HEAD>
<BODY>
<H1>Contact List Database</H1>
```

These lines identify the HTML file, give it a title, start the body of the file, and display a heading at the top of the page.

```
Click <A HREF="/fmpro?-db=contacts.fp3&-format=contacts/listview.htm&-
findall">here</A> to display a list of contacts.
```

This link tells FileMaker Pro to display all of the records in Contacts.fp3 using the listview.htm format file.

```
</BODY>
</HTML>
```

These two lines end the body and HTML document.

Check the code and save the file as default.htm in the contacts folder that you created.

listview.htm

The listview.htm format file displays the Name, Company, Phone, and Email fields for all records in the database in a table format. It also provides a link to detailed information about a specific record and a mailto link on each e-mail address.

Here's the **code** for listview.htm, along with my comments:

```
<HTML>
<HEAD>
<TITLE>Contact List</TITLE>
</HEAD>
<BODY>
<H1>Contact List</H1>
```

These lines identify the HTML file, give it a title, start the body of the file, and display a heading on the page.

```
<TABLE BORDER=1>
```

This line starts the table that will display database information.

```
<TR>
<TH>Name</TH>
<TH>Company</TH>
<TH>Phone</TH>
<TH>E-Mail</TH>
</TR>
```

These lines create a heading row that identifies the information in each column of the table.

```
[FMP-Record]
```

This CDML tag tells FileMaker Pro to repeat all code between it and the **[/FMP-Record]** tag for all records in the database.

```
<TR>
```

This code begins another table row.

```
<TD><A HREF="/fmpro?-db=contacts.fp3&-format=contacts/recordview.htm&
recid=[FMP-Field: recid]&-find">[FMP-Field: Name]</A></TD>
```

This code tells FileMaker Pro to display the name field in the first cell as a link to the same record displayed in the recordview.htm format file. The recid field is used to identify the record in the link.

```
<TD>[FMP-Field: Company]</TD>
```

This code tells FileMaker Pro to display the company field in a cell.

```
<TD>[FMP-Field: Phone]</TD>
```

This code tells FileMaker Pro to display the phone field in a cell.

```
<TD><A HREF="mailto:[FMP-Field: Email, url]">[FMP-Field: Email]</A></TD>
```

This code tells FileMaker Pro to display the email field in a cell as a mailto link. (Clicking this link in the Web browser window displays a pre-addressed e-mail form.)

```
</TR>
```

This code ends the row.

```
[/FMP-Record]
```

This code tells FileMaker Pro to stop repeating code.

```
</TABLE>
```

This code marks the end of the table.

```
</BODY>
</HTML>
```

These lines mark the end of the body and HTML document.

Check the code, then save it as listview.htm in the contacts folder.

recordview.htm

The recordview.htm format file displays the Name, Title, Company, Address, City, State, Zip, Phone, Extension, and Email fields for a specific database record when the name field for the record is clicked on the listview.htm page.

Here's the **code** and my comments for recordview.htm:

```
<HTML>
<HEAD>
<TITLE>Contacts: [FMP-Field: Name] Detail</TITLE>
</HEAD>
<BODY>
<H1>Record Detail</H1>
```

These lines identify the HTML file, give it a title, and display a heading on the page. Note the use of CDML tags in the TITLE; this enables you to display a database field in the Web browser's title bar.

```
<TABLE BORDER=0>
```

This line starts a borderless table.

```
<TR><TH ALIGN=RIGHT>Name:</TH><TD>[FMP-Field: Name]</TD></TR>
```

This line displays a two-column row with a heading in the left cell and the contents of the Name field in the right cell.

```
<TR><TH ALIGN=RIGHT>Title:</TH><TD>[FMP-Field: Title]</TD></TR>
```

This line displays a two-column row with a heading in the left cell and the contents of the Title field in the right cell.

```
<TR><TH ALIGN=RIGHT>Company:</TH><TD>[FMP-Field: Company]</TD></TR>
```

This line displays a two-column row with a heading in the left cell and the contents of the Company field in the right cell.

```
<TR><TH ALIGN=RIGHT>Address:</TH><TD>[FMP-Field: Address]<BR>[FMP-
Field: City], [FMP-Field: State]  [FMP-Field: Zip]</TD></TR>
```

This line displays a two-column row with a heading in the left cell and the contents of the Address, City, State, and Zip fields in the right cell. The fields are formatted with standard spacing and punctuation in two lines within the cell.

```
<TR><TH ALIGN=RIGHT>Voice Phone:</TH><TD>[FMP-Field: Phone] Ext. [FMP-
Field: Extension]</TD></TR>
```

This line displays a two-column row with a heading in the left cell and the contents of the Phone and Extension fields in the right cell. The abbreviation *Ext.* appears between the two fields to identify the extension portion of the phone number.

```
<TR><TH ALIGN=RIGHT>Email:</TH><TD><A HREF="mailto:[FMP-Field: Email,
url]">[FMP-Field: Email]</A></TD></TR>
```

This line displays a two-column row with a heading in the left cell and the contents of the Email field in the right cell. The Email field is formatted as a mailto link, just as it was in the listview.htm file.

```
</TABLE>
```

This line ends the table.

```
</BODY>
</HTML>
```

These lines end the body and the HTML document.

Check the code and save the document as recordview.htm in the contacts folder.

Checking the Custom Web Publishing Solution

To check your Custom Web Publishing solution, fire up your favorite Web browser and point it to the IP address of the database Web server followed by /contacts/default.htm. The default.htm format file with its single link should appear. Click the link to display the records in the listview.htm format file. Then click one of the names in the first column to display details for that record.

If your pages don't look like the ones illustrated at the beginning of this section, check the code in the format files. Remember, one misplaced angle bracket or slash can make a surprisingly big mess of things. The code in this chapter is correct so use it as a guide.

CHAPTER 9

Including Graphics in Published Data

In some databases, images are important pieces of data that should be included on Web pages that publish database information. A product catalog, like the one used throughout this chapter, is a good example. The old saying, "a picture's worth a thousand words," can also apply to Web publishing: "A page with pictures will get more attention than a page with a thousand words."

Including images with database information can offer additional challenges to Web publishers. How you tackle the problem depends on the Web publishing technique you plan to use. This chapter illustrates three methods for publishing a database that includes images: static Web publishing with calculation fields, Instant Web Publishing, and Custom Web Publishing. As you'll see, each method is different and offers its own set of challenges.

NOTE *You can download the solution files for this chapter from the companion Web site for this book, http://www.gilesrd.com/fmproweb/. That's also where you can find links to some of these solutions.*

About the Database

Products.fp3 provides information about products sold by Acme Office Supplies, a fictional office supply company. The database uses images in two different ways:

- A red "Sale Item" image displays for items that are on sale.
- Photographs illustrate each product.

The Web publishing requirement is to put the database information—including Sale Item image and product pictures—on the Web.

Here's some more specific information about Products.fp3. Use it if you want to create the file from scratch or explore the copy that you download from the book's companion Web site.

Database Fields

The database has the following fields:

FIELD NAME	TYPE	DESCRIPTION
recid	text	unique, auto-enter, non-modifiable serial number
Stock Number	text	item stock number
Item Name	text	name of item
Item Description	text	description of item
Unit Price	number	item price
Sale Item	text	sale item status; contents of field must be Yes or No as specified by a value list
Category	text	item category; value list options include: Business Machines, Writing Instruments, and Basic Office Supplies
Sale Item Image	global	container for Sale Item image
Image	container	item image
Sale	calculation	container that displays Sale Item image if the item is a sale item; formula is: **`If (Sale Item = "Yes" , Sale Item , "")`**

This list of fields excludes any fields created as part of a Web publishing solution. Fields created for a solution are discussed in the section about the solution.

Database Layouts

The database has two layouts:

- MAIN displays all fields except the recid, Sale Item Image, and Sale fields.
- GLOBALS displays the Sale Item Image global field.

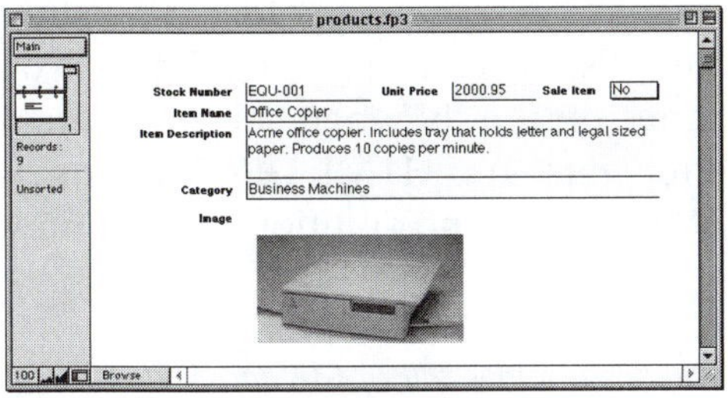

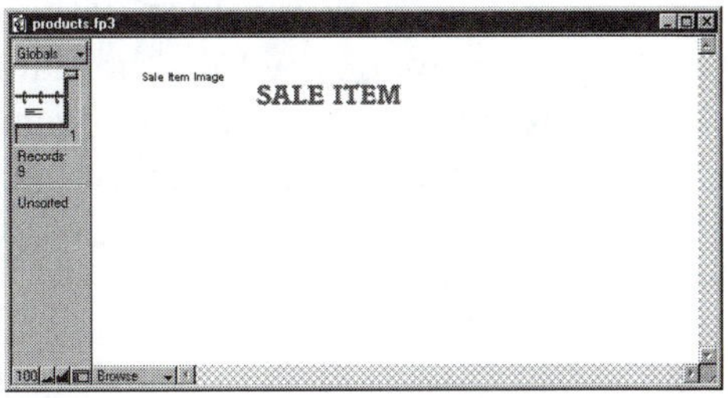

Database Records

The database has nine records, each with its own picture. There are at least two records for each category.

If you're creating the database from scratch, you can fill the records with any data you like. Be creative or get ideas from an office supply catalog sitting around on your desk.

About the Images

The database we created includes the Sale Item image in a global field and the individual item pictures for each record in a container field. Here are some important things to remember about where you store images to be published and how you set up FileMaker Pro for importing images.

Image Location

Where you store images to be published with a database depends on the Web publishing method you choose:

- For static Web publishing using exported calculation fields, the images do not need to be in the database at all. Instead, they should be stored in a folder on the Web server. (They can be in both places if desired.) They must be in either GIF or JPEG format so they can be interpreted by all graphic Web browsers. A field within the database should indicate the name or pathname to the image file; more on that in the Exporting Calculation Fields section later in this chapter.

- For Instant Web Publishing, the images for each record must be stored in a container field within the database file. Instant Web Publishing only displays the contents of a database; it cannot display images stored elsewhere. FileMaker Pro Web Companion automatically converts the images to JPEG format on the fly as it serves Web pages.
- For Custom Web Publishing, the images can be either within the database or in a separate folder within the solution's project folder. I recommend storing images within the database—it's easier to use FileMaker Pro Web Companion's ability to convert images on the fly when serving pages than to worry about pathnames, image formats, and HTML **IMG SRC** tags in format files. This is how the Custom Web Publishing solution in this chapter is developed.

The companion Web site for this book includes a folder full of GIF and JPEG images you can import into or use with a do-it-yourself copy of Products.fp3.

FileMaker Pro Image Preferences

Before importing or pasting images into a container field, be sure to turn on the Store Compatible Graphics option in FileMaker Pro's Document Preference dialog box. This ensures that the graphics are stored in a cross-platform format.

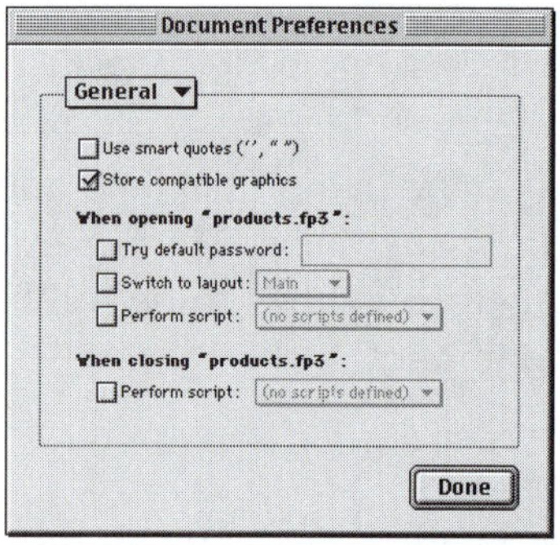

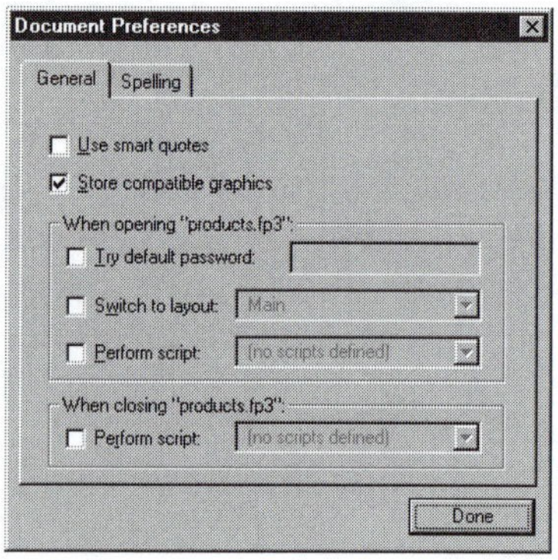

FileMaker Pro Import Picture Options

When importing images for use with Instant or Custom Web Publishing, do *not* turn on the Store only a reference to the file check box in the Import Picture dialog box. Doing so prevents the image from being stored in the database; instead FileMaker Pro looks for the image on disk each time it needs to display it.

Exporting Calculation Fields

One way to publish a database with images is to export calculation fields that generate a static HTML document with **IMG SRC** references to the images. This takes some time to develop, but once set up, it's a snap to update the page. I tell you more about this method in Chapter 4; in this section, I provide instructions for completing the task with Products.fp3. The finished solution looks like this:

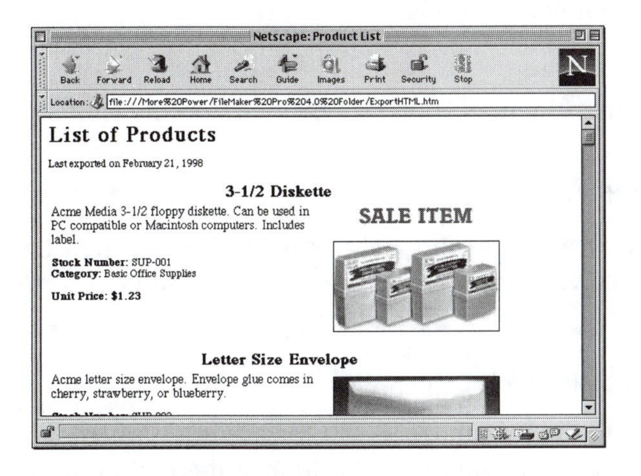

Creating the Fields

The solution requires that you create a number of additional text and calculation fields:

- **SALE IMG SRC**, **IMAGE FILE NAME** and **IMG SRC** are three fields that provide information about the location of image files that must be displayed for the Web publishing solution.
- **HEADER HTML**, **RECORD HTML**, and **FOOTER HTML** generate HTML that is exported for each field to create the complete HTML document.

NOTE

The Sale Item Image and Sale fields do not exist in our static Web publishing solution because they are not necessary. It doesn't matter whether they exist in the database file; they are not used in this solution.

Here's the information for each field, including a summary of its purpose, the formula (if necessary), and notes that explain what each part of the formula does. Use the Define Fields and Specify Calculation dialog box to create each of these fields.

TIP

It's a good idea to use Return and Space characters within complex formulas to help keep them straight in your mind as you create them. These three formulas are good examples. FileMaker Pro ignores Returns and Spaces unless they are enclosed within double quote characters.

Sale IMG SRC

The Sale IMG SRC field is a calculation field that evaluates whether the item is on sale and, if it is, calculates the HTML code necessary to display the Sale Image file.

Here's the **formula** and my comments:

```
If(Sale Item="Yes",
```

This first line evaluates whether the item is on sale by checking the contents of the Sale Item field.

```
"<IMG SRC=""images/sale.gif"">"
```

If the item is on sale, the field calculates the HTML code to display the sale.gif file, which is stored in the images folder in the same folder as the Web page.

```
,"")
```

If the item is not on sale, the field is left empty.

When you're finished entering the formula, check it for accuracy. Then choose Text from the Calculation result is menu at the bottom of the dialog box and click OK to save the formula.

Image File Name

The Image File Name field is a plain text field used to store the name of the image file for a record.

Once you create this field, you must return to Browse mode and enter data into it. Use the names of the image files for the items in the database. Be sure to enter the entire file name, including any file name extensions. If the file name contains a space character, that character should be encoded as %20. For example, a file named *sale picture.gif* should be entered as *sale%20picture.gif*. Otherwise, the file name will not be understood by Web browser software.

TIP

Do yourself a big favor: don't include spaces in file names that will be used in HTML documents. They'll be easier to code—and to troubleshoot.

IMG SRC

The IMG SRC field calculates the HTML code to display an image file on disk. Here's the **formula** with my comments:

```
If(Image File Name≠"",
```

This line determines whether an image file name has been recorded for the record by examining the contents of the Image File Name field.

```
"<IMG SRC=""images/" & Image File Name & """ BORDER=1>"
```

If the Image File Name field is not blank, FileMaker Pro calculates the HTML code to display the image by concatenating the name of the folder containing the image files with the image file name. The code also includes a **BORDER** tag which places a 1-pixel border around the image on the page.

```
,"")
```

If the Image File Name field is blank, the field is left empty.

When you're finished entering the formula, check it for accuracy. Then choose Text from the Calculation result is menu at the bottom of the dialog box. Click the OK button to save the formula.

header html

This calculation field determines whether the record being exported is the first record. Then:

- If it is the first record, the field provides HTML tags needed to start an HTML document.
- If it isn't the first record, the field is left blank.

Here's the formula for this field, along with my comments. The formula code is in **bold, sans serif type**; my comments are in this type. Don't enter my comments into the formula.

```
If(Status(CurrentRecordNumber)=1,
```

This tells FileMaker Pro to see if the current record is the first record.

```
"<HTML>¶
<HEAD><TITLE>Product List</TITLE></HEAD>¶
```

```
<BODY BGCOLOR=""#FFFFFF"">¶
<H1>List of Products</H1>
Last exported on "&MonthName(Today)&" "&Day(Today)&", "&Year(Today)&"¶
<P>¶"
```

If the record is the first record in the database, FileMaker Pro creates HTML code for the beginning of an HTML document titled Product List. The document displays a heading and the date the information was last exported at the top of the page.

```
,"")
```

If the current record is not the first record, FileMaker Pro leaves the field blank.

When you're finished entering the formula, check it for accuracy. Then choose Text from the Calculation result is menu at the bottom of the dialog box. Click the Storage Options button. In the Storage Options dialog box, turn on the Do not store calculation results check box and click OK.

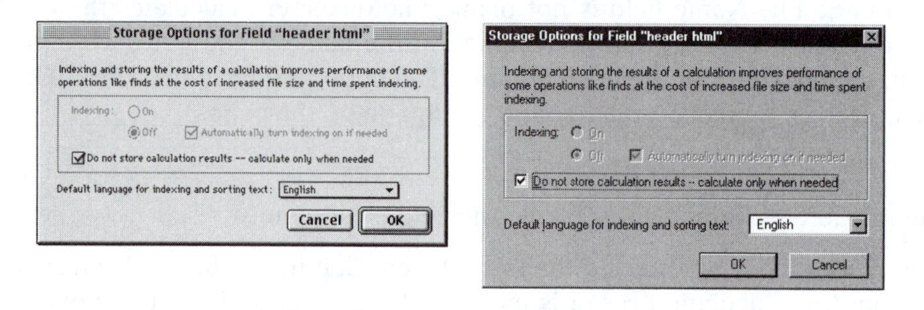

If you fail to turn on the Do not store calculation result check box, the header html code may appear for incorrect records.

Click OK in the Specify Calculation dialog box to save the formula.

record html

The record html field creates HTML code that displays a borderless table for each record that includes information and the image file. This field is calculated for every record of the database.

Here's the **formula** and my comments:

```
"<TABLE BORDER=0>¶
```

This starts the borderless table.

```
<TR>
<TD COLSPAN=2 BGCOLOR=""#FFFFCC"" ALIGN=""CENTER""><FONT
SIZE=+2><B>" & Item Name & "</B></FONT></TD>
```

```
</TR>¶
```

This code creates the first row of the table. It has a single cell that spans two columns and has a light yellow background color (which doesn't show up well in the illustration on the previous page). In that cell, centered and displayed in a bold font two sizes larger than normal, is the contents of the Item Name field for the record.

```
<TR>¶
```

This code starts the second row of the table.

```
<TD WIDTH=""300"" VALIGN=""TOP"">¶
<FONT SIZE=+1>"&Item Description&"</FONT>¶
<P>¶
<B>Stock Number:</B> " & Stock Number & "<BR>¶
<B>Category:</B> "& Category &"¶
<P>¶
<B>Unit Price: $" & Unit Price & "</B>¶
</TD>¶
```

This code displays the left cell in the row. It's 300 pixels wide and top-aligned. The first paragraph in the cell displays the item description in a font one size larger than normal. The next paragraph displays the Stock Number heading in bold, followed by the contents of the Stock Number field. The next line displays the Category heading in bold followed by the contents of the Category field. The next paragraph displays the Unit Price heading followed by the contents of the Unit Price field, both in bold.

```
<TD WIDTH=""200"" ALIGN=""CENTER"" VALIGN=""MIDDLE"">¶"
& Sale IMG SRC & "¶
<P>¶"
& IMG SRC & "¶
</TD>¶
```

This code displays the right cell in the row. It's 200 pixels wide and both center- and middle-aligned. The first paragraph displays the Sale Image file only if the item is on sale—it gets the path to the file from the Sale IMG SRC field. The second paragraph displays the picture of the item—it gets the path to the item's image file from the IMG SRC field.

```
</TR>¶
```

This code ends the row.

```
</TABLE>¶
```

This code ends the table.

```
<P>¶"
```

This code puts a blank paragraph between this record and the next one.

When you're finished entering the formula, check it, choose Text from the Calculation result is menu, and click OK.

footer html

The footer html field determines whether the record being exported is the last record. Then:

- If it is the last record, the field provides the tags needed to end the HTML document.
- If it isn't the last record, the field is left blank.

Here's the **formula** for record html, along with my comments:

```
If(Status(CurrentRecordNumber)=Status(CurrentRecordCount),
```

This tells FileMaker Pro to check if the current record is the last record in the database.

```
"</BODY>¶
</HTML>"
```

If the current record is the last record, FileMaker Pro creates the HTML code to end the document body and the HTML document.

```
,"")
```

If the current record is not the last record, FileMaker Pro leaves the field blank.

When you're finished entering the formula, check it, then choose Text from the Calculation result is menu. Click the Storage Options button and turn on the Do not store calculation results check box in the Storage Options dialog box. Click OK to save your setting, then click OK to save the formula.

WARNING

If you do not turn on the Do not store calculation result check box, the footer html code may appear for incorrect records.

Exporting the Records

Creating the calculation fields is the hard part. Exporting them to an HTML document is much easier. I tell you exactly how in Chapter 4, but here are some additional specifics for this example.

Use the Export Records command to export as a Tab-separated text file (not an HTML Table!). When you specify the fields to export, select the header html, record html, and footer html calculation fields you created, in that order. When you click the Export button, the HTML document is created.

Checking (and Troubleshooting) Your Work

Open the exported file with your favorite Web browser to check your work.

If the file doesn't look like the example shown at the beginning of this section, go back to FileMaker Pro and check your formulas. If you make any changes, you'll have to re-export the records and reload the file into your Web browser to check it again.

Publishing the Page

To make the page available on the Internet or your company intranet, you must copy it to the appropriate directory of your Web server. Then add links to the page on other pages or distribute the URL for the page so visitors can find it.

Instant Web Publishing

Instant Web Publishing, which I discuss in Chapter 1, makes it simple to publish databases with images on the Web—as long as the images have been properly pasted or imported into the database. Here are the instructions for publishing Products.fp3 and its images using Instant Web Publishing.

NOTE

The instructions for this solution assume that you have properly installed FileMaker Pro, enabled and configured the Web Companion Plug-In for Instant Web Publishing, and turned on Web Companion Sharing in the File Sharing dialog box. I provide detailed instructions for completing all of these tasks in Chapter 1.

Moving the File to the Web Folder

To publish a database using Instant Web Publishing, the database file must be in the Web folder inside the FileMaker Pro folder of the computer that will act as the database Web server.

If Products.fp3 is open, close it. Then move it to the Web folder. Double-click its icon to open it again.

Creating New Layouts

Instant Web Publishing creates Web pages (or views) by displaying fields that exist on specific layouts within the database file. Neither of the layouts in Products.fp3 is suitable for an Instant Web Publishing view so at least two new layouts must be created.

Table View Layout

The layout for Table View should include just a handful of useful fields. Switch to Layout mode, then create a new columnar report layout named Table View with the following fields: Category, Item Name, Sale, and Unit Price. When you're finished, the layout might look like this in Browse mode:

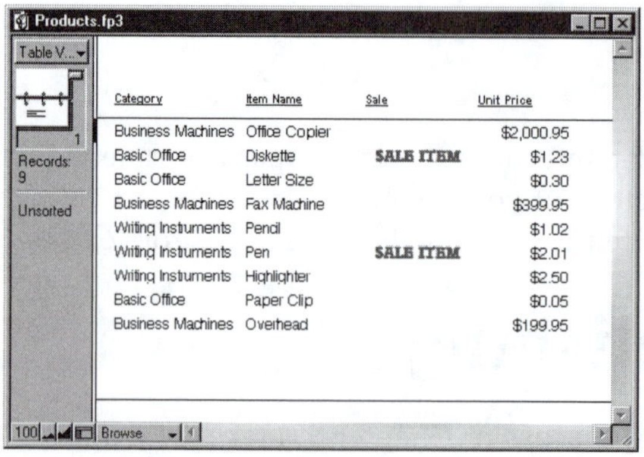

Form View Layout

The Layout for Form View should include all the fields that provide detailed information about the item, as well as the item's image. In Layout mode, create a new standard layout named Form View. Remove fields from the layout so that only the following fields remain, in this order: Item Name, Stock Number, Item Description, Sale, Unit Price, and Image. Resize the Item Description field so the entire description fits within the field boundaries. Then apply number formatting to the Unit Price field so it displays values with a leading currency symbol, thousands separator, and two decimal places. When you're finished, the layout might look like this:

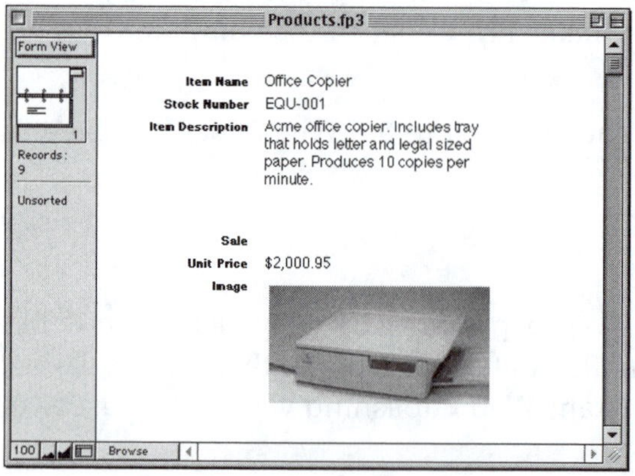

Search Layout

Although our solution isn't really concerned with the ability to search the database, searching cannot be disabled for Instant Web Publishing. Therefore, you may as well create a layout for searching.

In Layout mode, create a new standard layout called Search. Remove fields until only the following fields remain, in this order: Category, Item Name, Stock Number, Item Description, Sale Item, and Unit Price. When you're finished, the layout should look like this:

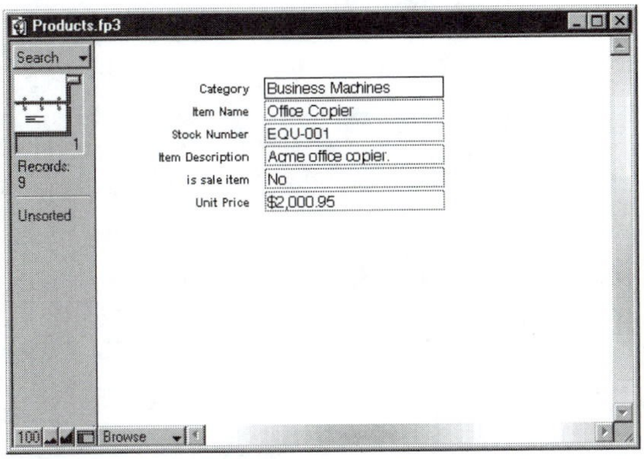

Setting Up Views

To display the correct fields on Web pages, you must specify the layout that should be used for each view. You do this in the Web Companion View Setup dialog box. I provide step-by-step instructions for setting up views in Chapter 1; here are some specifics for this example:

- For Table View, choose Table View from the Layout menu.
- For Form View, choose Form View from the Layout menu.
- For Search, choose Search from the Layout menu.
- For Sort, select the last radio button, then set the sort order by Category.

Here's what the Web Companion View Setup dialog box looks like with these options set:

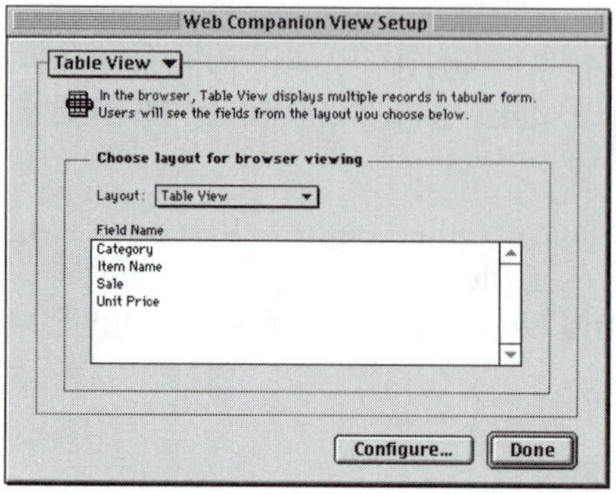

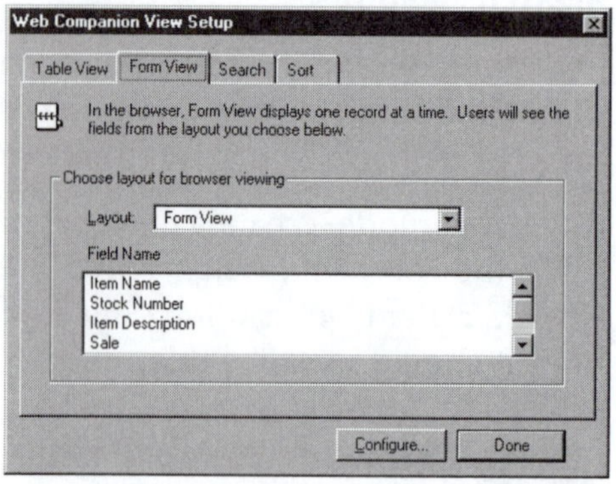

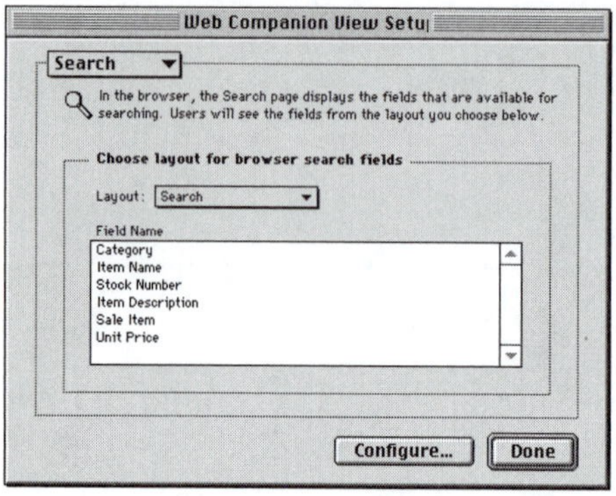

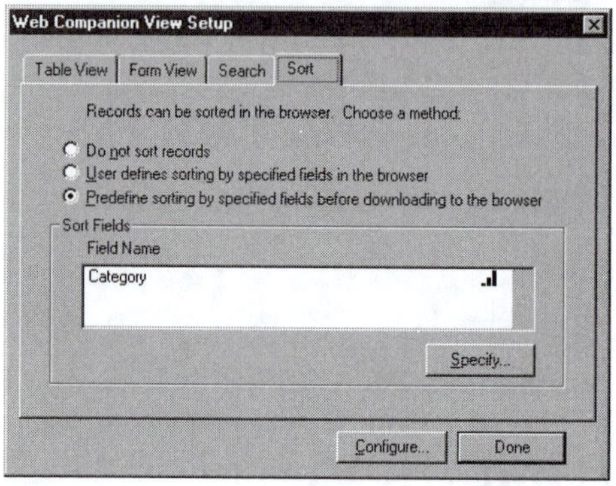

When you're finished, click the Done button to save your settings and dismiss the Web Companion View Setup dialog box.

Checking the Instant Web Publishing Solution

To check your Instant Web Publishing solution, fire up your favorite Web browser and point it to the IP address of the database Web server. FileMaker Pro Web Companion's built-in home page should list the file. Click its link to check your work. Here's what the Table and Form views look like in our solution:

If the wrong fields appear or the fields appear in the wrong order, check the layouts selected in the Web Companion View Setup dialog box, then look at the actual layouts themselves. Remember, fields appear on a page in the order in which they appear on a layout so you may have to rearrange the fields on a layout—or create a whole new layout—to get them to appear the way you want in Instant Web Publishing.

Custom Web Publishing

Custom Web Publishing also enables you to include images with database information on the Web. As I explain in Chapter 2, to successfully publish any database information on the Web with Custom Web Publishing, you must create format files that contain HTML and CDML tags.

Our Custom Web Publishing solution illustrates just how much control you have over page appearance by displaying database categories on one side of a frameset and the items within a specific category on the other side of the same frameset. Here's what it looks like when viewed with Web browser software:

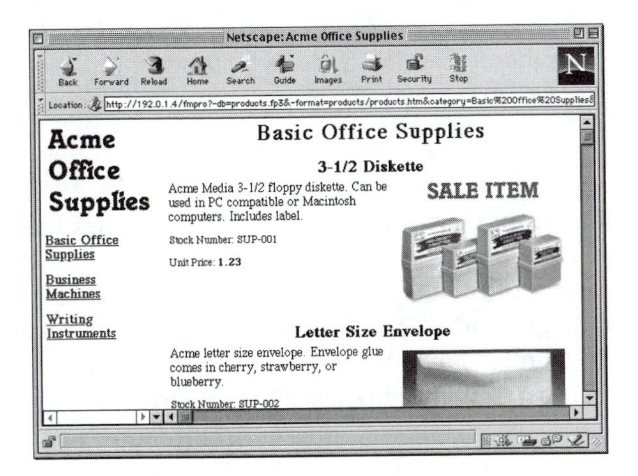

In this section, I provide instructions for creating this solution with FileMaker Pro's built-in Custom Web Publishing.

NOTE

The instructions for this solution assume that you have properly installed FileMaker Pro, enabled and configured the Web Companion Plug-In for Custom Web Publishing, and turned on Web Companion Sharing in the File Sharing dialog box. I provide detailed instructions for completing all of these tasks in Chapter 2.

Creating a Project Folder in the Web Folder

This example includes a number of format files that will be stored in a "project folder" inside the Web folder in the FileMaker Pro folder. The database file will be stored with them.

Create a folder named products inside the Web folder. Open the products folder and create a folder named images inside it. This folder is for images that are not stored inside the database, such as the Acme Office Supplies logo and other graphic elements that you may want to include on the Web page.

If the database file is open, close it. Then move it into the products folder. Double-click its icon to open it.

Creating the Format Files

This solution requires several format files that provide HTML and CDML commands for FileMaker Pro Web Companion.

Here's the information for each format file, including a discussion of its purpose, the HTML and CDML code within it, and notes that explain what each part of the code does. The code is in **bold, sans serif type**; my comments are in this type. Don't enter my comments in the format files!

TIP

Chapter 2 offers suggestions for using the CDML Tool that comes with FileMaker Pro or Claris Home Page to create format files. This is the best alternative to manually typing in the code for each format file.

default.htm

The default home page, default.htm, describes a frameset that, when loaded, automatically displays two format files. The left frame, which is named Categories, displays the contents of the Categories value list from the database file. The right frame, which is larger and named Products, displays instructions for using the Web page. What's nice about this format file is that it includes instructions for visitors who access it with a browser that isn't capable of displaying frames.

Here's the **code** for default.htm, along with my comments:

```
<HTML>
<HEAD>
<TITLE>Acme Office Supplies</TITLE>
</HEAD>
```

This code begins an HTML document and provides a head section with a title.

```
<FRAMESET COLS="140,*" FRAMEBORDER=0 BORDER=0>
```

This code describes the frameset. There are two frames, side by side. The left frame is 140 pixels wide while the right frame resizes depending on the width of the browser window. The frames have no border. (We used both the **FRAMEBORDER** and **BORDER** tags to make sure the border settings were read and understood by both Netscape Navigator and Microsoft Internet Explorer.)

```
<NOFRAMES><BODY BGCOLOR="#FFFFFF">
This page is displayed to browsers with no frame support.<P>
<A HREF="/fmpro?-db=products.fp3&-format=products/category.htm&
-findall">Click here to start</A>
</BODY>
</NOFRAMES>
```

This code provides HTML for browsers that are not capable of displaying frames. The page background color is set to white. A note explains that the page is displayed to browsers without frame support. Then a link that displays all categories using the category.htm file appears. Users who access the page with a browser that does not support frames must click this link to display the categories on a Web page.

```
<FRAME SRC="fmpro?-db=products.fp3&-format=category.htm&-findall"
FRAMEBORDER=0 NAME="CATEGORIES">
```

This code sets the left frame to display all categories in the database file using the category.htm format file. The frame has no border and is named Categories.

```
<FRAME SRC="blank.htm" FRAMEBORDER=0 NAME="PRODUCTS">
```

This code sets the right frame to display the blank.htm format file in a borderless frame named Products.

```
</FRAMESET>
```

This code ends the frameset.

```
</HTML>
```

This code ends the HTML document.

Check the code, then save the file as default.htm in the products folder.

category.htm

The category.htm file displays the Acme Office Supplies logo followed by a list of database categories. The categories, which are displayed using the Categories value list, are links. When clicked, they perform a find based on the clicked category and display all products from that category in the Products frame (for browsers with frame support) or in the main browser window (for browsers without frame support).

Here's the **code**, along with my comments:

```
<HTML>
<HEAD>
<TITLE>Acme Office Supplies - Categories</TITLE>
</HEAD>
<BODY BGCOLOR="#FFFFCC">
```

This code starts the HTML document, gives it a head with a title, and starts the body with a background color of pale yellow.

```
<IMG SRC="/products/images/logo.gif">
```

This code displays the Acme Office Supplies logo at the top of the page.

```
[FMP-ValueList: category, list=categories]
```

This code tells FileMaker Pro to repeat the code between it and the **[/FMP-Valuelist]** tag for every item in the Categories value list.

```
<A HREF="/fmpro?-db=products.fp3&-format=products/products.htm&category=
[FMP-ValueListItem,URL]&-sortfield=item+name&-find" target="PRODUCTS">
<H3>[FMP-ValueListItem]</H3></A>
```

This code displays a link consisting of a category name. When clicked, the link tells FileMaker Pro to display all the items in the category, sorted by name, using the products.htm format file. The target frame for the link is Products.

```
<P>
```

This code separates the categories with an empty line.

```
[/FMP-ValueList]
```

This code tells FileMaker Pro to stop repeating code.

```
</BODY>
</HTML>
```

This code ends the body and HTML document.

Check the code for accuracy, then save the file as category.htm in the products folder.

blank.htm

The blank.htm file provides simple instructions for using the Web publishing solution. This information appears in the Products frame when the default.htm file is opened with a browser capable of displaying frames; it does not appear at all for browsers that cannot display frames. In a real-life situation, you could use this file to provide additional information about the company, catalog items, or ordering procedures. We kept it simple.

Here's the **code** and my comments:

```
<HTML>
<HEAD>
<TITLE>Acme Office Supplies</TITLE>
</HEAD>
<BODY BGCOLOR="#FFFFFF">
```

This code starts the HTML document, gives it a head with a title, and starts the body with a background color of white.

```
<H1>Welcome to Acme!</H1>
<H3>Click on the name of one of the categories listed on the left side of this
page to display products within that category.</H3>
```

This code displays a heading and some instructions for viewing products.

```
<IMG SRC="images/arrow.gif">
```

This code displays an arrow image that points to the left frame. You don't need this; it's simply an example of another non-database image displayed on a page.

```
</BODY>
</HTML>
```

This code ends the body and HTML document.

As you can see, there's not a single CDML command in this code. It can say anything you like! When you're finished creating this document, save it as blank.htm in the products folder.

products.htm

The products.htm file displays each product in a two-column, borderless table that includes product information and the product image. If the product is a sale item, the Sale Item image displays right above the product image.

Here's the **code** for this file, along with my comments:

```
<HTML>
<HEAD>
<TITLE>Acme Office Supplies</TITLE>
```

```
</HEAD>
<BODY BGCOLOR="#FFFFFF">
```

This code starts the HTML document, gives it a head with a title, and starts the body with a background color of white.

```
<CENTER>
```

This tag starts centering.

```
<H1>[FMP-Field: category]</H1>
```

This code tells FileMaker Pro to display the category name as a heading.

```
<P>
```

This puts a blank line between the category name and the items to follow.

```
[FMP-Record]
```

This code tells FileMaker Pro to repeat all code between it and the **[/FMP-Record]** tag for every record in the found set.

```
<TABLE BORDER=0>
```

This code starts a borderless table.

```
<TR>
<TD COLSPAN=2 BGCOLOR=#FFFFCC ALIGN=CENTER><FONT SIZE=+2><B>
[FMP-Field: item name]</B></FONT></TD>
</TR>
```

This code displays the first row of a table, with a single cell that spans two columns. The cell background color is set to the same pale yellow as the categories.htm page. Inside the cell is the contents of the Item Name field, displayed centered in a bold font two sizes larger than normal.

```
<TR>
```

This code starts the second row of the table.

```
<TD WIDTH=300 VALIGN=TOP>
<FONT SIZE=+1>[FMP-Field: item description]</FONT>
<P>
Stock Number: [FMP-Field: stock number]<BR>
<P>
Unit Price:  <B>[FMP-Field: unit price]</B>
</TD>
```

This code displays the left cell of the second row of the table. Its width is set at 300 pixels; alignment is set to top. The first paragraph displays the contents of the Item Description field in a font one size larger than normal. The next paragraph displays the Stock Number heading followed by the contents of the Stock

Number field, then, on the next line, the Unit Price heading followed by the contents of the Unit Price field in bold.

```
<TD WIDTH=200 ALIGN=CENTER VALIGN=MIDDLE>
[FMP-If: Field: Sale Item .eq. Yes]
<img src="[FMP-Image: sale]"><P>
[/FMP-If]
<img src="[FMP-Image: image]">
</TD>
```

This code displays the right cell of the second row. Its width is set to 200 pixels with center and middle alignment. A CDML **[FMP-If]** tag tells FileMaker Pro to check the Sale Item field to see if the item is a sale item. If it is, it displays the image in the Sale field followed by a blank line; if it isn't the Sale image and blank line are omitted. FileMaker Pro then displays the contents of the Image field.

If the Image field is empty for a record, a missing image icon appears in the Web browser window. This code assumes that images are included in the database file for all records.

```
</TR>
```

This code ends the row.

```
</TABLE>
```

This code ends the table.

```
<P>
```

This code puts a blank line between the table and whatever follows it.

```
[/FMP-Record]
```

This code tells FileMaker Pro to stop repeating code.

```
</CENTER>
```

This code ends centering.

```
</BODY>
</HTML>
```

This code ends the body and HTML document.

Check the code for accuracy, then save it as products.htm in the products folder.

Checking the Custom Web Publishing Solution

To check your Custom Web Publishing solution, use your favorite Web browser to point to the IP address of the database Web server followed by

/products/default.htm. Then check the appearance and functionality of the pages that FileMaker Pro Web Companion serves.

Checking Frames

If your browser is capable of displaying frames, you should see something like the illustration below. Click category names in the left frame to display products in the right frame. The illustration at the beginning of this section gives you a good idea of how products are displayed.

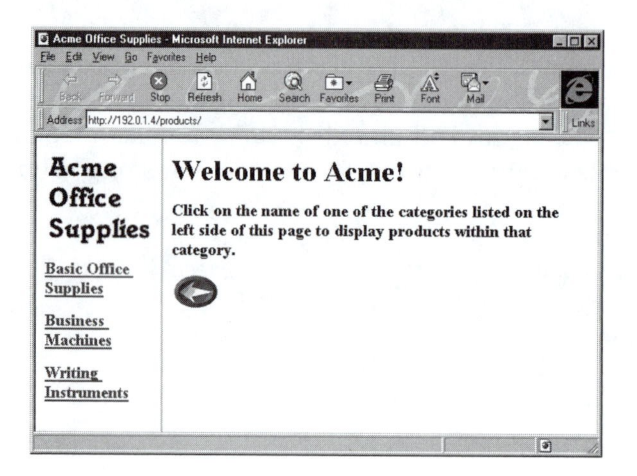

Checking without Frames

If your browser is not capable of displaying frames, an instruction page should appear. Click its link to display the category list. Then click one of the categories to display products. Here's what these pages might look like:

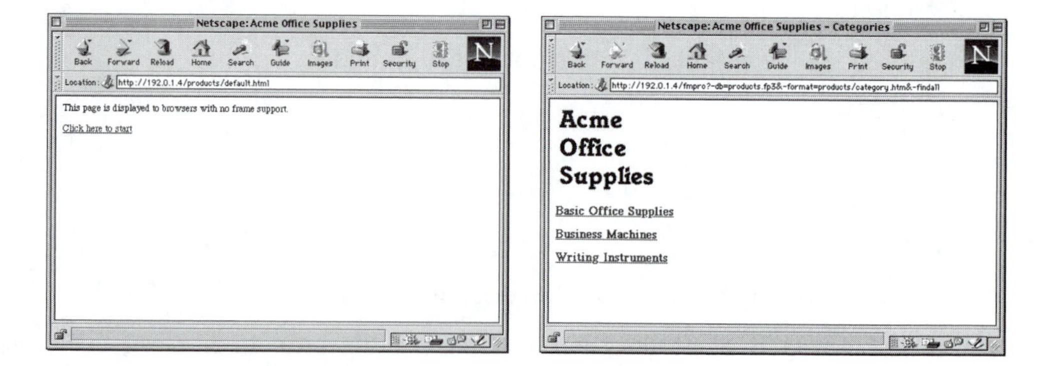

TIP

I'll be honest with you: I no longer have a browser that can't display frames. I threw them all away. But I was able to prepare the above screen shots by creating a default.html file that started with default.htm as described in this chapter but excluded all frame-related code. I loaded that into my browser. It was a good thing I did—I found (and fixed) two errors in the code that would have reared their ugly heads to the folks without frame support. This just proves something that I already knew: you should check all your HTML documents thoroughly!

Troubleshooting Problems

If your pages don't look like the ones illustrated here, check the code in the format files. Remember, one misplaced bracket can really screw things up.

CHAPTER 10

Making Published Data Interactive

For many database Web publishers, simply publishing database records on the Web isn't enough. They want interaction—the ability of Web site visitors to query, sort, change, or add database records.

Although some of the solutions in Chapters 8 and 9 include interaction—especially the Instant Web Publishing solutions—this chapter provides solutions that *require* interaction to work. It also provides examples of how security features can be included in the database or format files to limit the degree of interaction available to users.

In this chapter, I provide instructions for using Instant and Custom Web Publishing to publish a deluxe Guest Register on the Web.

NOTE

You can download the solution files for this chapter from the companion Web site for this book, http://www.gilesrd.com/fmproweb/. That's also where you can add your name to the site's Guest Register—the Custom Web Publishing solution in this chapter is the same solution I use for the Guest Register on my Web sites.

About the Database

Guest Register.fp3 provides fields for storing the names, e-mail addresses, Web site URLs, locations, and comments entered by Web site visitors. It also has a number of special features that help aid data entry and secure the database file.

The Guest Register requires that Web site visitors be able to see recent entries, get entry detail, add entries, and search for entries. Editing is not required, but may be useful.

Here's some more specific information about Guest Register.fp3. Use this information to create the file from scratch or explore the copy that you download from the book's companion Web site.

Database Fields

The database has the following fields:

Field Name	Type	Description
First Name	text	visitor's first name; required
Last Name	text	visitor's last name; required
Email Address	text	visitor's e-mail address
URL	text	visitor's Web site URL
City	text	visitor's city
State	text	visitor's state or province
Country	text	visitor's country; required
Date	date	auto-enter, non-modifiable, modification date
Time	time	auto-enter, non-modifiable, modification time
Referred By	text	where visitor heard about Web site; uses the Referral value list
Comments	text	visitor comments; required
Notification	text	visitor's preference for being contacted about revisions to the site; uses the Response value list

This list of fields excludes any fields created as part of a Web publishing solution. Fields created for a solution are discussed in the section about the solution.

Value Lists

The database uses two value lists for displaying options; these value lists can also be used in the Web publishing solution:

NAME	CONTENTS
Referral	"Database Publishing with FileMaker Pro on the Web" book Link from Peachpit Press Web Site Link from Giles Road Press Web Site Link from Maria Langer Web Site Link from another Web Site A Magazine Article or Review A Mailing List A Search Engine A Friend None of the Above
Response	Yes No

Database Layouts

The database has just one layout called Entry Form. It looks like this:

As you can see in this illustration, two of the fields have special formatting on the layout:

- **NOTIFICATION** is displayed as radio buttons using the Response value list.
- **REFERRED BY** is displayed as a pop-up menu using the Referral value list.

Database Records

The database we created has three records—there has to be something to publish! If you're creating the database from scratch, you can fill the records with the names, locations, and comments of your favorite fictional characters.

TIP

To see how fields appear when there's no data in them, it's a good idea to leave out optional data for one or more records.

Instant Web Publishing

Although Instant Web Publishing is not the best Web publishing technique for this database, it does offer a workable solution. And it certainly is easy to set up!

In this section, I provide instructions for publishing Guest Register.fp3 with Instant Web Publishing.

NOTE

The instructions for this solution assume that you have properly installed FileMaker Pro, enabled and configured the Web Companion Plug-In for Instant Web Publishing, and turned on Web Companion Sharing in the File Sharing dialog box. I provide detailed instructions for completing all of these tasks in Chapter 1.

Moving the File to the Web Folder

To publish a database using Instant Web Publishing, the database file must be in the Web folder inside the FileMaker Pro folder of the computer that will act as the database Web server.

If Guest Register.fp3 is open, close it. Then move it to the Web folder. Double-click its icon to open it again.

Creating New Layouts

Instant Web Publishing creates Web pages (or views) by displaying fields that exist on specific layouts within the database file. Although the layout in Guest Register.fp3 is suitable for the Form View, new layouts should be created for Table View and Search.

Table View Layout

The layout for Table View should include just a handful of fields that can provide basic information about a Guest Register entry.

Switch to Layout mode, then create a new columnar report layout named Entry List with the following fields: First Name, Last Name, City, State, and Date. When you're finished, the layout might look like this in Browse mode:

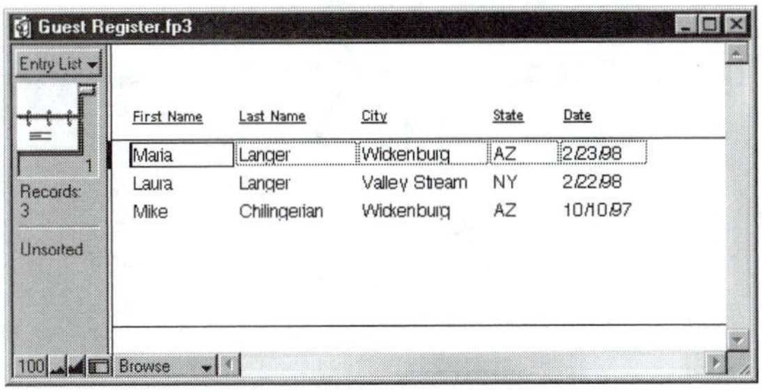

Search Layout

The Search page should display fields that users would be interested in using as search criteria.

In Layout mode, create a new standard layout called Search. Remove fields until only the following fields remain, in this order: First Name, Last Name, City, State, and Country. When you're finished, the layout should look like this:

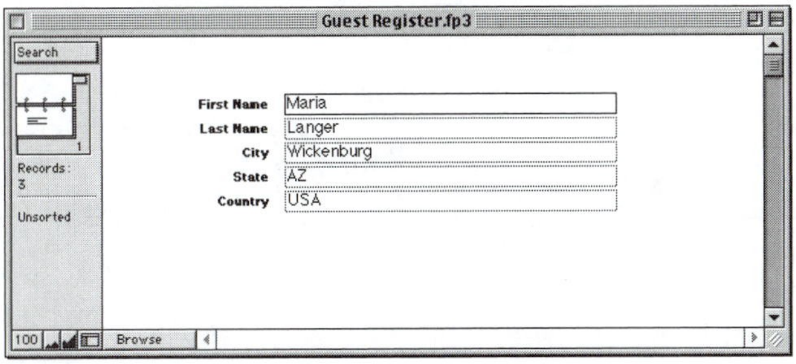

Setting Up Views

To display the correct fields on Web pages, you must specify the layout that should be used for each view. You do this in the Web Companion View Setup dialog box. I provide step-by-step instructions for setting up views in Chapter 1; here are some specifics for this example:

- For Table View, choose Entry List from the Layout menu.
- For Form View, choose Entry Form from the Layout menu.
- For Search, choose Search from the Layout menu.

◉ For Sort, select the middle radio button, then set the sort fields to Last Name, City, State, Country, and Date.

Here's what the Web Companion View Setup dialog box looks like with these options set:

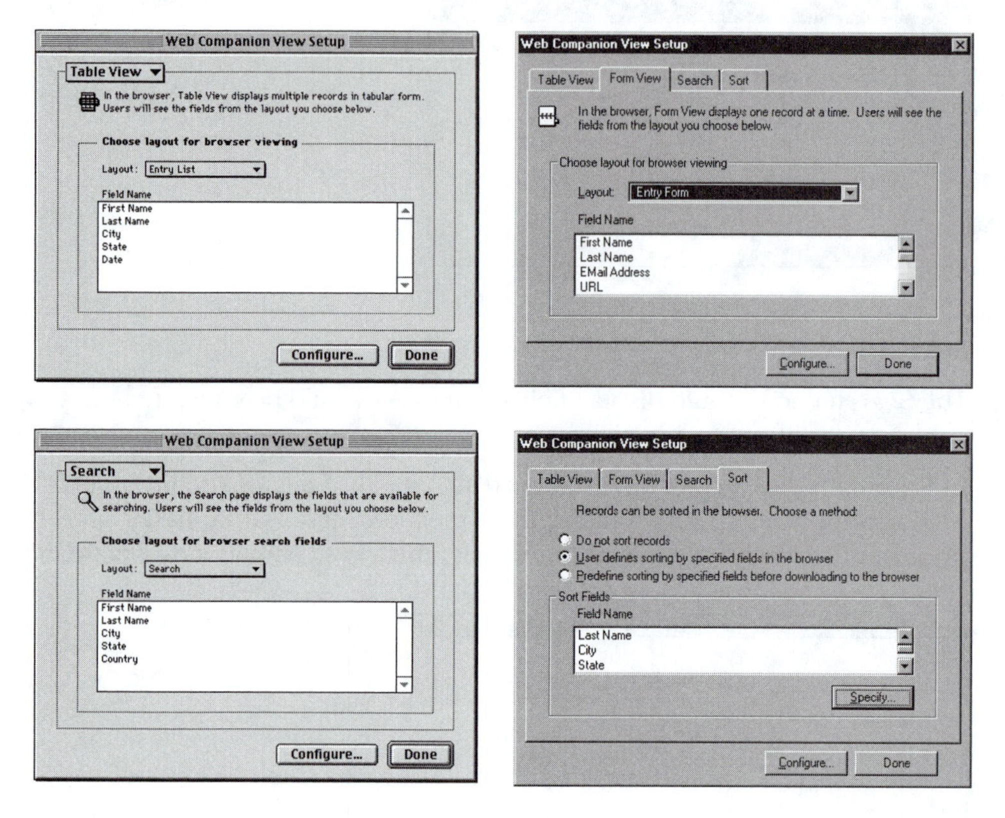

When you're finished, click the Done button to save your settings and dismiss the Web Companion View Setup dialog box.

Setting Access Privileges

Although our solution allows a lot of user interaction with the database file, one thing we don't want users doing is editing or deleting records. This would enable unscrupulous visitors to change or delete the comments entered by other visitors.

You can control the privileges of users by setting up access privileges. I discuss this in detail in Chapter 3. Here are a few specifics for this example.

About the Passwords

For this database, you need to set up two passwords:

- MASTER, the master password, allows all privileges. A master password is required for any database in which you set up security.
- (NO PASSWORD) allows Web users and others to access the database file without entering a password. This password should have editing and deleting records disabled.

Creating the Passwords

Start by choosing Define Passwords from the Access Privileges submenu under the File menu to display the Define Password dialog box.

Enter *master* in the Password edit box. Make sure all check boxes are turned on and click Create. The master password appears in the password list.

NOTE

You can make the master password anything you like—in fact, if you plan to use this solution on your Web site, you should choose something different. If you decide to use something other than master, don't forget what it is! You'll need the password to open the database file.

Clear the contents of the Password edit box. Turn off the Edit records and Delete records check box; the Access the entire file check box turns off automatically. Then click the Create button. The (no password) password appears in the password list.

Click the Done button. The Confirm dialog box appears so you can confirm that you know a password that allows access to the entire file.

Enter *master* in the edit box and click OK.

Setting Up a Default Password

To avoid displaying a password prompt every time you open the file, use FileMaker Pro's Document Preferences dialog box to set a default password. Otherwise, when the file opens, FileMaker Pro will display the Password dialog box and wait until you enter a password for the file—even if the database was opened automatically on system restart.

Choose Document from the Preferences submenu under the Edit menu. In the Document Preference dialog box that appears, turn on the Try default password check box. Leave the edit box beside it empty so the (no password) password is used each time the file is opened.

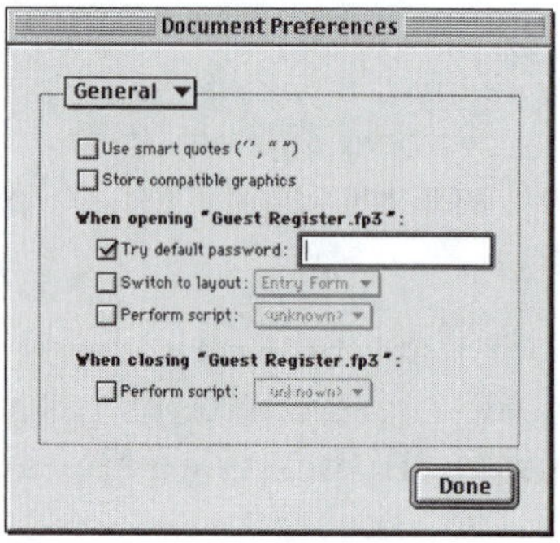

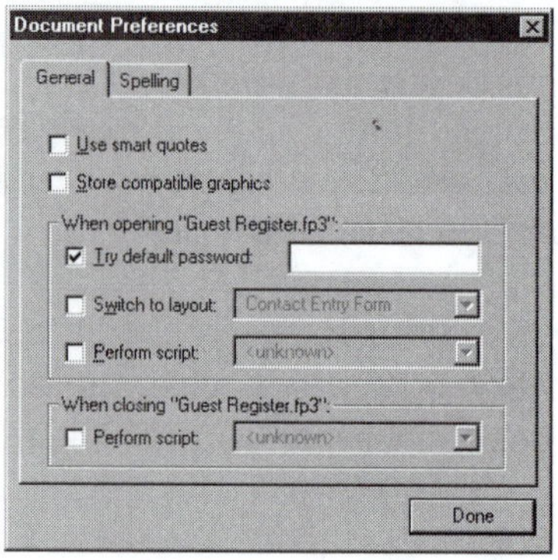

When you're finished, click OK to save your setting.

TIP

To display the Password dialog box after setting this option,, you'll have to hold down the Command and Option (Macintosh) or Shift and Control (Windows) keys when you open the file. Otherwise, the file will be opened with the default password.

Checking the Instant Web Publishing Solution

To check your Instant Web Publishing solution, fire up your favorite Web browser and point it to the IP address of the database Web server. FileMaker Pro Web Companion's built-in home page should list the file. Click its link to open the database file. Then check your work by viewing all Web pages, adding records, searching, and sorting. Can you edit or delete a record? Buttons for those options should not appear.

Here's what the Table, Form, Search, and Sort pages look like in our solution:

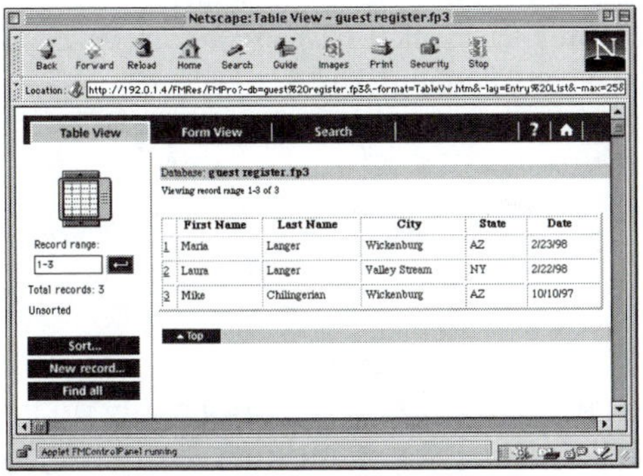

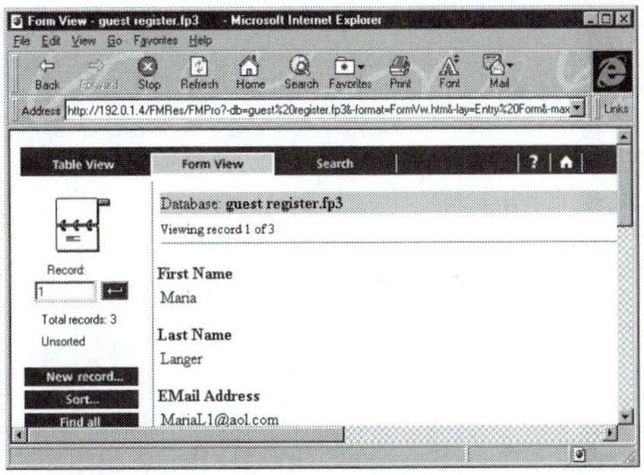

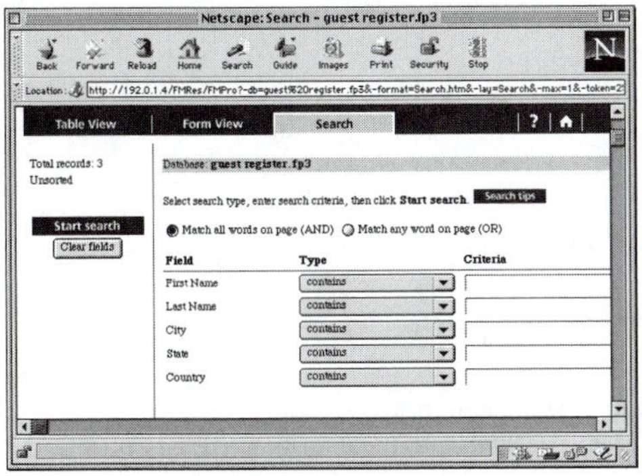

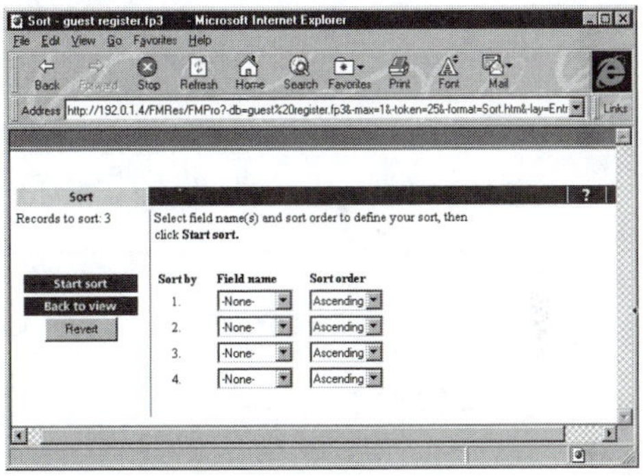

If the wrong fields appear or the fields appear in the wrong order, check the layouts selected in the Web Companion View Setup dialog box, then look at the actual layouts themselves. Remember, fields appear on a page in the order in which they appear on a layout, so you may have to rearrange the fields—or create a whole new layout—to get them to appear the way you want in Instant Web Publishing.

Custom Web Publishing

Custom Web Publishing is a far better method of publishing a Guest Register database—or any other database that requires flexible interaction—on the Web. It enables you to create custom Web pages to display data or allow interaction with the database.

Our Custom Web Publishing solution does everything the Instant Web Publishing solution does and more, including the ability for a visitor to edit or delete his own record. As you'll see in this section, it takes a lot of planning and many format files to create a solution like this, but I think the end product is well worth the effort put into it. I think you'll agree.

The instructions for this solution assume that you have properly installed FileMaker Pro, enabled and configured the Web Companion Plug-In for Custom Web Publishing, and turned on Web Companion Sharing in the File Sharing dialog box. I provide detailed instructions for completing all of these tasks in Chapter 2.

Planning the Solution

Since this Web publishing solution is a bit more complex than the ones in Chapters 8 and 9, it deserves some serious planning. What I normally do is create an organization or flow chart that illustrates the solution's format files and the way they interact.

Here's what I came up with for this solution:

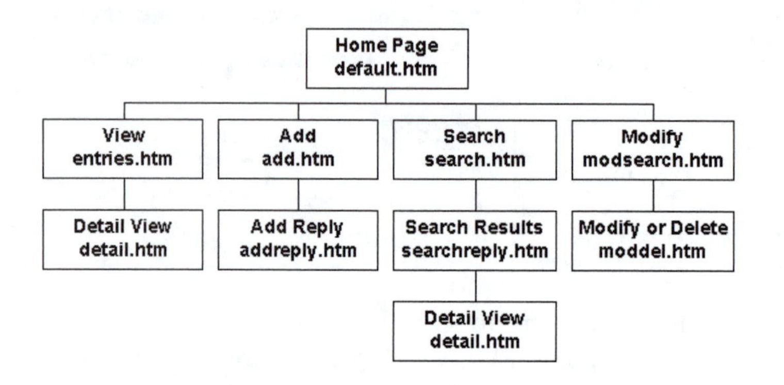

The solution starts with a Home Page named default.htm. The Home Page will offer four options:

- **VIEW** displays the most recent 15 entries using the entries.htm format file. Visitors will have the option of seeing additional entries in the same format or seeing detailed information about a specific entry using the detail.htm format file.
- **ADD** enables a visitor to add his information and comments to the database using the add.htm format file. The format file includes value list options from the database. When information has been entered, the addreply.htm format file confirms what has been added and provides the visitor with a password (more about that later).
- **SEARCH** enables a visitor to search the database for records matching criteria he enters in the search.htm format file. Results are displayed as a list in the searchreply.htm format file. Visitors can get details for a specific record using the same detail.htm format file utilized by the entries.htm file.

- **Modify** enables a visitor to search for his own entry with the modsearch.htm file, using the password he was given when he created it. A successful match displays the moddel.htm file, which allows the visitor to edit or delete the entry.

Along the way, various error pages appear if an error occurs while processing a request. In addition, visitors can branch back to the Home, Add, or Search options from most pages.

With this many format files, you can see how a simple chart can help keep relationships straight in your mind!

Creating a Project Folder in the Web Folder

This example's format files will be stored in a "project folder" inside the Web folder in the FileMaker Pro folder. The database file will be stored with them.

Create a folder named register inside the Web folder. Open the register folder and create a folder named images inside it. This folder is for images that will be included as graphic elements on the solution's Web pages.

If the database file is open, close it. Then move it into the register folder. Double-click its icon to open it.

Creating Additional Fields

The solution requires a few more fields to calculate and store data. Here's a description of each field. Use the Define Fields and, if necessary, Specify Calculation dialog boxes to create them.

Web Site

The Web Site field is a calculation field that displays the visitor's Web site URL—if he enters one in the URL field. Here's how it works.

The URL field will appear on the add.htm format file with the characters *http://* already in the field. This prompts the user to correctly enter his entire URL. (Although this doesn't guarantee that the URL will be correctly and consistently entered, it should help prevent errors.) If the visitor clears the contents of the URL field or doesn't enter anything after the default characters, the Web Site field will be blank. Otherwise, it will display the complete URL.

Here's the formula for the Web Site field:

```
If(URL > "http://", URL,"")
```

This formula checks the contents of URL. If more than just the default *http://* characters are in the field, the Web Site field equals the URL field. Otherwise the Web Site field is empty.

Random Number

The Random Number field is a text field that contains just that—a random number between 1 and 9999.

To create the field, use the Define Fields dialog box to create a text field named Random Number. Then click the Options button for the field. Turn on the Calculated value check box in the Auto Enter options area of the Entry Options dialog box.

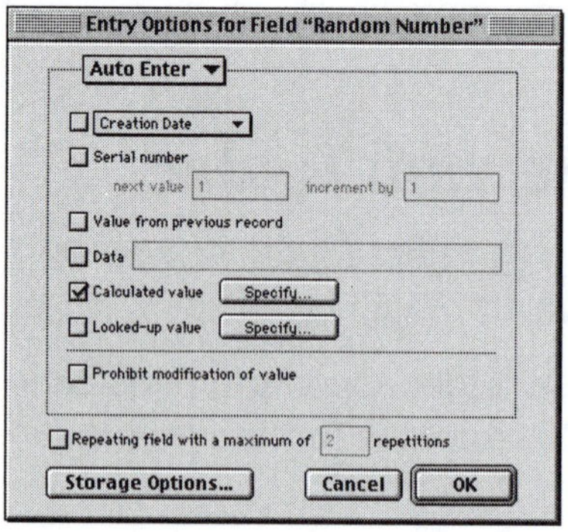

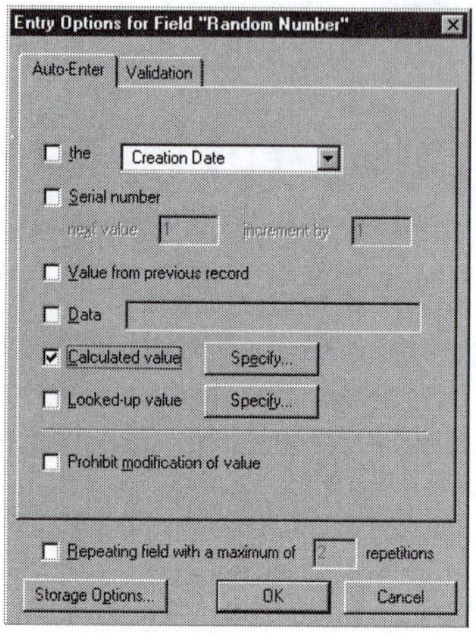

In the Specify Calculation dialog box that appears, enter the following formula:

```
Int (Random * 10000)
```

Click OK to save the formula, then click OK again to dismiss the Entry Options dialog box.

Password

The Password field is a calculation field that is designed for searching the database for a specific record. A visitor who wants to edit his entry must enter his password in the modsearch.htm format file. A successful search displays the moddel.htm format file, which enables the visitor to edit or delete the entry. By forcing a visitor to successfully search for a password before giving him access to the moddel.htm format file, you prevent unauthorized visitors from modifying or deleting entries while allowing a visitor to modify or delete his own entry.

This method of security is relatively easy to set up and use, but it is not bulletproof. For better security over database records, use record level security available via the Web Security Database. I tell you about security in detail in Chapter 3.

Here's the calculation for the Password field:

Left (Last Name, 4) & Random Number

After entering the formula in the Specify Calculation dialog box, choose Text from the Calculation result is menu at the bottom of the dialog box. Click the Storage Options button to display the Storage Options dialog box. Select the On radio button in the indexing area.

Click OK to save your settings, then click OK to save the formula.

Creating the Format Files

Creating the format files is the tough part, but just how tough it is depends on the tools you use to create them. Chapter 2 offers some suggestions.

TIP

To create the format files for this solution, we used Claris Home Page 3, taking full advantage of its two FileMaker Pro libraries. I tell you about using Claris Home Page to create format files in Chapter 2; if you don't already have this program, read up to see what you're missing. After creating many format files with a variety of different tools, I'm convinced that Claris Home Page is the quickest and easiest to use.

In this section, I provide an illustration of each format file, along with the HTML and CDML code that created it. The code appears in **bold, sans serif type like this**; my comments and descriptions appear in plain type like this. (If you create these files by typing in my code, don't type in my comments!)

TIP

Use copy and paste whenever possible to copy code from one format file to another. This not only saves typing, but it can prevent typos.

default.htm

The default.htm file is the Home Page for the solution. Here's what it looks like when viewed with a Web browser:

Most of this page is pure HTML. The View and Add buttons, however, are links that include CDML code.

Here's the **code** for default.htm along with my comments:

```
<HTML>
<HEAD>
<TITLE>Guest Register Home Page</TITLE>
</HEAD>
<BODY BGCOLOR="#FFFFFF">
```

This code sets up the document, giving it a title and a background color of white.

```
<H1><CENTER><IMG SRC="images/guestbook.gif" ALIGN=middle>Guest
Register Home Page</CENTER></H1>
```

This code displays the guestbook.gif image and the page heading.

```
<IMG SRC="images/powered_by_fmp.gif" ALIGN=right>
This database file records the names, e-mail addresses, Web sites, and comments
of visitors to this site. Click one of the buttons below to <B>view</B> recent
guest book entries, <B>add</B> an entry, <B>search</B> for an entry made
by you or a friend, or <B>modify</B> an entry you already made.
```

This code displays the Powered by FileMaker Pro image to the right of a paragraph with instructions for the visitor.

```
<P>
<HR>
```

This code inserts a blank line and then a full-width horizontal rule.

```
<CENTER>
```

This code starts centering.

```
<A HREF="FMPro?-Db=Guest%20Register.fp3&-Format=entries.htm&-Error=
error.htm&-SortField=Date&-SortOrder=Descend&-SortField=Time&-SortOrder=
Descend&-Max=15&-Findall"><IMG SRC="images/view.gif" BORDER=0
ALIGN=bottom></A>
```

This code creates a link for the View button that queries Guest Register.fp3 for the most recent 15 entries, sorted by the Date and Time fields in descending order. The entries.htm format file should be used to display the results; the error.htm format files should be displayed when there is an error.

```
<A HREF="FMPro?-Db=Guest%20Register.fp3&-Lay=Entry%20Form&-Format=
add.htm&-Error=error.htm&-View"><IMG SRC="images/add.gif" BORDER=0
ALIGN=bottom></A>
```

This code creates a link for the Add button that displays the add.htm format file. The CDML code is required because add.htm displays input fields that have values from the database file. If an error occurs, error.htm is displayed.

```
<A HREF="search.htm"><IMG SRC="images/search.gif" BORDER=0 ALIGN=
bottom></A>
```

This code creates a link for the Search button which displays the search.htm format file.

```
<A HREF="modsearch.htm"><IMG SRC="images/modify.gif" BORDER=0
ALIGN=bottom></A></CENTER>
```

This code creates a link for the Modify button which displays the modsearch.htm format file.

```
</BODY>
</HTML>
```

This code ends the HTML document.

Check the code—especially for the View and Add links—then save the file as default.htm in the register folder.

entries.htm

The entries.htm format file displays the most recent 15 entries from the database file. It offers links to get more detail, as well as to view the next or previous bunch of entries. Here's what it looks like in a Web browser with only three entries in the database:

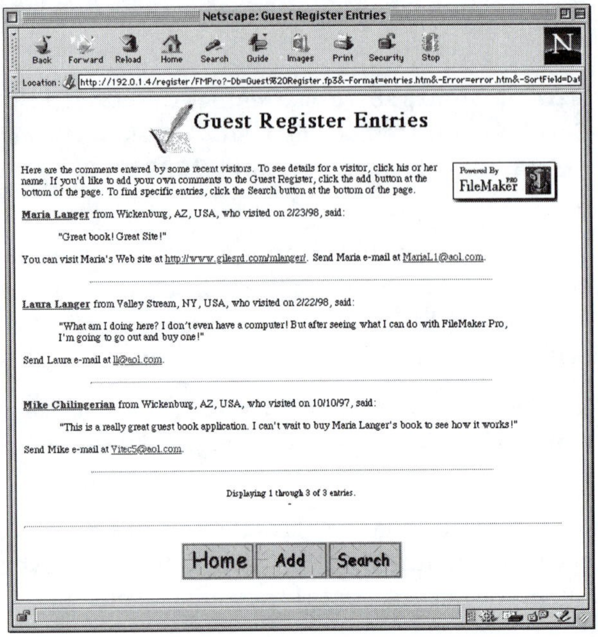

Here's the **code** and my comments for entries.htm:

```
<HTML>
<HEAD>
<TITLE>Guest Register Entries</TITLE></HEAD>
<BODY BGCOLOR="#FFFFFF">
```

This code starts the HTML document and sets the background color to white.

```
<H1><CENTER><IMG SRC="images/guestbook.gif" ALIGN=middle>Guest
Register Entries</CENTER></H1>
```

This code displays the guestbook.gif image and the page heading.

```
<IMG SRC="images/powered_by_fmp.gif" ALIGN=right>
Here are the comments entered by some recent visitors. To see details for a
visitor, click his or her name. If you'd like to add your own comments to the
Guest Register, click the add button at the bottom of the page. To find spe-
cific entries, click the Search button at the bottom of the page.
```

This code displays the Powered by FileMaker Pro image to the right of a paragraph with instructions for the visitor.

```
<P>
```

This code inserts a blank line.

```
[FMP-RECORD]
```

This code tells FileMaker Pro to repeat all code between it and the **[/FMP-RECORD]** tag for every record in the found set.

```
<A HREF="[FMP-LinkRecID:CurrentRecID,format=detail.htm]"><B>[FMP-FIELD:
First Name] [FMP-FIELD: Last Name]</B></A>
```

This code creates a link to detailed information presented with detail.htm. The linked text is the visitor's first and last name from the database, which is displayed in bold. This is the beginning of a sentence.

```
from
```

This code inserts the word *from* in the sentence.

```
[FMP-IF: Field: City .neq.][FMP-FIELD: City], [/FMP-IF]
```

This code evaluates whether the City field is empty. If it is not empty, it displays the City field, followed by a comma and a space. If it is empty, nothing is displayed.

```
[FMP-IF: Field: State .neq.][FMP-FIELD: State], [/FMP-IF]
```

This code evaluates whether the State field is empty. If it is not empty, it displays the State field, followed by a comma and a space. If it is empty, nothing is displayed.

```
[FMP-FIELD: Country],
```

This code displays the Country field followed by a comma and a space.

```
who visited on
```

This code displays the next part of the sentence.

```
[FMP-FIELD: Date],
```

This code displays the date field, followed by a comma and a space.

```
said:
```

This code adds to the sentence.

```
<BLOCKQUOTE>"[FMP-FIELD: Comments, Break]"</BLOCKQUOTE>
```

This code displays the contents of the Comments field, indented and between quote characters (like a quote).

```
[FMP-IF: Field: Web Site .neq.]You can visit [FMP-FIELD: First Name]'s Web
site at <A HREF="[FMP-Field:Web Site]">[FMP-FIELD: Web Site]</A>.
[/FMP-IF]
```

This code checks to see if the Web Site field is empty. If it is not empty, displays the contents of the Web Site field as a link to the Web site within a sentence. If it is empty, displays nothing.

```
[FMP-IF: Field: Email Address .neq.]Send [FMP-FIELD: First Name] e-mail at
<A HREF="mailto:[FMP-Field: Email Address]">[FMP-FIELD: Email
Address]</A>.[/FMP-IF]
```

This code checks to see if the Email Address field is empty. If it is not empty, displays the contents of the Email Address field as a mailto link to the e-mail address within a sentence. If it is empty, displays nothing.

```
<P>
<HR WIDTH="75%">
```

This code inserts a blank line and a 75% wide horizontal rule.

```
[/FMP-RECORD]
```

This code tells FileMaker Pro to stop repeating code.

```
<CENTER>
```

This code starts centering.

```
<FONT SIZE="-1">
```

This code reduces the font size.

```
Displaying [FMP-RANGESTART] through [FMP-RANGEEND] of
[FMP-CURRENTFOUNDCOUNT] entries.<BR>
```

This code displays a sentence that tells the visitor which records he's viewing and how many records are on the page.

```
[FMP-LINKPREVIOUS]Previous Bunch of Entries[/FMP-LINKPREVIOUS] - [FMP-
LINKNEXT]Next Bunch of Entries[/FMP-LINKNEXT]
```

This code displays two links: one to the previous 15 entries (which does not appear if the first 15 entries are being viewed) and the other to the next 15 entries (which does not appear if either there are less than 15 entries or the last 15 entries are being viewed. There's a dash between them. (The illustration of this format file shows just the dash because there are only three records and they are all being viewed.)

```
</FONT>
```

This code ends the font size change.

```
<P>
<HR>
```

This code inserts a blank line followed by a 100% width horizontal rule.

```
<A HREF="default.htm"><IMG SRC="images/home.gif" BORDER=0
ALIGN=bottom></A>
```

This code displays the Home button with a link to default.htm.

```
<A HREF="FMPro?-Db=Guest%20Register.fp3&-Lay=Entry%20Form&-Format=
add.htm&-Error=error.htm&-View"><IMG SRC="images/add.gif" BORDER=0
ALIGN=bottom></A>
```

This code displays the Add button with a link to add.htm. It's the same as the code on default.htm and can be copied and pasted from that file.

```
<A HREF="search.htm"><IMG SRC="images/search.gif" BORDER=0 ALIGN=
bottom></A>
```

This code displays the Search button with a link to search.htm. It's the same as the code on default.htm and can be copied and pasted from that file.

```
</CENTER>
```

This code stops centering.

```
</BODY>
</HTML>
```

This code ends the HTML document.

Check the code and save the file as entries.htm in the register folder.

detail.htm

The detail.htm format file displays detailed information about a specific record when a link on the entries.htm or searchreply.htm format file is clicked. Here's what it looks like when viewed with a Web browser:

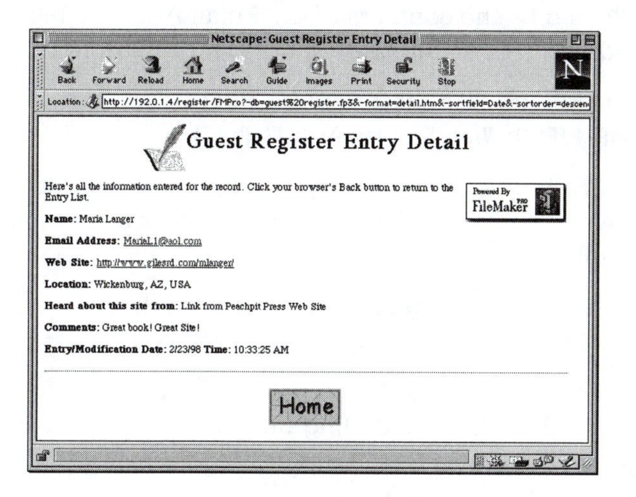

Here's the **code** for detail.htm, along with my comments. Pay close attention—a lot of this code is identical to the code in entries.htm so you can copy and paste it to save time.

```
<HTML>
```

```
<HEAD>
<TITLE>Guest Register Entry Detail</TITLE>
</HEAD>
<BODY BGCOLOR="#FFFFFF">
```

This code starts the HTML document and sets the background color to white.

```
<H1><CENTER><IMG SRC="images/guestbook.gif" ALIGN=middle>
Guest Register Entry Detail</CENTER></H1>
```

This code displays the guestbook.gif image and the page heading.

```
<IMG SRC="images/powered_by_fmp.gif" ALIGN=right>Here's all the information
entered for the record. Click your browser's Back button to return to the
Entry List.
```

This code displays the Powered by FileMaker Pro image to the right of a paragraph with instructions for the visitor.

```
<P><B>Name:</B> [FMP-FIELD: First Name] [FMP-FIELD: Last Name]
```

This code inserts a heading in bold followed by the contents of the First Name and Last Name fields.

```
[FMP-IF: Field: Email Address .neq.]<P><B>Email Address: </B>
<A HREF="mailto:[FMP-Field: Email Address]">[FMP-FIELD: Email Address]
</A>[/FMP-IF]
```

This code checks to see if the Email Address field is empty. If it is not empty, inserts a heading in bold, followed by the contents of the Email Address field as a mailto link to the e-mail address. If it is empty, does not insert anything.

```
[FMP-IF: Field: Web Site .neq.]<P><B>Web Site: </B><A HREF=
"[FMP-Field: Web Site]">[FMP-FIELD: Web Site]</A>[/FMP-IF]
```

This code checks to see if the Web Site field is empty. If it is not empty, inserts a heading in bold, followed by the contents of the Web Site field as a link to the web site. If it is empty, does not insert anything.

```
<P><B>Location:</B> [FMP-IF: Field: City .neq.][FMP-FIELD: City],
[/FMP-IF][FMP-IF: Field: State .neq.][FMP-FIELD: State], [/FMP-IF]
[FMP-FIELD: Country]
```

This code inserts a heading in bold, then, depending on field contents, inserts the City, State, and Country fields.

```
<P><B>Heard about this site from:</B> [FMP-FIELD: Referred By]
```

This code inserts a heading in bold, followed by the contents of the Referred By field.

```
<P><B>Comments:</B> [FMP-FIELD: Comments]
```

This code inserts a heading in bold, followed by the contents of the Comments field.

```
<P><B>Entry/Modification Date:</B> [FMP-FIELD: Date] <B>Time:</B>
[FMP-FIELD: Time]
```

This code displays headings in bold with the contents of the Date and Time fields.

```
<P>
<HR>
```

This code inserts a blank line and a horizontal rule.

```
<CENTER><A HREF="default.htm"><IMG SRC="images/home.gif" BORDER=0
ALIGN=bottom></A></CENTER>
```

This code displays the Home button, centered, with a link to default.htm.

```
</BODY>
</HTML>
```

This code ends the HTML document.

Check the code, then save the file as detail.htm in the register folder.

add.htm

The add.htm format file displays a form that the visitor can use to add his information and comments to the Guest Register. For some fields, the form displays options from the database file. In addition, some fields have default data already entered. Red field headings are used to indicate fields that require input.

On the following page you can see what add.htm looks like with a Web browser.

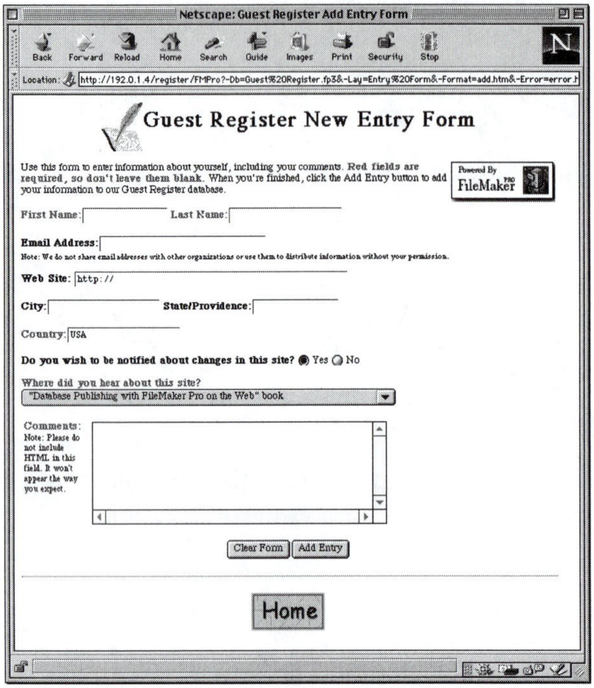

Netscape: Guest Register Add Entry Form
Back Forward Reload Home Search Guide Images Print Security Stop
Location: http://192.0.1.4/register/FMPro?-Db=Guest%20Register.fp3&-Lay=Entry%20Form&-Format=add.htm&-Error=error.h
Guest Register New Entry Form
Use this form to enter information about yourself, including your comments. Red fields are required, so don't leave them blank. When you're finished, click the Add Entry button to add your information to our Guest Register database.
Powered By FileMaker PRO
First Name: Last Name:
Email Address:
Note: We do not share email addresses with other organizations or use them to distribute information without your permission.
Web Site: http://
City: State/Providence:
Country: USA
Do you wish to be notified about changes in this site? Yes No
Where did you hear about this site?
"Database Publishing with FileMaker Pro on the Web" book
Comments:
Note: Please do not include HTML in this field. It won't appear the way you expect.
Clear Form Add Entry
Home

Here's the **code** and my comments for add.htm.

```
<HTML>
<HEAD>
<TITLE>Guest Register Add Entry Form</TITLE>
</HEAD>
<BODY BGCOLOR="#FFFFFF">
```

This code starts the HTML document, gives it a title, and sets the background color to white.

```
<H1><CENTER><IMG SRC="images/guestbook.gif" ALIGN=middle>Guest
Register New Entry Form</CENTER></H1>
```

This code displays the guestbook.gif image and the page heading.

```
<IMG SRC="images/powered_by_fmp.gif" ALIGN=right>
Use this form to enter information about yourself, including your comments.
<FONT COLOR="#FF3300"><B>Red fields are required, so don't leave them
blank.</B></FONT> When you're finished, click the Add Entry button to add
your information to our Guest Register database.
```

This code displays the Powered by FileMaker Pro image to the right of a paragraph with instructions for the visitor.

```
<P>
```

This code inserts a blank line.

```
<FORM ACTION="FMPro" METHOD="POST">
<INPUT TYPE="hidden" NAME="-db" VALUE="Guest Register.fp3">
<INPUT TYPE="hidden" NAME="-lay" VALUE="Entry Form">
<INPUT TYPE="hidden" NAME="-format" VALUE="addreply.htm">
<INPUT TYPE="hidden" NAME="-Error" VALUE="error.htm">
```

This code begins the form that will interact with FileMaker Pro. It specifies the database file name, layout containing fields, reply format file, and error format file. None of this appears on the Web page.

```
<P><FONT COLOR="#FF3300"><B>First Name:</B></FONT><INPUT TYPE=text
NAME="First Name" VALUE="" SIZE=15>
```

This code displays a heading in red, followed by a text field for entering data into the First Name field.

```
<FONT COLOR="#FF3300"><B>Last Name:</B></FONT><INPUT TYPE=text
NAME="Last Name" VALUE="" SIZE=20>
```

This code displays a heading in red, followed by a text field for entering data into the Last Name field.

```
<P><B>Email Address:</B><INPUT TYPE=text NAME="Email Address" VALUE=""
SIZE=30><BR>
<FONT SIZE="-2">Note: We do not share email addresses with other organiza-
tions or use them to distribute information without your permission.</FONT>
```

This code displays a heading, followed by a text field for entering data into the Email Address field. It also displays a note about e-mail address usage in a smaller font right below the input field.

```
<P><B>Web Site:</B> <INPUT TYPE=text NAME=URL VALUE="http://"
SIZE=50>
```

This code displays a heading, followed by a text field for entering data into the URL field. The field edit box displays the characters *http://* as a prompt so visitors enter their URL in the proper format.

```
<P><B>City:</B><INPUT TYPE=text NAME=City VALUE="" SIZE=20>
```

This code displays a heading, followed by a text field for entering data into the City field.

```
<B>State/Providence:</B><INPUT TYPE=text NAME=State VALUE=""
SIZE=15></P>
```

This code displays a heading, followed by a text field for entering data into the State field.

```
<P><FONT COLOR="#FF3300"><B>Country:</B></FONT><INPUT TYPE=text
NAME=Country VALUE="USA" SIZE=20>
```

This code displays a heading in red, followed by a text field for entering data into the Country field. The characters *USA* appear in the field's edit box as a default value.

```
<P><B>Do you wish to be notified about changes in this site?</B>
<INPUT TYPE=radio NAME=Notification VALUE=Yes CHECKED>Yes
<INPUT TYPE=radio NAME=Notification VALUE=No>No
```

This code displays a heading, followed by a pair of radio buttons for entering a Yes or No response for the Notification field. The Yes radio button is selected by default.

```
<P><FONT COLOR="#FF3300"><B>Where did you hear about this site? </B></FONT>
<Select name="Referred By">
[FMP-ValueList: Referred By, List=Referral]
<option [FMP-ValueListItem] Checked>[FMP-ValueListItem]
[/FMP-ValueList]
</Select>
```

This code displays a heading in red, followed by a pop-up menu with values from the Referral value list for entry into the Referred By field. The first option on the list is selected by default.

```
<P><TABLE BORDER=0>
<TR>
<TD VALIGN=top WIDTH=70>
<P><FONT COLOR="#FF3300"><B>Comments:</B></FONT>
<FONT SIZE="-1">Note: Please do not include HTML in this field. It won't
appear the way you expect.</FONT>
</TD>
<TD>
<TEXTAREA NAME=Comments ROWS=7 COLS=50 WRAP=virtual></TEXTAREA>
</TD>
</TR>
</TABLE>
```

This code displays a borderless, two-column table. The left column displays a heading in red, followed by a note in a smaller font. The right column displays a text area for entering data into the Comments field. We used the table strictly to position the note beneath the heading; it isn't required.

```
<CENTER><INPUT TYPE=reset VALUE="Clear Form"><INPUT TYPE="submit"
NAME="-New" VALUE="Add Entry"></CENTER>
```

This code displays a reset button labeled Clear Form and a submit button to create the new record labeled Add Entry. Both buttons are centered.

```
</FORM>
```

This code ends the form.

```
<CENTER>
<P>
<HR>
<P><A HREF="default.htm"><IMG SRC="images/home.gif" BORDER=0
ALIGN=bottom></A>
</CENTER>
```

This code displays a horizontal rule, followed by the Home button, centered, with a link to default.htm.

```
</BODY>
</HTML>
```

This code ends the HTML document.

Check the code, then save the file as add.htm in the register folder.

addreply.htm

The addreply.htm format file confirms that information has been added to the database, and displays the information that was added in the same format used in entries.htm. (You know what that means: copy and paste!).

Here's what the file looks like when viewed with a Web browser:

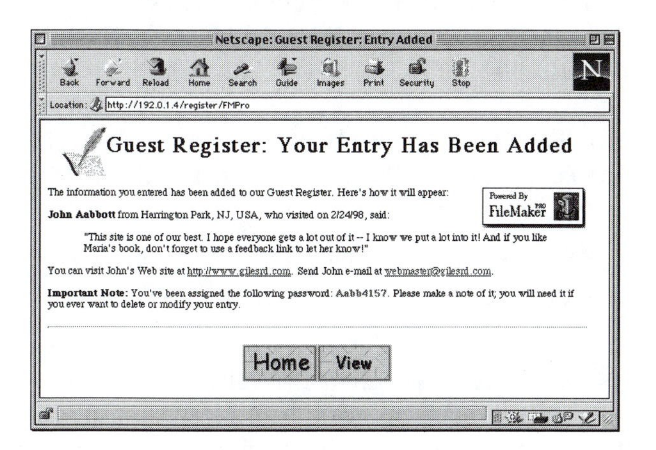

Here's the **code** for this file, along with my comments. If you're typing this in manually, leave the entries.htm file open and remember the Copy and Paste commands!

```
<HTML>
<HEAD>
<TITLE>Guest Register: Entry Added</TITLE>
</HEAD>
<BODY BGCOLOR="#FFFFFF">
```

This code starts the HTML document, gives it a title, and sets the background color to white.

```
<H1><CENTER><IMG SRC="images/guestbook.gif" ALIGN=middle>
Guest Register: Your Entry Has Been Added</CENTER></H1>
```

This code displays the guestbook.gif image with a page heading beside it.

```
<IMG SRC="images/powered_by_fmp.gif" ALIGN=right>The information you
entered has been added to our Guest Register. Here's how it will appear:
```

This code displays the Powered by FileMaker Pro image to the right of a paragraph with information for the visitor.

```
<P><B>[FMP-FIELD: First Name] [FMP-FIELD: Last Name]</B>
from
[FMP-IF: Field: City .neq.][FMP-FIELD: City], [/FMP-IF]
[FMP-IF: Field: State .neq.][FMP-FIELD: State][/FMP-IF]
[FMP-FIELD: Country],
who visited on
[FMP-FIELD: Date],
said:
<BLOCKQUOTE>"[FMP-FIELD: Comments, Break]"</BLOCKQUOTE>
<P>[FMP-IF: Field: Web Site .neq.]You can visit [FMP-FIELD: First Name]'s
Web site at <A HREF="[FMP-Field:Web Site]">[FMP-FIELD: Web Site]</A>.
[/FMP-IF]
[FMP-IF: Field: Email Address .neq.]Send [FMP-FIELD: First Name] e-mail at
<A HREF="mailto:[FMP-Field: Email Address]">[FMP-FIELD: Email
Address]</A>.[/FMP-IF]
```

This code is almost identical to the code in entries.htm, so I won't explain it again here. The only thing it omits is the link from the visitor's name to the detail.htm format file.

```
<P><B>Important Note:</B> You've been assigned the following password:
<FONT COLOR="#FF3300"><B>[FMP-FIELD: Password]</B></FONT>. Please
make a note of it; you will need it if you ever want to delete or modify your
entry.
```

This code displays the visitor's password in red as part of a note on the page.

```
<P>
<HR>
```

This code displays a blank line and a horizontal rule.

```
<CENTER>
```

This code starts centering.

```
<A HREF="default.htm"><IMG SRC="images/home.gif" BORDER=0
ALIGN=bottom></A>
```

This code displays the Home button with a link to default.htm.

```
<A HREF="FMPro?-Db=Guest%20Register.fp3&-Format=entries.htm&
-Error=error.htm&-SortField=Date&-SortOrder=Descend&-SortField=Time&
-SortOrder=Descend&-Max=10&-Findall"><IMG SRC="images/view.gif"
BORDER=0 ALIGN=bottom></A>
```

This code displays the View button with a link to the entries.htm format file that includes all instructions needed to display the most recent 15 entries in the database.

```
</CENTER>
```

This code ends centering.

```
</BODY>
</HTML>
```

This code ends the HTML document.

When you're finished, check the code, then save the file as addreply.htm in the register folder.

search.htm

The search.htm file displays a form that visitors can use to search for entries by specific fields. It also allows the visitor to specify up to two sort fields to arrange database information.

Here's what the search.htm format file looks like when viewed with a Web browser:

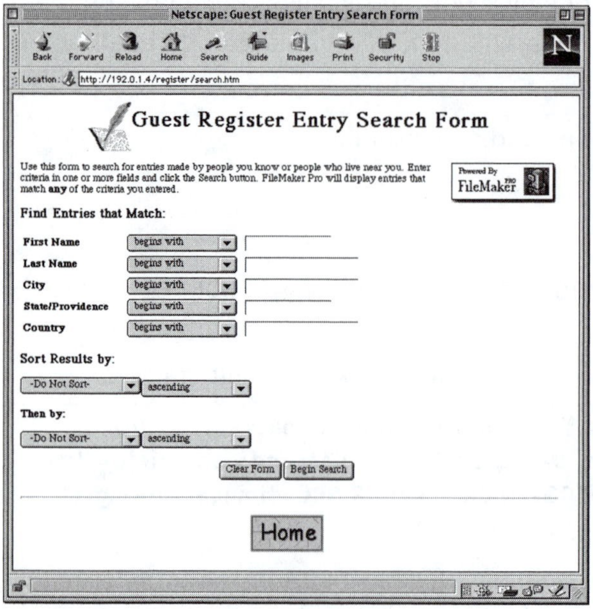

Here's the **code** and my comments for this file:

```
<HTML>
<HEAD>
<TITLE>Guest Register Entry Search Form</TITLE>
</HEAD>
<BODY BGCOLOR="#FFFFFF">
```

This code starts the HTML document, gives it a title, and sets the background color to white.

```
<H1><CENTER><IMG SRC="images/guestbook.gif" ALIGN=middle>
Guest Register Entry Search Form</CENTER></H1>
```

This code displays the guestbook.gif image with a page heading beside it.

```
<IMG SRC="images/powered_by_fmp.gif" ALIGN=right>Use this form to search
for entries made by people you know or people who live near you. Enter cri-
teria in one or more fields and click the Search button. FileMaker Pro will
display entries that match <B>any</B> of the criteria you entered.</P>
```

This code displays the Powered by FileMaker Pro image to the right of a paragraph with instructions and information for the visitor.

```
<FORM ACTION="FMPro" METHOD="POST">
<INPUT TYPE="hidden" NAME="-db" VALUE="Guest Register.fp3">
<INPUT TYPE="hidden" NAME="-lay" VALUE="Entry Form">
<INPUT TYPE="hidden" NAME="-format" VALUE="searchreply.htm">
<INPUT TYPE="hidden" NAME="-Error" VALUE="searcherror.htm">
<INPUT TYPE="hidden" NAME="-Max" VALUE="20">
<INPUT TYPE="hidden" NAME="-LOP" VALUE=OR>
```

This code starts the form that will work with FileMaker Pro. It provides the name of the database file, the name of the layout containing fields that are accessed, the name of the format file that will display results, the name of the format file that appears in case of an error, the maximum number of records to display at a time, and the search logical operator, which is set to OR.

```
<H3>Find Entries that Match:</H3>
```

This code displays a heading.

```
<P><TABLE BORDER=0>
```

This code starts a borderless table in which search field options are presented. We used a table to keep the layout looking neat.

```
<TR>
<TD WIDTH=110>
<B>First Name</B>
</TD>
<TD WIDTH=130>
<CENTER><SELECT NAME="-op">
<OPTION VALUE=bw SELECTED>begins with
<OPTION VALUE=eq>equals
<OPTION VALUE=cn>contains
<OPTION VALUE=ew>ends with
<OPTION VALUE=ne>not equal
</SELECT></CENTER>
</TD>
<TD>
<INPUT TYPE=text NAME="First Name" VALUE="" SIZE=15>
</TD>
</TR>
```

This code displays the first row of the table. The first cell displays a heading, the second displays a pop-up menu with a choice of search operators, and the third cell displays a text field for entering search criteria for the First Name field.

```
<TR>
<TD>
Last Name</B>
</TD>
<TD>
<CENTER><SELECT NAME="-op">
<OPTION VALUE=bw SELECTED>begins with
<OPTION VALUE=eq>equals
<OPTION VALUE=cn>contains
<OPTION VALUE=ew>ends with
<OPTION VALUE=ne>not equal
</SELECT></CENTER>
</TD>
<TD>
<INPUT TYPE=text NAME="Last Name" VALUE="" SIZE=20>
</TD>
</TR>
```

This code displays the second row, which displays the same information as the first row, but for the Last Name field.

```
<TR>
<TD>
<B>City</B>
</TD>
<TD>
<CENTER><SELECT NAME="-op">
<OPTION VALUE=bw SELECTED>begins with
<OPTION VALUE=eq>equals
<OPTION VALUE=cn>contains
<OPTION VALUE=ew>ends with
<OPTION VALUE=ne>not equal
</SELECT></CENTER>
</TD>
<TD>
<INPUT TYPE=text NAME=City VALUE="" SIZE=20>
</TD>
</TR>
```

This code displays the same information in the third row for the City field.

```
<TR>
<TD>
<B>State/Providence</B>
</TD>
<TD>
```

```
<CENTER><SELECT NAME="-op">
<OPTION VALUE=bw SELECTED>begins with
<OPTION VALUE=eq>equals
<OPTION VALUE=cn>contains
<OPTION VALUE=ew>ends with
<OPTION VALUE=ne>not equal
</SELECT></CENTER>
</TD>
<TD>
<INPUT TYPE=text NAME=State VALUE="" SIZE=15>
</TD>
</TR>
```

This code displays the same information in the fourth row, for the State field.

```
<TR>
<TD>
<B>Country</B>
</TD>
<TD>
<CENTER><SELECT NAME="-op">
<OPTION VALUE=bw SELECTED>begins with
<OPTION VALUE=eq>equals
<OPTION VALUE=cn>contains
<OPTION VALUE=ew>ends with
<OPTION VALUE=ne>not equal
</SELECT></CENTER>
</TD>
<TD>
<INPUT TYPE=text NAME=Country VALUE="" SIZE=20>
</TD>
</TR>
```

This code displays the same information in the last row of the table, for the Country field.

```
</TABLE>
```

This code ends the table.

```
<H3>Sort Results by:</H3>
```

This code displays a heading.

```
<SELECT NAME="-SortField">
<OPTION>-Do Not Sort-
<OPTION>Last Name
<OPTION>City
```

```
<OPTION>State
<OPTION>Country
<OPTION>Date
</SELECT>
```

This code displays a pop-up menu offering a variety of fields by which to sort results. The visitor's choice is used by the **-SortField** CDML tag.

```
<SELECT NAME="-sortorder">
<OPTION VALUE=ascend SELECTED>ascending
<OPTION VALUE=descend>descending
</SELECT>
```

This code displays a pop-up menu offering two choices for sort order. The choice is used by the **-sortorder** CDML tag.

```
<H4>Then by:</H4>
```

This code displays another heading.

```
<SELECT NAME="-SortField">
<OPTION>-Do Not Sort-
<OPTION>Last Name
<OPTION>City
<OPTION>State
<OPTION>Country
<OPTION>Date
  </SELECT>
<SELECT NAME="-sortorder">
 <OPTION VALUE=ascend SELECTED>ascending
<OPTION VALUE=descend>descending
</SELECT>
```

This code is identical to the code above the *Then By* heading, offering a secondary sort field and sort order.

```
<CENTER>
<INPUT TYPE=reset VALUE="Clear Form">
<INPUT TYPE="submit" NAME="-Find" VALUE="Begin Search">
</CENTER>
```

This code displays the reset and submit buttons, centered. The submit button uses the **-Find** CDML command to begin the search.

```
</FORM>
```

This code ends the form.

```
<CENTER>
<P>
<HR>
<P>
```

This code starts centering, then displays a horizontal rule between two blank lines.

```
<A HREF="default.htm"><IMG SRC="images/home.gif" BORDER=0
ALIGN=bottom></A>
```

This code displays the Home button with a link to default.htm.

```
</CENTER>
```

This code ends centering.

```
</BODY>
</HTML>
```

This code ends the HTML document.

Check the code, then save the file as search.htm in the register folder.

searchreply.htm

The searchreply.htm file displays the results of the search as a list within a table. Only the First Name, Last Name, City, State, and Country fields are displayed. A link on the name fields displays detailed information about the entry using the detail.htm file.

Here's what the searchreply.htm file looks like when viewed with a Web browser:

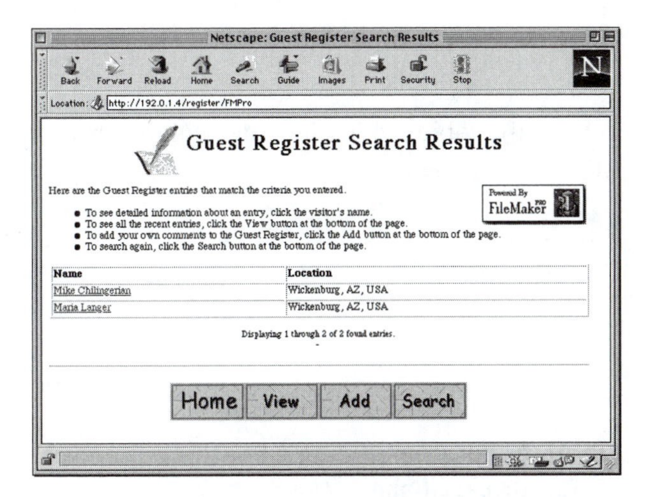

Here's the **code** for the file, along with my comments:

```
<HTML>
<HEAD>
<TITLE>Guest Register Search Results</TITLE>
</HEAD>
<BODY BGCOLOR="#FFFFFF">
```

This code starts the HTML document, gives it a title, and sets the background color to white.

```
<H1><CENTER><IMG SRC="images/guestbook.gif" ALIGN=middle>
Guest Register Search Results</CENTER></H1>
```

This code displays the guestbook.gif image and a page heading.

```
<IMG SRC="images/powered_by_fmp.gif" ALIGN=right>Here are the Guest
Register entries that match the criteria you entered.
<UL>
<LI>To see detailed information about an entry, click the visitor's name.
<LI>To see all the recent entries, click the View button at the bottom of the page.
<LI>To add your own comments to the Guest Register, click the Add button at
the bottom of the page.
<LI>To search again, click the Search button at the bottom of the page.
</UL>
```

This code displays the Powered by FileMaker Pro image to the right of a paragraph with instructions for the visitor.

```
<TABLE BORDER=1 WIDTH="100%">
```

This code begins an HTML table.

```
<TR>
<TH><ALIGN=left>Name</TH>
<TH><ALIGN=left>Location</TH>
</TR>
```

This code displays the first row of the table, which includes column headings.

```
[FMP-RECORD]
```

This CDML tag tells FileMaker Pro to repeat all code between it and the **[/FMP-RECORD]** tag for every record in the found set.

```
<TR>
```

This code starts the next row.

```
<TD>
<A HREF="[FMP-LinkRecID:CurrentRecID,format=detail.htm]">
[FMP-FIELD: First Name][FMP-FIELD: Last Name]</A>
</TD>
```

This code displays the contents of the First Name and Last Name fields for a record in a cell as a link to the detailed information for the record.

```
<TD>
[FMP-IF: Field: City .neq.][FMP-FIELD: City], [/FMP-IF]
[FMP-IF: Field: State .neq.][FMP-FIELD: State], [/FMP-IF]
[FMP-FIELD: Country]
</TD>
```

This code displays the City, State, and Country fields, depending on their contents, in a cell. It's the same code used in entries.htm and addreply.htm, entered between **<TD>** and **</TD>** tags.

```
</TR>
```

This code ends the row.

```
[/FMP-RECORD]
```

This CDML tag tells FileMaker Pro to stop repeating code.

```
</TABLE>
```

This code ends the table.

```
<P>
<CENTER>
```

This code inserts a blank line and begins centering.

```
<FONT SIZE="-1">
Displaying [FMP-RANGESTART] through [FMP-RANGEEND] of [FMP-CURRENT-
FOUNDCOUNT] found entries.<BR>
[FMP-LINKPREVIOUS]Previous Bunch of Entries[/FMP-LINKPREVIOUS] - [FMP-
LINKNEXT]Next Bunch of Entries[/FMP-LINKNEXT]
</FONT>
```

This code reduces the font size to indicate the records being displayed and number of records found. It also displays two links: one to the previous 20 entries (which does not appear if the first 20 entries are being viewed) and the other to the next 20 entries (which does not appear if either there are less than 20 entries or the last 20 entries are being viewed. There's a dash between them. (The illustration of this format file shows just the dash because there are only two records in the found set and they are both being viewed.)

```
<P>
<HR>
```

This code inserts a blank line and a horizontal rule.

```
<A HREF="default.htm"><IMG SRC="images/home.gif" BORDER=0
ALIGN=bottom></A>
<A HREF="FMPro?-Db=Guest%20Register.fp3&-Format=entries.htm&-Error=
error.htm&-SortField=Date&-SortOrder=Descend&-SortField=Time&-SortOrder=
Descend&-Max=15&-Findall"><IMG SRC="images/view.gif" BORDER=0
ALIGN=bottom></A>
<A HREF="FMPro?-Db=Guest%20Register.fp3&-Lay=Entry%20Form&-Format=
add.htm&-Error=error.htm&-View"><IMG SRC="images/add.gif" BORDER=0
ALIGN=bottom></A>
<A HREF="search.htm"><IMG SRC="images/search.gif" BORDER=0
ALIGN=bottom></A>
```

This code displays the Home, View, Add, and Search buttons, providing appropriate code for their links. These buttons use the same code here as they do on the other format files on which they appear, so you can copy and paste them.

```
</CENTER>
```

This code ends centering.

```
</BODY>
</HTML>
```

This code ends the HTML document.

When you're finished creating this document, check the code, then save it as searchreply.htm.

modsearch.htm

The modsearch.htm format file offers a simple search form with only one field. The user must enter an exact match for the field to successfully display results with the moddel.htm format file.

WARNING

Although I mentioned this earlier in this chapter, it's important enough to repeat here...This method of security is not bulletproof. For better security over database records, use record level security available via the Web Security Database. I tell you about security in detail in Chapter 3.

Here's what modsearch.htm looks like when viewed with a Web browser:

Here's the **code** for this file, along with my comments:

```
<HTML>
<HEAD>
<TITLE>Guest Register Modify/Delete Entry Search Form</TITLE>
</HEAD>
<BODY BGCOLOR="#FFFFFF">
```

This code starts the HTML document, gives it a title, and sets the background color to white.

```
<H1><CENTER><IMG SRC="images/guestbook.gif" ALIGN=middle>
Guest Register Modify/Delete Entry Search Form</CENTER></H1>
```

This code displays the guestbook.gif image and a page heading.

```
<IMG SRC="images/powered_by_fmp.gif" ALIGN=right>
Use this form to search for your entry in the database. You <B>must</B>
enter the password that you were assigned when you created your entry.
FileMaker Pro will only display entries that exactly match the password you
enter.
```

This code displays the Powered by FileMaker Pro image to the right of a paragraph with instructions for the visitor.

```
<FORM ACTION="FMPro" METHOD="POST">
<INPUT TYPE="hidden" NAME="-db" VALUE="Guest Register.fp3">
<INPUT TYPE="hidden" NAME="-lay" VALUE="Entry Form">
<INPUT TYPE="hidden" NAME="-format" VALUE="moddel.htm">
<INPUT TYPE="hidden" NAME="-Error" VALUE="moderror.htm">
```

This code sets up the form that will work with FileMaker Pro. It provides the name of the database, layout on which the field appears, format file for displaying results, and format file for displaying an error message.

```
<CENTER>
```

This tag starts centering.

```
<B>Password: </B><INPUT TYPE="hidden" NAME="-op" VALUE=eq><INPUT
TYPE=text NAME=Password VALUE="" SIZE=10>
```

This code displays a heading, then sets the search operator to equals and provides a field for inputting search criteria in the Password field.

```
<INPUT TYPE=reset VALUE="Clear Form">
<INPUT TYPE="submit" NAME="-Find" VALUE="Find My Entry">
```

This code displays the reset and submit buttons. The submit button uses the **-Find** CDML tag.

```
</CENTER>
```

This code ends centering.

```
</FORM>
```

This code ends the form.

```
<CENTER>
<P>
<HR>
```

This code starts centering, inserts a blank line, and displays a horizontal rule.

```
<P><A HREF="default.htm"><IMG SRC="images/home.gif" BORDER=0
ALIGN=bottom></A>
```

This code displays the Home button with a link to default.htm.

```
</CENTER>
```

This code ends centering

```
</BODY>
</HTML>
```

This code ends the HTML document.

Check the code, then save the file as modsearch.htm in the register folder.

moddel.htm

The moddel.htm format file appears only to visitors who correctly enter their password in the modsearch.htm format file's search form. It displays the visitor's record and enables him to modify or delete it.

Here's what moddel.htm looks like when viewed with a Web browser:

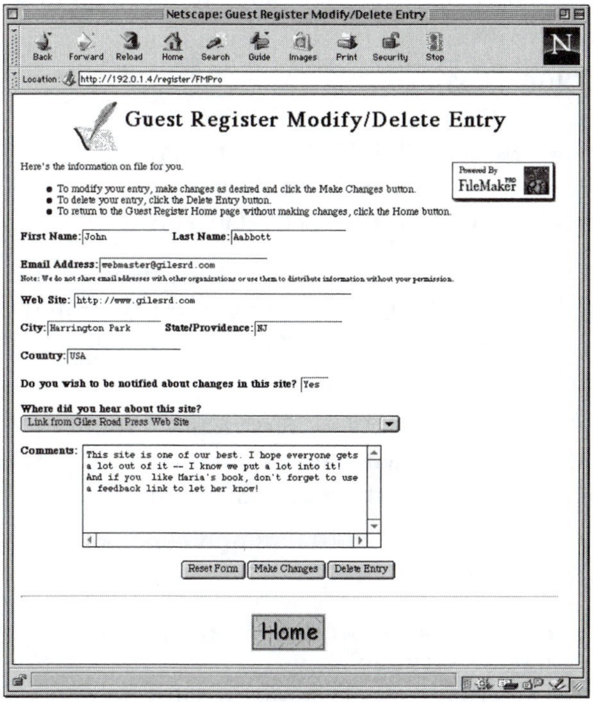

Here's the **code** and comments for this file:

```
<HTML>
<HEAD>
<TITLE>Guest Register Modify/Delete Entry</TITLE>
</HEAD>
<BODY BGCOLOR="#FFFFFF">
```

This code starts the HTML file, gives it a title, and sets the background color to white.

```
<H1><CENTER><IMG SRC="images/guestbook.gif" ALIGN=middle>
Guest Register Modify/Delete Entry</CENTER></H1>
```

This code displays the guestbook.gif image and a page heading.

```
<IMG SRC="images/powered_by_fmp.gif" ALIGN=right>Here's the information
on file for you.
<UL>
<LI>To modify your entry, make changes as desired and click the Make
Changes button.
<LI>To delete your entry, click the Delete Entry button.
<LI>To return to the Guest Register Home page without making changes, click
the Home button.
</UL>
```

This code displays the Powered by FileMaker Pro image to the right of a paragraph with instructions for the visitor.

```
<FORM ACTION="FMPro" METHOD="POST">
<INPUT TYPE="hidden" NAME="-DB" VALUE="Guest Register.fp3">
<INPUT TYPE="hidden" NAME="-Format" VALUE="default.htm">
<INPUT TYPE="hidden" NAME="-Error" VALUE="error.htm">
<INPUT TYPE="hidden" NAME="-RecID" VALUE="[FMP-CurrentRecID]">
```

This code sets up the form for FileMaker Pro. It provides the name of the database, the name of the format file to display after successful processing of the form, the name of the format file to display if an error occurs, and identification of the current record.

```
<P><B>First Name:</B><INPUT TYPE=text NAME="First Name" VALUE=
"[FMP-Field: First Name]" SIZE=15> <B>Last Name:</B><INPUT TYPE=text
NAME="Last Name" VALUE="[FMP-Field: Last Name]" SIZE=20>
```

This code displays headings and text fields for the First Name and Last Name fields. Each field displays data from the database.

```
<P><B>Email Address:</B><INPUT TYPE=text NAME="Email Address"
VALUE="[FMP-Field: Email Address]" SIZE=30><BR>
<FONT SIZE="-2">Note: We do not share email addresses with other
organizations or use them to distribute information without your
permission.</FONT>
```

This code displays a heading and text field for the Email Address field. The field displays information from the database. The code also includes a note in tiny print, just like the one in the add.htm format file.

```
<P><B>Web Site:</B> <INPUT TYPE=text NAME=URL VALUE="[FMP-Field: URL]"
SIZE=50>
```

This code displays a heading and text field for the Web Site field, with information from the database.

```
<P><B>City:</B><INPUT TYPE=text NAME=City VALUE="[FMP-Field: City]"
SIZE=20> <B>State/Providence:</B><INPUT TYPE=text NAME=State
VALUE="[FMP-Field: State]" SIZE=15>
```

This code displays headings and text fields for the City and State fields, with information from the database.

```
<P><B>Country:</B><INPUT TYPE=text NAME=Country VALUE=
"[FMP-Field: Country]" SIZE=20>
```

This code displays a heading and text field for the Country field, with information from the database.

```
<P><B>Do you wish to be notified about changes in this site?</B>
<INPUT TYPE=text NAME=Notification VALUE="[FMP-Field: Notification]"
SIZE=4>
```

This field displays a heading and text field for the Notification field, with information from the database.

```
<P><B>Where did you hear about this site?</B>
<SELECT NAME="Referred By">
<option>[FMP-Field: Referred By]
[FMP-ValueList: Referred By, List=Referral]
<option>[FMP-ValueListItem]
[/FMP-ValueList]
</SELECT>
```

This code displays a heading and pop-up menu for the Referred By field. The field displays information from the database and offers options from the Referral value list.

```
<P><B>Comments: </B><TEXTAREA NAME=Comments ROWS=7 COLS=50
WRAP=virtual>[FMP-Field: Comments]</TEXTAREA>
```

This code displays a heading and text area for the Comments field, with information from the database.

```
<CENTER>
```

This code starts centering.

```
<INPUT TYPE=reset VALUE="Reset Form">
<INPUT TYPE="submit" NAME="-Edit" VALUE="Make Changes">
<INPUT TYPE="submit" NAME="-Delete" VALUE="Delete Entry"
onclick="return confirm('Really delete this record?')">
```

This code displays a reset button and two submit buttons. One submit button uses the **-Edit** CDML tag to modify the record based on the contents of fields. The other submit button uses the **-Delete** CDML tag to delete the entry. When a user clicks the Delete button, the browser displays a confirmation dialog box created with a very short JavaScript. (This dialog box only appears when the page is viewed with a Java-enabled Web browser.)

```
</CENTER>
```

This tag ends centering.

```
</FORM>
```

This tag ends the form.

```
<P>
<HR>
```

This code inserts a blank line and a horizontal rule.

```
<CENTER>
<A HREF="default.htm"><IMG SRC="images/home.gif" BORDER=0
ALIGN=bottom></A>
</CENTER>
```

This code displays the Home button with a link to default.htm.

```
</BODY>
</HTML>
```

This code ends the HTML document.

Check the code, then save the file as moddel.htm in the register folder.

error.htm

The error.htm format file is a generic format file that appears if an error occurs while processing a number of the format files.

The error.htm file looks like this in a Web browser:

Here's the **code** for this file. Comments really aren't necessary; this is straight HTML.

```
<HTML>
<HEAD>
<TITLE>Guest Register Error</TITLE>
</HEAD>
<BODY BGCOLOR="#FFFFFF">
<H1><CENTER><IMG SRC="images/guestbook.gif" ALIGN=middle>Guest
Register Error</CENTER></H1>
Oops! An error occurred while processing your request. Click your browser's
back button to try again. Otherwise, click the Home button to return to the
Guest Register Home page.
<P>
```

```
<HR>
<CENTER><A HREF="default.htm"><IMG SRC="images/home.gif" BORDER=0
ALIGN=bottom></A></CENTER>
</BODY>
</HTML>
```

Save this file as error.htm in the register folder.

searcherror.htm

The searcherror.htm format file appears when no records are found as the result of a search. It's very much like the generic error format file, but gives a specific reason for its appearance.

The searcherror.htm file looks like this:

Here's the **code**:

```
<HTML>
<HEAD>
<TITLE>Guest Register Error</TITLE>
</HEAD>
<BODY BGCOLOR="#FFFFFF">
<H1><CENTER><IMG SRC="images/guestbook.gif" WIDTH=50 HEIGHT=52
ALIGN=middle>Guest Register Error</CENTER></H1>
Sorry! No records match the criteria you entered. Click the Search
button to try again. Otherwise, click the Home button to return to
the Guest Register Home page.
<P>
<HR>
<CENTER><A HREF="default.htm"><IMG SRC="images/home.gif" BORDER=0
ALIGN=bottom></A><A HREF="search.htm"><IMG SRC="images/search.gif"
BORDER=0 ALIGN=bottom></A></CENTER>
</BODY>
</HTML>
```

Save this file as searcherror.htm in the register folder.

moderror.htm

The moderror.htm format file appears when a visitor enters the wrong password in the modsearch.htm search form. It gives a very specific reason for its appearance, as you can see:

Here's the **code** for this file:

```
<HTML>
<HEAD>
<TITLE>Guest Register Modify/Delete Error</TITLE>
</HEAD>
<BODY BGCOLOR="#FFFFFF">
<H1><CENTER><IMG SRC="images/guestbook.gif" ALIGN=middle>Guest
Register Error</CENTER></H1>
<P>Oops! You did not correctly enter the Password information as required.
To modify or delete your entry, you <B>must</B> correctly enter the
Password that you were assigned when you created your entry.
<P>To try again, click the Modify button. Otherwise, click the Home
button to return to the Guest Register Home Page.
<P>
<HR>
<CENTER><A HREF="default.htm"><IMG SRC="images/home.gif"
BORDER=0 ALIGN=bottom></A><A HREF="modsearch.htm"><IMG
SRC="images/modify.gif" BORDER=0 ALIGN=bottom></A></CENTER>
</BODY>
</HTML>
```

Save this file as moderror.htm in the register folder.

Checking the Custom Web Publishing Solution

To try out this solution, use your favorite Web browser to point to the IP address of the database Web server followed by /register/default.htm. Then check the appearance and functionality of the pages that FileMaker Pro Web Companion serves.

If your pages don't look like the ones illustrated here, it's time to troubleshoot. First, identify the format file that's causing the problem. Then check its code. Remember:

- HTML controls the way pages appear.
- CDML controls the way the solution interacts with FileMaker Pro.

A typographical error, such as a missing or misplaced character, can really mess things up.

CHAPTER 11

Performing Calculations

One of the most powerful features of FileMaker Pro is its ability to perform calculations. Calculation fields defined with formulas that refer to other database fields enable you to perform virtually any calculation with data. Why not harness the power of calculation fields to provide information to Web visitors?

This chapter offers a FileMaker Pro Custom Web Publishing solution that gathers information about automobile purchase and lease deals, uses calculation fields to determine which is the better deal, and displays the results on a Web page.

NOTE

You can download the solution files for this chapter from the companion Web site for this book, http://www.gilesrd.com/fmproweb/. That's also where you can find links to try out the solution in this chapter.

WARNING

These solution files are provided as examples only. Neither Peachpit Press nor I can take responsibility for the accuracy of the formulas they contain. Do not use this solution for real-life buy vs. lease decision making!

About the Database

BuyOrLease.fp3 is a database that includes fields for inputting information about purchase and lease deals. A number of calculation fields calculate monthly payments on the loan, total payments for the loan and a lease, and the present value of loan and lease payments. A final calculation field compares the present values of the purchase and lease deals and displays which is less expensive.

Here are some specifics about the database file. Use this information to create the database from scratch or explore the database that you download from the book's companion Web site.

Database Fields

The database includes the following number fields:

- PurchasePrice is the full amount of the purchase.
- PurchaseDownpayment is the downpayment amount for the purchase.
- LeaseDownpayment is the downpayment amount for the lease.
- AnnualInterestRate is the annual interest rate of the loan. This value is also used for present value calculations.
- TermInYears is the number of years for the loan and lease.
- MonthlyLeasePayment is the monthly payment for the lease.
- LeaseEndPrice is the buyout amount at the end of the lease.

The database also includes the following calculation fields:

- Amount Financed is the amount of the loan. Its formula is:
  ```
  If(TermInYears <> 0, PurchasePrice - PurchaseDownpayment, 0)
  ```
- MonthlyLoanPayment is the monthly payment for the loan. Its formula is:
  ```
  If( TermInYears <> 0, Round( PMT( AmountFinanced ,
  AnnualInterestRate/100/12, TermInYears * 12 ) , 2 ) , 0 )
  ```
- PurchaseTotalPayments is the total amount of all payments made for the purchase deal. Its formula is:
  ```
  Round(If(TermInYears * 12 <> 0, MonthlyLoanPayment * TermInYears * 12
  + PurchaseDownpayment, PurchasePrice), 2)
  ```
- LeaseTotalPayments is the total amount of all payments made for the lease deal. Its formula is:
  ```
  Round(MonthlyLeasePayment * TermInYears * 12 + LeaseEndPrice +
  LeaseDownpayment,2)
  ```

- PurchasePresentValue is the present value of all payments for the purchase deal. Its formula is:

```
Round(If(TermInYears * 12 <> 0, (PV(MonthlyLoanPayment,
AnnualInterestRate / 100/12, TermInYears*12)) + PurchaseDownpayment,
PurchasePrice), 2)
```

- LeasePresentValue is the present value of all payments for the lease deal. Its formula is:

```
Round(PV(MonthlyLeasePayment, AnnualInterestRate / 100/12,
TermInYears*12) + LeaseDownpayment + LeaseEndPrice, 2)
```

- LeastExpensive compares the two present value calculations to specify which is the better deal. Its formula is:

```
If(PurchasePresentValue < LeasePresentValue, "Buy",
If(PurchasePresentValue > LeasePresentValue, "Lease", "Either -- No
Difference"))
```

Database Layouts

The database has one layout called EntryForm. This layout presents all fields in a nice-looking data-entry form, with asterisks identifying the fields that must be filled in for the calculation to work.

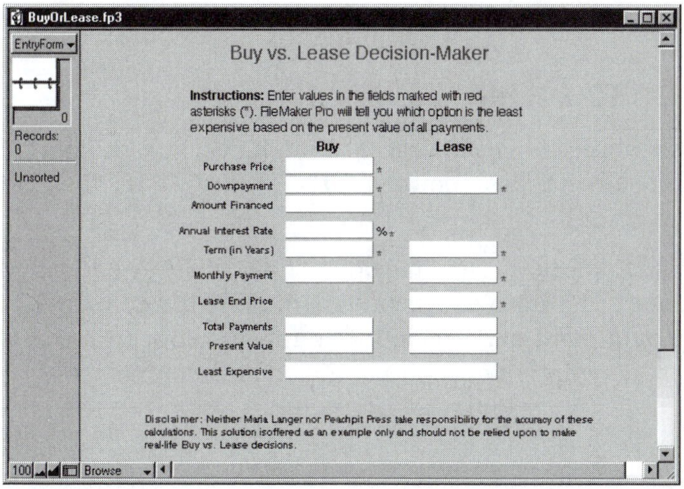

Database Records

Unlike the other databases Web publishing examples in this book, this one doesn't need any records. Instead, it creates a new record each time it is accessed, and publishes the results calculated based on the entered data. In fact, the Custom Web Publishing solution in this chapter can actually delete the record when the user is finished.

Custom Web Publishing Solution

The FileMaker Pro Custom Web Publishing solution we developed uses three format files—one to gather information, one to display calculated results, and a third in case there's an error processing the request. It's a relatively simple solution, but as you'll see throughout the rest of this chapter, it includes a few useful tricks that you can apply to other Custom Web Publishing solutions you develop.

The instructions in this section assume that you have properly installed FileMaker Pro, enabled and configured the Web Companion Plug-In for Custom Web Publishing, and turned on Web Companion Sharing in the File Sharing dialog box. I provide detailed instructions for completing all of these tasks in Chapter 2.

Creating a Project Folder

Like the other Web publishing solution examples in this book, this solution will be stored in its own folder.

Create a folder named buyorlease in the Web folder inside the FileMaker Pro folder. If BuyOrLease.fp3 is open, close it. Move BuyOrLease.fp3 into the new folder and open it.

Creating the Format Files

This solution requires three format files: default.htm, response.htm, and error.htm. The first two format files combine HTML with CDML; the third is strictly HTML.

In this section, I explain what each format file does, show you how it looks when viewed with a Web browser, and provide its underlying HTML and CDML code. The code appears in a **bold, sans serif type**; my comments appear in this type. If you create these files by typing in code, don't include my comments!

default.htm

The default.htm format file displays a form for gathering purchase and lease deal information. The fields, which appear in a borderless table, are filled in with zeros (or in the case of the TermInYears field, the number 4). A reset button labeled Start Over clears the form. A submit button labeled Calculate adds the data to the database so it can be calculated.

Here's what default.htm looks like when viewed with a Web browser:

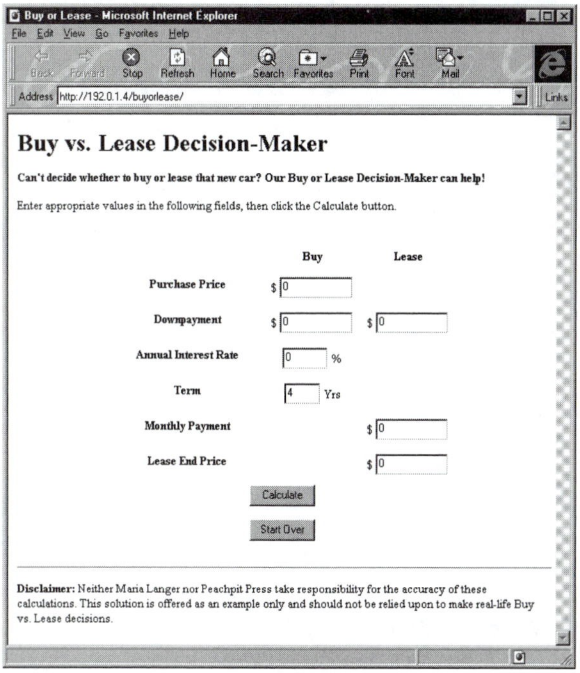

Here's the **code** and my comments for default.htm:

```
<HTML>
<HEAD>
<TITLE>Buy or Lease</TITLE>
</HEAD>
<BODY BGCOLOR="#FFFFFF">
```

This code starts the HTML document, gives it a title, and sets the background color to white.

```
<H1>Buy vs. Lease Decision-Maker</H1>
<H4>Can't decide whether to buy or lease that new car? Our Buy or
Lease Decision-Maker can help!</H4>
<P>Enter appropriate values in the following fields, then click the
Calculate button.
```

This code puts two headings and some instructions at the top of the page.

```
<FORM ACTION="FMPro" METHOD="post">
<INPUT TYPE="hidden" NAME="-DB" VALUE="BuyOrLease.fp3">
<INPUT TYPE="hidden" NAME="-Lay" VALUE="EntryForm">
<INPUT TYPE="hidden" NAME="-Format" VALUE="response.htm">
<INPUT TYPE="hidden" NAME="-Error" VALUE="error.html">
```

This code sets up the form that will work with FileMaker Pro. It specifies the name of the database, layout, response format file, and error format file.

```
<CENTER>
```

This tag starts centering.

```
<TABLE BORDER=0 CELLSPACING=5 CELLPADDING=5 WIDTH=380>
```

This code begins a borderless, fixed-width HTML table.

```
<TR>
<TD></TD>
<TH WIDTH=100>Buy</TH>
<TH WIDTH=100>Lease</TH>
</TR>
```

This code for the first row of the table displays column headings for the second and third columns.

```
<TR>
<TH><ALIGN=right>Purchase Price</TH>
<TD>$ <INPUT TYPE=text NAME=PurchasePrice VALUE="0" SIZE=12
MAXLENGTH=12></TD>
<TD></TD>
</TR>
```

This code for the second row of the table displays a row heading, then provides a text field for entering data into the PurchasePrice field. The default entry value is set to 0.

```
<TR>
<TH><ALIGN=right>Downpayment</TH>
<TD>$ <INPUT TYPE=text NAME=PurchaseDownpayment VALUE="0" SIZE=12
MAXLENGTH=12></TD>
<TD>$ <INPUT TYPE=text NAME=LeaseDownpayment VALUE="0" SIZE=12
MAXLENGTH=12></TD>
</TR>
```

This code for the third row of the table displays a row heading, then provides text fields for entering data into the PurchaseDownpayment and LeaseDownpayment fields. The default entry value is set to 0 for each field.

```
<TR>
<TH><ALIGN=right>Annual Interest Rate</TH>
<TD><CENTER><INPUT TYPE=text NAME=AnnualInterestRate VALUE="0" SIZE=6
MAXLENGTH=12>%</CENTER></TD>
<TD</TD>
</TR>
```

This code for the fourth row of the table displays a row heading, then provides a text field for entering data into the AnnualInterestRate field. The default entry value is set to 0.

```
<TR>
<TH><ALIGN=right>Term</TH>
<TD><CENTER><INPUT TYPE=text NAME=TermInYears VALUE="4" SIZE=4
MAXLENGTH=12> Yrs</CENTER></TD>
<TD></TD>
</TR>
```

This code for the fifth row of the table displays a row heading, then provides a text field for entering data into the TermInYears field. The default entry value is set to 4.

```
<TR>
<TH><ALIGN=right>Monthly Payment</TH>
<TD></TD>
<TD>$ <INPUT TYPE=text NAME=MonthlyLeasePayment VALUE="0" SIZE=12
MAXLENGTH=12></TD>
</TR>
```

This code for the sixth row of the table displays a row heading, then provides a text field for entering data into the MonthlyLeasePayment field. The default entry value is set to 0.

```
<TR>
<TH><ALIGN=right>Lease End Price</TH>
<TD></TD>
<TD>$ <INPUT TYPE=text NAME=LeaseEndPrice VALUE="0" SIZE=12
MAXLENGTH=12></TD>
</TR>
```

This code for the last row of the table displays a row heading, then provides a text field for entering data into the LeaseEndPrice field. The default entry value is set to 0.

```
</TABLE>
```

This code ends the table.

```
<P><INPUT TYPE="submit" NAME="-New" VALUE="Calculate">
<P><INPUT TYPE=reset VALUE="Start Over">
```

This code displays the submit and reset buttons, one above the other. The submit button, which is labeled Calculate, uses the **-New** CDML command to create a new database record.

```
</CENTER>
```

This tag ends centering.

```
</FORM>
```

This tag ends the form.

```
<P>
<HR>
<P>
```

This code inserts two blank lines with a horizontal rule between them.

```
<B>Disclaimer:</B> Neither Maria Langer nor Peachpit Press take
responsibility for the accuracy of these calculations. This solution is
offered as an example only and should not be relied upon to make
real-life Buy vs. Lease decisions.
```

This code displays a disclaimer. (You can leave this out if you want—just don't forget what it says!)

```
</BODY>
</HTML>
```

This code ends the HTML document.

When you are finished, check the code, then save the file as default.htm in the buyorlease folder.

response.htm

The response.htm format file displays a borderless table with field entries. The data already entered appears in form fields so it can be modified. A submit button labeled Recalculate modifies the data in the record and redisplays the response.htm format file. All this is handled through one form. A second form displays only a submit button labeled Start Over. When clicked, it deletes the record and displays the default.htm format file.

Another way to create this file would be to display calculated results without allowing the user to edit fields. To do so, eliminate the input fields and simply display the contents of FileMaker Pro fields with the Start Over button to delete the newly added record and return to default.htm.

Here's what this format file looks like when viewed with a Web browser. As you can see, it's very similar to the default.htm format file. The big difference is the inclusion of entered data and two additional rows to display the calculated results.

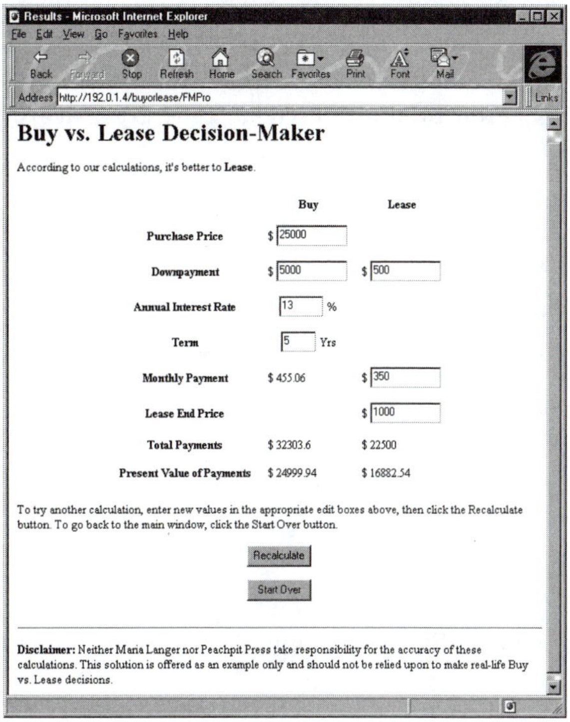

Results - Microsoft Internet Explorer

File Edit View Go Favorites Help

Back Forward Stop Refresh Home Search Favorites Print Font Mail

Address http://192.0.1.4/buyorlease/FMPro

Links

Buy vs. Lease Decision-Maker

According to our calculations, it's better to **Lease**.

	Buy	Lease
Purchase Price	$ 25000	
Downpayment	$ 5000	$ 500
Annual Interest Rate	13 %	
Term	5 Yrs	
Monthly Payment	$ 455.06	$ 350
Lease End Price		$ 1000
Total Payments	$ 32303.6	$ 22500
Present Value of Payments	$ 24999.94	$ 16882.54

To try another calculation, enter new values in the appropriate edit boxes above, then click the Recalculate button. To go back to the main window, click the Start Over button.

Recalculate

Start Over

Disclaimer: Neither Maria Langer nor Peachpit Press take responsibility for the accuracy of these calculations. This solution is offered as an example only and should not be relied upon to make real-life Buy vs. Lease decisions.

Here's the **code** and my comments for response.htm:

```
<HTML>
<HEAD>
<TITLE>Results</TITLE>
</HEAD>
<BODY BGCOLOR="#FFFFFF">
```

This code begins the HTML document, gives it a title, and sets the background color to white.

```
<H1>Buy vs. Lease Decision-Maker</H1>
```

This code displays a heading at the top of the page.

```
<FORM ACTION="FMPro" METHOD="POST">
<INPUT TYPE="hidden" NAME="-DB" VALUE="BuyOrLease.fp3">
<INPUT TYPE="hidden" NAME="-Lay" VALUE="EntryForm">
<INPUT TYPE="hidden" NAME="-Format" VALUE="response.htm">
<INPUT TYPE="hidden" NAME="-Error" VALUE="error.htm">
<INPUT TYPE="hidden" NAME="-RecID" VALUE="[FMP-CurrentRecID]">
```

This code sets up a form that will interact with FileMaker Pro. It provides the name of the database, layout, response format file, error format file, and identification of the current record. Note that the response format file is the same file—this enables the user to keep modifying the calculation without starting over from scratch.

```
According to our calculations, it's better to <B>[FMP-FIELD: LeastExpensive]</B>.
```

This displays a sentence that includes the contents of the LeastExpensive field to announce which deal is better.

```
<CENTER>
```

This tag starts centering.

```
<TABLE BORDER=0 CELLSPACING=5 CELLPADDING=5 WIDTH=380>
```

This code starts a borderless, fixed width table.

```
<TR>
<TD></TD>
<TH WIDTH=100>Buy<</TH>
<TH WIDTH=100>Lease</TH>
</TR>
```

This code for the first row of the table displays column headings for the second and third columns.

```
<TR>
<TH><ALIGN=right>Purchase Price</TH>
<TD>$ <INPUT TYPE=text NAME=PurchasePrice VALUE="[FMP-Field:
PurchasePrice]" SIZE=12 MAXLENGTH=12></TD>
<TD></TD>
</TR>
```

This code for the second row of the table displays a row heading, then provides a text field containing the contents of the PurchasePrice field.

```
<TR>
<TH><ALIGN=right>Downpayment</TH>
<TD>$ <INPUT TYPE=text NAME=PurchaseDownpayment VALUE="[FMP-Field:
PurchaseDownpayment]" SIZE=12 MAXLENGTH=12></TD>
<TD>$ <INPUT TYPE=text NAME=LeaseDownpayment VALUE="[FMP-Field:
LeaseDownpayment]" SIZE=12 MAXLENGTH=12></TD>
</TR>
```

This code for the third row of the table displays a row heading, then provides text fields containing the contents of the PurchaseDownpayment and Lease Downpayment fields.

```
<TR>
<TH><ALIGN=right>Annual Interest Rate</TH>
<TD><CENTER><INPUT TYPE=text NAME=AnnualInterestRate VALUE="[FMP-
Field: AnnualInterestRate]" SIZE=6 MAXLENGTH=12>%</CENTER></TD>
<TD></TD>
</TR>
```

This code for the fourth row of the table displays a row heading, then provides a text field containing the contents of the AnnualInterestRate field.

```
<TR>
<TH><ALIGN=right>Term</TH>
<TD><CENTER><INPUT TYPE=text NAME=TermInYears VALUE="[FMP-Field:
TermInYears]" SIZE=4 MAXLENGTH=12> Yrs</CENTER></TD>
<TD></TD>
</TR>
```

This code for the fifth row of the table displays a row heading, then provides a text field containing the contents of the TermInYears field.

```
<TR>
<TH><ALIGN=right>Monthly Payment</TH>
<TD>$ [FMP-FIELD: MonthlyLoanPayment]</TD>
<TD>$ <INPUT TYPE=text NAME=MonthlyLeasePayment VALUE="[FMP-Field:
MonthlyLeasePayment]" SIZE=12 MAXLENGTH=12></TD>
</TR>
```

This code for the sixth row of the table displays a row heading in the first cell, the calculated amount in the MonthlyLoanPayment field in the second cell, and a text field containing the contents of the MonthlyLeasePayment field in the third cell.

```
<TR>
<TH><ALIGN=right>Lease End Price</TH>
<TD></TD>
<TD>$ <INPUT TYPE=text NAME=LeaseEndPrice VALUE="[FMP-Field:
LeaseEndPrice]" SIZE=12 MAXLENGTH=12></TD>
</TR>
```

This code for the seventh row of the table displays a row heading, then provides a text field containing the contents of the LeaseEndPrice field.

```
<TR>
<TH><ALIGN=right>Total Payments</TH>
<TD>$ [FMP-FIELD: PurchaseTotalPayments]
</TD>
<TD>$ [FMP-FIELD: LeaseTotalPayments]</TD>
</TR>
```

This code for the eighth row of the table displays a row heading, then displays the calculated results in the PurchaseTotalPayments and LeaseTotalPayments fields.

```
<TR>
<TH><ALIGN=right>Present Value of Payments</TH>
<TD>$ [FMP-FIELD: PurchasePresentValue]</TD>
<TD>$ [FMP-FIELD: LeasePresentValue]</TD>
</TR>
```

This code for the last row of the table displays a row heading, then displays the calculated results in the PurchasePresentValue and LeasePresentValue fields.

```
</TABLE>
```

This tag ends the table.

```
<P>To try another calculation, enter new values in the appropriate
edit boxes above, then click the Recalculate button. To go back to
the main window, click the Start Over button.
```

This code displays additional instructions for the user.

```
<INPUT TYPE="submit" NAME="-Edit" VALUE="Recalculate">
```

This code displays a submit button which uses the **-Edit** CDML tag to tell FileMaker Pro to edit the current record using revised entries.

```
</FORM>
```

This tag ends the form.

```
<FORM ACTION="FMPro" METHOD="POST">
<INPUT TYPE="hidden" NAME="-DB" VALUE="BuyOrLease.fp3">
<INPUT TYPE="hidden" NAME="-Lay" VALUE="EntryForm">
<INPUT TYPE="hidden" NAME="-Format" VALUE="default.htm">
<INPUT TYPE="hidden" NAME="-Error" VALUE="error.htm">
<INPUT TYPE="hidden" NAME="-RecID" VALUE="[FMP-CurrentRecID]">
<INPUT TYPE="Submit" NAME="-Delete" VALUE="Start Over">
</FORM>
```

This is a neat trick. It creates a second form to display another submit button. This button uses the **-Delete** CDML tag to delete the current record, then displays the default.htm file, enabling the user to start from scratch. Cool, huh?

```
</CENTER>
```

This tag ends centering.

```
<P>
<HR>
<P>
```

This code inserts two blank lines with a horizontal rule between them.

```
<B>Disclaimer:</B> Neither Maria Langer nor Peachpit Press take responsibil-
ity for the accuracy of these calculations. This solution is offered as an
example only and should not be relied upon to make real-life Buy vs. Lease
decisions.
```

This code displays a disclaimer. (You don't have to type it.)

```
</BODY>
</HTML>
```

This code ends the HTML document.

Check the code, then save the file as response.htm in the buyorlease folder.

Creating error.htm

The error.htm file is merely an HTML file telling users what to do if an error occurs. Here's what it looks like:

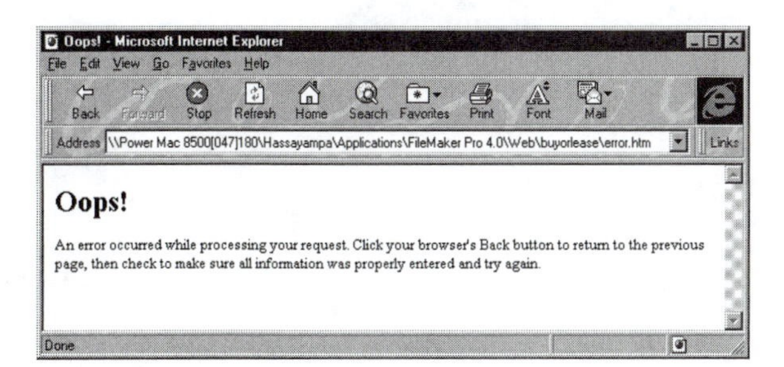

Here's its **code**. No explanation should be necessary. Save it as error.htm in the buyorlease folder.

```
<HTML>
<HEAD>
<TITLE>Oops!</TITLE>
</HEAD>
<BODY BGCOLOR="#FFFFFF">
<H1>Oops!</H1>
<P>An error occurred while processing your request. Click your browser's
Back button to return to the previous page, then check to make sure all
information was properly entered and try again.
</BODY>
</HTML>
```

Checking the Solution

To check your Custom Web Publishing solution, fire up your favorite Web browser and point it to the IP address of the database Web server followed by /buyorlease/default.htm. The default.htm format file should appear. Fill in the form and click the Calculate button. The results of the calculation should appear. Now edit one or more of the previously entered values and click the Recalculate button. The revised results should appear. Click the Start Over button to return to the original page. If you examine the FileMaker Pro database, you'll find that the record you created was deleted.

If your pages don't look or work right, check the code in the format files. Remember:

- HTML controls the way pages appear.
- CDML controls the way the solution interacts with FileMaker Pro.

CHAPTER 12

Handling Transactions

These days, more and more companies are doing business on the Web. One important component of any online commerce system is the ability to sell products or services. As shown in Chapters 8 through 11, you can use database Web publishing to display database information and images; allow visitors to search, display, add, and edit database records; and perform calculations on the contents of database fields. By combining these capabilities in one solution, you can allow visitors to shop—and purchase—the products and services that you promote on your Web site.

This chapter provides detailed information and instructions for creating an online "shopping cart" using FileMaker Pro Custom Web Publishing. The solution enables users to browse or search a catalog, select items, enter shipping and billing information, and enter a sales transaction.

You can download the solution files for this chapter from the companion Web site for this book, http://www.gilesrd.com/fmproweb/. That's also where you can find links to try out the solution in this chapter.

About the Databases

This solution is relatively complex and requires multiple related databases:

- **PRODUCTS.FP3** is a product catalog very similar to the one in Chapter 9.
- **ORDERITEMS.FP3** is a database of items selected by customers during the shopping process.
- **CUSTOMERS.FP3** is a database of customers.
- **ORDERS.FP3** is a database of customer orders.

Here's how it works. When the visitor first accesses the Web publishing solution, he can browse or search Products.fp3 to find items that interest him. When he adds an item to his "cart" the information about the item and quantity is added to OrderItems.fp3 for his order number. The visitor can add or remove as many items as desired.

When the visitor clicks a Checkout button, he is given an opportunity to enter his customer number and password to search the Customers.fp3 file. If his information is found, it is displayed; if his information is not found, he enters it to create a new record in that file. The information is also entered in a new record of the Orders.fp3 file, which calculates the order total, including shipping. When the visitor confirms the order, an Order In report is printed from the database Web server for processing. Orders.fp3 has additional features for managing and processing orders locally (not via the Web).

TIP

This solution does not include automatic verification of credit card information. Macintosh users can add this feature using AppleScript and a program such as MacAuthorize by Tellan Software, Inc. Check the Tellan Web site, http://www.tellan.com/, for examples of how this feature can be added to a shopping cart solution like the one in this chapter.

In this section, I describe each of the database files, providing detailed information about each file so you can either create it from scratch or analyze the files you download from this book's companion Web site.

TIP

I highly recommend downloading the files we already created. Why reinvent (or rebuild) the wheel? Start with our wheel, learn how it works, and modify it for your own needs.

Products.fp3

Products.fp3 is a database of products sold by Acme Office Supplies, a fictional office supply company. It's basically the same database file used in Chapter 9.

Here's some detailed information about this database file.

Database Fields

Here's a list of the fields in Products.fp3:

FIELD NAME	TYPE	DESCRIPTION
Product ID	number	unique, auto-enter serial number to identify item
Stock Number	text	item stock number
Item Name	text	name of item
Item Description	text	description of item
Unit Price	number	item price
Sale Item	text	sale item status; uses Yes No value list for validation (more on that later)
Category	text	item category; generates Categories value list (more on that later)
Sale Item Image	global	container for Sale Item image
Picture	container	item image
Sale	calculation	container that displays Sale Item image if the item is a sale item; formula is: **If(Sale Item="Yes",Sale Item Image,"")**
Display Unit Price	calculation	calculation that displays the unit price as properly formatted text; formula is: **If(IsEmpty(Unit Price), "", "$") & If(Round (Unit Price, 2) > 1000, Int(Round(Unit Price, 2) / 1000) & ",", "") & Right(Int(Round (Unit Price, 2)), 3) & Left(Round(Unit Price, 2) - Int(Round(Unit Price, 2)) + .001, 3)**

Value Lists

Products.fp3 has two value lists:

VALUE LIST NAME	CONTENTS
Yes No	Yes No
Categories	Uses values from the Category field of the database

Database Layouts

The database has two layouts:

- **WEB** displays all fields, except the Sale Item Image field, on a form suitable for data entry.
- **GLOBALS** displays just the Sale Item Image field.

Here's what these two layouts look like:

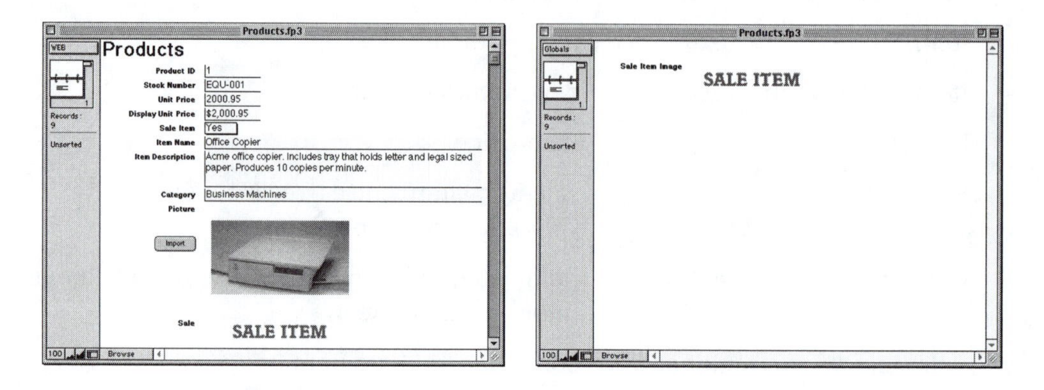

Database Records

The database has nine records—the same nine records found in Products.fp3 in Chapter 9. Each record includes information in all fields for a product, including a picture of the product.

Database Scripts

This particular database includes a script for importing images into the Picture field. This script is not utilized by the Web publishing solution. It's designed to quickly import an image into the file when adding a new product.

OrderItems.fp3

The order items file contains information about the items that a Web site visitor adds to his shopping cart. Here's some detailed information about this file.

Database Fields

The database has the following fields:

FIELD NAME	TYPE	DESCRIPTION
Order ID	number	order identification number set by solution; indexed for quick searching

Product ID	number	item identification number; used as match field for relationship to Products.fp3 (more about that later)
Qty	number	quantity of item desired
Item Name	text	name of item; auto-entered via a lookup to Products.fp3
Unit Price	number	price of item; auto-entered via a lookup to Products.fp3
Item Total	calculation	line item extension; formula is: `Unit Price * Qty`
Display Unit Price	calculation	calculation that displays the unit price as properly formatted text; formula is: `If(IsEmpty(Unit Price), "", "$") & If(Round (Unit Price, 2) > 1000, Int(Round(Unit Price, 2) / 1000) & ",", "") & Right(Int(Round (Unit Price, 2 )), 3) & Left(Round(Unit Price, 2) - Int(Round(Unit Price, 2)) + .001, 3)`
Display Item Total	calculation	calculation that displays the item total as properly formatted text; formula is: `If(IsEmpty(Item Total), "", "$") & If(Round(Item Total, 2) > 1000, Int(Round (Item Total, 2) / 1000) & ",", "") & Right(Int (Round(Item Total, 2)), 3) & Left(Round (Item Total, 2) - Int(Round(Item Total, 2)) + .001, 3)`

Database Relationships

The database has one relationship named Products. It matches the Product ID field in the OrderItems.fp3 file to the Product ID field in the Products.fp3 file. The relationship is used by lookups for the Item Name and Unit Price fields.

Database Layouts

OrderItems.fp3 has one layout named WEB, which displays the Order ID, Qty, Product ID, Item Name, Display Unit Price, and Display Item Total fields. It looks like this:

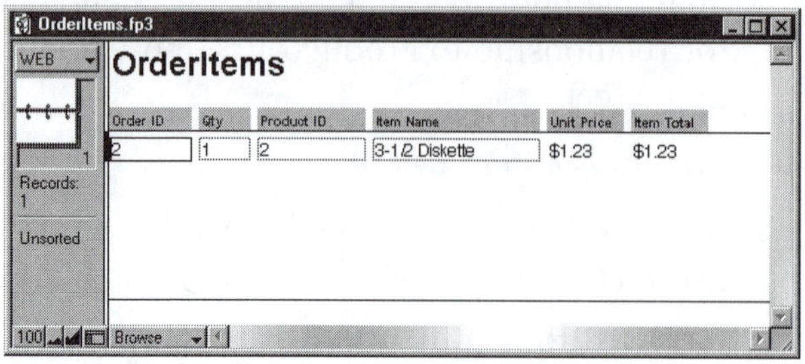

Database Records

The database doesn't come with records. Instead, records are added by shoppers as they add items to their virtual shopping cart.

Customers.fp3

The Customers.fp3 database is used to gather and store information about customers. Customers enter this information when they place an order. If they have ordered before, they can use a search feature within the Web publishing solution to automatically enter this information in a new order form.

Here are the details for this file.

Database Fields

Customers.fp3 has the following fields:

FIELD NAME	TYPE	DESCRIPTION
Customer ID	number	unique, auto-enter serial number to identify customer
First Name	text	customer's first name; required
Last Name	text	customer's last name; required
Password	text	customer's password; required
Username	calculation	calculation that concatenates characters from the customer's name with the Customer ID field; formula is: **`Left(Last Name, 2) & Left(First Name, 2) & Customer ID`**
Organization	text	customer's shipping organization name
Address	text	customer's shipping street address; required
City	text	customer's shipping address city; required
State	text	customer's shipping address state; required

Zip	text	customer's shipping address zip code; required
Email	text	customer's e-mail address; required
Phone	text	customer's telephone number; required
Fax	text	customer's fax number
Billing First Name	text	customer's billing first name; required
Billing Last Name	text	customer's billing last name; required
Billing Organization	text	customer's billing organization name
Billing Address	text	customer's billing street address; required
Billing City	text	customer's billing address city; required
Billing State	text	customer's billing address state; required
Billing Zip	text	customer's billing address zip; required
Billing Phone	text	customer's billing phone number; required
Billing Fax	text	customer's billing fax number

Database Layouts

The database has one layout named WEB. It displays all fields in an entry-form like this:

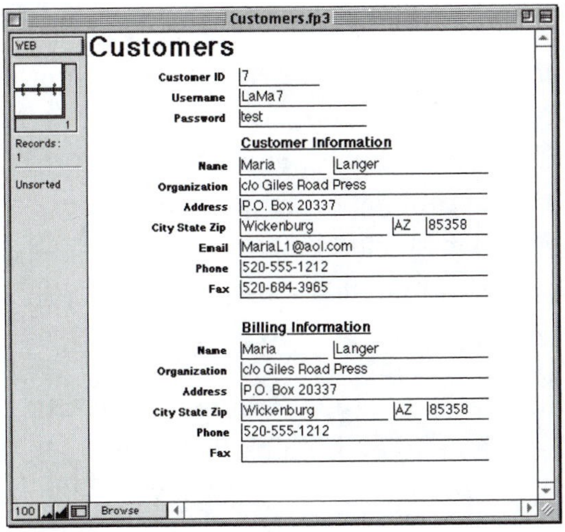

Database Records

The database doesn't need any records when you first start out. Instead, customers add records for you when they place orders.

TIP

If you use this solution on your Web site, you should periodically check the contents of the database to remove invalid data entered by customers who did not complete orders or placed orders with false information.

Orders.fp3

The Orders.fp3 database file gathers information about orders placed by Web visitors. It has a number of features that not only gather information from customers, but help you to process orders.

Here's the information about this file.

Database Fields

The database includes the following fields, most of which are used to collect payment information about the order:

FIELD NAME	TYPE	DESCRIPTION
Order ID	number	unique number to identify order; indexed
Customer ID	number	customer identification number
Order Date	date	date order was placed
Subtotal	calculation	the sum of all items in the order; uses fields from a relationship with OrderItems.fp3 (more on that later); formula is: **Sum(OrderItems::Item Total)**
Shipping	calculation	calculates the shipping based on the subtotal; formula is: **Case(Subtotal>100, 15, Subtotal >50 , 10, 5)**
Order Total	calculation	adds the subtotal to shipping; formula is: **Subtotal + Shipping**
Display Subtotal	calculation	calculation that displays the Subtotal field as properly formatted text; formula is: **If(IsEmpty(Subtotal), "", "$") & If(Round (Subtotal, 2) > 1000, Int(Round(Subtotal, 2) / 1000) & ",", "") & Right(Int(Round (Subtotal, 2)), 3) & Left(Round(Subtotal, 2) Int(Round(Subtotal, 2)) + .001, 3)**

Display Shipping	calculation	calculation that displays the Shipping field as properly formatted text; formula is: **If(IsEmpty(Shipping), "", "$") & If(Round (Shipping, 2) > 1000, Int(Round(Shipping, 2) / 1000) & ",", "") & Right(Int(Round (Shipping, 2)), 3) & Left(Round(Shipping, 2) Int(Round(Shipping, 2)) + .001, 3)**
Display Order Total	calculation	calculation that displays the Order Total field as properly formatted text; formula is: **If(IsEmpty(Order Total), "", "$") & If(Round (Order Total, 2) > 1000, Int(Round (Order Total, 2) / 1000) & ",", "") & Right(Int(Round(Order Total, 2)), 3) & Left(Round(Order Total, 2) Int(Round(Order Total, 2)) + .001, 3)**
Payment Type	text	method of payment; uses the Payment Type value list for validation
Credit Card Number	number	credit card number for purchase
Credit Card Exp	text	credit card expiration date
Order Status	text	status of order processing; uses the Order Status value list for validation
Category	global	the product categories
IP Number	text	the IP address of the visitor who placed the order

Value Lists

The database has three value lists that are used by its fields:

VALUE LIST NAME	CONTENTS
Payment Type	Money Order Visa MasterCard American Express Discover
Order Status	New Order Processing Paid
Categories	uses values from Category field in Products.fp3 file

Database Relationships

The database has two relationships to other files. This enables it to access and display information from other database files without actually storing the information.

- **OrderItems** matches the Order ID field in Order.fp3 to the Order ID field in OrderItems.fp3.
- **Customers** matches the Customer ID field in Orders.fp3 to the Customer ID field in Customers.fp3.

Database Layouts

The database has four layouts:

- WEB displays the fields used in the Web publishing solution.
- Order In provides information about the order so it can be processed. This layout is printed automatically each time an order is submitted.
- Packing Slip provides a packing slip for preparing the order for shipping. This layout is printed automatically when the order has been approved.
- Invoice provides an invoice for the customer. This layout is printed automatically when the order has been approved.

Here's what these layouts look like:

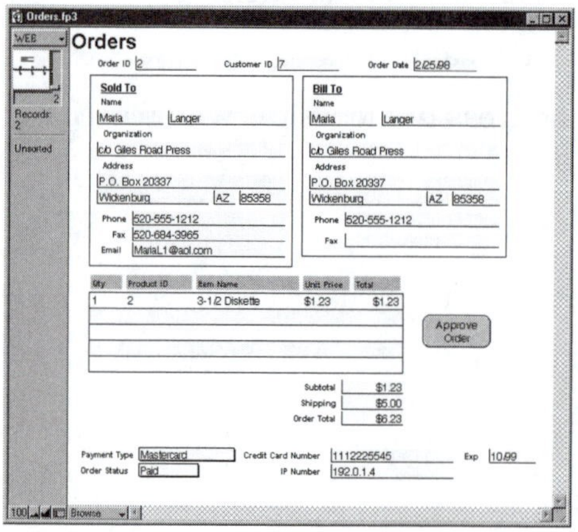

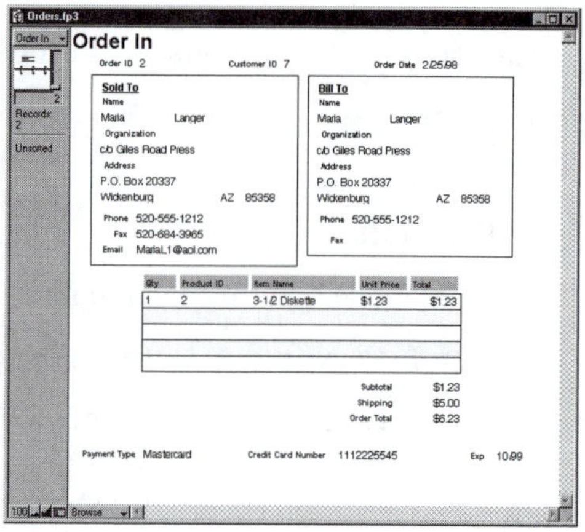

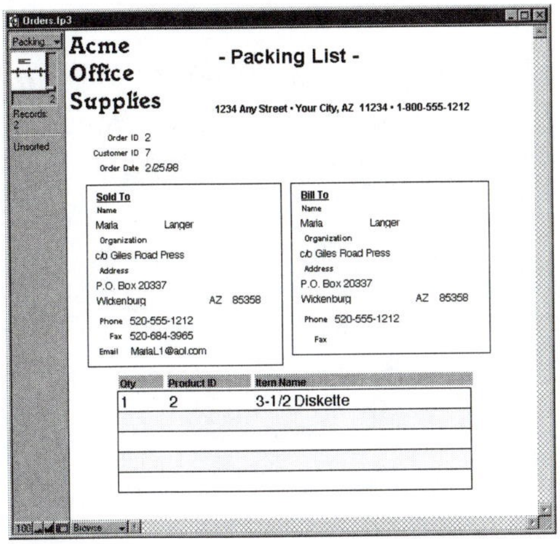

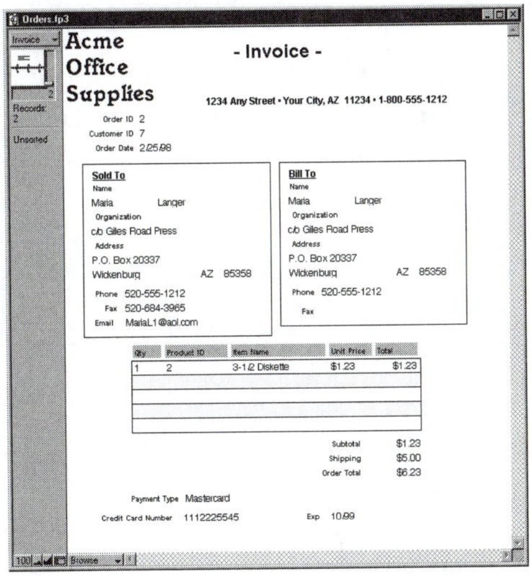

Database Records

No database records are necessary when you first use this file. Database records are created when visitors place orders.

Database Scripts

This database also includes two scripts, one of which is used by the Web publishing solution.

- **PRINT ORDER** prints the Order In layout for an incoming order.
- **APPROVE** sets the Order Status field to Paid and prints the Packing Slip and Invoice layouts for the active order record. This script is designed to be used by individuals who access the database directly to process orders.

Custom Web Publishing Solution

The FileMaker Pro Custom Web Publishing solution we developed uses 13 format files, some images, and an include file to handle all interaction between the Web site visitor and database files. It's a complex solution, but I explain it in detail in this section.

The instructions in this section assume that you have properly installed FileMaker Pro, enabled and configured the Web Companion Plug-In for Custom Web Publishing, and turned on Web Companion Sharing in the File Sharing dialog box. I provide detailed instructions for completing all of these tasks in Chapter 2.

Planning the Solution

Like the Guest Register solution in Chapter 10, this Web publishing solution is complex and deserves some serious planning. Here's the chart I came up with to illustrate the way format files should interact for the shopping cart solution:

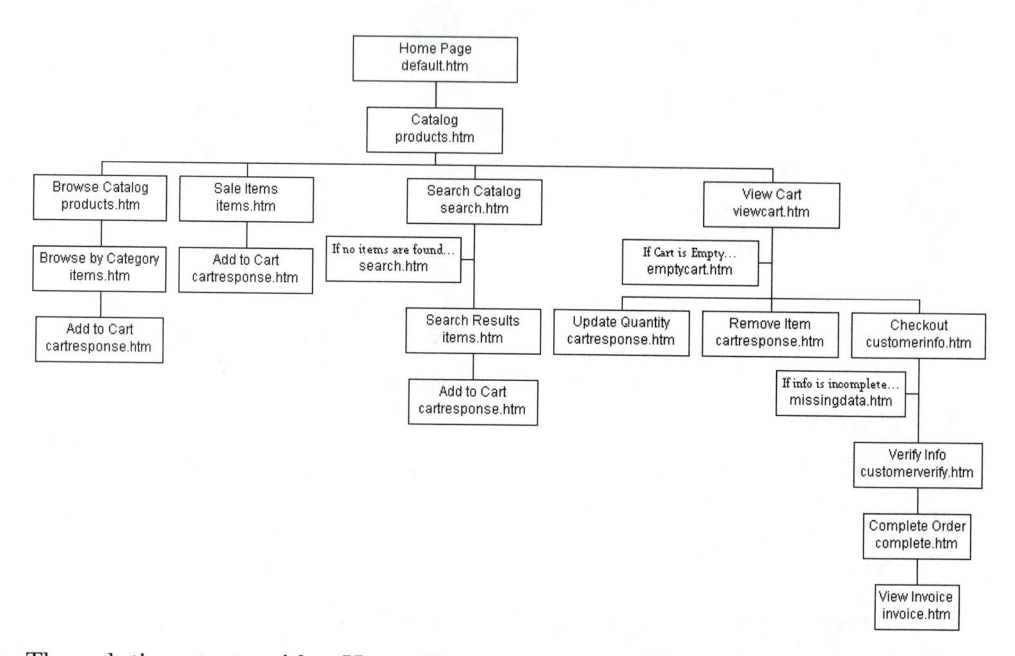

The solution starts with a Home Page named default.htm. Visitors click a link on the page to view the products.htm format file, start shopping, and eventually complete an order.

Shopping

The products.htm format file—and most other format files in the solution—includes four buttons to browse the catalog (Products.fp3) and check the contents of the virtual shopping cart (OrderItems.fp3):

- **Browse Catalog** displays a list of item categories. This is the same view that appears when the visitor clicks the link on default.htm. Clicking a product category displays all of the items in that category using the items.htm format file.
- **Sale Items** displays a list of the items that are on sale, using the items.htm format file.
- **Search Catalog** displays the search.htm format file, which enables the visitor to enter search criteria. A successful search displays the items found using the items.htm format file. An unsuccessful search displays a message in the search.htm format file, enabling the visitor to try another search.

- **VIEW CART** displays either the cartview.htm or emptycart.htm format files—depending on whether the shopping cart contains items. More on that in a moment.

Adding Items to the Shopping Cart

The items.htm file includes fields for entering quantities for any item and an Add to Cart button to add an item to a virtual shopping cart. This creates a new record in OrderItems.fp3. The cartresponse.htm format file confirms that the item has been added. This feature is available when browsing by category, viewing sale items, or searching for items that match criteria.

Working with the Shopping Cart

At any time, a visitor can click the View Cart button to view the contents of his virtual shopping cart, which is determined by the customer's Order ID number for items in OrderItems.fp3. If the cart is empty, the emptycart.htm format file appears. If the cart is not empty, the items in the cart are listed using the viewcart.htm format file, which offers three options:

- **UPDATE** enables the shopper to change the quantity of an item. Clicking the update button modifies the OrderItems.fp3 record and displays the cartresponse.htm format file.
- **DELETE** (a trash can icon) enables the shopper to remove an item from the shopping cart. Clicking the trash can icon deletes the OrderItems.fp3 record and displays the cartresponse.htm format file.
- **CHECKOUT** enables the shopper to complete the order. More on that next.

Checking Out

Clicking the Checkout button in the viewcart.htm format file displays the customerinfo.htm format file. This page can be used two ways:

- A repeat customer can enter his username and password to search Customers.fp3 for his information. The information appears on the customerverify.htm format file.
- A first-time customer can enter his information into fields, then add his record to the Customers.fp3 format file. If the entered information is complete, it appears on the customerverify.htm format file. If the entered information is not complete, the missingdata.htm format file appears. The shopper must then go back to the customerinfo.htm format file to enter the missing information.

When a shopper clicks the Continue button on the customerverify.htm format file, the complete.htm format file appears. It provides order total information from Orders.fp3 and enables the shopper to enter payment information. When the customer clicks the Process button on this page, the invoice.htm format file appears. This file, which is designed to be printed by the shopper, summarizes the order. Meanwhile, the Order In layout of Orders.p3 prints from the database Web server.

Finishing Up

When the order is complete, the customer can click the Home button on the invoices.htm format file page to return to Products.fp3. His order is completed and closed.

About Token Passing

One of the important components of this solution is the passing of a token from one format file to the next. Throughout the solution, the current order number, which is obtained when the user first enters the virtual store, is tracked. This is vital for preventing one customer's order from being mixed up with that of another who is shopping at the same time.

You'll see token passing code like this throughout this solution's format files:

```
-token=[FMP-if:currentdatabase.eq.Orders.fp3][FMP-currentrecid]
[FMP-else][FMP-currenttoken][/FMP-if]
```

This code checks to see what the current database is. If it is Orders.fp3, where the Order ID is first assigned, it assigns the current record number of that file as the token. Otherwise, it uses the token already in memory.

```
<INPUT TYPE="hidden" NAME="-token" VALUE="[FMP-currenttoken]">
```

Code like this simply confirms the existing token value to pass it to another format file.

```
<INPUT TYPE="hidden" NAME="Order ID" VALUE="[FMP-currenttoken]">
```

Code like this uses the token contents within forms to locate records and enter data into the correct order.

When the shopper clicks the Home button on the invoice.htm format file page, the tokens are cleared. Any additional items he adds to a shopping cart become part of a brand new order.

WARNING

Without the token passing code, a shopper's order could not be properly tracked!

Creating Project Folders

Like the other Web publishing solution examples in this book, this solution's files will be stored in their own folder.

Start by creating a folder named cart in the Web folder inside the FileMaker Pro folder. Open the folder and create a folder called databases inside it. If the database files are open, close them. Move them into the databases folder, then open them.

Create two more folders inside the cart folder: images, which will be used to store image files for buttons and logos, and includes, which will be used to store the include file.

Creating the Format Files

This solution requires a total of 13 format files, each of which combine HTML and CDML tags. Chapter 2 provides information about the CDML Tool and Claris Home Page 3, each of which can make creating these files easier.

TIP

As I mention earlier in this chapter, I recommend that you download the solution files from this book's companion Web site. Then use the information in this section to analyze and, if desired, modify the format files for your own use.

In this section, I explain what each format file does, show you how it looks when viewed with a Web browser, and provide its underlying HTML and CDML code. The code appears in a **bold, sans serif type**; my comments appear in this type. If you create these files by typing in code, be sure to exclude my comments!

default.htm

The default.htm format file is a simple Home page for the solution. Here's what it looks like when viewed with a Web browser:

Here's the **code** and my comments for this file:

```
<HTML>
<HEAD>
<TITLE>Welcome to Acme Office Supplies</TITLE>
</HEAD>
<BODY BGCOLOR="#FFFFFF">
```

This code starts the HTML document, gives it a title, and sets the background color to white.

```
<CENTER>
<A HREF="FMPro?-db=Orders.fp3&-format=products.htm&-New"><IMG
SRC="images/welcome.gif" BORDER=0></A>
</CENTER>
```

This code displays an image with a CDML link, centered on the page. The link creates a new record in the Orders.fp3 file and displays products.htm.

```
</BODY>
</HTML>
```

This code ends the HTML document.

When you're finished creating this file, save it as default.htm in the cart folder.

products.htm

The products.htm file is the first file that displays the shopping cart interface. It includes a number of buttons along the left side of the screen that enable the visitor to view products and the contents of his virtual shopping cart. Here's what this file looks like when viewed with a Web browser:

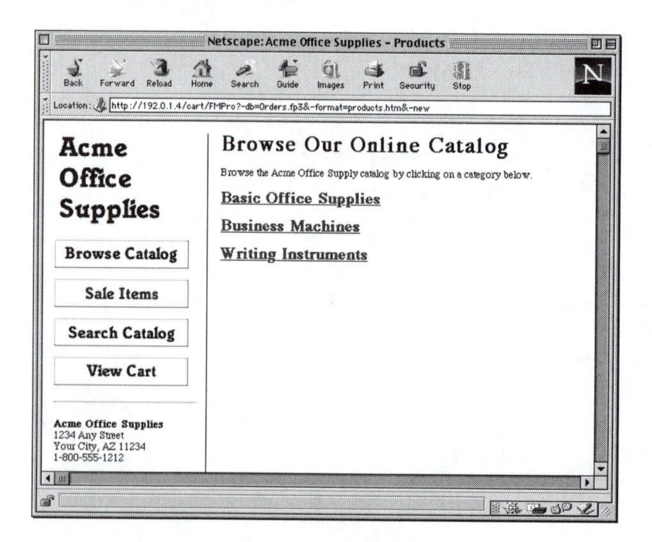

Here's the **code** for the products.htm file, along with my comments:

```
<HTML>
<HEAD>
<TITLE>Acme Office Supplies - Products</TITLE>
</HEAD>
<BODY BGCOLOR="#FFFFFF">
```

This code starts the HTML document, gives it a title, and sets the background color to white.

```
<TABLE BORDER="0" CELLPADDING="5" CELLSPACING="0" WIDTH="600">
```

This code starts a fixed-width, borderless table.

```
<TR>
```

This code starts the table row.

```
<TD ALIGN=LEFT VALIGN=TOP WIDTH="160">
```

This code starts the first cell, by setting alignment to left and top and fixing the width at 160 pixels.

```
<IMG SRC="images/logo.gif">
<BR>
```

This code displays the Acme Office Supplies logo and ends the line.

```
<P><A HREF="FMPro?-token=[FMP-if:currentdatabase.eq.Orders.fp3]
[FMP-currentrecid][FMP-else][FMP-currenttoken][/FMP-if]&-db=Products.fp3&
-format=products.htm&-findall"><IMG SRC="images/browse.gif" BORDER=0></A>
```

This code displays and creates a link for the Browse button that finds all records in Products.fp3 and displays the products.htm format file. (It does basically the same thing as the link on default.htm.)

```
<P><A HREF="FMPro?-token=[FMP-if:currentdatabase.eq.Orders.fp3]
[FMP-currentrecid][FMP-else][FMP-currenttoken][/FMP-if]&-db=Products.fp3&
sale%20item=yes&-sortfield=item%20name&-format=items.htm&-find">
<IMG SRC="images/sale.gif" BORDER=0></A>
```

This code displays and creates a link for the Sale Items button that finds all records in Products.fp3 that are sale items and displays them in the items.htm format file.

```
<P><A HREF="FMPro?-token=[FMP-if:currentdatabase.eq.Orders.fp3]
[FMP-currentrecid][FMP-else][FMP-currenttoken][/FMP-if]&-db=Products.fp3&
-format=search.htm&-findall"><IMG SRC="images/search.gif" BORDER=0></A>
```

This code displays and creates a link for the Search button that finds all records in the Products.fp3 file and displays the search.htm format file.

```
<P><A HREF="FMPro?-token=[FMP-if:currentdatabase.eq.Orders.fp3]
[FMP-currentrecid][FMP-else][FMP-currenttoken][/FMP-if]&-db=OrderItems.fp3&
-error=emptycart.htm&order%20id=[FMP-if:currentdatabase.eq.Orders.fp3]
[FMP-currentrecid][FMP-else][FMP-currenttoken][/FMP-if]&-format=viewcart.htm&
-find"><IMG SRC="images/viewcart.gif" BORDER=0></A>
```

This code displays and creates a link for the View Cart button. It uses the token with the **-Find** CDML tag to determine which items are included in the visitor's cart. If the cart is not empty, it displays all items for that order number using the viewcart.htm format file. If there are no items for that order number, it displays the emptycart.htm format file (the error format file).

```
<P>
<HR>
<P>
```

This code inserts two blank lines with a horizontal rule between them.

```
<B>Acme Office Supplies</B><BR>
1234 Any Street<BR>
Your City, AZ  11234<BR>
1-800-555-1212
```

This code displays the Acme Office Supplies address and phone number. (Remember, this is a *fictional* company; don't bother toll-free directory services!)

```
</TD>
```

This code ends the first cell of the table.

```
<TD ALIGN=LEFT VALIGN=TOP WIDTH="5">
```

This code sets up the second cell of the table with left and top alignment and a fixed pixel width of 5.

```
<IMG SRC="images/pixel.gif" WIDTH="1" HEIGHT="450" BORDER="0">
```

This code displays a vertical rule in the cell by stretching a single pixel image to a height of 450 pixels. (Think of it as a digital rubber band.)

```
</TD>
```

This code ends the second cell of the table.

```
<TD ALIGN=LEFT VALIGN=TOP WIDTH="425">
```

This code sets up the third cell of the table with left and top alignment and a fixed width of 425 pixels.

```
<H1>Browse Our Online Catalog</H1>
Browse the Acme Office Supply catalog by clicking on a category below.
<P>
```

This code provides a heading and some instructions, followed by a blank line.

```
[FMP-valuelist:Category,list=Categories]
<A HREF="FMPro?-token=[FMP-if:currentdatabase.eq.Orders.fp3][FMP-curren-
trecid][FMP-else][FMP-currenttoken][/FMP-if]&-db=Products.fp3&-lay=WEB&-
format=items.htm&-sortfield=item%20name&category=[FMP-valuelistitem,url]
&-find"><H2>[FMP-valuelistitem]</H2></A>
[/FMP-valuelist]
```

This code displays each of the entries in the Category value list of the Products.fp3 or Orders.fp3 file (whichever is in the foreground) as a link. Clicking the link uses the **-Find** CDML tag to display all of the items in the category using the items.htm format file.

```
</TD>
```

This tag ends the cell.

```
</TR>
```

This tag ends the row.

```
</TABLE>
```

This tag ends the table.

```
</BODY>
</HTML>
```

This tag ends the HTML document.

When you're finished creating this file, save it as products.htm in the cart folder.

items.htm

The items.htm file displays the same buttons along the left side of the window with items from Products.fp3 beside it. This format file is used to display items when a visitor clicks a category name or the Sale Items button in products.htm or successfully completes a search. It includes the Add to Cart button, along with the Qty field for each item so visitors can add items to their virtual shopping carts.

On the following page you can see what items.htm looks like when you click the Sale Items button.

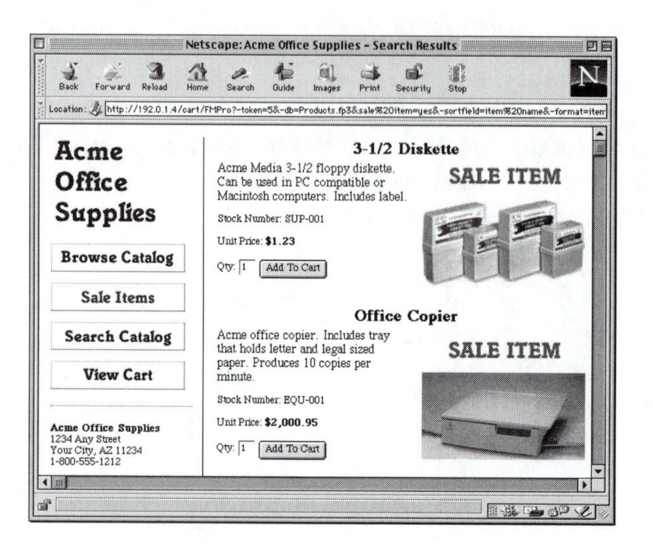

Here's the **code** and my comments for items.htm:

```
<HTML>
<HEAD>
<TITLE>Acme Office Supplies - Search Results</TITLE>
</HEAD>
<BODY BGCOLOR="#FFFFFF">
```

This code starts the HTML document, gives it a title, and sets the background color to white.

```
<TABLE BORDER="0" CELLPADDING="5" CELLSPACING="0" WIDTH="600">
```

This code sets up a borderless, fixed width table.

```
<TR>
```

This code starts the table row.

```
<TD ALIGN=LEFT VALIGN=TOP WIDTH="160">
[FMP-include:includes/sidebar.txt]
</TD>
```

This code displays the first cell of the table with HTML and CDML tags from the sidebar.txt include file.

TIP

Using an include file enables you to include the same code in multiple files without having to enter that code in each file. The main benefit of using an include file is that when you change the single file, the HTML and CDML it contains is automatically changed in each file that references it.

```
<TD ALIGN=LEFT VALIGN=TOP WIDTH="5">
<IMG SRC="images/pixel.gif" WIDTH="1" HEIGHT="450" BORDER="0">
</TD>
```

This code displays a 450-pixel long vertical line in the second cell.

```
<TD ALIGN=LEFT VALIGN=TOP WIDTH="425">
```

This code sets up the third cell with left and top alignment and a fixed width.

```
[FMP-Record]
```

This tag tells FileMaker Pro to repeat the code between it and the **[/FMP-Record]** tag for every record in the found set.

```
<TABLE BORDER=0>
```

This code starts a nested table within the third cell of the outer table.

```
<TR>
<TD COLSPAN=2 BGCOLOR=#FFFFCC ALIGN=CENTER>
<FONT SIZE=+2>
<B>[FMP-Field: Item Name]</B>
</FONT>
</TD>
</TR>
```

This code displays the contents of the Item Name field in the first row of the nested table.

```
<TR>
```

This code starts the second row of the nested table.

```
<TD WIDTH=300 VALIGN=TOP>
```

This code starts the first cell in the second row of the nested table.

```
<FONT SIZE=+1>[FMP-Field: item description]</FONT>
<P>
Stock Number: [FMP-Field: stock number]<BR>
<P>
Unit Price:  <B>[FMP-Field: display unit price]</B>
<P>
```

This code displays information about a product.

```
<FORM METHOD="POST" ACTION="FMPro">
<INPUT TYPE="hidden" NAME="-db" VALUE="OrderItems.fp3">
<INPUT TYPE="hidden" NAME="-format" VALUE="cartresponse.htm">
<INPUT TYPE="hidden" NAME="-token" VALUE="[FMP-currenttoken]">
<INPUT TYPE="hidden" NAME="-lay" VALUE="WEB">
<INPUT TYPE="hidden" NAME="Product ID" VALUE="[FMP-field: product ID]">
<INPUT TYPE="hidden" NAME="Order ID" VALUE="[FMP-currenttoken]">
Qty: <INPUT TYPE="text" SIZE="2" NAME="Qty" VALUE="1">
<INPUT TYPE="submit" NAME="-NEW"  VALUE="Add To Cart">
</FORM>
```

This code displays a form that enables the visitor to add the desired number of a particular item to his shopping cart. It provides all the information needed to properly record the item in OrderItems.fp3 for the correct order number. If the submit (Add to Cart) button is clicked, a new record is added to OrderItems.fp3 and the cartresponse.htm format file is displayed.

```
</TD>
```

This code ends the table cell.

```
<TD WIDTH=200 ALIGN=CENTER VALIGN=MIDDLE>
[FMP-If: Field: Sale Item .eq. Yes]
<img src="[FMP-Image: sale]"><P>
[/FMP-If]
<img src="[FMP-Image: picture]">
</TD>
```

This code displays the second cell of the second row of the nested table. It includes the Sale Item image if the item is a sale item, followed by a picture of the item.

```
</TR>
```

This tag ends the second row of the nested table.

```
</TABLE>
```

This tag ends the nested table.

```
<P>
```

This tag inserts a blank line.

```
[/FMP-Record]
```

This tag tells FileMaker Pro to stop repeating code.

```
</TD>
```

This tag ends the third cell of the the outer table.

```
</TR>
```

This tag ends the row of the outer table.

```
</TABLE>
```

This tag ends the table.

```
</BODY>
</HTML>
```

This code ends the HTML document.

When you are finished creating this file, check its code and save it as items.htm in the cart folder.

search.htm

The search.htm file appears when the Search button is clicked. It provides fields and buttons that can be used to search Products.fp3 for items that match visitor criteria.

Here's what search.htm looks like when viewed with a Web browser:

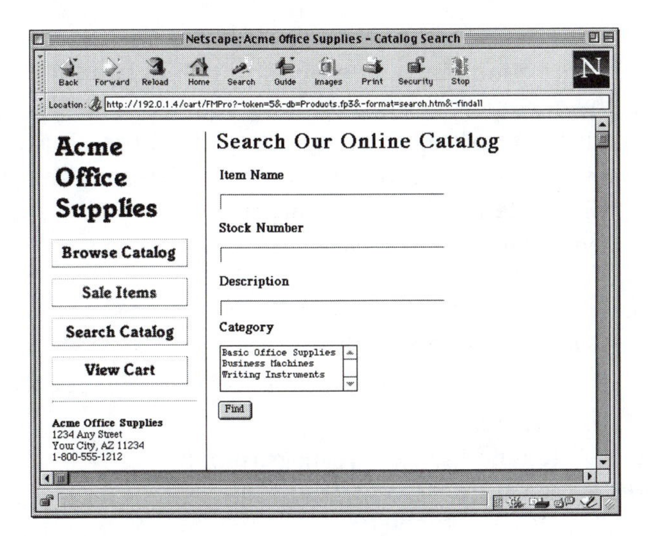

Here's the **code** for search.htm, along with my comments.

```
<HTML>
<HEAD>
<TITLE>Acme Office Supplies - Catalog Search</TITLE>
</HEAD>
<BODY BGCOLOR="#FFFFFF">
<TABLE BORDER="0" CELLPADDING="5" CELLSPACING="0" WIDTH="600">
```

```
<TR>
<TD ALIGN=LEFT VALIGN=TOP WIDTH="160">
[FMP-include:includes/sidebar.txt]
</TD>
<IMG SRC="images/pixel.gif" WIDTH="1" HEIGHT="450" BORDER="0">
</TD>
<TD ALIGN=LEFT VALIGN=TOP WIDTH="425">
```

This code is the same as the code at the beginning of items.htm, so check my comments about that file for an explanation. If you're creating this file by typing in code, remember the Copy and Paste commands!

```
<H1>Search Our Online Catalog</H1>
```

This code displays a heading in the third cell of the table.

```
[FMP-if:currentaction.eq.find]
[FMP-if:currentfoundcount.eq.0]
<B>No matching records found.</B> Please try again.
<P>
[/FMP-if]
[/FMP-if]
```

This code checks whether the last command issued was the **-Find** command. If it was, the code then checks the current found count. If the found count is 0, displays a message that no records were found. If the found count was greater than 0 or if the **-Find** command was not the command last used, displays nothing. This code enables the search.htm file to be used as an error format file, automatically giving visitors another chance to search the database.

In reality, if the the last command used was the **-Find** *command but records were found, a different format file would be displayed.*

```
<FORM METHOD="POST" ACTION="FMPro">
<INPUT TYPE="hidden" NAME="-token" VALUE="[FMP-currenttoken]">
<INPUT TYPE="hidden" NAME=-DB VALUE="Products.fp3">
<INPUT TYPE="hidden" NAME=-LAY VALUE="WEB">
<INPUT TYPE="hidden" NAME="-format" VALUE="items.htm">
<INPUT TYPE="hidden" NAME="-error" VALUE="search.htm">
<INPUT TYPE="hidden" NAME="-sortfield" VALUE="item name">
<INPUT TYPE="hidden" NAME="-sortorder" VALUE="descending">
```

This code sets up a form for searching and reporting results from the Products.fp3 file.

```
<H3>Item Name</H3>
<INPUT TYPE="text" NAME="Item Name" VALUE="" SIZE="40">
<H3>Stock Number</H3>
<INPUT TYPE="text" NAME="Stock Number" VALUE="" SIZE="40">
<H3>Description</H3>
<INPUT TYPE="text" NAME="Item Description" VALUE="" SIZE="40">
```

This code displays headings and text fields for inputting search criteria into the Item Name, Stock Number, or Item Description fields.

```
<H3>Category</H3>
<SELECT NAME="Category" MULTIPLE SIZE=4>
[FMP-valuelist:Category,list=Categories]
<OPTION>[FMP-valuelistitem]
[/FMP-valuelist]
</SELECT>
```

This code displays a heading followed by a scrolling list of options for the Category field from the Categories value list in Products.fp3.

```
<P>
<INPUT TYPE="submit" NAME="-FIND" VALUE="Find">
```

This code displays a submit button that uses the **-Find** CDML tag to search Products.fp3.

```
</FORM>
```

This tag ends the form.

```
</TD>
</TR>
</TABLE>
</BODY>
</HTML>
```

This code is the same as the code at the end of items.htm; check my comments about that file for details.

When you're finished, check the code and save the file as search.htm in the cart folder.

cartresponse.htm

The cartresponse.htm format file is used to reply to any action that changes the contents of the visitor's virtual shopping cart. By checking the last command used, it displays an appropriate message for the most recent action.

Here's what the cartresponse.htm file looks like when viewed with a Web browser just after adding an item to the shopping cart:

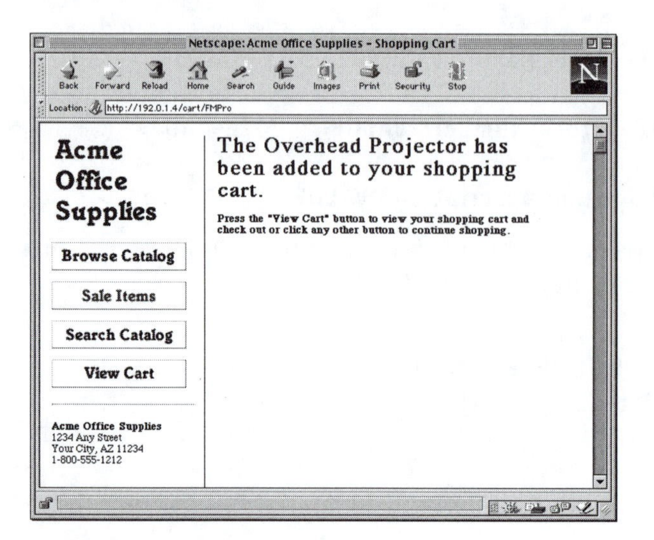

Here's the **code** for cartresponse.htm, along with my comments:

```
<HTML>
<HEAD>
<TITLE>Acme Office Supplies - Shopping Cart</TITLE>
</HEAD>
<BODY BGCOLOR="#FFFFFF">
<TABLE BORDER="0" CELLPADDING="5" CELLSPACING="0" WIDTH="575">
<TR>
<TD ALIGN=LEFT VALIGN=TOP WIDTH="160">
[FMP-include:includes/sidebar.txt]
</TD>
<TD ALIGN=LEFT VALIGN=TOP WIDTH="5">
<IMG SRC="images/pixel.gif" WIDTH="1" HEIGHT="450" BORDER="0">
</TD>
<TD ALIGN=LEFT VALIGN=TOP WIDTH="425">
```

This code is the same as the code at the beginning of items.htm, so check my comments about that file for an explanation.

```
[FMP-if:currentaction.eq.delete]
<H1>Your selection has been deleted.</H1>
[FMP-else]
[FMP-if:currentaction.eq.new]
<H1>The [FMP-Field: Item Name] has been added to your shopping cart.</H1>
[FMP-else]
<H1>The [FMP-Field: Item Name] has been updated in your cart.</H1>
[/FMP-if]
[/FMP-if]
```

This code uses nested **[FMP-If]** tags to determine what the last command issued was and respond appropriately. If the last command was the **-Delete** command, informs the visitor that the item has been deleted. If the last command was the **-New** command, informs the visitor that the item has been added, referring to the item by name with the **[FMP-Field: Item Name]** tag. The only other action that uses this format file is the **-Edit** command; if it was the last command, informs the visitor that the item has been updated, referring to the item by name with the **[FMP-Field: Item Name]** tag. This code enables you to use one format file for three different responses!

```
<B>Press the "View Cart" button to view your shopping cart and check out or
click any other button to continue shopping.</B>
```

This code provides instructions for the online shopper.

```
</TD>
</TR>
</TABLE>
</BODY>
</HTML>
```

This code is the same as the code at the end of items.htm; check my comments about that file for details.

Check the code and save the file as cartresponse.htm in the cart folder.

viewcart.htm

The viewcart.htm format file displays the contents of the visitor's shopping cart, enabling him to change quantities or remove items. Here's what it looks like with a Web browser during my shopping spree:

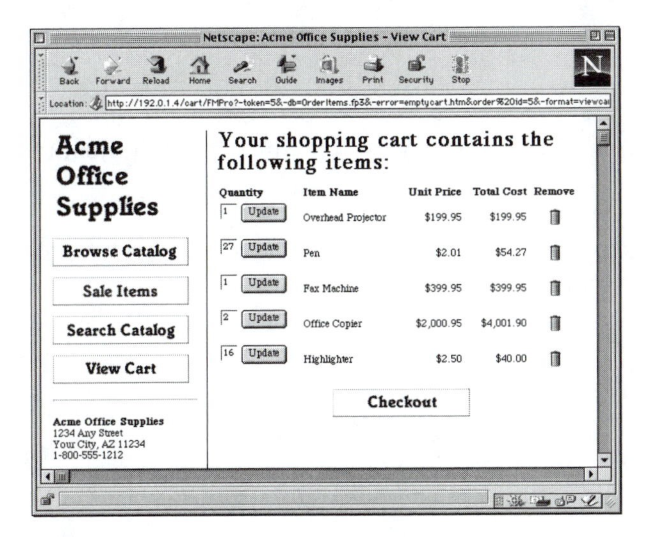

Here's the **code** for this format file with my comments:

```
<HTML>
<HEAD>
<TITLE>Acme Office Supplies - View Cart</TITLE>
</HEAD>
<BODY BGCOLOR="#FFFFFF">
<TABLE BORDER="0" CELLPADDING="5" CELLSPACING="0" WIDTH="600">
<TR>
<TD ALIGN=LEFT VALIGN=TOP WIDTH="160">
[FMP-include:includes/sidebar.txt]
</TD>
<TD ALIGN=LEFT VALIGN=TOP WIDTH="5">
<IMG SRC="images/pixel.gif" WIDTH="1" HEIGHT="450" BORDER="0">
</TD>
<TD ALIGN=LEFT VALIGN=TOP WIDTH="425">
```

This code is the same as the code near the beginning of items.htm, so check my comments about that file for an explanation.

```
<H1>Your shopping cart contains the following items:</H1>
```

This code displays a heading.

```
<TABLE BORDER="0" CELLPADDING="2" CELLSPACING="0" WIDTH="400">
```

This code begins a fixed-width, borderless, nested table.

```
<TR>
<TH ALIGN=LEFT>Quantity</TH>
<TH ALIGN=LEFT>Item Name</TH>
<TH ALIGN=RIGHT>Unit Price</TH>
<TH ALIGN=RIGHT>Total Cost</TH>
<TH>Remove</TH>
</TR>
```

This code displays the first row of the table, which includes column headings.

```
[FMP-Record]
```

This tag tells FileMaker Pro to repeat all code between it and the **[/FMP-Record]** tag for every record in the found set.

```
<TR>
```

This tag starts the second row of the nested table.

```
<TD VALIGN="CENTER">
<FORM METHOD="POST" ACTION="FMPro">
<INPUT TYPE="hidden" NAME="-db" VALUE="OrderItems.fp3">
<INPUT TYPE="hidden" NAME="-format" VALUE="cartresponse.htm">
<INPUT TYPE="hidden" NAME="-lay" VALUE="WEB">
<INPUT TYPE="hidden" NAME="-token" VALUE="[FMP-currenttoken]">
<INPUT TYPE="hidden" NAME="-recid" VALUE="[FMP-currentrecid]">
<INPUT TYPE="text" SIZE="2" NAME="Qty" VALUE="[FMP-field:Qty]">
<INPUT TYPE="submit" NAME="-edit" Value="Update">
</FORM>
</TD>
```

This code displays a little form in the first cell of the second row of the nested table. The form includes the contents of the Qty field for a record in a text field and an Update button that uses the **-Edit** CDML tag to modify the record. When successfully used, the cartresponse.htm format file is displayed.

```
<TD VALIGN="CENTER">
[FMP-Field: item name]
</TD>
```

This code displays the contents of the Item Name field vertically centered in a cell.

```
<TD ALIGN=RIGHT VALIGN="CENTER">
[FMP-Field: Display Unit Price]
</TD>
```

This code displays the contents of the Display Unit Price field vertically centered in a cell.

```
<TD ALIGN=RIGHT VALIGN="CENTER">
[FMP-Field: Display Item Total]
</TD>
```

This code displays the contents of the Display Item Total field vertically centered in a cell.

```
<TD ALIGN=MIDDLE VALIGN="CENTER">
<A HREF="FMPro?-db=OrderItems.fp3&-format=cartresponse.htm&
-lay=WEB&-token=[FMP-currenttoken]&-recid=[FMP-currentrecid]&
-delete"><IMG SRC="images/delete.gif" BORDER=0></A>
</TD>
```

This code displays a little trash can icon with a link to CDML code. When the trash can beside an item is clicked, the item is deleted from OrderItems.fp3 and the cartresponse.htm format file is displayed to confirm the deletion.

```
</TR>
```

This tag ends the table row.

```
[/FMP-Record]
```

This tag tells FileMaker Pro to stop repeating code.

```
</TABLE>
```

This tag ends the nested table.

```
<P>
```

This tag inserts a blank line.

```
<CENTER>
<A HREF="FMPro?-db=Orders.fp3&-format=customerinfo.htm&
Order%20ID=[FMP-currenttoken]&-recid=[FMP-currenttoken]&
-token=[FMP-currenttoken]&-edit"><IMG SRC="images/checkout.gif"
BORDER=0 ALT="Checkout"></A>
</CENTER>
```

This code displays the Checkout button, with a CDML link. When clicked, the customerinfo.htm format file is displayed to gather information for the Orders.fp3 file. The -Edit CDML tag is used because the record for the Order ID (which is passed by the token yet again) already exists.

```
</TD>
</TR>
</TABLE>
</BODY>
</HTML>
```

This code is the same as the code at the end of items.htm; check my comments about that file for details.

When you're finished creating this file, check the code, then save it as viewcart.htm in the cart folder.

emptycart.htm

The emptycart.htm format file appears when a shopper clicks the View Cart button but has not yet added any items to his shopping cart. Here's what it looks like when viewed with a Web browser:

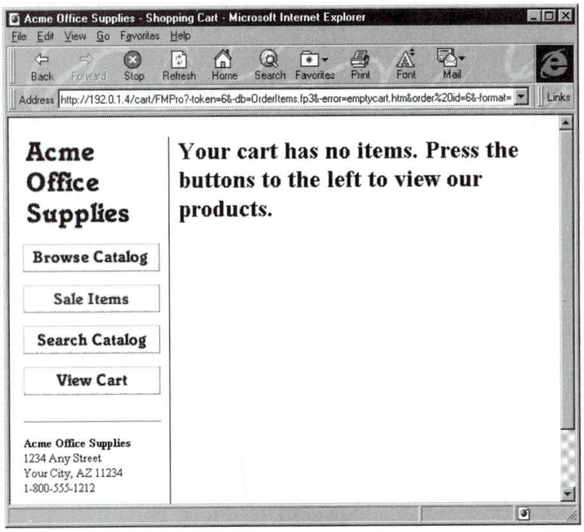

Here's the **code** for this file, along with my comments:

```
<HTML>
<HEAD>
<TITLE>Acme Office Supplies - Shopping Cart</TITLE>
</HEAD>
<BODY BGCOLOR="#FFFFFF">
<TABLE BORDER="0" CELLPADDING="5" CELLSPACING="0" WIDTH="575">
<TR>
<TD ALIGN=LEFT VALIGN=TOP WIDTH="160">
[FMP-include:includes/sidebar.txt]
</TD>
ALIGN=LEFT VALIGN=TOP WIDTH="5">
<IMG SRC="images/pixel.gif" WIDTH="1" HEIGHT="450" BORDER="0">
</TD>
<TD ALIGN=LEFT VALIGN=TOP WIDTH="425">
```

This code is the same as the code at the beginning of items.htm; check my comments about that file for details.

```
<H1>Your cart has no items. Press the buttons to the left to view our
products.</H1>
```

This code displays a message with instructions as a heading.

```
</TD>
</TR>
</TABLE>
</BODY>
</HTML>
```

This code is the same as the code at the end of items.htm; check my comments about that file for details.

When you're finished creating this simple format file, save it as emptycart.htm in the cart folder.

customerinfo.htm

The customerinfo.htm file appears when a visitor clicks the Checkout button in the viewcart.htm format file. It enables a repeat customer to search for his record or a new customer to enter customer information. This format file works with the Customers.fp3 database file.

Here's what customerinfo.htm looks like when viewed with a Web browser:

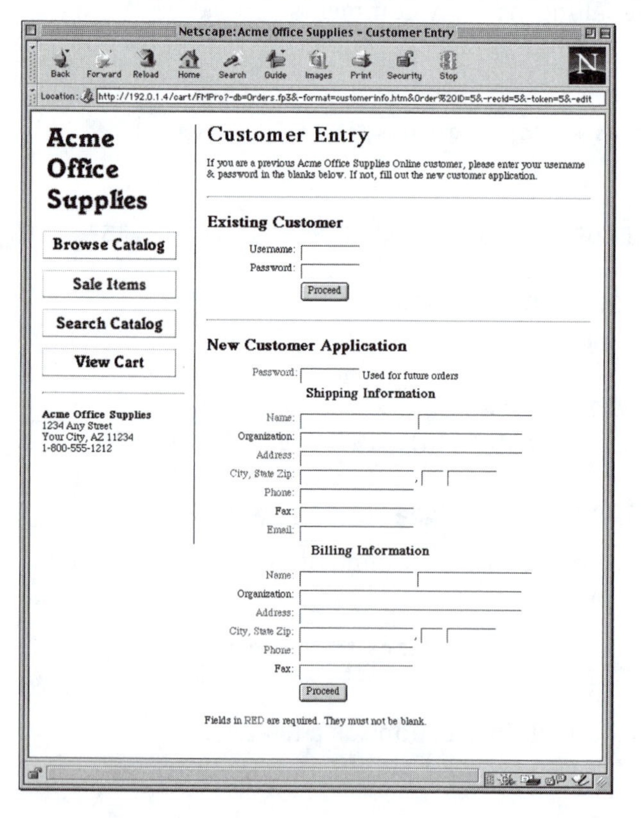

Here's the **code** for customerinfo.htm, along with my comments:

```
<HTML>
<HEAD>
<TITLE>Acme Office Supplies - Customer Entry</TITLE>
</HEAD>
<BODY BGCOLOR="#FFFFFF">
<TABLE BORDER="0" CELLPADDING="5" CELLSPACING="0" WIDTH="600">
<TR>
<TD ALIGN=LEFT VALIGN=TOP WIDTH="160">
[FMP-include:includes/sidebar.txt]
</TD>
<TD ALIGN=LEFT VALIGN=TOP WIDTH="5">
<IMG SRC="images/pixel.gif" WIDTH="1" HEIGHT="450" BORDER="0">
</TD>
<TD ALIGN=LEFT VALIGN=TOP WIDTH="425">
```

This code is the same as the code in the beginning of items.htm; check my comments about that format file for details.

```
<H1>Customer Entry</H1>
If you are a previous Acme Office Supplies Online customer, please enter your
username & password in the blanks below. If not, fill out the new customer
application.
```

This code displays a heading, followed by some instructions.

```
<P>
<HR>
<P>
```

This code inserts two blank lines with a horizontal rule between them.

```
<H2>Existing Customer</H2>
```

This code displays a heading for the Existing Customer section of the page.

```
[FMP-if:currentdatabase.eq.Customers.fp3]
<FONT COLOR="#FF0000"><B>Your username and password do not match any
entries in our database.<BR>
Please fill out the new customer application below.</B></FONT>
[/FMP-if]
```

This code checks to see if the active database file is Customers.fp3. If it is, the code displays a message that the visitor's information has not been found. If it isn't, displays nothing. The logic here is that if Customers.fp3 is the active file, it must have been searched and if this format file is displayed, the search must have come up empty. This enables you to use the customerinfo.htm format file as an error file when the user searches for his information in the Customers.fp3 database.

```
<FORM METHOD="POST" ACTION="FMPro">
<INPUT TYPE="hidden" NAME="-db" VALUE="Customers.fp3">
<INPUT TYPE="hidden" NAME="-lay" VALUE="WEB">
<INPUT TYPE="hidden" NAME="-token" VALUE="[FMP-currenttoken]">
<INPUT TYPE="hidden" NAME="-format" VALUE="customerverify.htm">
<INPUT TYPE="hidden" NAME="-error" VALUE="customerinfo.htm">
```

This code sets up a form for searching for a customer record in Customers.fp3.

```
<TABLE BORDER="0" CELLPADDING="0" CELLSPACING="2">
<TR><TD ALIGN=RIGHT VALIGN=TOP WIDTH="100">Username:</TD>
<TD VALIGN=TOP><INPUT TYPE="text" SIZE="10" NAME="Username"></TD>
</TR>
<TR>
<TD ALIGN=RIGHT VALIGN=TOP WIDTH="100">Password:</TD>
<TD VALIGN=TOP><INPUT TYPE="text" SIZE="10" NAME="Password"></TD>
</TR>
<TR>
<TD></TD>
<TD><INPUT TYPE="submit" NAME="-find" VALUE="Proceed"></TD>
</TR>
</TABLE>
```

This code sets up a nested table that displays the Username and Password prompts with corresponding text fields, as well as a submit button for searching the Customers.fp3 database.

```
</FORM>
```

This tag ends the form.

```
<P>
<HR>
<P>
```

This code inserts two blank lines with a horizontal rule between them.

```
<H2>New Customer Application</H2>
```

This code displays a heading for the New Customer Application part of the page.

```
<FORM METHOD="POST" ACTION="FMPro">
<INPUT TYPE="hidden" NAME="-db" VALUE="Customers.fp3">
<INPUT TYPE="hidden" NAME="-lay" VALUE="WEB">
<INPUT TYPE="hidden" NAME="-token" VALUE="[FMP-currenttoken]">
<INPUT TYPE="hidden" NAME="-format" VALUE="customerverify.htm">
<INPUT TYPE="hidden" NAME="-error" VALUE="missingdata.htm">
```

This code sets up a form for creating a new record in Customers.fp3.

```
<TABLE BORDER="0" CELLPADDING="0" CELLSPACING="2">
<TR>
<TD ALIGN=RIGHT VALIGN=TOP WIDTH="100">
<FONT COLOR="#FF0000">Password:</FONT>
</TD>
<TD VALIGN=TOP>
<INPUT TYPE="text" SIZE="10" NAME="Password"> Used for future orders
</TD>
</TR>
<TR>
<TD COLSPAN=2 ALIGN=CENTER>
<H3>Shipping Information</H3>
</TD>
</TR>
<TR>
<TD ALIGN=RIGHT VALIGN=TOP WIDTH="100">
<FONT COLOR="#FF0000">Name:</FONT>
</TD>
<TD VALIGN=TOP>
<INPUT TYPE="text" SIZE="20" NAME="first name">
<INPUT TYPE="text" SIZE="20" NAME="last name"
</TD>
</TR>
<TR>
<TD ALIGN=RIGHT VALIGN=TOP WIDTH="100">
Organization:
</TD>
<TD VALIGN=TOP>
<INPUT TYPE="text" SIZE="40" NAME="organization">
</TD>
</TR>
<TR>
<TD ALIGN=RIGHT VALIGN=TOP WIDTH="100">
<FONT COLOR="#FF0000">Address:</FONT>
</TD>
<TD VALIGN=TOP>
<INPUT TYPE="text" SIZE="40" NAME="address">
</TD>
</TR>
<TR>
<TD ALIGN=RIGHT VALIGN=TOP WIDTH="100">
<FONT COLOR="#FF0000">City, State  Zip:</FONT>
</TD>
```

```
<TD VALIGN=TOP>
<INPUT TYPE="text" SIZE="20" NAME="city">,
<INPUT TYPE="text" SIZE="3" NAME="state">
<INPUT TYPE="text" SIZE="8" NAME="zip">
</TD>
</TR>
<TR>
<TD ALIGN=RIGHT VALIGN=TOP WIDTH="100">
<FONT COLOR="#FF0000">Phone:</FONT>
</TD>
<TD VALIGN=TOP>
<INPUT TYPE="text" SIZE="20" NAME="phone">
</TD>
</TR>
<TR>
<TD ALIGN=RIGHT VALIGN=TOP WIDTH="100">
Fax:
</TD>
<TD VALIGN=TOP>
<INPUT TYPE="text" SIZE="20" NAME="fax">
</TD>
</TR>
<TR>
<TD ALIGN=RIGHT VALIGN=TOP WIDTH="100">
<FONT COLOR="#FF0000">Email:</FONT>
</TD>
<TD VALIGN=TOP>
<INPUT TYPE="text" SIZE="20" NAME="email">
</TD>
</TR>
<TR>
<TD COLSPAN=2 ALIGN=CENTER>
<H3>Billing Information</H3>
</TD>
</TR>
<TR>
<TD ALIGN=RIGHT VALIGN=TOP WIDTH="100">
<FONT COLOR="#FF0000">Name:</FONT>
</TD>
<TD VALIGN=TOP>
<INPUT TYPE="text" SIZE="20" NAME="billing first name">
<INPUT TYPE="text" SIZE="20" NAME="billing last name"
</TD>
```

```
</TR>
<TR>
<TD ALIGN=RIGHT VALIGN=TOP WIDTH="100">
Organization:
</TD>
<TD VALIGN=TOP>
<INPUT TYPE="text" SIZE="40" NAME="billing organization">
</TD>
</TR>
<TR>
<TD ALIGN=RIGHT VALIGN=TOP WIDTH="100">
<FONT COLOR="#FF0000">Address:</FONT>
</TD>
<TD VALIGN=TOP>
<INPUT TYPE="text" SIZE="40" NAME="billing address">
</TD>
</TR>
<TR>
<TD ALIGN=RIGHT VALIGN=TOP WIDTH="100">
<FONT COLOR="#FF0000">City, State  Zip:</FONT>
</TD>
<TD VALIGN=TOP>
<INPUT TYPE="text" SIZE="20" NAME="billing city">,
<INPUT TYPE="text" SIZE="3" NAME="billing state">
<INPUT TYPE="text" SIZE="8" NAME="billing zip">
</TD>
</TR>
<TR>
<TD ALIGN=RIGHT VALIGN=TOP WIDTH="100">
<FONT COLOR="#FF0000">Phone:</FONT>
</TD>
<TD VALIGN=TOP>
<INPUT TYPE="text" SIZE="20" NAME="billing phone">
</TD>
</TR>
<TR>
<TD ALIGN=RIGHT VALIGN=TOP WIDTH="100">
Fax:
</TD>
<TD VALIGN=TOP>
<INPUT TYPE="text" SIZE="20" NAME="billing fax">
</TD>
</TR>
```

```
<TR>
<TD></TD>
<TD>
<INPUT TYPE="submit" NAME="-new" VALUE="Proceed">
</TD>
</TR>
</TABLE>
```

Whew! All of that code displays a borderless, nested table that contains input fields for customer information. The headings for required fields appear in red. The submit button, when clicked, creates a new record with this information in the Customers.fp3 file.

```
</FORM>
```

This tag ends the form.

```
<P>
Fields in <FONT COLOR="#FF0000">RED</FONT> are required. They must not
be blank.
```

This code tells customers that the fields in red are required.

```
</TD>
</TR>
</TABLE>
</BODY>
</HTML>
```

This code is the same as the code at the end of items.htm; check my comments about that file for details.

When you're finished creating this file, check the code and save it as customerinfo.htm in the cart folder.

customerverify.htm

The customerverify.htm format file appears when an existing customer has successfully searched for his record in customers.fp3 using customerinfo.htm or a new customer has properly completed the form in customerinfo.htm. It displays all the information for the customer's record and enables him to modify it if required.

The customerverify.htm format file looks like this:

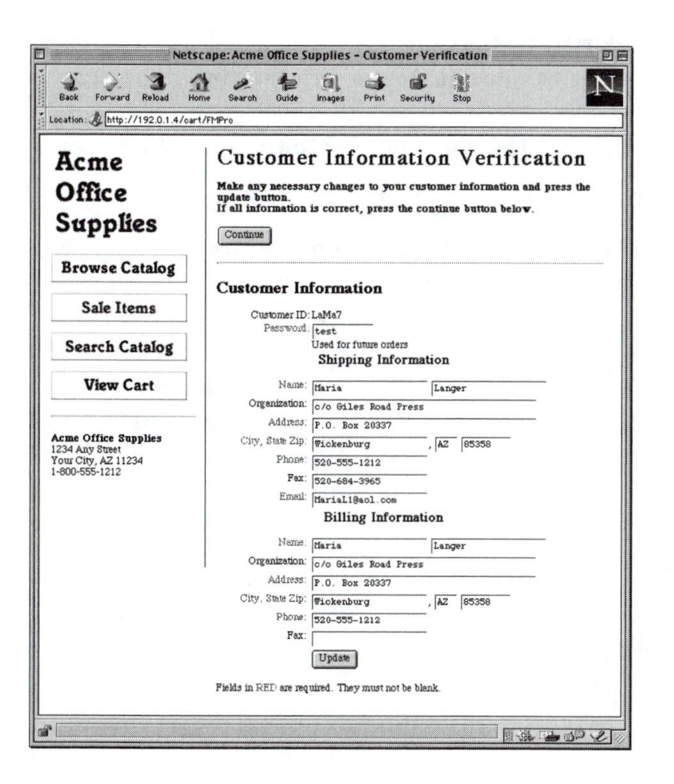

Here's the **code** for this file, along with my comments:

```
<HTML>
<HEAD>
<TITLE>Acme Office Supplies - Customer Verification</TITLE>
</HEAD>
<BODY BGCOLOR="#FFFFFF">
<TABLE BORDER="0" CELLPADDING="5" CELLSPACING="0" WIDTH="600">
<TR>
<TD ALIGN=LEFT VALIGN=TOP WIDTH="160">
[FMP-include:includes/sidebar.txt]
</TD>
<TD ALIGN=LEFT VALIGN=TOP WIDTH="5">
<IMG SRC="images/pixel.gif" WIDTH="1" HEIGHT="450" BORDER="0">
</TD>
<TD ALIGN=LEFT VALIGN=TOP WIDTH="425">
```

This code is the same as the code at the beginning of items.htm; check my comments about that format file for details.

```
<H1>Customer Information Verification</H1>
<B>Make any necessary changes to your customer information and press the
update button.<BR>
If all information is correct, press the continue button below.</B>
```

This code displays a heading and some instructions.

```
<FORM METHOD="POST" ACTION="FMPro" NAME="confirmform">
<INPUT TYPE="hidden" NAME="-db" VALUE="Orders.fp3">
<INPUT TYPE="hidden" NAME="-lay" VALUE="WEB">
<INPUT TYPE="hidden" NAME="-token" VALUE="[FMP-currenttoken]">
<INPUT TYPE="hidden" NAME="-format" VALUE="complete.htm">
<INPUT TYPE="hidden" NAME="Customer ID" VALUE="[FMP-field:customer id]">
<INPUT TYPE="hidden" NAME="-recid" VALUE="[FMP-currenttoken]">
<INPUT TYPE="submit" NAME="-edit" VALUE="Continue">
</FORM>
```

This code displays a form with a single button labeled Continue. When clicked, it uses the **-Edit** CDML tag to accept the data in the format file and move on to the complete.htm format file.

NOTE

*The **-View** CDML tag would also work in this code.*

```
<P>
<HR>
<P>
```

This code inserts two blank lines with a horizontal rule between them.

```
<H2>Customer Information</H2>
```

This code displays a heading.

```
<FORM METHOD="POST" ACTION="FMPro">
<INPUT TYPE="hidden" NAME="-db" VALUE="Customers.fp3">
<INPUT TYPE="hidden" NAME="-lay" VALUE="WEB">
<INPUT TYPE="hidden" NAME="-token" VALUE="[FMP-currenttoken]">
<INPUT TYPE="hidden" NAME="-recid" VALUE="[FMP-currentrecid]">
<INPUT TYPE="hidden" NAME="-format" VALUE="customerverify.htm">
<INPUT TYPE="hidden" NAME="-error" VALUE="missingdata.htm">
```

This code sets up a form for interacting with Customers.fp3.

```
<TABLE BORDER="0" CELLPADDING="0" CELLSPACING="2">
<TR>
<TD ALIGN=RIGHT VALIGN=TOP WIDTH="100">
Customer ID:
</TD>
<TD ALIGN=LEFT VALIGN=TOP>[FMP-Field: Username]
</TD>
</TR>
<TR>
<TD ALIGN=RIGHT VALIGN=TOP WIDTH="100">
<FONT COLOR="#FF0000">Password:</FONT>
</TD>
<TD ALIGN=LEFT VALIGN=TOP>
<INPUT TYPE="text" SIZE="10" NAME="Password" VALUE="[FMP-Field: Password]">
<BR>Used for future orders
</TD>
</TR>
<TR>
<TD COLSPAN=2 ALIGN=CENTER>
<H3>Shipping Information</H3>
</TD>
</TR>
<TR>
<TD ALIGN=RIGHT VALIGN=TOP WIDTH="100">
<FONT COLOR="#FF0000">Name:</FONT>
</TD>
<TD ALIGN=LEFT VALIGN=TOP>
<INPUT TYPE="text" SIZE="20" NAME="first name" VALUE="[FMP-Field: first name]">
<INPUT TYPE="text" SIZE="20" NAME="last name" VALUE="[FMP-Field: last name]">
</TD>
</TR>
<TR>
<TD ALIGN=RIGHT VALIGN=TOP WIDTH="100">
Organization:
</TD>
<TD ALIGN=LEFT VALIGN=TOP>
<INPUT TYPE="text" SIZE="40" NAME="organization" VALUE=
"[FMP-Field: organization]">
</TD>
</TR>
<TR>
<TD ALIGN=RIGHT VALIGN=TOP WIDTH="100">
<FONT COLOR="#FF0000">Address:</FONT>
```

```
</TD>
<TD ALIGN=LEFT VALIGN=TOP>
<INPUT TYPE="text" SIZE="40" NAME="address" VALUE="[FMP-Field: address]">
</TD>
</TR>
<TR>
<TD ALIGN=RIGHT VALIGN=TOP WIDTH="100">
<FONT COLOR="#FF0000">City, State  Zip:</FONT>
</TD>
<TD ALIGN=LEFT VALIGN=TOP>
<INPUT TYPE="text" SIZE="20" NAME="city" VALUE="[FMP-Field: city]">,
<INPUT TYPE="text" SIZE="3" NAME="state" VALUE="[FMP-Field: state]">
<INPUT TYPE="text" SIZE="8" NAME="zip" VALUE="[FMP-Field: zip]">
</TD>
</TR>
<TR>
<TD ALIGN=RIGHT VALIGN=TOP WIDTH="100">
<FONT COLOR="#FF0000">Phone:</FONT>
</TD>
<TD ALIGN=LEFT VALIGN=TOP>
<INPUT TYPE="text" SIZE="20" NAME="phone" VALUE="[FMP-Field: phone]">
</TD>
</TR>
<TR>
<TD ALIGN=RIGHT VALIGN=TOP WIDTH="100">
Fax:
</TD>
<TD ALIGN=LEFT VALIGN=TOP>
<INPUT TYPE="text" SIZE="20" NAME="fax" VALUE="[FMP-Field: fax]">
</TD>
</TR>
<TR>
<TD ALIGN=RIGHT VALIGN=TOP WIDTH="100">
<FONT COLOR="#FF0000">Email:</FONT>
</TD>
<TD ALIGN=LEFT VALIGN=TOP>
<INPUT TYPE="text" SIZE="20" NAME="email" VALUE="[FMP-Field: email]">
</TD>
</TR>
<TR>
<TD COLSPAN=2 ALIGN=CENTER>
<H3>Billing Information</H3>
</TD>
```

```
</TR>
<TR>
<TD ALIGN=RIGHT VALIGN=TOP WIDTH="100">
<FONT COLOR="#FF0000">Name:</FONT>
</TD>
<TD ALIGN=LEFT VALIGN=TOP>
<INPUT TYPE="text" SIZE="20" NAME="billing first name" VALUE=
"[FMP-Field: billing first name]">
<INPUT TYPE="text" SIZE="20" NAME="billing last name" VALUE=
"[FMP-Field: billing last name]">
</TD>
</TR>
<TR>
<TD ALIGN=RIGHT VALIGN=TOP WIDTH="100">
Organization:
</TD>
<TD ALIGN=LEFT VALIGN=TOP>
<INPUT TYPE="text" SIZE="40" NAME="billing organization" VALUE=
"[FMP-Field: billing organization]">
</TD>
</TR>
<TR>
<TD ALIGN=RIGHT VALIGN=TOP WIDTH="100">
<FONT COLOR="#FF0000">Address:</FONT>
</TD>
<TD ALIGN=LEFT VALIGN=TOP>
<INPUT TYPE="text" SIZE="40" NAME="billing address" VALUE=
"[FMP-Field: billing address]">
</TD>
</TR>
<TR>
<TD ALIGN=RIGHT VALIGN=TOP WIDTH="100">
<FONT COLOR="#FF0000">City, State  Zip:</FONT>
</TD>
<TD ALIGN=LEFT VALIGN=TOP>
<INPUT TYPE="text" SIZE="20" NAME="billing city" VALUE=
"[FMP-Field: billing city]">,
<INPUT TYPE="text" SIZE="3" NAME="billing state" VALUE=
"[FMP-Field: billing state]">
<INPUT TYPE="text" SIZE="8" NAME="billing zip" VALUE=
"[FMP-Field: billing zip]">
</TD>
</TR>
```

```
<TR>
<TD ALIGN=RIGHT VALIGN=TOP WIDTH="100">
<FONT COLOR="#FF0000">Phone:</FONT>
</TD>
<TD ALIGN=LEFT VALIGN=TOP>
<INPUT TYPE="text" SIZE="20" NAME="billing phone" VALUE=
"[FMP-Field: billing phone]">
</TD>
</TR>
<TR>
<TD ALIGN=RIGHT VALIGN=TOP WIDTH="100">
Fax:
</TD>
<TD ALIGN=LEFT VALIGN=TOP>
<INPUT TYPE="text" SIZE="20" NAME="billing fax" VALUE=
"[FMP-Field: billing fax]">
</TD>
</TR>
<TR>
<TD></TD>
<TD>
<INPUT TYPE="submit" NAME="-Edit" VALUE="Update">
</TD>
</TR>
</TABLE>
```

All of this code displays the text fields for customer information with data from the Customer.fp3 database in the fields. Customers can edit the information as desired, then click the Update button at the bottom of the form to invoke the **-Edit** CDML command and edit their customer record.

```
</FORM>
```

This code ends the form.

```
<P>
Fields in <FONT COLOR="#FF0000">RED</FONT> are required. They must not
be blank.
```

This code adds a message stating that field names in red are required.

```
</TD>
</TR>
</TABLE>
</BODY>
</HTML>
```

This code is the same as the code at the end of items.htm; check my comments about that file for details.

When you're finished creating this file, check the code and save it as customerverify.htm in the cart folder.

missingdata.htm

The missingdata.htm file appears if a customer leaves required fields empty while filling out the customerinfo.htm form. It looks like this:

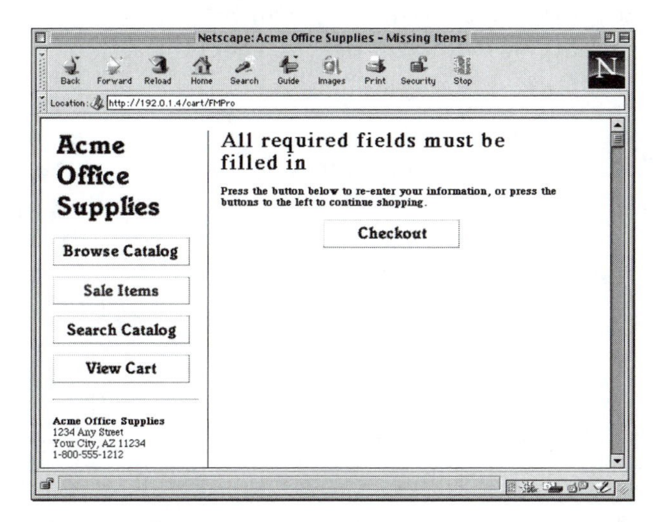

Here's the **code** for missingdata.htm, along with my comments:

```
<HTML>
<HEAD>
<TITLE>Acme Office Supplies - Missing Items</TITLE>
</HEAD>
<BODY BGCOLOR="#FFFFFF">
<TABLE BORDER="0" CELLPADDING="5" CELLSPACING="0" WIDTH="575">
<TR>
<TD ALIGN=LEFT VALIGN=TOP WIDTH="160">
[FMP-include:includes/sidebar.txt]
</TD>
<TD ALIGN=LEFT VALIGN=TOP WIDTH="5">
<IMG SRC="images/pixel.gif" WIDTH="1" HEIGHT="450" BORDER="0">
</TD>
<TD ALIGN=LEFT VALIGN=TOP WIDTH="425">
```

This code is the same as the code for items.htm; check my comments about that file for details.

```
<H1>All required fields must be filled in</H1>
<B>Press the button below to re-enter your information, or press the buttons
to the left to continue shopping.</B>
<P>
```

This code provides a heading, an explanation of the problem, and instructions, followed by a blank line.

```
<CENTER>
<A HREF="FMPro?-db=Orders.fp3&-format=customerinfo.htm&
Order%20ID=[FMP-currenttoken]&-recid=[FMP-currenttoken]&
-token=[FMP-currenttoken]&-edit"><IMG SRC="images/checkout.gif"
BORDER=0 ALT="Checkout"></A>
</CENTER>
```

This code displays the Checkout button and returns the shopper to the customerinfo.htm format file.

```
</TD>
</TR>
</TABLE>
</BODY>
</HTML>
```

This code is the same as the code at the end of items.htm; check my comments about that format file for more information.

When you're finished creating this file, check it for errors, then save it as missingdata.htm in the cart folder.

complete.htm

The complete.htm format file appears when the customer has clicked the Continue button on the customerverify.htm format file page. It summarizes the order and enables the customer to enter payment information.

Here's what complete.htm looks like when viewed with a Web browser:

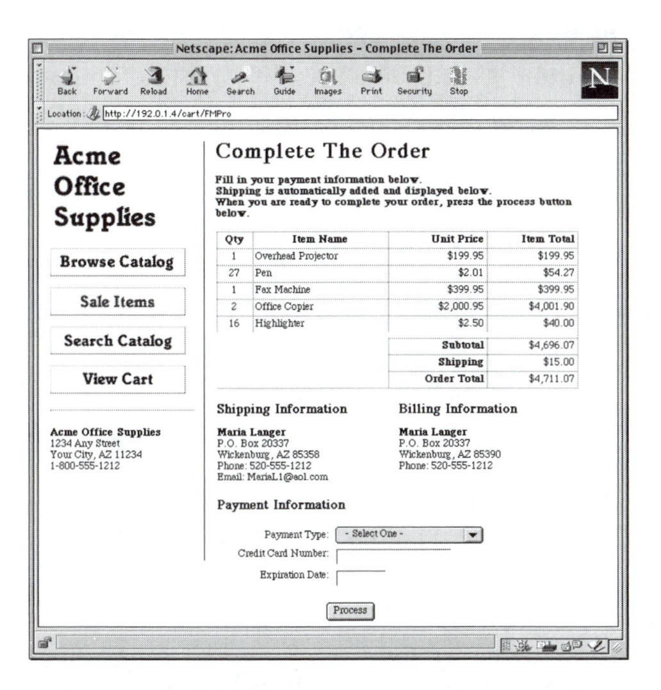

Here's the **code** and my comments for this file:

```
<HTML>
<HEAD>
<TITLE>Acme Office Supplies - Complete The Order</TITLE>
</HEAD>
<BODY BGCOLOR="#FFFFFF">
<TABLE BORDER="0" CELLPADDING="5" CELLSPACING="0" WIDTH="600">
<TR>
<TD ALIGN=LEFT VALIGN=TOP WIDTH="160">
[FMP-include:includes/sidebar.txt]
</TD>
<TD ALIGN=LEFT VALIGN=TOP WIDTH="5">
<IMG SRC="images/pixel.gif" WIDTH="1" HEIGHT="450" BORDER="0">
</TD>
<TD ALIGN=LEFT VALIGN=TOP WIDTH="425">
```

This code is the same as the code in items.htm; check my comments about that file for more information.

```
<H1>Complete The Order</H1>
<B>Fill in your payment information below.<BR>
Shipping is automatically added and displayed below.<BR>
When you are ready to complete your order, press the process button
below.</B>
<P>
```

This code displays a heading and some instructions, followed by a blank line.

```
<TABLE BORDER="1" CELLPADDING="2" CELLSPACING="0" WIDTH="400">
```

This code starts a borderless, nested table.

```
<TR>
<TH>Qty</TH>
<TH>Item Name</TH>
<TH ALIGN="RIGHT">Unit Price</TH>
<TH ALIGN="RIGHT">Item Total</TH>
</TR>
```

This code displays headings in the first row of the table.

```
[FMP-portal:OrderItems]
```

This tag tells FileMaker Pro to repeat all code between it and the **[/FMP-Portal]** tag for every record in the Portal for the relationship named OrderItems.

```
<TR>
<TD ALIGN="CENTER">[FMP-field:OrderItems::Qty]</TD>
<TD>[FMP-field:OrderItems::Item Name]</TD>
<TD ALIGN="RIGHT">[FMP-field:OrderItems::Display Unit Price]</TD>
<TD ALIGN="RIGHT">[FMP-field:OrderItems::Display Item Total]</TD>
</TR>
```

This code displays the contents of related fields that exist in the OrderItems.fp3 file but are displayed on the WEB layout of the Order.fp3 file. Each field appears in a separate cell beneath the appropriate heading.

```
[/FMP-portal]
```

This tag tells FileMaker Pro to stop repeating code.

```
<TR>
<TD COLSPAN=4>
</TD>
</TR
```

This code displays an empty row with a single cell that spans the width of the table.

```
<TR>
<TD COLSPAN=2></TD>
<TD ALIGN="RIGHT"><B>Subtotal</B></TD>
<TD ALIGN="RIGHT">[FMP-Field: Display Subtotal]</TD>
</TR>
```

This code displays a heading and the contents of the Display Subtotal field in the last two columns of the table.

```
<TR>
<TD COLSPAN=2></TD>
<TD ALIGN="RIGHT"><B>Shipping</B></TD>
<TD ALIGN="RIGHT">[FMP-Field: Display Shipping]</TD>
</TR>
```

This code displays a heading and the contents of the Display Shipping field in the last two columns of the table.

```
<TR>
<TD COLSPAN=2></TD>
<TD ALIGN="RIGHT"><B>Order Total</B></TD>
<TD ALIGN="RIGHT">[FMP-Field: Display Order Total]</TD>
</TR>
```

This code displays a heading and the contents of the Display Order Total field in the last two columns of the table.

```
</TABLE>
```

This tag ends the nested table.

```
<P>
```

This tag inserts a blank line.

```
<TABLE BORDER="0" CELLPADDING="2" CELLSPACING="0" WIDTH="400">
<TR>
<TD WIDTH=50% VALIGN="TOP">
<H3>Shipping Information</H3>
<B>[FMP-Field: Customers::First Name] [FMP-Field: Customers::Last Name]</B>
<BR>
[FMP-If: Customers::Organization .neq.]
[FMP-Field: Customers::Organization]<BR>
[/FMP-If]
[FMP-Field: Customers::Address]<BR>
[FMP-Field: Customers::City], [FMP-Field: Customers::State]
[FMP-Field: Customers::Zip]<BR>
Phone: [FMP-Field: Customers::Phone]<BR>
[FMP-If: Customers::Fax .neq.]
Fax: [FMP-Field: Customers::Fax]<BR>
[/FMP-If]
Email: [FMP-Field: Customers::Email]
</TD>
<TD WIDTH=50% VALIGN="TOP">
<H3>Billing Information</H3>
<B>[FMP-Field: Customers::Billing First Name]
[FMP-Field: Customers::Billing Last Name]</B><BR>
```

```
[FMP-If: Customers::Billing Organization .neq.]
[FMP-Field: Customers::Billing Organization]<BR>
[/FMP-If]
[FMP-Field: Customers::Billing Address]<BR>
[FMP-Field: Customers::Billing City], [FMP-Field: Customers::Billing State]
[FMP-Field: Customers::Billing Zip]<BR>
Phone: [FMP-Field: Customers::Billing Phone]<BR>
[FMP-If: Customers::Billing Fax .neq.]
Fax: [FMP-Field: Customers::Billing Fax]<BR>
[/FMP-If]
</TD>
</TR>
</TABLE>
```

This code displays a borderless, nested table with the customer's shipping information in the left column and billing information in the right column. The information comes from related fields that exist in the Customers.fp3 file and are displayed on the WEB layout of the Orders.fp3 file. The **[FMP-If]** CDML tag is used throughout to skip lines where fields are blank.

```
<P>
```

This tag inserts a blank line.

```
<TABLE BORDER="0" CELLPADDING="2" CELLSPACING="0" WIDTH="300">
```

This code starts yet another borderless, nested table.

```
<TR>
<TD COLSPAN=2>
<H3>Payment Information</H3>
```

This code starts the first row and cell, which spans two columns. It also displays a heading in the cell.

```
[FMP-if:currenterror.neq.0]
<B>These fields must not be blank!</B>
[/FMP-if]
```

This code checks whether an error occurred as a result of the last command. If an error did occur, displays a message reminding customers that all fields must be filled in.

```
</TD>
```

This tag ends the cell.

```
<FORM METHOD="POST" ACTION="FMPro" NAME="checkoutform">
<INPUT TYPE="hidden" NAME="-db" VALUE="Orders.fp3">
<INPUT TYPE="hidden" NAME="-format" VALUE="invoice.htm">
<INPUT TYPE="hidden" NAME="-lay" VALUE="WEB">
<INPUT TYPE="hidden" NAME="-token" VALUE="[FMP-currenttoken]">
<INPUT TYPE="hidden" NAME="-script" VALUE="Print Order">
<INPUT TYPE="hidden" NAME="-recid" VALUE="[FMP-currenttoken]">
<INPUT TYPE="hidden" NAME="Order ID" VALUE="[FMP-currenttoken]">
<INPUT TYPE="hidden" NAME="Order Status" VALUE="New Order">
<INPUT TYPE="hidden" NAME="IP Number" VALUE="[FMP-ClientIP]">
```

This code sets up a form for interacting with the Orders.fp3 file. Note that the **-Script** CDML tag is included; when the submit button for this form is clicked, the Print Order script in the Orders.fp3 database file will run.

FileMaker Pro must be the foreground application for the Print Order script to run. If it is not, an error will occur in FileMaker Pro and the entire solution will come to a halt! (For best performance using Custom Web Publishing, FileMaker Pro should be the foreground application anyway.)

```
</TR>
```

This tag ends the table row.

```
<TR>
<TD ALIGN=RIGHT WIDTH="150">
Payment Type:
</TD>
<TD ALIGN=LEFT>
<SELECT NAME="Payment Type" VALUE="">
<OPTION VALUE="">- Select One -
[FMP-valuelist:Payment Type,list=Payment Type]
<OPTION VALUE="[FMP-valuelistitem]">[FMP-valuelistitem]
[/FMP-valuelist]
</SELECT>
</TD>
</TR>
```

This code displays a row with a heading and a pop-up menu for selecting a value for the Payment Type field. The Payment Type value list in Orders.fp3 is used to populate the pop-up menu.

```
<TR>
<TD ALIGN=RIGHT VALIGN=TOP WIDTH="150">
Credit Card Number:
</TD>
<TD ALIGN=LEFT VALIGN=TOP>
<INPUT TYPE="text" SIZE="20" NAME="Credit Card Number" VALUE="">
</TD>
</TR>
```

This code displays a row with a heading and text field for entering a value for the Credit Card Number field.

```
<TR>
<TD ALIGN=RIGHT VALIGN=TOP WIDTH="150">
Expiration Date:
</TD>
<TD ALIGN=LEFT VALIGN=TOP>
<INPUT TYPE="text" SIZE="8" NAME="Credit Card Exp" VALUE="">
</TD>
</TR>
```

This code displays a row with a heading and text field for entering a value for the Credit Card Exp field.

```
<TR>
<TD COLSPAN=2 ALIGN="MIDDLE">
<INPUT TYPE="submit" NAME="-edit" VALUE="Process">
</TD>
</TR>
```

This code displays a submit button labeled Process which edits the Orders.fp3 record to add the payment information.

```
</FORM>
```

This code ends the form.

```
</TABLE>
```

This code ends the nested table.

```
</TD>
</TR>
</TABLE>
</BODY>
</HTML>
```

This code is the same as the code at the end of items.htm; check my comments about that file for details.

When you're finished creating this file, check the code and save it as complete.htm in the cart folder.

invoice.htm

The invoice.htm format file is the last format file that the shopper sees when he completes his order. Designed to be printed by the visitor, it summarizes the entire transaction. It looks like this:

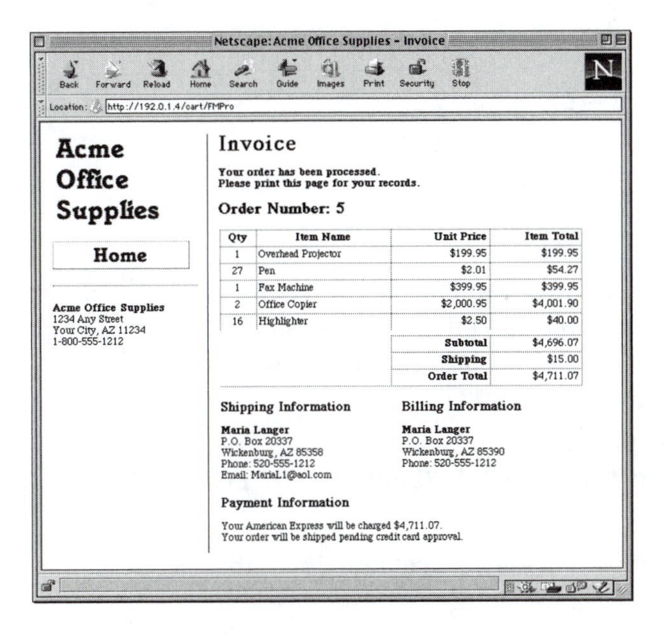

Here's the **code** for invoice.htm, along with my comments:

```
<HTML>
<HEAD>
<TITLE>Acme Office Supplies - Invoice</TITLE>
</HEAD>
<BODY BGCOLOR="#FFFFFF">
```

This code starts the HTML document, gives it a title, and sets the background color to white.

```
<TABLE BORDER="0" CELLPADDING="5" CELLSPACING="0" WIDTH="600">
```

This code starts a borderless HTML table.

```
<TR>
```

This tag starts the first row of the table.

```
<TD ALIGN=LEFT VALIGN=TOP WIDTH="160">
<IMG SRC="images/logo.gif">
<BR>
<P>
<A HREF="FMPro?-db=Orders.fp3&-format=products.htm&-new">
<IMG SRC="images/home.gif" BORDER=0><
/A>
<P>
<HR>
<P>
<B>Acme Office Supplies</B><BR>
1234 Any Street<BR>
Your City, AZ  11234<BR>
1-800-555-1212
</TD>
```

This code displays the Acme Office Supplies log, a Home button, and contact information for Acme Office Supplies in the first column of the table. The Home button has a link to the products.htm format file that does basically the same thing as the link on the default.htm page.

```
<TD ALIGN=LEFT VALIGN=TOP WIDTH="5">
<IMG SRC="images/pixel.gif" WIDTH="1" HEIGHT="450" BORDER="0">
</TD>
```

This code displays a single pixel wide vertical line down the second column of the table.

```
<TD ALIGN=LEFT VALIGN=TOP WIDTH="425">
```

This code begins the third cell (column) of the table.

```
<H1>Invoice</H1>
<B>Your order has been processed.<BR>
Please print this page for your records.</B>
<H2>Order Number: [FMP-Field: Order ID]</H2>
<P>
```

This code displays a heading and some information, including the contents of the Order ID field.

```
<TABLE BORDER="1" CELLPADDING="2" CELLSPACING="0" WIDTH="400">
```

This code starts a nested table.

```
<TR>
<TH>Qty</TH>
<TH>Item Name</TH>
<TH ALIGN="RIGHT">Unit Price</TH>
<TH ALIGN="RIGHT">Item Total</TH>
</TR>
```

This code puts headings across the first row of the table.

```
[FMP-portal:OrderItems]
<TR>
<TD ALIGN="CENTER">[FMP-field:OrderItems::Qty]</TD>
<TD>[FMP-field:OrderItems::Item Name]</TD>
<TD ALIGN="RIGHT">[FMP-field:OrderItems::Display Unit Price]</TD>
<TD ALIGN="RIGHT">[FMP-field:OrderItems::Display Item Total]</TD>
</TR>
[/FMP-portal]
```

This code uses the **[FMP-Portal]** and **[FMP-Field]** CDML tags to display related fields containing information about items ordered in table rows.

```
<TR>
<TD COLSPAN=4>
</TD>
</TR
```

This code displays an empty table row.

```
<TR>
<TD COLSPAN=2></TD>
<TD ALIGN="RIGHT"><B>Subtotal</B></TD>
<TD ALIGN="RIGHT">[FMP-Field: Display Subtotal]</TD>
</TR>
<TR>
<TD COLSPAN=2></TD>
<TD ALIGN="RIGHT"><B>Shipping</B></TD>
<TD ALIGN="RIGHT">[FMP-Field: Display Shipping]</TD>
</TR>
<TR>
<TD COLSPAN=2></TD>
<TD ALIGN="RIGHT"><B>Order Total</B></TD>
<TD ALIGN="RIGHT">[FMP-Field: Display Order Total]</TD>
</TR>
```

This code displays order subtotal, shipping, and order total amounts with headings in table rows.

```
</TABLE>
```

This code ends the table.

```
<P>
```

This code inserts a blank line.

```
<TABLE BORDER="0" CELLPADDING="2" CELLSPACING="0" WIDTH="400">
<TR>
<TD WIDTH=50% VALIGN="TOP">
<H3>Shipping Information</H3>
<B>[FMP-Field: Customers::First Name] [FMP-Field: Customers::Last Name]</B><BR>
[FMP-If: Customers::Organization .neq.]
[FMP-Field: Customers::Organization]<BR>
[/FMP-If]
[FMP-Field: Customers::Address]<BR>
[FMP-Field: Customers::City], [FMP-Field: Customers::State]
[FMP-Field: Customers::Zip]<BR>
Phone: [FMP-Field: Customers::Phone]<BR>
[FMP-If: Customers::Fax .neq.]
Fax: [FMP-Field: Customers::Fax]<BR>
[/FMP-If]
Email: [FMP-Field: Customers::Email]
</TD>
<TD WIDTH=50% VALIGN="TOP">
<H3>Billing Information</H3>
<B>[FMP-Field: Customers::Billing First Name]
[FMP-Field: Customers::Billing Last Name]</B><BR>
[FMP-If: Customers::Billing Organization .neq.]
[FMP-Field: Customers::Billing Organization]<BR>
[/FMP-If]
[FMP-Field: Customers::Billing Address]<BR>
[FMP-Field: Customers::Billing City], [FMP-Field: Customers::Billing State]
[FMP-Field: Customers::Billing Zip]<BR>
Phone: [FMP-Field: Customers::Billing Phone]<BR>
[FMP-If: Customers::Billing Fax .neq.]
Fax: [FMP-Field: Customers::Billing Fax]<BR>
[/FMP-If]
</TD>
</TR>
</TABLE>
```

All of this code is the same as code used in the complete.htm format file to summarize shipping and billing information in a nested table. Check my comments about that file for details.

```
<H3>Payment Information</H3>
[FMP-If: Payment Type .eq. Money Order]
Your order will be shipped upon receipt of your payment.<BR>
Please reference <B>Order Number [FMP-Field: Order ID]</B> on your money
order.<BR>
Payments should be submitted to:<BR>
<B>Acme Office Supplies</B><BR>
PO Box 12345<BR>
Your City, AZ  11234<BR>
[FMP-Else]
Your [FMP-Field: Payment Type] will be charged [FMP-Field: Display Order Total].
<BR>
Your order will be shipped pending credit card approval.
[/FMP-If]
```

This code displays information about payment. The **[FMP-If]** tag checks whether the contents of the Payment Type field is Money Order. If it is, it displays a message telling the customer where to send payment. If it isn't, it displays information about which credit card will be charged.

```
</TD>
```

This tag ends the table cell.

```
</TR>
```

This tag ends the table row.

```
</TABLE>
```

This tag ends the table.

```
</BODY>
</HTML>
```

This code ends the HTML document.

When you're finished creating this format file, check it and save it as invoice.htm in the cart folder.

Creating the Include File

If you read the descriptions of the format files carefully, you probably noticed that almost all of them refer to an include file. This makes it possible to include the same code in a bunch of format files without actually typing it into the files.

The include file for this solution is called sidebar.txt. It displays the Acme Office Supplies logo and the shopping buttons you can see down the left side of every Web page in the solution except invoice.htm.

Here's the code for sidebar.txt, along with my comments:

```
<IMG SRC="images/logo.gif">
<BR>
```

This code displays the Acme Office Supplies logo and ends the line.

```
<P><A HREF="FMPro?-token=[FMP-if:currentdatabase.eq.Orders.fp3]
[FMP-currentrecid][FMP-else][FMP-currenttoken][/FMP-if]&-db=Products.fp3&
-format=products.htm&-findall"><IMG SRC="images/browse.gif" BORDER=0></A>
```

This code displays and creates a link for the Browse button that finds all records in Products.fp3 and displays the products.htm format file. (It does basically the same thing as the link on default.htm.)

```
<P><A HREF="FMPro?-token=[FMP-if:currentdatabase.eq.Orders.fp3]
[FMP-currentrecid][FMP-else][FMP-currenttoken][/FMP-if]&-db=Products.fp3&
sale%20item=yes&-sortfield=item%20name&-format=items.htm&-find">
<IMG SRC="images/sale.gif" BORDER=0></A>
```

This code displays and creates a link for the Sale Items button that finds all records in Products.fp3 that are sale items and displays them in the items.htm format file.

```
<P><A HREF="FMPro?-token=[FMP-if:currentdatabase.eq.Orders.fp3]
[FMP-currentrecid][FMP-else][FMP-currenttoken][/FMP-if]&-db=Products.fp3&
-format=search.htm&-findall"><IMG SRC="images/search.gif" BORDER=0></A>
```

This code displays and creates a link for the Search button that finds all records in the Products.fp3 file and displays the search.htm format file.

```
<P><A HREF="FMPro?-token=[FMP-if:currentdatabase.eq.Orders.fp3]
[FMP-currentrecid][FMP-else][FMP-currenttoken][/FMP-if]&-db=OrderItems.fp3&
-error=emptycart.htm&order%20id=[FMP-if:currentdatabase.eq.Orders.fp3]
[FMP-currentrecid][FMP-else][FMP-currenttoken][/FMP-if]&-format=viewcart.htm&
-find"><IMG SRC="images/viewcart.gif" BORDER=0></A>
```

This code displays and creates a link for the View Cart button. It uses the token with the **-Find** CDML tag to determine which items are included in the visitor's cart. If the cart is not empty, it displays all items for that order number using the viewcart.htm format file. If there are no items for that order number, it displays the emptycart.htm format file (the error format file).

```
<P>
<HR>
<P>
```

This code inserts two blank lines with a horizontal rule between them.

```
<B>Acme Office Supplies</B><BR>
```

```
1234 Any Street<BR>
Your City, AZ  11234<BR>
1-800-555-1212
```

This code displays the Acme Office Supplies address and phone number.

When you're finished entering this code, save the file as sidebar.txt in the includes folder.

Checking the Solution

As Corbin would say at this point, "All righty then." It's time to test your work.

Trying It for Yourself

Make sure that all four of the database files are open and that FileMaker Pro is the foreground application on the database Web server computer. Then fire up your favorite Web browser and point it to the IP address of the database Web server followed by /cart/default.htm. The default.htm format file should appear.

Now go shopping! Add whatever you like to the shopping cart, change quantities, remove items—try every button and link available to you. Then complete the checkout process.

Troubleshooting

If you created the format files following my instructions, you may encounter errors. It's not because my instructions are wrong—all the code in this chapter works! It's because you're human and may have made an error.

Remember these two rules if you need to troubleshoot:

- HTML controls the way pages appear.
- CDML controls the way the solution interacts with FileMaker Pro.

To troubleshoot, start by identifying the format file that's causing the problem. Then check its code against the code in this book. You know the drill: one misplaced character can cause a heck of a big mess. If your eyes start to blur, take a break and consider this: reading all that code is not anywhere near as tedious as writing and commenting on it! Good luck!

A

Appendixes

The best place for reference information is usually where it's easiest to find: at the back of the book. That's what you'll find here: some reference material you might find helpful when searching for database Web publishing information or developing a Custom Web Publishing solution. The two appendixes are:

Appendix A: Online Resources

Appendix B: Claris Dynamic Markup Language Tags

Online Resources

I'm not an Internet surfer. (I'd rather spend my free time doing things that don't involve a computer.) When I get on the net, I zero in on the information that I want, I learn what I need to know, and I get off.

One thing I'm sure of: the World Wide Web is an excellent source of up-to-date information about computer related topics such as database Web publishing. Best of all, this information is available 24 hours a day, 7 days a week.

With that in mind, here are some online resources that you can check to get additional information about Web publishing with FileMaker Pro.

Companion Web Site

I started creating so-called "companion Web sites" for my books back in 1997 as a way to provide additional information to readers. The trouble with books is that they can't usually be updated on a timely basis. A Web page, however, can be updated within minutes, providing visitors with up-to-date information any time.

As mentioned throughout this book, the book's companion Web site includes information about the book and the files you can use to try out the practice exercises. It also has an entire page with links to other Web pages and sites—including those listed in this appendix. This page will be updated regularly so you should check it any time you start a search for new FileMaker Pro Web publishing information.

The companion Web site for this book can be found at:

http://www.gilesrd.com/fmproweb/

Peachpit Press will be mirroring this site. Check Peachpit's Web site for details. You can find it at:

http://www.peachpit.com/

FileMaker, Inc. Pages

FileMaker, Inc. (formerly Claris Corporation) is a great source of information about FileMaker Pro and Web publishing. Not only can you find detailed information about FileMaker, but you can also get technical support and read articles about Web publishing. Here are some URLs to get you started:

The FileMaker, Inc. Home Page can be found at:

http://www.filemaker.com/

A good page to start looking for support and specific information about Web publishing is:

http://www.claris.com/support/products/filemakerpro/filemakerpro.html

Third-Party Solution Pages

Lasso, Tango for FileMaker Pro, and WEB•FM are the three third-party solutions I discuss in Part II of this book. Each organization maintains its own Web site with information about its products as well as sample solutions and/or trial versions of the software.

Blue World Communications

Blue World's Web site is extremely informative—and not just for Lasso users. On it, you'll find useful documents about Web publishing, as well as links to join FileMaker Pro and Lasso e-mail discussion lists.

You can visit Blue World Communication at:

http://www.blueworld.com/

Everyware Development

Everyware's site has more information about its other products than it does for Tango for FileMaker, but it does provide some useful information. Its URL is:

http://www.everyware.com/

Web Broadcasting

Web Broadcasting's site provides information about WEB•FM and related products, as well as links to get on mailing lists about WEB•FM, Web publishing with FileMaker Pro, and other topics.

You can visit Web Broadcasting at:

http://macweb.com/

Finding Other Sites

These are only a few sites to get you started. From these sites, you can find links to other pages with more information. There's a lot out there, but with URLs changing all the time, I'd prefer not to list them here. The best way to find good quality sites to to follow links from other good quality sites.

Another thing you can do to find sites—although I don't recommend it—it to use search engines such as AltaVista, Excite, WebCrawler, etc. Trouble is, if you enter a search phrase like *"FileMaker Pro"* or *"FileMaker Pro" AND Web*, you'll come up with thousands of matches that you'll have to inspect one at a time to find anything useful.

Frankly, I've been pretty disgusted with search engines lately. Most of what they find is garbage and a good portion of the links are bad.

E-Mail Discussion Lists

One last recommendation: if you're serious about database Web publishing and want to keep up to date on all the latest information about the Web publishing tools you select, subscribe to an appropiate mailing list. These two links list the best ones for FileMaker Pro users and Web publishers:

http://www.blueworld.com/lists/

http://macweb.com/lists/

TIP

If you do subscribe to any of these lists, remember to read the list rules before posting a message. An inappropriate message is a good way to make a lot of enemies all over the world.

APPENDIX B

Claris Dynamic Markup Language Tags

This appendix provides a complete list of Claris Dynamic Markup Language tags used for FileMaker Pro Custom Web Publishing. The following information is provided for most tags:

- Tag Name
- Tag
- Other Required Tags
- Syntax
- Sample Syntax

Syntax code appears in the same bold, sans serif type used for code throughout this book. Variables within code appear in an italic version of the same type. Parameters separated by a vertical line (|) are actual options.

Action Tags

Action tags perform an action on the database. Beginning on the following page is a complete list of the CDML action tags.

Delete Record

-Delete

Deletes the record specified by -RecID.

Other Required Tags

```
-DB -RecID
```

Sample Syntax for a Link

```
<A HREF="FMPro?-DB=databasename.fp3&-Format=formatfilename.htm&
-RecID=[FMP-CurrentRecID]&-Delete">Delete this Record</A>
```

Sample Syntax for a Form

```
<input type="submit" name="-Delete" value="Delete this Record">
```

Duplicate Record

-Dup

Duplicates the record specified by -RecID

Other Required Tags

```
-DB -RecID -Format
```

Sample Syntax for a Link

```
<A HREF="FMPro?-DB=databasename.fp3&-Format=formatfilename.htm&
-RecID=[FMP-CurrentRecID]&-Dup">Duplicate this Record</A>
```

Sample Syntax for a Form

```
<input type="submit" name="-Dup" value="Duplicate this Record">
```

Edit Record

-Edit

Updates the record specified by -RecID using the contents of name/value pairs.

Other Required Tags

```
-DB -RecID fieldname
```

Sample Syntax for a Link

```
<A HREF="FMPro?-DB=databasename.fp3&-Format=formatfilename.htm&
-RecID=[FMP-CurrentRecID]&fieldname=Yes&-Edit">Change Response to
Yes</A>
```

Sample Syntax for a Form

```
<input type="submit" name="-Edit" value="Update this Record">
```

Find Record

-Find

Submits a find request using defined criteria.

Other Required Tags

-DB -Format *fieldname*

Sample Syntax for a Link

```
<A HREF="FMPro?-DB=databasename.fp3&-Format=formatfilename.htm&
fieldname=Yes&-Find">Find records with a response of Yes</A>
```

Sample Syntax for a Form

```
<input type="submit" name="-Find" value="Begin Search">
```

Find All Records

-FindAll

Finds all records, then displays them using the specified format file.

Other Required Tags

-DB -Format

Sample Syntax for a Link

```
<A HREF="FMPro?-DB=databasename.fp3&-Format=formatfilename.htm&
-FindAll">Display all records</A>
```

Sample Syntax for a Form

```
<input type="submit" name="-FindAll" value="Display All Records">
```

Find Any Record

-FindAny

Displays a single random record using the specified format file.

Other Required Tags

`-DB -Format`

Sample Syntax for a Link

```
<A HREF="FMPro?-DB=databasename.fp3&-Format=formatfilename.htm&
-FindAny">Display Random Record</A>
```

Sample Syntax for a Form

```
<input type="submit" name="-FindAny" value="Display Random Record">
```

New Record

-New

Creates a new record, populating it with the contents of specified field name/value pairs.

Other Required Tags

`-DB` *fieldname*

Sample Syntax for a Link

```
<A HREF="FMPro?-DB=databasename.fp3&-Format=formatfilename.htm&
fieldname=Smith&-New">Create a new record for Smith</A>
```

Sample Syntax for a Form

```
<input type="submit" name="-New" value="Add Record">
```

View

-view

Displays a search or add format file. Use to display a format file without obtaining data from the database.

Other Required Tags

`-DB -Format`

Sample Syntax for a Link

```
<A HREF="FMPro?-DB=databasename.fp3&-Format=formatfilename.htm&
-View">View Search Page</A>
```

Sample Syntax for a Link

```
<input type="submit" name="-View" value="View Search Page">
```

Variable Tags

Variable tags provide additional information for use with action tags. Here's a complete list of the variable CDML tags:

Blind Carbon Copy for Email

-mailbcc

Specifies the e-mail address of a person who should be blind carbon copied on a message.

Other Required Tags

-DB -Mailto -MailFrom -MailSub -MailHost -MailFormat *actiontag*

Sample Syntax for a Form

```
<input type="hidden" name="-mailbcc" value="name@domain.com">
```

Carbon Copy for Email

-mailcc

Specifies the e-mail address of a person who should be carbon copied on a message.

Other Required Tags

-DB -Mailto -MailFrom -MailSub -MailHost -MailFormat *actiontag*

Sample Syntax for a Form

```
<input type="hidden" name="-mailcc" value="name@domain.com">
```

Database Name

-DB

Specifies the name of the database with which the request will interact.

Other Required Tags

actiontag

Sample Syntax for a Link

```
<A HREF="FMPro?-DB=databasename.fp3&-Format=formatfilename.htm&
-RecID=[FMP-CurrentRecID]&-Delete">Delete this Record</A>
```

Sample Syntax for a Form

```
<input type="hidden" name="-DB" value="databasename.fp3">
```

Error Response

-Error

Specifies the format file to be used to display a response when an error occurs while processing the request.

Other Required Tags

-DB *actiontag*

Sample Syntax for a Link

```
<A HREF="FMPro?-DB=databasename.fp3&-Format=formatfilename.htm&
-Error=errorfilename.htm&-RecID=[FMP-CurrentRecID]&-Delete">Delete this
Record</A>
```

Sample Syntax for a Form

```
<input type="hidden" name="-Error" value="errorfilename.htm">
```

Format File

-Format

Specifies the format file to be used to display a response after processing a successful request.

Other Required Tags

-DB *actiontag*

Sample Syntax for a Link

```
<A HREF="FMPro?-DB=databasename.fp3&-Format=formatfilename.htm&
-Error=errorfilename.htm&-RecID=[FMP-CurrentRecID]&-Delete">Delete this
Record</A>
```

Sample Syntax for a Form

```
<input type="hidden" name="-Format" value="formatfilename.htm">
```

Format File for Email

-mailformat

Specifies the format file that should be used to create the body of an e-mail message.

Other Required Tags

-DB -Mailto -MailFrom -MailSub -MailHost *actiontag*

Sample Syntax for a Form

```
<input type="hidden" name="-mailformat" value="format.htm">
```

From for Email

-mailfrom

Specifies the e-mail address of the person who is sending the message.

Other Required Tags

-DB -Mailto -MailSub -MailHost -MailFormat *actiontag*

Sample Syntax for a Form

```
<input type="hidden" name="-mailfrom" value="name@domain.com">
```

Host for Email

-mailhost

Specifies the address of the SMTP server host that will send the e-mail message.

Other Required Tags

-DB -Mailto -MailFrom -MailSub -MailFormat *actiontag*

Sample Syntax for a Form

```
<input type="hidden" name="-mailhost" value="smtp.sendersdomain.com">
```

Layout Name

-Lay

Specifies the name of the layout that is used for processing the request.

Other Required Tags

-DB ***actiontag***

Sample Syntax for a Link

```
<A HREF="FMPro?-DB=databasename.fp3&-Format=formatfilename.htm&
-Lay=layoutname&-RecID=[FMP-CurrentRecID]&-Delete">Delete this
Record</A>
```

Sample Syntax for a Form

```
<input type="hidden" name="-Lay" value="layoutname">
```

Logical Operator

-LOP

Specifies the logical operator to be used for a find request. Value can be either **AND** or **OR**.

Other Required Tags

-DB -Find -Format ***fieldname***

Sample Syntax for a Link

```
<A HREF="FMPro?-DB=databasename.fp3&-Format=formatfilename.htm&
fieldname=Yes+Maybe&-LOP=AND&-Find">Find records with a response of
Yes</A>
```

Sample Syntax for a Form

```
<input type="hidden" name="-LOP" value="AND">
```

Max Records

-Max

Specifies the maximum number of records that should be returned per page as a result of a find request.

Other Required Tags

-DB -Find (or -FindAll) -Format

Sample Syntax for a Link

```
<A HREF="FMPro?-DB=databasename.fp3&-Format=formatfilename.htm&
fieldname=Yes&-Max=15&-Find">Find records with a response of Yes</A>
```

Sample Syntax for a Form

```
<input type="hidden" name="-Max" value="15">
```

Operator

-Op

Specifies the operator to be used with the field name/value pair that follows it in a **-Find** action.

Possible Values

The following values are valid:

eq	equals
cn	contains
bw	begins with
ew	ends with
gt	greater than
gte	greater than or equals
lt	less than
lte	less than or equals
neq	not equals

Other Required Tags

-DB -Find -Format *fieldname*

Sample Syntax for a Link

```
<A HREF="FMPro?-DB=databasename.fp3&-Format=formatfilename.htm&
-Op=eq&fieldname=Yes&-Max=15&-Find">Find records with a response of
Yes</A>
```

Sample Syntax for a Form

```
<input type="hidden" name="-Op" value="equals">
```

Perform Script

-Script

Specifies the FileMaker Pro script that should be perform after the finding and sorting of records (if any) during the processing of a request.

Other Required Tags

-DB ***actiontag***

Sample Syntax for a Link

```
<A HREF="FMPro?-DB=databasename.fp3&-Format=formatfilename.htm
&fieldname=Yes&-Max=15&-Script=PrintReport&-Find">Find records with a
response of Yes & Print Report</A>
```

Sample Syntax for a Form

```
<input type="hidden" name="-Script" value="scriptname">
```

Perform Script before Find

-Script.PreFind

Specifies the FileMaker Pro script that should be perform before the finding and sorting of records (if any) during the processing of a request.

Other Required Tags

-DB ***actiontag***

Sample Syntax for a Link

```
<A HREF="FMPro?-DB=databasename.fp3&-Format=formatfilename.htm
&fieldname=Yes&-Max=15&-Script.PreFind=PrintRequest&-Find">Print Request
and Find records with a response of Yes</A>
```

Sample Syntax for a Form

```
<input type="hidden" name="-Script.PreFind" value="scriptname">
```

Perform Script before Sort

-Script.PreSort

Specifies the FileMaker Pro script that should be perform after the finding and before the sorting of records (if any) during the processing of a request.

Other Required Tags

-DB ***actiontag***

Sample Syntax for a Link

```
<A HREF="FMPro?-DB=databasename.fp3&-Format=formatfilename.htm
&fieldname=Yes&-Max=15&-Script.PreSort=PrintRequest&-Find">Find records
with a response of Yes and Print Unsorted Report</A>
```

Sample Syntax for a Form

```
<input type="hidden" name="-Script.PreSort" value="scriptname">
```

Record ID

-RedID

Specifies the record that should be operated on. Usually used with the **-Edit**, **-Dup**, and **-Delete** CDML tags.

Other Required Tags

-DB -Format ***actiontag***

Sample Syntax for a Link

```
<A HREF="FMPro?-DB=databasename.fp3&-Format=formatfilename.htm&
-RecID=[FMP-CurrentRecID]&-Delete">Delete this Record</A>
```

Sample Syntax for a Form

```
<input type="submit" name="-RecID" value="[FMP-CurrentRecID]">
```

Skip Records

-Skip

Specifies the number of records that should be skipped before displaying records.

Other Required Tags

-DB -Find (or -FindAll) -Format

Sample Syntax for a Link

```
<A HREF="FMPro?-DB=databasename.fp3&-Format=formatfilename.htm&
fieldname=Yes&-Max=15&-Skip=5&-Find">Find records with a response of
Yes</A>
```

Sample Syntax for a Form

```
<input type="hidden" name="-Skip" value="5">
```

Sort Field

-SortField

Specifies the field that should be used for sorting results.

Other Required Tags

-DB -Find (or -FindAll) -Format

Sample Syntax for a Link

```
<A HREF="FMPro?-DB=databasename.fp3&-Format=formatfilename.htm&
fieldname=Yes&-SortField=fieldname&-Find">Find records with a response of
Yes</A>
```

Sample Syntax for a Form

```
<input type="hidden" name="-SortField" value="fieldname">
```

Sort Order

-SortOrder

Specifies the order in which a field should be sorted.

Possible Values

The following values are valid:

Ascend	Ascending
Descend	Descending
Custom=*valuelistname*	

Other Required Tags

-DB -Lay (if using a custom sort order) -Find (or -FindAll) -Format

Sample Syntax for a Link

```
<A HREF="FMPro?-DB=databasename.fp3&-Format=formatfilename.htm&
fieldname=Yes&-SortField=fieldname&-SortOrder=Descending&-Find">Find
records with a response of Yes</A>
```

Sample Syntax for a Form

```
<input type="hidden" name="-SortOrder" value="Descending">
```

Subject for Email

-mailsub

Specifies the subject of the e-mail message.

Other Required Tags

-DB -Mailto -MailFrom -MailHost -MailFormat *actiontag*

Sample Syntax for a Form

```
<input type="hidden" name="-mailsub" value="The Subject Goes Here">
```

To Address for Email

-mailto

Specifies the e-mail address of the person who should receive the message.

Other Required Tags

-DB -MailFrom -MailSub -MailHost -MailFormat *actiontag*

Sample Syntax for a Form

```
<input type="hidden" name="-mailto" value="name@domain.com">
```

Token

-Token

Passes any value from one format file to another.

Other Required Tags

-DB -Format *actiontag*

Sample Syntax for a Link

```
<A HREF="FMPro?-DB=databasename.fp3&-Format=formatfilename.htm&
-Token=Anything&-FindAll">Display all Records</A>
```

Sample Syntax for a Form

```
<input type="hidden" name="-Token" value="Anything">
```

Replacement Tags

Replacement tags are replaced by database data or other information. Here is a complete list of the CDML replacement tags.

Client Address

[FMP-ClientAddress]

Replaced with the current client's domain name or IP address (if the domain name is unavailable).

Sample Syntax

```
Your Domain Name is: [FMP-ClientAddress]
```

Client IP Address

[FMP-ClientIP]

Replaced with the current client's IP address.

Sample Syntax

```
Your IP Address is: [FMP-ClientIP]
```

Client Password

[FMP-ClientPassword]

Replaced with the current HTTP-authenticated client password—the last password entered in the Password dialog box.

Sample Syntax

```
Your password is: [FMP-ClientPassword]
```

Client Type

[FMP-ClientType]

Replaced with the current Web browser client type.

Sample Syntax

```
Your Web browser is: [FMP-ClientType]
```

Client User Name

[FMP-ClientUserName]

Replaced with the current HTTP-authenticated client name—the last User ID entered in the Password dialog box.

Sample Syntax

```
Your User ID is: [FMP-ClientUserName]
```

Client MIME Type

[FMP-ClientMIMEType]

Changes the MIME type returned to the browser.

Syntax

```
[FMP-ContentMIMEType: MIMEType]
```

Cookie

[FMP-Cookie]

Replaced by the current value of a specified cookie.

Syntax

```
[FMP-Cookie: cookiename, Raw|URL]
```

Current Action

[FMP-CurrentAction]

Replaced by the name of the most recently used action tag.

Syntax

```
[FMP-CurrentAction: HTML|Display]
```

Sample Syntax

```
The last action performed was: [FMP-CurrentAction]
```

Current Database

[FMP-CurrentDatabase]

Replaced with the name of the database last accessed.

Syntax

```
[FMP-CurrentDatabase: Raw|URL|HTML]
```

Sample Syntax

```
You are accessing the database  named [FMP-CurrentDatabase: HTML]
```

Current Date

[FMP-CurrentDate]

Replaced with the current date.

Syntax

```
[FMP-CurrentDate: Short|Abbrev|Long]
```

Sample Syntax

```
Today's date is [FMP-CurrentDate]
```

Current Day

[FMP-CurrentDay]

Replaced with the name of the current day of the week.

Syntax

```
[FMP-CurrentDay: Short|Long]
```

Sample Syntax

```
Today's is [FMP-CurrentDay: Long]
```

Current Error

[FMP-CurrentError]

Replaced with the error number that resulted from the most recent action.

Sample Syntax

```
The last action failed, resulting in an error code of [FMP-Error]
```

Current Find

[FMP-CurrentFind]...[/FMP-CurrentFind]

Repeats the HTML between the two tags for each find criteria that created the current page.

Sample Syntax

```
The current found set is based on the following search criteria:
[FMP-CurrentFind]
[FMP-FindFieldItem] [FMP-FieldOpItem] [FMP-FindValueItem]<BR>
[/FMP-CurrentFind]
```

Current Format File

[FMP-CurrentFormat]

Replaced with the name of the format file being processed.

Syntax

```
[FMP-CurrentFormat: Raw|URL|HTML]
```

Sample Syntax

```
This page is displayed using the format file named [FMP-CurrentFormat]
```

Current Found Count

[FMP-CurrentFoundCount]

Replaced with the total number of records in the found set.

Sample Syntax

```
Your search resulted in [FMP-CurrentFoundCount] record(s) found.
```

Current Layout

[FMP-CurrentLayout]

Replaced with the name of the FileMaker Pro layout used to process the page.

Syntax

```
[FMP-CurrentLayout: Raw|URL|HTML]
```

Sample Syntax

```
The fields on this page are included in the [FMP-CurrentLayout] layout.
```

Current Logical Operator

[FMP-CurrentLOP]

Replaced with the logical operator used for the current search.

Sample Syntax

```
Your search used the [FMP-CurrentLOP] logical operator.
```

Current Max

[FMP-CurrentMax]

Replaced with the maximum number of records specified to be displayed on the page using the **-Max** variable.

Sample Syntax

```
This page displays up to [FMP-Max] of the records found.
```

Current Record Count

[FMP-CurrentRecordCount]

Replaced with the total number of records in the database.

Sample Syntax

```
The database contains [FMP-CurrentRecordCount] records.
```

Current Record ID

[FMP-CurrentRecID]

Replaced with the record key, an identifying number for the current record.

Sample Syntax for a Link

```
<A HREF="FMPro?-DB=databasename.fp3&-Format=formatfilename.htm&
-RecID=[FMP-CurrentRecID]&-Dup">Duplicate this Record</A>
```

Sample Syntax for a Form

```
<input type="hidden" name="-RecID" value="[FMP-CurrentRecID]">
```

Current Record Number

[FMP-CurrentRecordNumber]

Replaced with the total record's position in the found set.

Sample Syntax

```
This is record number [FMP-CurrentRecordNumber] of the [FMP-
CurrentFoundCount] records in the found set.
```

Current Skip

[FMP-CurrentSkip]

Replaced with the number of records skipped from the beginning of the found set.

Sample Syntax

```
The first [FMP-CurrentSkip] records of the found set have been skipped.
```

Current Sort

[FMP-CurrentSort]...[/FMP-CurrentSort]

Repeats the HTML between the two tags for each sort argument that was used to create the current page.

Sample Syntax

```
These records are sorted by:
[FMP-CurrentSort]
[FMP-SortFieldItem] in [FMP-SortOrderItem] order<BR>
[/FMP-CurrentSort]
```

Current Time

[FMP-CurrentTime]

Replaced with the current time.

Syntax

```
[FMP-CurrentTime: Short|Long]
```

Sample Syntax

```
The time is now [FMP-CurrentTime]
```

Current Token

[FMP-CurrentToken]

Replaced with the value set with the **-Token** variable tag when creating the current page.

Syntax

`[FMP-CurrentToken: Raw|URL|HTML]`

Sample Syntax

```
Your last entry in the response field was [FMP-CurrentToken].
```

Field

[FMP-Field]

Replaced with the contents of the specified field.

Syntax

`[FMP-Field:` *`fieldname`*`, Raw|URL|HTML|Break]`

Sample Syntax for Displaying Data

```
Name: [FMP-Field: Name]
```

Sample Syntax for Displaying Data in an Editable Field

```
Name: <input type="text" name="Name" value="[FMP-Field: Name, Raw]">
```

Field Name

[FMP-FieldName]

Replaced with the name of the current field when used between the `[FMP-LayoutFields]` and `[/FMP-LayoutFields]` tags.

Other Required Tags

`[FMP-LayoutFields] [/FMP-LayoutFields]`

Syntax

`[FMP-FieldName: Raw|URL|HTML]`

Sample Syntax for a Form

```
<select name="-SortField">
<option value="">-Select a Sort Field [FMP-LayoutFields]
<option>[FMP-FieldName: raw] [/FMP-LayoutFields]
</select>
```

Find Field Item

[FMP-FindFieldItem]

Replaced with the field name used for the find request that created the page when used between the **[FMP-CurrentFind]** and **[/FMP-CurrentFind]** tags.

Other Required Tags

[FMP-CurrentFind] [/FMP-CurrentFind]

Syntax

[FMP-FindFieldItem: Raw|URL|HTML]

Sample Syntax

```
The current found set is based on the following search criteria:
[FMP-CurrentFind]
[FMP-FindFieldItem] [FMP-FieldOpItem] [FMP-FindValueItem]<BR>
[/FMP-CurrentFind]
```

Find Operator Item

[FMP-FindOpItem]

Replaced with the search operator used for the find request that created the page when used between the **[FMP-CurrentFind]** and **[/FMP-CurrentFind]** tags.

Other Required Tags

[FMP-CurrentFind] [/FMP-CurrentFind]

Syntax

[FMP-FindOpItem: Short|Long|Display]

Sample Syntax

```
The current found set is based on the following search criteria:
[FMP-CurrentFind]
[FMP-FindFieldItem] [FMP-FieldOpItem] [FMP-FindValueItem]<BR>
[/FMP-CurrentFind]
```

Find ValueItem

[FMP-FindValueItem]

Replaced with the value of the search criteria used for the find request that created the page when used between the **[FMP-CurrentFind]** and **[/FMP-CurrentFind]** tags.

Other Required Tags

[FMP-CurrentFind] [/FMP-CurrentFind]

Syntax

[FMP-FindValueItem: Raw|URL|HTML]

Sample Syntax

```
The current found set is based on the following search criteria:
[FMP-CurrentFind]
[FMP-FindFieldItem] [FMP-FieldOpItem] [FMP-FindValueItem]<BR>
[/FMP-CurrentFind]
```

Header

[FMP-Header]...[/FMP-Header]

Replaces the default HTTP header of the page with what's between the tags. Must be placed before the **[FMP-ContentMIMEType]** and **[FMP-SetCookie]** tags.

Sample Syntax

```
[FMP-Header]
HTTP/1.0 302 Moved Temporary
Location: http://www.peachpit.com/
[/FMP-Header]
```

If

[FMP-IF]...[FMP-Else]...[/FMP-If]

Controls what HTML is displayed by evaluating a condition and displaying the appropriate HTML for that condition's result.

Syntax

[FMP-If: ***LeftSide operator RightSide*****]**

where:

LeftSide can be any of the following reserved words:

CanDelete
CanEdit
CanNew
IsSorted
CurrentError
CurrentFoundCount
CurrentMax
CurrentRecordCount
CurrentRecordNumber
CurrentSkip
RangeEnd
RangeSize
RangeStart
ClientPassword
ClientType
ClientUserName
CurrentAction
CurrentCookie
CurrentDatabase
CurrentFormat
CurrentLayout
CurrentToken
Field: *fieldname*
ValueListItem
CurrentDate
CurrentDay
CurrentTime
ClientAddress
ClientIP

operator can be any of the following:

.eq. **.gt.** **.lt.** **.cn.**
.neq. **.gte.** **.lte.** **.ncn.**

RightSide can be any of the following reserved words (depending on the ***LeftSide*** and ***operator***):

False
True
Field: *fieldname*
Literal Numeric Value
Literal Text Value
Checked
List of Literal Values

Image

[FMP-Image]

Replaced by an the URL to display an image in a FileMaker Pro container field.

Syntax

```
[FMP-Image: fieldname]
```

Sample Syntax

```
<IMG SRC="[FMP-Image: Pictures]">
```

Include

[FMP-Include]

Replaced with the contents of another file, usually in text or HTML format.

Syntax

[FMP-Include: *filename*]

Sample Syntax

[FMP-Include: copyrightblurb.txt]

Layout Fields

[FMP-LayoutFields]...[/FMP-LayoutFields]

Repeats the HTML between the two tags for each field on the layout that was used to create the current page.

Sample Syntax for a Form

```
<select name="-SortField">
<option value="">-Select a Sort Field [FMP-LayoutFields]
<option>[FMP-FieldName: raw] [/FMP-LayoutFields]
</select>
```

Link

[FMP-Link]

Replaced with a URL that points to the page it is on. The URL is a shortcut for find and sort criteria used to create the page.

Syntax

[FMP-Link: d|r|l|s|f|m|k|t|a]

where parameter codes specify the parts of the URL to omit as follows:

d - database

r - format file

l - layout

s - sort criteria

f - find criteria

m - max

k - skip

t - token

a - action

Sample Syntax for a Link

```
<A HREF="[FMP-Link: rm]&-Format=showall.htm&-Find">Show All Matches</A>
```

Link First

[FMP-LinkFirst]...[/FMP-LinkFirst]

Replaces the HTML between the tags with a link to the first range of records based on the **-Max** value used to create the current page.

Sample Syntax

```
[FMP-LinkFirst]View First Group of Records[/FMP-LinkFirst]
```

Link Last

[FMP-LinkLast]...[/FMP-LinkLast]

Replaces the HTML between the tags with a link to the last range of records based on the **-Max** value used to create the current page.

Sample Syntax

```
[FMP-LinkLast]View Last Group of Records[/FMP-LinkLast]
```

Link Next

[FMP-LinkNext]...[/FMP-LinkNext]

Replaces the HTML between the tags with a link to the next range of records based on the **-Max** value used to create the current page.

Sample Syntax

```
[FMP-LinkNext]View Next Group of Records[/FMP-LinkNext]
```

Link Previous

[FMP-LinkPrevious]...[/FMP-LinkPrevious]

Replaces the HTML between the tags with a link to the last range of records based on the **-Max** and **-Skip** values used to create the current page.

Sample Syntax

```
[FMP-LinkPrevious]View Previous Group of Records[/FMP-LinkPrevious]
```

Link to a Record ID

[FMP-LinkRecID]

Replaced with a URL to display a specific record in the database.

Syntax

[FMP-LinkRecID: Format=*formatfilepath*, Layout=*layoutname*]

Sample Syntax

```
<A HREF="[FMP-LinkRecID: Format=detail.htm]">View Details</A>
```

Option

[FMP-Option]

Replaced with all the values in the value list of a field in the specified layout.

Syntax

[FMP-Option: *fieldname*, List=*valuelistname*]

Sample Syntax

```
<select name="Category">
[FMP-option: Category, list=CategoryList]
</select>
```

Portal

[FMP-Portal]...[/FMP-Portal]

Repeats the HTML between the two tags for each record in a specific portal.

Syntax

[FMP-Portal: *relationshipname*]

Sample Syntax

```
[FMP-Portal: OrderItems]
[FMP-Field: OrderItems::Item Name]<BR>
[/FMP-Portal]
```

Range End

[FMP-RangeEnd]

Replaced with the record number of the last record being displayed.

Sample Syntax

```
You are viewing record [FMP-RangeStart] through [FMP-RangeEnd] of the
[FMP-CurrentFoundCount] records found.
```

Range Size

[FMP-RangeSize]

Replaced with the total number of records displayed on the page.

Sample Syntax

```
You are viewing [FMP-RangeSize] records.
```

Range Start

[FMP-RangeStart]

Replaced with the record number of the first record being displayed.

Sample Syntax

```
You are viewing record [FMP-RangeStart] through [FMP-RangeEnd] of the
[FMP-CurrentFoundCount] records found.
```

Record

[FMP-Record]...[/FMP-Record]

Repeats the HTML between the two tags for each record in the found set.

Sample Syntax

```
[FMP-Record]
[FMP-Field: Name] [FMP-Field: Email]<BR>
[/FMP-Record]
```

Repeating

[FMP-Repeating]

Repeats the HTML between the tags for each repetition of a repeating field.

Other Required Tags

-DB

Syntax

[FMP-Repeating: *fieldname*]

Sample Syntax

```
Sales Reps:<BR>
[FMP-Repeating: Sales Rep Names]
[FMP-RepeatingItem]<BR>
[/FMP-Repeating]
```

Repeating Item

[FMP-RepeatingItem]

Replaced with the contents of the next repetition when used between the **[FMP-Repeating]** and **[/FMP-Repeating]** tags.

Other Required Tags

-DB [FMP-Repeating] [/FMP-Repeating]

Syntax

```
[FMP-RepeatingItem: Raw|URL|HTML|Break]
```

Sample Syntax

```
Sales Reps:<BR>
[FMP-Repeating: Sales Rep Names]
[FMP-RepeatingItem]<BR>
[/FMP-Repeating]
```

Set Cookie

[FMP-SetCookie]

Used to set a cookie with the specified name and value in the client's browser. Usually used to store information that will be used in future visits.

Syntax

[FMP-SetCookie: *cookiename=cookievalue*, Expires=*minutes*, Path=*pathname*, Domain=*domainname*]

Sample Syntax

```
[FMP-SetCookie: EmailResponse=Field: Response, Expires=50000]
```

Sort Field Item

[FMP-SortFieldItem]

Replaced with the sort field name that was part of the request that created the page when placed within the **[FMP-CurrentSort]** and **[/FMP-CurrentSort]** tags.

Other Required Tags

[FMP-CurrentSort] [/FMP-CurrentSort]

Syntax

[FMP-SortFieldItem: Raw|URL|HTML]

Sample Syntax

```
These records are sorted by:
[FMP-CurrentSort]
[FMP-SortFieldItem] in [FMP-SortOrderItem] order<BR>
[/FMP-CurrentSort]
```

Sort Order Item

[FMP-SortOrderItem]

Replaced with the sort order (ascending or descending) that was part of the request that created the page when placed within the **[FMP-CurrentSort]** and **[/FMP-CurrentSort]** tags.

Other Required Tags

[FMP-CurrentSort] [/FMP-CurrentSort]

Syntax

[FMP-SortOrderItem: Raw|URL|HTML|Display]

Sample Syntax

```
These records are sorted by:
[FMP-CurrentSort]
[FMP-SortFieldItem] in [FMP-SortOrderItem] order<BR>
[/FMP-CurrentSort]
```

Value List

[FMP-ValueList]...[/FMP-ValueList]

Repeats the HTML between the tags for each value of a specific value list.

Syntax

[FMP-ValueList: ***fieldname*****, List=*****valuelistname*****]**

Sample Syntax

```
[FMP-ValueList: CategoryList]
<input type="radio" name="Category" value="[FMP-ValueListItem]">
[FMP-ValueListItem]
[/FMP-ValueList]
```

Value List Checked

[FMP-ValueListChecked]

Replaced with the word “checked” for every value list item that has been selected for the specified field when placed within the **[FMP-ValueList]** and **[/FMP-Valuelist]** tags.

Other Required Tags

[FMP-ValueList] [/FMP-ValueList]

Sample Syntax

```
[FMP-ValueList: CategoryList]
<input type="radio" name="Category" value="[FMP-ValueListItem]"
[FMP-ValueListChecked]>[FMP-ValueListItem]
[/FMP-ValueList]
```

Value List Item

[FMP-ValueListItem]

Replaced with the next value of a value list when placed within the **[FMP-ValueList]** and **[/FMP-Valuelist]** tags.

Other Required Tags

-DB [FMP-ValueList] [/FMP-ValueList]

Syntax

```
[FMP-ValueListItem: checked|always, Raw|URL|HTML]
```

Sample Syntax

```
[FMP-ValueList: CategoryList]
<input type="radio" name="Category" value="[FMP-ValueListItem]"
[FMP-ValueListChecked]>[FMP-ValueListItem]
[/FMP-ValueList]
```

Value Names

[FMP-ValueNames]...[/FMP-ValueNames]

Repeats the HTML between the tags for every value list in the database.

Sample Syntax

```
This database has the following value lists:<B>
[FMP-ValueNames]
[FMP-ValueNameItem]<BR>
[/FMP-ValueNames]
```

Value Name Item

[FMP-ValueNameItem]

Replaced with the of a value list when placed within the **[FMP-ValueNames]** and **[/FMP-ValueNames]** tags.

Other Required Tags

[FMP-ValueNames] [/FMP-ValueNames]

Syntax

```
[FMP-ValueNametItem: Raw|URL|HTML]
```

Sample Syntax

```
This database has the following value lists:<B>
[FMP-ValueNames]
[FMP-ValueNameItem]<BR>
[/FMP-ValueNames]
```

Index

%20 encoding 41, 116, 188

A

Access privileges 20, 61, 71, 73–76, 84

Access Privileges dialog box 73, 75–76

Accessing data
- Custom Web Publishing 64-66
- Instant Web Publishing 24–34
- Lasso 143–145
- Tango 179–180
- WEB•FM 211–212

Adobe PageMill
- *See* Web authoring tools

AltaVista 379

Amazon.com 1

AppleScript 4

Application Preferences dialog box 17–18, 58

B

BBEdit 105

BigBook 1, 3

Blue World Communications, Inc. 5, 36, 103, 104, 378

Book icon 27

Buy vs. Lease Calculation example 301–314

C

C/C++ 4

Calculation fields
- generating HTML for static Web publishing 93–99
- using with WEB•FM 183

Campmor 1

Castro, Elizabeth 2

CDML 5, 36, 40–44
- action tags 40, 381–385
- generating code with the CDML Tool 45–49
- in a form 43–44
- in a link 42–43
- replacement tags 40, 394–411
- tag syntax 40–41
- types of tags 40
- variable tags 40, 385–393

CDML Reference 44

CDML Tool 45–49
- tags tab 46–48
- templates tab 45–46
- using with Web authoring tools 48–49

CGI 4

Change Password dialog box (WEB•FM) 208

Claris Dynamic Markup Language
- *See* CDML

Claris Home Page 49–57
FileMaker Pro Connection Assistant 49–56, 64
FileMaker Pro Libraries 56–57
with WEB•FM 193
See also Web authoring tools
Common Gateway Interface *See* CGI
Companion Web site 10, 377–378
Contact database example 215–230
Creator code 142
Custom Web Publishing 5, 35–66
accessing a database 64–66
CDML See CDML
configuration options 67–72
examples 225–230, 245–253, 263–299, 304–314, 325–374
format files 36, 38–40, 61–63
overview 35–37
security options 61, 72–87
setting up 57–65
testing a solution 64–65
troubleshooting 65–66

D

Data Sources window (Tango) 155, 157–158
Define Fields dialog box 95, 199, 203–204
Define Groups dialog box 73, 74
Define Passwords dialog box 73, 74–75
Document Preferences dialog box 234
Dynamic forms 39–40
Dynamic Web publishing 2–4
hardware requirements 6
Internet or Intranet connection requirements 7–8
options 5–6
software requirements 7

E

E-mail discussion lists 379–380
Everyware Development Corp. 5, 147, 379
Excite 379
Export Calculation Fields 6, 89, 93–99
examples 218–222, 235–241
Export Field Order dialog box 92, 99
Export privileges 75
Export to HTML Table 6, 89, 90–93
examples 217–218

F

File Sharing control panel 156–157, 207
File Sharing dialog box 21, 63, 75
FileMaker Application dialog box (Tango) 155–156
FileMaker Connection Assistant 49–56, 64
FileMaker Form Library 56–57
FileMaker Pro Runtime/SDK 104, 182
FileMaker Pro Web Companion 5, 15–16
See also Web Companion plug-in
FileMaker Reference Library 56–57
FileMaker, Inc. 378
FileTyper 142
FM Link 105, 115, 119–130
Databases tab 120, 123
Fields tab 123–124, 127–129
Help window 121, 124–125
Lasso commands 119, 124–127
Lasso Tags tab 120, 124–127, 129
Layouts tab 123
templates 119, 120–122

using to build a format file from scratch 122–130
using with Web authoring tools 130–131
Form view 19, 20
browsing records 26–27
setting up 21–22
Format files
creating for Custom Web Publishing 61–63
creating for Lasso 134–135
Custom Web Publishing 36, 38–40
Lasso 106–112
tools for creating for Custom Web Publishing 44–57

G

Groups 73–76
Guest Register example 255–300

H

Home page
Custom Web Publishing 59, 68–69
Instant Web Publishing 18, 68–69, 84
HTML 2, 36
generating with calculation fields 93–99
Custom Web Publishing format file 39
Lasso format file 106, 109
Tango query document 149
tables 90
WEB•FM 183–185, 205–207
HTML for the World Wide Web: Visual QuickStart Guide 2
Hypertext Markup Language *See* HTML

I

Image
example of publishing a database with 231–254
import options 234–235
location and format 233–234
preferences 234
Instant Web Publishing 5, 15–34
accessing a database 24–34
adding records 32–33
browsing records 25–32
configuration options 67–72
deleting records 33–34
disabling 59, 68, 84
editing records 33
enabling 18, 68
examples 222–225, 241–245, 258–263
getting help 34
language 69
modifying the database 32–34
overview 15–16
returning to the Home page 34
searching for records 27–29
security options 20, 72–87
setting up 17–24
sorting records 30–31
unsorting records 31–32
Internet commerce 72
Internet connection 7–8
Intranet connection 8

J

Java applets 104
Java-enabled Web browser 26, 27

L

LAN access to FileMaker Pro databases 75

Lasso 4, 5, 36, 77, 103–145
accessing a database 143–145
CGI 5, 104, 105–106, 109–110, 131–132, 140
format files 106–112
installing and registering 131–133
modes 111
overview 105–107
Plug-in 5, 104, 105–106, 110–111, 132
preparing a database for publishing 133–134
security 135–143
Server 5, 105, 106, 110–111, 132–133, 140
Tag Converter 105
tags *See* LDML
vs. Web Companion Plug-In

Lasso Dynamic Markup Language See LDML

Lasso Security Database 77, 136–141
clearing a user or field entry 139–140
creating a database record 137
creating custom security violation pages 140–141
defining field-level and record-level security 138–139
defining names, passwords, and permissions 137–138
deleting settings for a database 140–141
opening 136
remote administration 142–142
reviewing default settings 137
specifying an Admin Password 137

Layouts
Custom Web Publishing 60–61
Instant Web Publishing 19–20
Lasso 133–134
WEB•FM 205

LDML 103, 106
action tags 112
command tags 112–113
container tags 114
sub-container tags 114–115
substitution tags 113–114
syntax 115–116
tags in a form action 117–118
types of tags 112–115
to specify Lasso actions for the Lasso CGI 109–110
to specify Lasso actions for the Lasso Plug-In or Server 110–111
URL-embedded tags 116–117

Log activity 70–71

LOG•FM 182

M

Mac Companies Database Online 4, 94

Macintosh Tips & Tricks 11

Meta tags 149, 152–153

Microsoft FrontPage See Web authoring tools

Microsoft Internet Explorer 7

Modify Data Source dialog box (Tango) 157

N

Netscape Navigator 7

New Document dialog box (Tango) 158

No password password 75

O

Odd Couple 11

OfficeMax 1, 3

Online resources 377–380
Opened Databases dialog box (Tango) 157

P

Passwords 73–76
Peachpit Press 378
PICT•FM 6, 182
Port number 24, 64, 71–72
Preferences dialog box
  Tango 154
  WEB•FM 191
Product Catalog example 231–254
Program Linking 156
Project folder
  Custom Web Publishing 62
  Lasso 134–135
  WEB•FM 206

Q

Query documents 149, 150–152, 178
  contents 151
  creating a link to 178–179
  creating with Tango Editor 153–176
  types 150
Quote characters 97, 202

R

Record Range icon 26
Related fields 22, 142
Relative references 62, 135
Remote administration
  FileMaker Pro built-in Web publishing 70
  Web Security Database 85–87
ResEdit 142

S

Scripting 94
Search engines 379
Search form 19, 20
  setting up 21–22
  using 27–29
Security
  accessing a secured database file 83–84, 141
  FileMaker Pro built-in Web publishing 72–87
  Lasso 135–143
  loopholes 84–85, 141–142
  WEB•FM 207–211
Shopping Cart example 315–374
Smart quotes 97, 202
Sort form
  setting up 23–24
  using 30–32
Space characters
  Custom Web Publishing format files 41
  Lasso format files 116
  WEB•FM 188
Specify Calculation dialog box 96, 193, 200–204
Specify Field Order for Export dialog box 92, 99
Specify Sort dialog box 23
Specify Sort Order dialog box 23
SSL server 72, 104
Static forms 39–40
Static Web publishing 2–4, 89–99
  hardware requirements 6
  Internet or Intranet connection requirements 8
  options 6, 89
  software requirements 7
System requirements 6–8

T

Table view 16, 19, 20
  browsing records 25–26
  setting up 21–22
TAG•FM 6, 182, 187, 190–193
  adding codes to an HTML document 192–193
  All Fields window 191
  creating required fields 197–199
  FileMaker Calculations window 192
  Layouts window 191
  opening a database 190
  preferences 191
  Preformatted HTML Snippets window 192
  Reserved Field Names window 191
  using with Web authoring tools 191
Tango Editor 5, 148, 151, 153–176
  allowing records to be deleted 170
  button titles 165, 170, 173
  data sources 155, 159
  Debug Mode 179–180
  Delete Response page 170–171
  field options 161–164, 167, 169, 172
  fields 169, 171
  fields and sort order 166
  format options 164, 167–168, 170, 172
  generating a query document 173–174
  header and footer 164, 168, 170, 172
  maximum matches 167
  New Record Query Builder 171–173
  New Record Response page 173
  No Results HTML 165
  preferences 154–155
  Query Document Builder 153, 158–174
  Query Document Editor 153, 174–176
  Record Detail tab 168–171
  Record List tab 165–168
  saving files 159–160
  Search Query Builder 158–171
  Search tab 160–165
  starting 153–154
  test drive mode 177
  Update Response page 170–171
  using the database palette 160
Tango for FileMaker 4, 5–6, 147–180
  accessing a database 179–180
  action attributes 151–152
  actions 151
  CGI 5, 148
  data source 178
  installing 176–177
  meta tags see Meta tags
  overview 148–150
  query documents
    See Query documents
  Server Plug-in 148, 174
  troubleshooting 180
TCP/IP port number See Port number
Third-party Web publishing solutions 5–6
Token passing 328

U

UNIX 4

W

Web authoring tools 2, 7, 43, 48–49, 62–63, 69, 83, 90, 93, 118, 122, 130–131, 189, 204
Web Broadcasting Corporation 6, 181, 379

Web browser 7
Web Companion Configuration dialog box 18–19, 68–72, 78, 83
Web Companion Configuration Options 67–72
  log activity 70–71
  remote administration 70
  security 71
  TCP/IP port number 71–72
  user interface 68–69
Web Companion plug-in
  Custom Web Publishing 57–59
  Instant Web Publishing 17–19
  vs. Lasso 104
Web Companion sharing
  disabling 84
  enabling and configuring for Instant Web Publishing 20–24
  enabling for Custom Web Publishing 63
Web Companion View Setup dialog box 21–24, 68
Web publishing
  options 4–6
  requirements 6–8
Web Security Database 20, 61, 71, 76–82, 84, 135
  clearing a user or field entry 81
  creating a database record 79
  creating custom security violation pages 82–83
  defining field-level and record-level security 80–81
  defining names, passwords, and permissions 79–80
  deleting settings for a database 81
  opening 77
  remote administration 85–87
  reviewing default options 78
  using with Instant Web Publishing 82
Web server
  realm 142, 208
  software 7, 106, 148
WEB•FM 4, 6, 181–212
  accessing a database 211–212
  Admin Database 207–211
  administrator name and password 195
  installing 194–197
  optional fields 203–204
  overview 182–183
  preparing the database 197–204
  required fields 197–202
  security-related fields 205
WEB•FM SDK 182
WEB•FM actions 184–185
  specifying in a form 184–185, 188, 189–190
  specifying in a link/URL 185, 188–189
WEB•FM codes 185–190
  basic commands 185, 186
  incoming tokens 187
  INPUT variables 185, 186
  outgoing tokens 187
  reserved field names 185, 186
  substitution tokens 185, 187
  syntax 187–188
WEB•FM Security 207–211
  accessing a secured file 209
  database-level 208–209
  field-level 210–211
  record-level 211
  securing database files 208–211
  securing the Admin Database 207–208
  task-level 209–210
  using the .fm suffix 207
WebCrawler 379
WebSTAR 7, 106, 142, 148, 176, 182
WebSTAR SSL 72
Wickenburg, AZ 1, 11

more from Peachpit Press

If you'd like to hear from us when we release new books, join our "New Books" e-mail list.

Every few weeks, you'll receive a brief e-mail announcement describing our newly released titles, giving you a sneak peek at our latest books on Web authoring, graphic design techniques, animation, multimedia, and more—even before the ink dries.

To subscribe to the list, please send us a message at **newbooks@peachpit.com** with "subscribe" in the subject line.

For more information please visit our Web site at **www.peachpit.com** or call us at 1-800-283-9444.

Audio on the Web: The Official IUMA Guide

INCLUDES CD-ROM

By Jeff Patterson and Ryan Melcher

Whether it's music, voice, or ambient noise, your Web site is crying out for sound. Let the geniuses behind the Internet Underground Music Archive (IUMA) teach you how to create, compress, and optimize downloadable and streaming audio for the Web, then post clips to your site for peak user experience. The accompanying CD contains a variety of software utilities and sample digitized songs.

$39.95 U.S. (208 PAGES, W/CD-ROM)
ISBN 0-201-69613-4

Animation on the Web

INCLUDES CD-ROM

By Sean Wagstaff

This book covers basic through advanced animation techniques from the point of view of Web development and traditional animation. It offers insider advice on using DHTML, animated GIFs, QuickTime, Shockwave, RealMedia, mBedlets, and other Web animation technologies, and includes a vivid 32-page color graphics section. The CD is packed with sample animations, examples from the book, shareware, and demos of popular animation software.

$39.95 U.S. (448 PAGES, W/CD-ROM)
ISBN 0-201-69687-8

Creating Stores on the Web

By Joe Cataudella, Dave Greeley, and Ben Sawyer

Who better to give advice on creating and running an online store than a successful online store owner? Let an experienced expert save you time and grief by explaining exactly what you need to survive and profit on the Web. From technical, legal, and software issues to marketing, shipping, distribution, ad banners, customer service, and common-sense philosophy, this book covers everything you need to know to succeed in Web retail.

$32.95 U.S. (544 PAGES)
ISBN 0-201-69681-9

Elements of Web Design, 2nd Edition

By Darcy DiNucci
with Maria Giudice and Lynne Stiles

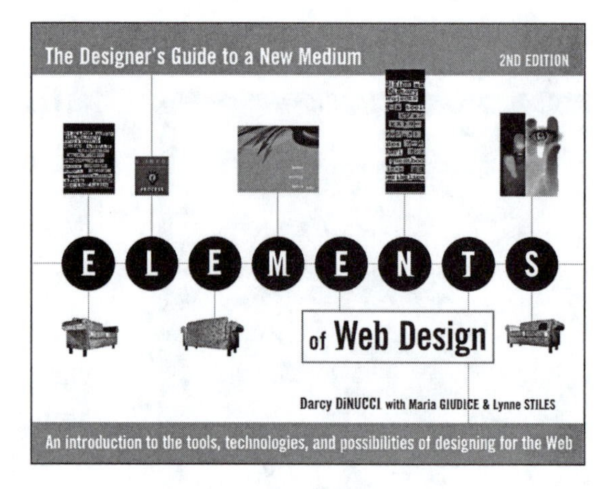

Fully revised to cover the latest developments in Web design, including cascading style sheets, typography, and dynamic HTML, *Elements of Web Design* remains a favorite four-color text for graphic designers new to the Web. This is the only book that covers the entire process, from assembling a team and working with contracts, through designing for interactivity and understanding the new technologies involved in the wild world of Web design.

$39.95 U.S. (240 PAGES)
ISBN 0-201-69698-3

Web Graphics Tools and Techniques

By Peter Kentie

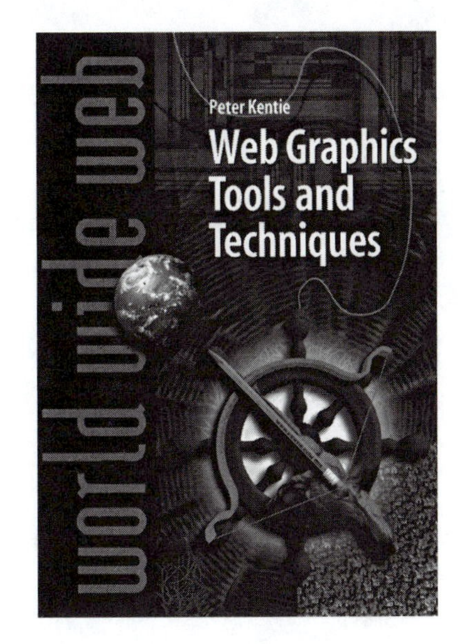

An indispensable, richly illustrated, full-color resource for Web site creators needing to master a variety of authoring and graphics tools. After covering the specifics of formatting graphics, text, and tables with HTML, it moves deeper into graphics techniques and tools, explaining the use of Photoshop, Painter, Poser, KPT Welder, GIF Construction Set, and Director. It also covers tables, clickable maps, 3D images, and user interaction.

$39.95 U.S. (320 PAGES)
ISBN 0-201-68813-1

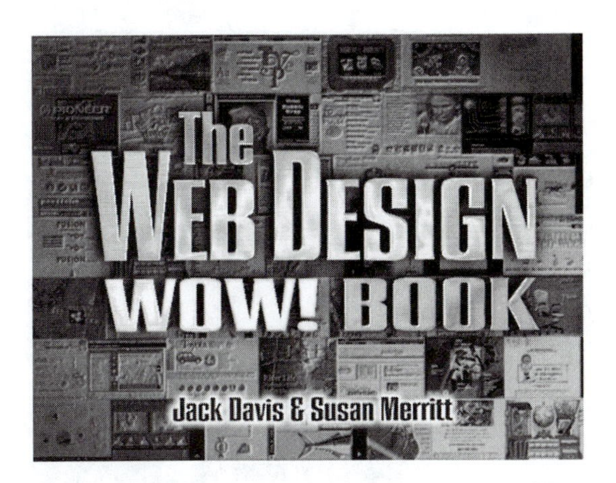

The Web Design Wow! Book

INCLUDES CD-ROM

By Jack Davis and Susan Merritt

Here's an indispensable source of practical advice and creative inspiration for anyone designing screen-based communications—from Web to CD-ROM and beyond. From Susan Merritt and Jack Davis, co-author of the award-winning *Photoshop Wow! Book*, this book covers the conceptual process, design fundamentals, and interface components, includes over 50 case studies, and features hundreds of full-color samples showcasing some of the most successful and creative interfaces for marketing, education, sales, and portfolio presentations.

$39.95 U.S. (224 PAGES, W/CD-ROM)
ISBN 0-201-88678-2

The Non-Designer's Web Book

By Robin Williams and John Tollett

In the best-selling *The Non-Designer's Design Book*, Robin Williams explained design principles and techniques to novices. Now Robin does it again, but this time for the Web. This book explores basic, universal Web design principles. Using full-color examples, the book demonstrates how Web design is different from print design, how to use typography on the Web, where to get graphics, and how to get your well-designed Web site up for all to admire.

$29.95 U.S. (288 PAGES)
ISBN 0-201-68859-X

Getting Hits

By Don Sellers

Building a world-class Web site doesn't mean people will come flocking—Web sites must be promoted to be successful. *Getting Hits* is your guide to advertising and publicizing your site. Topics include: posting your site to a search engine; links that give the biggest hits; guerrilla marketing strategies; producing hits offline; creating your own Web campaign; and how to keep visitors coming back to your site.

$19.95 U.S. (208 PAGES)
ISBN 0-201-68815-8

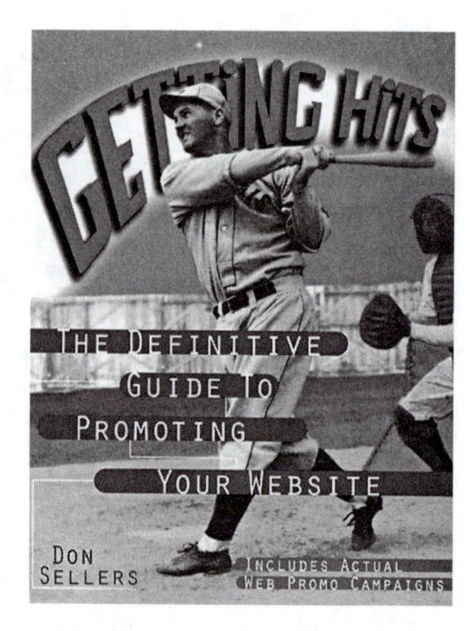

Order Form

usa 800-283-9444 ▪ 510-524-2178 ▪ fax 510-524-2221
canada 800-387-8028 ▪ 416-447-1779 ▪ fax 800-456-0536 or 416-443-0948

You can also place your orders online at www.peachpit.com

Qty	Title	Price	Total
	Subtotal		
	Add Applicable Sales Tax*		
	Shipping		
	TOTAL		

Shipping is by UPS ground: $4 for first item, $1 each add'l.

*We are required to pay sales tax in all states with the exceptions of AK, DE, MT, NH, and OR. Please include appropriate sales tax if you live in any state not mentioned above.

Customer Information

Name

Company

Street Address

City State Zip

Phone ( ) Fax ( )

[Phone number is required for credit card orders]

E-Mail

Payment Method

❑ Check enclosed ❑ VISA ❑ MasterCard ❑ AMEX

Credit Card # Exp. date

Company Purchase Order #

Tell Us What You Think

Please tell us what you thought of this book: Title:

What other books would you like us to publish?

Peachpit Press • 1249 Eighth Street • Berkeley, CA 94710

Get Started With FileMaker

Listing 1: Search.htm page—Here's an example of the HTML code needed to generate this page.

```
<HTML>
  <HEAD><TITLE>Search</TITLE></HEAD>
  <BODY BGCOLOR=#FFFFFF>
    <FORM ACTION="FMPro" METHOD="POST">

      <INPUT TYPE="hidden" NAME="-db" VALUE="cars.fp3">
      <INPUT TYPE="hidden" NAME="-lay" VALUE="web">
      <INPUT TYPE="hidden" NAME="-format" VALUE="list.h
      <INPUT TYPE="hidden" NAME="-error" VALUE="errors."
      <TABLE>
        <TR>
          <TD ALIGN=CENTER COLSPAN=2>
            <FONT SIZE=5>Search For A Car/Van/Sport Utilit
          </TD>
        </TR>
        <TR>
          <TD ALIGN=RIGHT
            <B>Make:</B>
          </TD>
          <TD>
            <SELECT NAME="make">
              <OPTION VALUE="" SELECTED>- Sele
              <OPTION>Chevrolet
              <OPTION>GMC
              <OPTION>Nissan
              <OPTION>Toyota
            </SELECT>
          </TD>
        </TR>
        <TR>
          <TD ALIGN=RIGHT>
            <B>Type:</B>
          </TD>
          <TD>
            <SELECT NAME="Type">
              <OPTION VALUE="" SELECTED>- Sel
              <OPTION>Car
              <OPTION>Van
              <OPTION>Sport Utility
            </SELECT>
          </TD>
        </TR>
        <TR>
          <TD ALIGN=RIGHT>
```

by, and all **<OPTION>** tags specify values w
you know to exist in your database.

Use the pop-up menu to search the make
and type (i.e., car, van, and sport utility). T
menus listed are cool! They let you specify
to sort the search results by. For you
the **<OPTION VALUE="" SELECTED>-**
beginning of each pop-up menu will be e
VALUE=") if you don't select anythi
menu. So, if you click the Search butt
anything to search by, then you'll
the database.

These sort pop-up menus dif
simple way: Rather than
NAME="-sortfield" and
the field names that you
of these **"-sortfield"** c
than one, the results w
field" tags are placed i
the first sortfield to
field to be **"Model"**
"Make" field then

We interrupt this book

to announce that database development with FileMaker® Pro just got even easier...

800-336-6060

Outside US (619)278-5600 • Fax (619)279-4728

E-mail: subscribe@advisor.com • www.advisor.com

6 issues US $39, Canada $49, All Other Countries $59.